C000072395

CORIOLIS
Technology Press

NT5
The Next Revolution

Ari Kaplan
Morten Strunge Nielsen

NT5: The Next Revolution

The Coriolis Group, Inc.
An International Thomson Publishing Company
14455 N. Hayden Road, Suite 220
Scottsdale, Arizona 85260

602.483.0192
FAX 602.483.0193
http://www.coriolis.com

Library of Congress Cataloging-In-Publication Data

Kaplan, Ari
  NT 5 : the next revolution / by Ari Kaplan and Morten Strunge Nielsen
   p. cm.
  Includes index.
  ISBN 1-57610-288-2
   1. Microsoft Windows NT. 2. Operating systems (Computers)
I. Nielsen, Morten Strunge. II. Title.
QA76.76.O63K364 1998
005.4'469—dc21   98-25094
Printed in the United States of America   CIP

10 9 8 7 6 5 4 3 2 1

Publisher
Keith Weiskamp

Acquisitions Editor
Stephanie Wall

Project Editor
Toni Zuccarini

Production Coordinator
Wendy Littley

Cover Design
Anthony Stock

Layout Design
April Nielsen

an International Thomson Publishing company

Albany, NY • Belmont, CA • Bonn • Boston • Cincinnati • Detroit
Johannesburg • London • Madrid • Melbourne • Mexico City
New York • Paris • Singapore • Tokyo • Toronto • Washington

*To Raoul Wallenberg, wherever you are,
and to my family.*

—Ari Kaplan

*This book is dedicated to my wife, Helena Strunge Nielsen,
and our daughter, Camilla Strunge Nielsen,
in heartfelt gratitude for their interest
and patience during the long days and nights
I spent in preparing this book.
They were a constant source of comfort and love.*

—Morton Strunge Nielsen

Acknowledgments

Many thanks to the California Institute of Technology, their Alumni Office, and their Summer Undergraduate Research Fellowship program. Special thanks to Bill Gates and Melinda French.

Table Of Contents

Introduction

If we were asked to mention one, and only one, story of success in the world of computers, we know exactly what we would choose: It would be the story of Microsoft.

Microsoft's success can be ascribed to three outstanding products: MS-DOS, Windows, and Microsoft Office. These three products dominate the global computer market to an astonishing degree. DOS is now rapidly on the decline, and will soon die, because it is technologically outdated due to Windows 95/98 and Windows NT. It is estimated that by 1999, 95 percent of all desktop computers will contain a Microsoft operating system.

This book will deal with the venture that is intended to ensure Microsoft's next great success: Windows NT 5.0. Microsoft has already declared that Windows NT 5.0 will be the sole Windows operating system for PCs in the future.

Microsoft's goal is to have this operating system be the magic solution that makes it possible to use the same operating system base for everything: the individual PC user, workstations, small servers, and large mission-critical servers. The only other Windows operating system anticipated to "survive" after the year 2000 is Windows CE, which is used in consumer electronics and lightweight portable computers.

Microsoft intends to bury all future competition in the upper and lower segments of the PC market by means of Windows NT 5.0 and Windows 98, respectively. The new version of NT will gradually erode the Windows 98 market, and its successor will completely eliminate the old 16-bit-based Windows 98 generation around the year 2000.

Soon we are bound to hear loud praises of the wonderful advantages of NT 5.0. Microsoft's highly efficient public relations people will be in top gear in the fourth quarter of 1998, and they will remain so until NT 5.0 has been launched. There is no doubt in our minds that the world will marvel at a lavish PR display that will surpass what we experienced when Microsoft introduced Windows 95, which included parades and gala celebrations in cities around the world.

How This Book Came About

Everybody all over the world will sooner or later want to voice his or her opinion on the next Windows edition. We are certainly two of them. However, while others express their thoughts and ideas verbally in close-knit circles, we have felt a great urge to put them down on paper in an attempt to reach a wider audience.

Contrary to many of our colleagues, we are advocates to some degree of all alternatives to Microsoft's operating system products. The world would be an extremely boring place in which to live if Microsoft succeeds in winning the last few percentages of the market that it doesn't already dominate. All things considered, we feel that the consumers will bear the brunt if the operating systems belong to a single company. A market share that is like a monopoly has never led to something good, certainly not in the ever-changing world of computers.

Unfortunately, apart from Microsoft's Windows products, it is increasingly difficult in recent years to find other operating systems worth mentioning. Since Windows 95 (and later Windows 98) was launched, there has not really been anything worth writing home about. Microsoft dominates the market of server operating systems. Novell and IBM seem to have come to a complete standstill, while NT Server is conquering the world at lightning speed.

We certainly see no alternatives to Windows NT Server on the horizon currently. As an experiment, we implemented Windows NT Server and Novell NetWare 4.1 in two computer environments of approximately the same size—slightly more than 1,000 PC users. The implementation of NetWare 4.1 with Windows 95/98 on the clients created far greater problems than did the corresponding purely Windows NT installation (Windows NT Server on all servers and Windows NT Workstation on all clients). To be fair, there were two years' experience that were drawn upon when implementing the NT installation, yet many more challenges remained in the previous NetWare installation at the end of the two-year period. This is because very few computer specialists actually have much experience with Novell 4.x's directory service (NDS).

Guidance For The Reader

This book focuses a lot on the purely commercial perspectives of Windows NT 5.0 and its closest competitors. The concentration is on Windows NT Server, but all the features of NT Workstation will also be described. The other goal of this book is to present the most important features and facilities in Windows NT 5.0, and wherever possible to compare them with competing products.

This book contains a three-step launching pad:

- An outline of the Microsoft Windows strategy today, leading up to the year 2000, as compared with the computer market as a whole (Chapters 1 and 2). These chapters describe in detail the commercial problems with NT 5.0. This section is reader-friendly to a broad section of professional IT users, including IT decision-makers, programmers, support personnel, curious computer experts, and NT administrators. The chapters don't require any particular knowledge of Windows NT, which we hope will make them all the more valuable to all the organizations that are considering changing to NT.

- A fairly simple discussion of the most important features in NT 5.0 (Chapters 3 through 9). Chapter 3 is a survey chapter that discusses in short the contents of the next six chapters. This more advanced section discusses Active Directory in detail, as this technology marks a radical break with the past. We know only too well from our own experience when we had to come to grips with the Novell NDS that it will give those of you already familiar with domains plenty of food for thought. We have also gone to great lengths to ensure that this section gives you all the information necessary to start the transition of your company from Windows NT 3.51 or 4.0 to Windows NT 5.0—or to construct a whole new Windows NT 5.0-based infrastructure.

  It should be emphasized that it is a good idea to start such planning now. It will be necessary to carry out some fairly radical adjustments within your organization—you might just as well address and tackle them now. Your company is likely to avoid this trouble entirely by ensuring that all decisions take into account the fundamentals of Windows NT 5.0.

- A technical in-depth survey of the most important changes in NT 5.0 as compared with its predecessors (Chapters 10 through 20). This is the most advanced section of the book, and also includes a small appendix telling you how to migrate from NetWare if your company plans to change to Windows NT Server, either in part or in full. The last two chapters finish the book with a commercial perspective of Windows NT 5.0.

Anybody, with or without a prior knowledge of the computer world and Windows, can benefit from the first part of the book. Most professional users of IT, from IT decision-makers to advanced users, will benefit from the second part. The third part is devoted to the truly advanced systems and operations people in the IT department.

The book is prepared on the basis of the Windows NT 5.0 beta 1 (or build 1671), approximately 6,000 copies of which were released at the Professional Developer's conference in San Diego in September 1997. Beta 1 was subsequently forwarded to the approximately 200,000 other Microsoft customers who are members of Microsoft Developer's Network (MSDN).

Although Windows NT 5.0 beta 1 is an early version of NT 5.0 (Microsoft has announced that they plan beta 2 and beta 3 versions in 1998), it is fairly complete. Experience with Microsoft's Windows products so far shows that there are very few changes, if any, in how it functions once the beta phase has started—even if it is an early beta, which some might say should instead be dubbed an alpha version.

If you enjoy reading the book just half as much as we have enjoyed writing it, our goal will be achieved.

—Ari Kaplan and Morten Strunge Nielsen

Windows Everywhere

A few years have passed since the computer market acknowledged that Windows had effectively wiped out all competition with respect to the graphical user interface (GUI) for PCs. In 1995, more than 60 million Windows 3.1x-based PCs were in use globally, and to this figure can be added several million IBM OS/2-based PC-compatible computers with Windows built in.

In June 1997, Microsoft announced that it had sold more than 77 million copies of Windows 95. Microsoft stated that this number equated to 4 million copies of Windows 95 sold per month since it was launched. In other words, more than one copy was sold per second. In late 1997, Microsoft announced that it had sold more than 100 million copies of Windows 95.

Windows 95's "big brother," Windows NT Workstation, is also beginning to make its presence felt. As of May 1997, more than 3 million copies of NT Workstation were sold, and the growth rate was approximately 400,000 copies of NT Workstation per month. This figure is still increasing very sharply. Microsoft announced that by the middle of November 1997, more than 11 million copies of its NT Workstation had been sold.

The sale of Windows NT Server licenses also is impressive. Microsoft has stated that by mid-May 1997, 1 million copies of NT Server 4.0 had been sold since its launch in August 1996. For each server system, one or more workstations usually exist, depending on the server's business implementation. Some servers have hundreds or more workstations attached to them. In a typical NT Server 4.0 environment, the workstations comprise NT Workstation 4.0 and/or Windows 95 as their operating system.

Nevertheless, Windows NT Server and NT Workstation still have some ways to go before they capture their respective market segments. Microsoft still needs to install several million more NT Servers just to be on par with the number of Novell NetWare Server installations. This does not even include the larger Unix server market, which has many vendors, including Sun, Silicon Graphics, Hewlett-Packard, and others. For every NT Workstation license sold daily, 10 times as many Windows 95 licenses are sold, which means that the gap between the two operating systems is increasing.

But even so, the market is very encouraging for Microsoft. Microsoft's declared goal is to have its two NT products take over the market for PC clients and PC servers, respectively, in the years to come.

Why Windows?

The reason why 16-bit Windows environments dominate the market is due neither to superiority nor to user-friendliness. Windows has always lagged behind in these two vital areas (see Figure 1.1).

Up until the launch of Windows 95, Apple's Macintosh user interface was generally accepted as being far superior to Windows. Likewise, several operating systems (notably OS/2, Windows NT, SCO Unix, and others) were set up with considerably more-detailed technical solutions. Even if the least-biased observers are convinced that Windows 95 is behind in technology and user-friendliness, Windows 95 clearly has

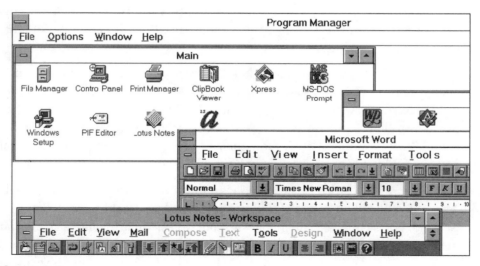

Figure 1.1
User-friendliness and technology were not predominant in Microsoft's Windows 3.1 design. Regardless, Windows 3.1 is far more user-friendly than the previous text-based interfaces (for example, MS-DOS) that dominated the earlier market.

narrowed the degree of superiority between it and its competitors (see Figure 1.2). Before Windows 95 appeared, the large gaps in technology and user-friendliness were much more noticeable.

From the start, the success of the Windows platform has been due to the fact that it works reasonably well with the majority of existing PCs. Also, Microsoft is extremely talented and professional in its sales drives.

In the past, Microsoft has focused a lot of attention on the smallest common denominator for PCs by means of compromises in the technological field. They did this to ensure that Windows would work on the small, consumer-level computers (with little memory and processor power), thus increasing their overall sales. For instance, the earlier versions of Windows—as opposed to OS/2 and Mac—were not independent operating systems, per se. The previous Windows versions can fairly be called the lowest common denominator for graphical user interface systems, with DOS being the lowest common denominator for operating systems having a text-based user interface. Much functionality had been added to Windows 95, and the tremendous improvements have extended to Windows 98 and NT 5.0.

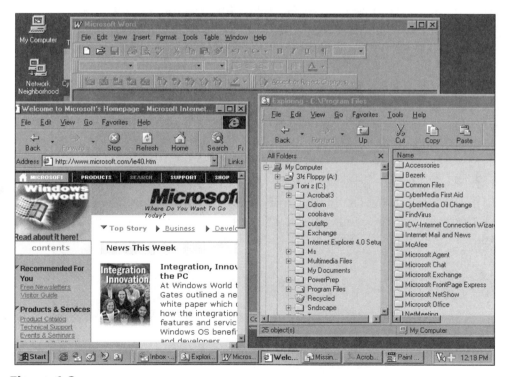

Figure 1.2
Windows 95 fixes many of the shortcomings and errors of Windows 3.1—including the lack of user-friendliness and technology.

Microsoft's business strategy has been the subject of discussion ever since the first version of Windows was launched. Die-hard computer professionals viewed the original Windows operating system with contempt. Instead, they favored OS/2, which was launched a few years after the first, much-criticized version of Windows.

Windows 95's subsequent market dominance vindicated Microsoft's business strategy. The majority of PC owners don't buy software based strictly on technology. They choose by weighing such factors as the options available, range of applications, purchase price, user-friendliness, and whether a brand dominates the market. This constitutes the typical consumer's order of priorities. Microsoft was aware of these priorities when designing Windows, which soon outsold its competitors, and is now number one on the market.

Program developers were drawn to Windows, which wasn't true for its competitors, causing more applications to be developed for Windows than any other OS on the market with a GUI. Developers were drawn to Windows because of the great momentum in gaining market share. In many ways, Windows was not necessarily the best technological operating system, but due to the potentially large sales of their products, developers chose Windows as their primary operating system.

Microsoft's history illustrates that it doesn't mind creating products with non-cutting-edge technology in a given market—as long as it tops the sales charts. Microsoft's history also shows that it fully realized it could possibly lose its number-one position in the technology field, which is one reason why it developed Windows NT and refined Windows 3.1 into Windows 95. Also, Windows 95 was created because Windows 3.1 simply could not handle the multitasking, networked environments in which it was being used. Windows 95 has mended many of the fundamental restrictions of the 16-bit Windows OS, without losing its compatibility with the old applications that were made for Windows 3.1 and MS-DOS.

Microsoft certainly held on to the traditional virtues of Windows in the Windows 95 product, while at the same time making great strides to correct the two weakest points in the earlier Windows series: technology and user-friendliness.

Network—Where And How?

Microsoft has also established and maintained another Windows product series, Windows NT, despite the overwhelming success of the Windows 3.1x series (which later became Windows 95 and Windows 98). Windows NT has both a client version (NT Workstation) and a version for servers (NT Server).

One reason that Microsoft may have decided to create Windows NT was because its working relationship with IBM on OS/2 was not going very well in the late 1980s. Windows NT was also necessary on a technical level, because the Windows 3.x and Windows 95 operating systems simply could not handle the functionality of an advanced networked operating system, the way Unix and Novell could. Windows NT is Microsoft's offer of an uncompromising operating system along the lines of OS/2—a "big brother" of sorts to the 16-bit Windows and LAN Manager.

It's unclear whether Microsoft initially regarded NT as a player on the server operating systems market or clients just came along as a result of market events. It is more probable that Microsoft regarded Windows NT as the natural successor to its first (and not very successful) attempt at network solutions: MS-Net, and later, LAN Manager.

To place network solutions in a historical perspective, it is necessary to go back to the early 1980s, at which time network solutions for PCs was a new concept. In 1982, a little-known Utah firm by the name of Novell Data Systems introduced a file-service solution called ShareNet (for copyright reasons, this name was later changed to NetWare). Novell clearly surpassed the solutions devised by its competitors, who were using a disk-server method that made sharing hard disks possible, but that didn't offer any possibility of file-level admission control. Novell's file service offered file-level admission control, as well as high performance and security.

In 1985, Microsoft launched MS-Net, which was based on DOS 3.x and influenced by several network products, notably IBM PC Network and the 3Com 3+ program. As was the case with the existing disk-server products, MS-Net was based on a number of DOS extensions, with one slight difference: MS-Net contained a genuine file service with file-level admission control. MS-Net's disadvantage was that it was decidedly slower and less safe than Novell's solution.

Nevertheless, Microsoft launched MS-Net as the future solution in network handling. However, a lot of customers continued to buy Novell's NetWare because they felt that it was a "tactical" solution that filled both their technical and business needs, rather than wait for the "strategic" products from Microsoft and IBM that were bound to follow.

In 1987, these strategic products were finally launched: IBM released OS/2, followed shortly by Microsoft's LAN Manager, 3Com's 3+ Open LAN Manager, and IBM's LAN Server, all three of which were based on OS/2. These three solutions became the market winners.

The Gartner Group, among others, proclaimed that these three solutions would dominate the market by 1991, thus counting out Novell. This is one of the reasons (other reasons involved some minor license conditions) why quite a few versions of Microsoft

LAN Manager started appearing at more-established companies. LAN Manager was incorporated in the following systems (among others):

- AT&T's Unix-based StarGROUP network operating system, ported to Sun Solaris, which was based on the same AT&T Unix System V-nucleus

- Digital's PathWorks NETWORK operating system

- Hewlett-Packard's HP-UX operating system (on the HP 9000 series)

Microsoft LAN Manager and its competitors were successful. LAN Manager made Microsoft the third largest provider of PC-based network operating systems, behind Novell and Banyan Systems, respectively. A closer look at the LAN Manager market share (estimated to be 2 to 7 percent, depending on the market research firm and statistical method used) demonstrates that Microsoft wasn't extremely successful, contrary to what Gartner Group had predicted.

Why was this so? The answer lies with Novell. In 1987, Novell launched the NetWare 386 OS (later known as NetWare 3). NetWare 386 was tailored for Intel's 80386 processors, as opposed to LAN Manager and the other products, which were based on Intel's 80286 processor. NetWare 386 soon proved to be far superior in every sense to the three OS/2-based solutions, and Novell consequently increased its market share greatly in the following years.

In further support of Novell's position, cooperation between Microsoft and IBM started to crack in a very bad way in the latter years of the 1980s. In late 1990, IBM and Microsoft parted company. This prompted Microsoft to focus on Windows rather than OS/2. Microsoft also launched a new 32-bit operating system platform called Windows NT, which stands for New Technology. NT was launched as Microsoft's alternative to OS/2, and as its future network platform.

In 1993, after many frustrating delays, NT was finally launched. From its beginning, Windows NT consisted of two products: Windows NT for Workstations and Windows NT Advanced Server for servers. While OS/2 was centered around the Intel processor family, Microsoft tried to be different from its competitors by making NT compatible with other processor platforms. Windows NT thus was later supplied in versions for Digital Alpha, SGI MIPS, IBM/Motorola PowerPC processors, and, of course, the Intel processor family. The development of Windows NT is shown in Figure 1.3.

Windows NT Advanced Server replaced Microsoft's OS/2 LAN Manager, which was not being used much, despite many analysts' predictions to the contrary. NT Advanced Server was functionally almost identical to LAN Manager 2.2, although many details had been changed regarding how it was to be handled administratively.

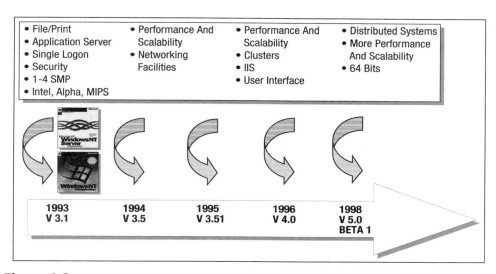

Figure 1.3
Microsoft Windows NT Server's development up to the present.

In 1993, Novell, with its NetWare 2.x and 3.x network operating systems, dominated the market. To further hinder Microsoft's launch of NT Advanced Server, Novell launched the NetWare 4 OS in 1993, which was far superior to Microsoft's OS. NetWare 4 also contained NDS (Novell Directory Services), a global catalogue of network services that is known as a *directory service* (see Chapter 4 for an in-depth definition). NDS makes it possible to gather all information in one central location.

However, NetWare 4 experienced too many adjustment problems to establish itself in the OS market. In fact, NetWare disappointed consumers because Novell was unable to fulfill public expectations.

Microsoft had some great advantages in trying to take over Novell's share of the market: Everybody was very confounded by the problems with NetWare 4 and the confusing signals being received from Novell, which was purchasing a variety of companies and products in the early 1990s.

Despite the fact that NetWare 4.0 is technologically more advanced than Windows NT Advanced Server, NT Advanced Server started to win a market "mindshare" in the mid-1990s. At the same time, Microsoft made a great effort to copy what it regarded as the key to Novell's success: a large number of dealers, an extremely successful certification program of NetWare technicians, and a strong position on the workgroup market. This was, after all, the route NetWare had taken to win the market starting when they introduced the 2.x version of the product.

Microsoft has been successful in its strategy. In recent years, Windows NT Server (as Windows NT Advanced Server is now called) has sold in ever-increasing numbers. This has made Microsoft's closest competitor, namely Novell, very uneasy.

Microsoft's Universal Windows Plan

To fully understand Microsoft's universal Windows strategy, it is worthwhile to review the point in time when Windows 95 was launched.

Until September 5, 1995, the Windows line of products comprised Windows 3.1 and Windows for Workgroups 3.11. Both items were developed with a view to selling standard programs with a GUI on the PC platform. Windows NT Workstation 3.51 and NT Server 3.51 operating systems were designed to handle applications on high-end workstations and servers, respectively (see Figure 1.4). Windows NT versions for traditional Intel-based PCs and a number of the most popular RISC-based workstations existed.

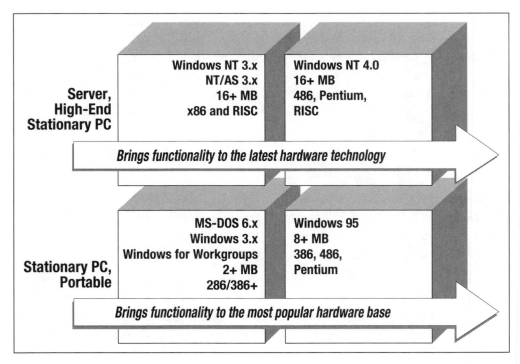

Figure 1.4
Microsoft's view of its Windows line in 1995; Windows NT would handle servers and high-end users, while Windows 95 would focus on general PC users.

As of September 5, 1995, Microsoft stopped selling Windows 3.1 and Windows for Workgroups 3.11. Both of these products were replaced by Windows 95.

Microsoft clearly wanted a quick transition to Windows 95. It wanted to remove any kind of competition on the market for the 32-bit operating systems for PCs, and it wanted to move up its customer base to a more uniform level, which would also reduce support costs. This was also the reason why, in 1995, Microsoft focused so much on its message that Windows 95 is easier to use and contains a wider range of functions than the previous Windows versions. Added to this, of course, is the fact that Windows 95 is fully compatible with the programs of its predecessors, and does not require much in terms of hardware.

Microsoft wanted to force the transition to Windows 95 because the OS forms an integral part of Microsoft's strategy, started in 1990. (Bill Gates often is quoted as saying "Information at your fingertips.") The transition to Windows 95 was also a source of enormous wealth for the company.

The *philosophy* behind "information at your fingertips" is to create a world where all information is only a mouse-click away from the user. Nevertheless, the *essence* of the strategy is Bill Gates' "Windows Everywhere" vision from 1987. Microsoft wants to be present—and number one—within all segments of the computer market. This strategy is tripartite: PCs today, servers tomorrow, and in the future, everything that requires an OS, including PDAs (Personal Digital Assistants), office equipment, consumer durables, TV decoder boxes, and video servers. Many suspect that Microsoft hopes, en route, to be able to mix the applications layer into the operating system, thus making Microsoft Office just as indispensable as the Windows OS.

Microsoft's plan is to use its strong position on the broad PC market as a sort of Trojan Horse to succeed in the low- and high-end computer markets. Microsoft's "Trojan Horse" consists of offering versions of Windows that are tailored to the low- and high-end markets, yet with the same user interface and programming environment that make its line of products easier to use than its competitors' products, for both users and program developers.

So far, everything has gone according to Microsoft's plan. Windows 95 established the Win32 API (Application Programming Interface), which is also used in Windows NT as the natural point of departure for developing programs. OLE 2.0 (Object Linking and Embedding) established Microsoft's technology for integration among various application programs and client/server solutions. OLE 2.0 and the newer Common Object Model technology enable Microsoft, in many instances, to introduce Microsoft Office and its program packages (not the least of which is Visual Basic) through the back door (see Figure 1.5).

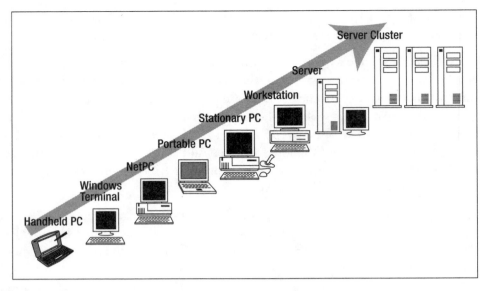

Figure 1.5
Microsoft's view of its Windows package today. Note in particular the top and bottom of this figure.

Windows 95 upheld Microsoft's best expectations by selling very well. As soon as Windows 95 was launched, all other independent application programmers had to alter their existing 16-bit DOS and Windows programs to 32-bit Windows, to avoid losing market share. In September 1997, the sale of 32-bit applications in the U.S. and the rest of the world amounted to 94 percent and 85 percent, respectively, of the total sale of Windows applications. At the same point in 1997, Microsoft estimated that 100,000 applications were compatible with Windows 95. More than 8,000 of these applications had already been developed for use on Windows NT Workstation. Significantly, almost all of the most popular computer programs were Windows 95-compatible. Microsoft says that many more such applications will follow.

Windows NT Workstation Sets The Pace

How does Microsoft plan to move forward from Windows 98? The answer is NT. In recent years, Microsoft has been telling the market that, of its present two operating systems, NT will endure the longest on the market. Since 1995, Microsoft hasn't concealed its goal of having only one OS on the market, and it wants that OS to be Windows NT, which has been a 32-bit operating system from its inception.

Microsoft periodically declares that Windows 98 likely will be the last "old" Windows version. After Windows 98, Microsoft wants to see all PC users transfer to

Windows NT Workstation (see Figure 1.6). And if Microsoft has its way, its current two lines of products—a high-end NT range and a broad Windows 95/Windows 98 range—will be on the market only a short while. Otherwise, Microsoft has to maintain program code for two different operating systems, when just one will suffice.

Microsoft's plan from the start has been for the Windows NT products to approximate the Windows 95/98 technologies, which has been very successful for NT Workstation 4.0 thus far. NT Workstation 4.0 looks and feels entirely like Windows 95 with regard to the user interface and the basic underlying programming structures

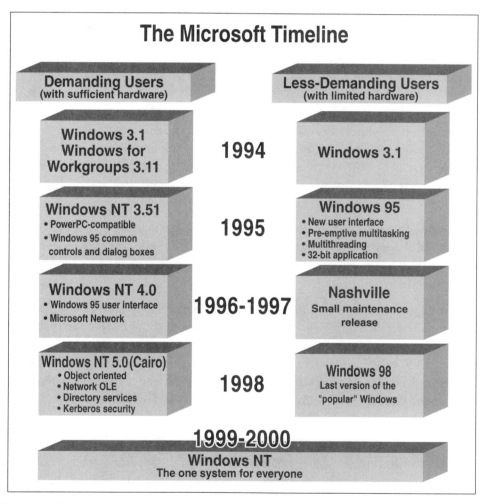

Figure 1.6
Microsoft announced its operating system plans two years ago, and already knew its strategy: one operating system for everybody.

(the APIs) are the same in both operating systems. A major part of Windows 95's program components have been re-created in Windows NT 4.0, which is great because rebuilding Windows 95 programs to run on NT is usually a minor effort for most programmers.

> **Note:** When NT Workstation 4.0 was launched, Microsoft touted it as the right choice for professional users, while promoting Windows 95 as the OS for everyday users. Jonathan Roberts, head of Windows' marketing division, describes the difference like this: "We say that Windows 95 is the easiest way to handle 32-bit application programs. It is supported by a wider range in hardware and requires less RAM. This design measure was greater compatibility. NT is simply a stronger operating system. Its design measure was higher reliability, scalability, and safety."
>
> So far, buyers have reacted somewhat coolly to Microsoft's plans for NT Workstation. Microsoft states that it has sold more than 11 million NT Workstations, which seems insignificant when compared with the 100 million copies of Windows 95 sold.

Microsoft has a lot of work ahead of it for Windows NT Workstation to spread to a larger number of ordinary PC users. To date, most companies that have implemented NT Workstation tend to use the operating system for workstations, which are used for complex tasks, rather than as ordinary PCs. Other companies that have implemented NT Workstation may have done so for the high security features or the greater control over user privileges.

One reason Windows NT Workstation has not gained popularity with PC users is that it technologically has always been slightly ahead of end users. It requires a larger RAM and processor size, and is markedly less compatible with older hardware and software products.

But Microsoft remains very optimistic. At WINHEC '97 (Windows Hardware Engineering Conference and Exhibition), Bill Gates stated, "We have started to see a migration from Windows 95 to Windows NT," but he was quick to add, "Microsoft is very careful in trying not to force the market to make the transition until it is ready for it. Here, the drop in prices on memory has been very helpful, so that a new computer now tends to have 32MB or even 64MB today, which makes it a really good computer for handling Windows NT."

Microsoft hasn't moved forward with its marketing of NT Workstation to PC users in recent months. However, since Microsoft constantly tells users that it anticipates NT Workstation will be the standard OS for company use in the coming years, its tone toward PC users has been more conciliatory in the last few months.

Microsoft's remarks on the differences between NT Workstation and Windows 95/98 are somewhat more cautious than they were originally. Now Microsoft is trying to *sell* NT Workstation to companies rather than forcing it on them. According to Microsoft, its strategy is to emphasize the obvious advantages of the NT Workstation operating system over Windows 95: better security facilities, greater integration with NT Server, better use of Pentium Pro processors, and improved performance on computers with more than 16MB RAM.

Parallel to this strategy, Microsoft is aiming ruthlessly at establishing itself on the market for high-end workstations, which is currently dominated by Unix. Microsoft has been fairly successful, with the most important suppliers of workstation applications now porting their products to Windows NT. This success has made many potential buyers consider changing to NT Workstation for simple financial reasons: A high-end PC and extra components are far cheaper than an identical Unix-based workstation. Microsoft has published several independent investigations that show NT-based workstations offer a significantly lower *cost of ownership* (the total cost, taking into account working expenses, the yield, and system lifetime) than corresponding Unix-based workstations.

Microsoft undoubtedly intends to initiate a more aggressive sales drive of NT Workstation to the wider computing public when NT Server and NT Workstation 5.0 become available. A manifestation of Microsoft's intentions is already very clear in its pitch that NT Workstation 5.0 is capable of reducing administrative expenses for PCs to one-third of the expenses for an identical Windows 95-based network. And Microsoft is bound to focus on administrative expenses in its sales promotions.

Windows NT Server At Full Tilt

According to Microsoft, Windows NT has made it the second largest supplier of operating systems. Novell NetWare is still the biggest, with IBM Warp Server a distant third. In 1996, more copies of NT Server were sold than NetWare or Warp Server. Novell is in first place only because of its extremely large existing base of NetWare 3.x servers.

By mid-May 1997, more than 1 million copies of Windows NT Server 4.0 had been sold since its August 1996 launch date. According to Microsoft, this means that more copies of NT Server 4.0 were sold than NT Server 3.51 and NetWare 4.x (the latest version of NetWare, which had been on the market for more than four years), and that, currently, more NT-based servers exist than Unix-based servers.

This information should be considered in its proper context; it comes from Microsoft, who, of course, has chosen the figures that best represent NT Server. Alas, much confusion exists as to how to calculate the sales of operating systems for network use, and manipulating these calculations for a particular company's benefit isn't very difficult.

Some analysts focus on the number of server licenses, others on the number of client licenses, and still others on sales figures. As NT Server is currently sold to small and medium-sized enterprises (enterprises with a few thousand PCs), the number of *server licenses sold* best represents NT Server, and that is what Microsoft stakes its claims on.

What Is Scalability?

Scalability is the capability of a software or hardware product to grow almost unrestrained in processing throughput, provided the right technology is installed.

With regard to operating systems, scalability means that it is possible to increase throughput, which adjusts with the increase in horsepower of the underlying hardware platform. So, for instance, if a server is extended from two to four processors, you may get almost double the throughput in the given applications.

With respect to Microsoft's plans, scalability also refers to maximizing the various hardware technologies across all the different versions of Windows using the same user interface.

Windows NT Server's position on the market appears more moderate when based on one of the other two methods for calculating market share. Regardless, many analysts agree that the market in recent years has tended to move fairly rapidly in the direction of Windows NT Server. So, even if NT Server hasn't yet overtaken NetWare 4.x in the number of client licenses sold (because many people have bought NetWare 4.x licenses rather than NetWare 3.x licenses, without using the NetWare 4.x facilities), and its distribution is still significantly lower than the number of Unix clients, the clear trend is that Novell, Unix, and all other competitors are losing their market shares to NT Server.

According to the latest figures from International Data Corporation (IDC), more than 1.3 million NT Server licenses were sold in 1997. By comparison, 717,000 Unix server licenses, 900,000 NetWare server licenses, and 226,000 OS/2 server licenses were sold.

Windows NT Server sales are doing nicely, and, consequently, Microsoft doesn't spend nearly as much time trying to convince the public that its product is better than its competitors' products. Instead, Microsoft is focusing on conquering the high-end server market, where none of its servers have come close to gaining market share. The Unix-based servers, OS/400-based minicomputers (AS/400), MVS-based mainframes, and a host of other large operating systems currently dominate this high end of the market. These are operating systems that tend to be available from a supplier on their own hardware platform.

Microsoft's avowed intention for the future is that PC servers must be able to handle any situation, and must be scaled to meet even the most complex problems. This applies to both the Windows NT Server operating system and the entire BackOffice line of products.

May 20, 1997 was Microsoft's "Scalability Day," the purpose of which was to demonstrate the NT Server operating system and the scalability of Microsoft's BackOffice products. Microsoft's ambitions were fulfilled, helped by (among others) Tandem, Digital, NCR, and Unisys on the hardware side. Microsoft also was successful with regard to fault tolerance, despite the very limited functionality of NT Server 4.0 in this area. Despite criticism of Scalability Day as lacking a "sense of reality" in many of its configuration settings, it displayed two important factors: Microsoft is focusing intensely on the scalability area, and its collaborators are very keen on not only being present, but also in outdoing one another in the market.

Many independent programmers have also started holding similar scalability demonstrations on NT Server, in order to be well placed within a promising market. Position on the market could turn out to be just as important for every programmer as it is for Microsoft. For example, NT's share of SAP's total license turnover rose from 10 percent to 25 percent during the period 1994 to 1996, and in August 1997, SAP reported that the share of new SAP R/3 licenses taken out for NT Server was 42 percent. These figures are impressive, considering that SAP is currently the biggest supplier of integrated company systems for trade and industry. (People tend to associate SAP only with big mainframes and minicomputers.) Even more impressive, SAP actually recommends NT Server 4.0 for solutions having up to 1,500 users. This covers everything except the most extreme business requirements.

Other trends on the NT Server market look positive for Microsoft, notably the focus by heavyweights like Baan, PeopleSoft, and IBM on creating applications for Windows NT Server, which could make NT even more popular. A greater variety of server applications means that NT Server will be a real winner. Stories abound in the computer market that prove buyers choose solutions rather than technology. According to Microsoft, there are approximately 1,800 more applications available for NT Server than for any other operating system.

Despite these promising trends for NT Server, Microsoft still isn't satisfied. It is already talking about focusing on better scalability on every single server. Presently, its aim is to make Windows NT Server 5.0 capable of delivering scalability of up to 16 processors per server, whereas today, scalability can be sensibly handled only with up to 4 processors for most applications. The topic of clustering (with respect to Microsoft's Cluster Server) is also very prominent: The goal is to have several servers working together on the same job, so that the task is accomplished that much faster.

Likewise, Microsoft is very focused on improving the clustering system. It is improving fault tolerance via its Cluster Server, and is improving the administrative facilities by introducing the directory service, adding safety facilities, and augmenting the service and support structure of NT Server. Many of these improvements will be introduced in NT Server 5.0.

What Is Windows CE?

Having set the PC and server platforms off to a good start with Windows 98, NT Workstation 4.0, and NT Server 4.0, Microsoft set its sights on its Achilles' heel with regard to its strategy of "information at your fingertips": small, cheap units for communication, entertainment, and mobile treatment of data.

Microsoft has previously carried out some unsuccessful attacks in this area with, among others, Windows for Pen Computing (for PDA and pen computers) and Microsoft Bob (for entertainment). But with Windows CE, Microsoft is geared toward a new and wholehearted entry into the consumer market.

Windows CE is an entirely new, 32-bit, processor-independent, multitasking, and multithreading operating system that is built for the purpose of accessing the broad consumer market. Two important common denominators exist between Windows CE and the other Windows products: Windows CE is equipped with the same user interface as Windows 95/98 and NT 4.0, and Windows CE operates with a portion of the Win32 API (not the entire Windows API), making it compatible with regular Windows. Windows CE also has a special version of Internet Explorer (to access the Internet), facilities for exchanging data with existing Windows-based PCs, and various standard applications for a scaled-down Microsoft Office.

Microsoft predicts Windows CE will be a contender in the new hand-held PC (HPC) mobile computer category. HPCs are geared towards the same market as portable PCs, but HPCs are much smaller, lighter, and cheaper than current portable PCs. Microsoft also anticipates that Windows CE will be used for most other types of consumer units, such as portable PCs, units for cordless communication (such as cellular telephones and Global-Positioning Satellite [GPS] receivers), multimedia playing machines, and perhaps specially built Internet units (for example, Internet TV, digital TV boxes, and Internet telephones).

Microsoft is also considering using Windows CE as a linkup with WebTV technology, which it has already bought. And rumors are circulating that Microsoft will use Windows CE as a possible Windows visual display terminal product. The role of Windows CE in Microsoft's sales is shown in Figure 1.7.

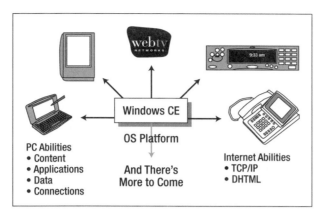

Figure 1.7
Windows CE plays a crucial role in a majority of Microsoft's sales drives in markets closely related to the PC.

Windows CE is not available as a software package, simply because it is supposed to be an operating system for consumer units. Windows CE will only be sold directly to those who develop these hardware units, and not to regular consumers. Microsoft thus depends a lot on companies that develop hardware. Otherwise, Microsoft would have to expand its resources to cater to such items. Currently, nothing indicates that Microsoft is likely to make such changes, although Windows CE is slowly catching on. Twenty-five products for Windows CE already exist, and they are being developed by prominent companies such as Casio, Compaq, Hewlett-Packard, Hitachi, NEC, and Phillips.

Windows CE is far from dominating the HPC market, but Bill Gates' strategy of "information at your fingertips" will likely be effective by the year 2000, simply because only a few real competitors exists in Windows CE's market, and most users are accustomed to Windows 95's user interface.

Coming Soon: NetPCs

NetPC (or Network PC) will be the latest addition to the family of PCs supported by Microsoft's operating systems. NetPC is specially developed to cut the expenses and reduce the complexity of managing a distributed PC environment.

NetPC is basically an ordinary PC from which all hardware that requires administration has been removed. NetPC has no CD-ROM drive, disk drive, or internal extension space. NetPC is based on a PCI-bus, Advanced Configuration and Power Interface (ACPI), wake-on LAN (the PC can be turned on centrally, enabling settings to be changed even if the individual PC is off). It is delivered in a sealed box, which prevents the user from tampering with the insides.

A NetPC must be equipped with a remote-boot ROM so that the OS can be placed on the network and the PC can be booted via a network server. A NetPC can also be equipped with a hard disk, so that the OS, applications, and any user data can still be placed locally.

NetPC is not a new and different type of PC—it's just a simplified PC, cheap in price and cheap to run. Microsoft has defined NetPC in collaboration with Intel, Compaq, and Hewlett-Packard, and the PC producers thus are likely to launch it very aggressively on the market.

NetPC's specification was completed in mid-May 1997, and the first NetPCs were ready for delivery in the third quarter of 1997. The cheapest NetPCs sell at less than $1,000. This price will need to lower for NetPCs to become more popular, because many more-powerful desktop PCs now cost under $1,000.

On Its Way: Windows Terminals

Recently, Microsoft began concentrating on the concept of *thin clients*, clients that have very little program code and that don't require very much hardware. Microsoft claims that the majority of its customers want simplicity rather than thin clients, but this claim seems to be a marketing "truth," intended to conceal the fact that Microsoft is unable to muster any opposition to the hard-pressed, Java-based thin clients of its competitors, without having to reach a compromise on its current Windows strategy. With the Internet quickly becoming extremely popular, Microsoft will find it very difficult to compete head-on with Java, as Java has already established itself as one of the leading programming environments. This is why Microsoft has adopted this marketing strategy.

Windows CE is Microsoft's only possible thin client solution. Yet Microsoft continuously emphasizes that Windows CE is not written for personal computers, which require Windows 95 or NT Workstation. Windows CE's existence, however, means that Microsoft can change its decision at any time and market Windows CE as its thin client, which could stop possible infiltration to Windows' low-end market share.

Microsoft has chosen to focus on an existing technology to meet the possible threat from thin clients. Rather than completely extending Windows to the low-end market, this technology consists of simply transmitting pictures on screen to the client, and transmitting the client's keyboard and mouse movements back to the computer that handles Windows. In other words, this technology is based on the well-known and thoroughly tested technology of visual display terminals. Microsoft calls its product a *Windows terminal*, or by its project code name, *Hydra*.

Microsoft has taken out a license on the technologies from Citrix (WinFrame)—a company that has many years of experience handling multiuser technologies and terminal emulation for its Windows terminals. Under this license, Microsoft and Citrix will cooperate in developing the fundamental multiuser facilities. This technology is based on the Citrix ICA protocol (already used in the Citrix WinFrame product) and the T.Share/T.120 protocol (an international protocol for multichannel conferences, optimized for network environments with high bandwidth; the protocol is used in Microsoft NetMeeting).

Microsoft's plan is that Windows clients will use the T.Share protocol, and other types of clients will use the ICA protocol. The baseline product, Hydra, will be a supplementary item for Windows NT Server 4.0 and 5.0. Citrix and Microsoft will develop and market extra components, all based on Hydra.

Microsoft anticipates that it will develop Windows terminals (consisting of a screen, keyboard, mouse, and computer unit that functions on par with common visual display terminals) costing no more than $500. Microsoft estimates that many Windows terminals will be based on the Windows CE operating system. Presently, questions of when, how, and who will start producing such units are unclear. Microsoft hopes that the first Windows terminals will be launched in 1998, to coincide with the anticipated launching of Hydra.

Compared with other thin clients, Windows terminals may not be very interesting or attractive. This is due to the Microsoft NetPC specification, which has more functions and costs only about $1,000. In addition, because conventional PCs are continually falling in price, many PCs already cost the same as NetPCs cost. The vast number of outdated PCs, however, makes the Windows terminal concept far more attractive. Practically every company has outdated PCs, which can be used for a few more years if they are converted to Windows terminals for less-demanding users. This conversion also could be advantageous to a company that wants to use a certain application that requires a more modern OS than the one being used on its PCs. The advantage over competing companies is that existing hardware can be utilized with Windows terminals, meaning the purchase of new hardware isn't necessarily required.

The Windows terminals may be one way of incorporating the remaining terminal users into the Microsoft universe. More than 2 million visual display terminals are sold worldwide every year, and Microsoft would like to own a piece of that market.

Microsoft Has Its Eyes On Consumers

Microsoft is also busy investigating the market opportunities for really low-end consumer electronics. Recently, Microsoft purchased the WebTV product. WebTV units can be connected to any television set, and can supply roughly the same functions as an Internet browser, while everything is operated from the usual Windows user interface. Any new WebTV products likely will be based on Microsoft's Windows CE operating system.

Microsoft is not limiting itself to the WebTV concept. It is looking into other market opportunities for consumer electronics that have TV and DVD players (the likely next consumer hit) as their point of entry. Microsoft recently invested $1 billion in Comcast Corporation, the fourth largest U.S. cable TV operator, which also has various other interests in telecommunications.

What Is The PC 98 Reference Specification?

Together with the producers of PCs, Microsoft released a new specification in which it predicts the developments in the computer market that are likely to appear in the coming year. Microsoft's reference specification is connected to the tools and products that require the necessary hardware that it wants to introduce in its operating systems.

Although Microsoft is powerful, it can't force PC producers to follow its reference specification. Yet it is difficult for the producers to ignore, because the specification is connected to the highly prestigious Windows logo for hardware components, and the logo greatly influences buyers' purchasing decisions.

Microsoft's sudden interest in the cable TV market is fairly simple: Probably the biggest growth opportunity for Windows is greater access in homes. Today, only 40 percent of all U.S. households have a computer. Compare this to the fact that over 90 percent of all U.S. households have television sets. Microsoft's chances of exploiting this lucrative market further (with units such as WebTV) depend on TV and telephone companies investing heavily in updating their infrastructure from analog to digital. Digital transmissions generate far better images, and will increase the likelihood that more people have access to the Web and other digital services.

Microsoft invested in Comcast because it wanted to put digitizing of the infrastructure at the top of Comcast's agenda. This would develop investment interest in the digital communication market, thus giving other telecommunications businesses more money—and incentive—to invest in digitizing their own infrastructures. Microsoft's strategy seems to be successful, because after Microsoft's moderate investment in Comcast shares, the value of shares in cable TV and telephone companies rose sharply.

Microsoft's investment also means that telephone and cable TV companies have been exposed to a new dimension in their choice of digital technologies and standards. This is a vital detail, because work is ongoing in setting the formats for digital TV images. Before Microsoft's investment in Comcast and its declaration that the PC 98 reference specification for PCs also covers digital TV (in the shape of a 480- and 720-frame-line film format), the TV industry had ignored PCs in its discussions of the decisive parameters for the new digital standards. Now the PC may very well hold the balance: Millions more personal computers currently exist that can accept digital TV signals than there are conventional TV sets that can do the same.

Make no mistake about Microsoft's intentions: Although the company might be investing more in various businesses these days, Microsoft goes to great lengths to emphasize that its core products remain Windows 95/98, Office, Windows NT Server, and BackOffice (Microsoft's central server applications).

Microsoft Sees No Limits To Growth Within The Windows Family

First there was the PC, then portable computers, and now Microsoft is working hard at establishing itself in the high-end markets for workstations and servers, with Windows NT Workstation and NT Server, respectively (see Figure 1.8).

Microsoft has even made radical changes in its marketing strategy. In 1995, Microsoft discovered the Internet and the fact that Microsoft could be shut out of Web media if it didn't act quickly. Microsoft also realized that this could eventually deal a deathblow to

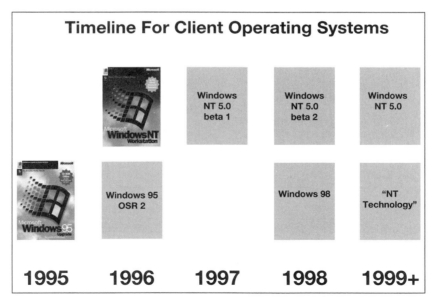

Figure 1.8
Microsoft's short-term plans for the Windows family.

Windows. Microsoft's fear was caused by a small company named Netscape, which had an extremely firm grip on the market with its Navigator Web browser. Together with workstation-powerhouse Sun Microsystems' Java language, Netscape seemed to have created a new type of operating system.

Recognizing the threat, Microsoft announced in December 1995 that Internet standards would be built into all its products. Bill Gates seemed overly optimistic when he announced that Microsoft would capture the market for Web browsers and Web servers in a matter of years. How could Microsoft possibly do so at such a comparatively late stage in the Web market?

Microsoft successfully fulfilled all of its Internet-related promises during 1996, and its progress on the market since has been phenomenal (see Figure 1.9). Microsoft's Internet Explorer Web browser dominates 25 to 30 percent of the total market, with close to 50 percent of the market in Europe (which was slower to embrace the Web than the U.S.). Microsoft's Internet Information Services is well on its way to becoming the most-used commercial Web server product, largely because it comes free with Windows NT Server. Finally, Microsoft has made the Java programming language an integral part of all its program-development tools and its product strategies.

Microsoft's competitors must feel very uneasy when they see that Microsoft is well on its way to opening numerous new, promising markets for Windows, including:

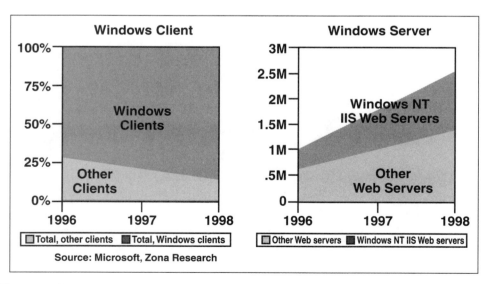

Figure 1.9
Microsoft is doing well in the Internet market, despite its late start.

- Small handheld Windows units (Windows CE)

- Very high-end servers (through more-scalable server software and increased versions of NT Server)

- Terminals with Windows, as well as actual Windows terminals (under the project name Hydra)

- Simpler and cheaper PCs (the NetPC thin clients)

Microsoft is concentrating its efforts on making Windows a truly scalable platform, from the very low-end (and hence low-cost) Windows CE, to the very high-end Windows NT Server, with its clustering and multiprocessing capabilities (see Figure 1.10). Everything, of course, comes with the same user interface and the same APIs, so that the applications stretch from top to bottom without costly changes for businesses or individuals.

After the failure of OS/2 and Microsoft's approximately $1 billion investment in Apple, it's hard to imagine who can stop Microsoft. As far as I know, Microsoft's investment in Apple means that Microsoft has the right to utilize all present and future Apple patents and technologies. One effect of this may actually prevent Apple from ever becoming a serious competitor to the various Windows operating systems.

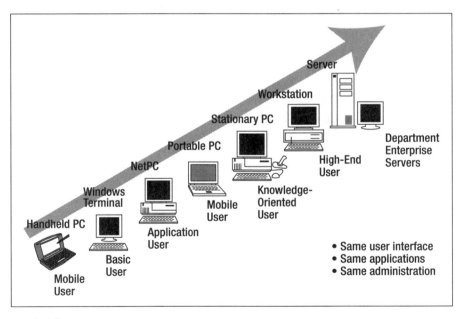

Figure 1.10
Microsoft introduces its "Windows Everywhere" business strategy.

Microsoft's Only Fear: The Network Computer

Interestingly, the only real competitor to Windows' domination is Oracle's Network Computer (NC), a product that has filled more marketing space than shelf space. NC isn't available quite yet, and very little experience with NC installations exists. This is, perhaps, the irony of the situation, because Microsoft undoubtedly is considered the world's leading IT marketing force, but so far, Oracle's NC has proven its value primarily through marketing (including expensive Super Bowl and World Series commercials).

Microsoft has spent a lot of energy fighting NCs in recent years. But while Microsoft has done everything possible to bring the NC concept into disrepute, it has also become extremely interested in total cost of ownership (TCO). As far as I know, Microsoft never mentioned the NC term prior to its introduction by Oracle Corporation. Furthermore, Microsoft has joined forces with Intel to make the reference specification for NetPC, which is nothing more than a tuned-down Windows PC, and a Windows terminal is on the drawing board.

> **Note:** You can read more about total cost of ownership (TCO) in Chapter 7. Chapter 8 discusses the possibilities for saving TCO for a Windows 95- or Windows 98-based PC network. This is a good starting point for the subsequent, thorough treatment of all NT 5.0 TCO-saving facilities on the customer side.

Microsoft just doesn't take many chances. If it doesn't succeed at ruining NC's chances on the market, it certainly has made the NC concept less interesting by explaining to the world that Microsoft can achieve the same low TCO with a Windows platform and an NC. And, according to Microsoft, if customers want an NC, they might just as well buy a NetPC instead.

More than anything else, the Windows terminal is Microsoft's struggle against the NC. Microsoft suddenly is interested in building an actual Windows visual display terminal based on Windows CE (see "What Is Windows CE?" and "On Its Way: Windows Terminals," earlier in this chapter). The Windows terminal quite clearly will be a very big and direct competitor to the visual display terminals on the market, and possibly to the low end of the NC market.

Several hardware producers aren't waiting for Microsoft's seal of approval—they are already making their own Windows CE-based notebook-style computers, which could very easily compete with Windows 95-based notebooks. This situation more than likely will continue, because Windows CE 2.0 has been launched, which contains support for higher-end solutions (namely Java) and gives access to network services.

Microsoft is already looking more closely at the production plans of Windows CE licensees, to prevent unwanted direct competition between Windows CE and Windows 95/98. (Microsoft earns more on Windows 95/98 licenses.)

I am convinced that Microsoft will successfully compete with the NC, one way or another. The NC is already at a disadvantage because it isn't a Windows-standard product, but rather a concept that anybody can shape to their personal liking. This will cause mutual incompatibility at various levels, something that Microsoft has been explaining to anyone who cares to listen.

In principle, all NC technologies can be mutually incompatible, except for the Java programming language, which covers only the applications that can be run on the NCs. NCs do not include the user interface, the underlying operating system, the type of processor, or connecting external units. NCs work contrary in almost every way to the four pillars of the PC: uniformity, openness, crystal-clear (yet possibly more or less proprietary) standards, and *personal* (which, of course, forms one half of "PC").

Very few applications are available in Java, which is probably the NC's biggest problem. A computer has never gained a foothold in the market without already having a tangible advantage software-wise, either in the range of software available, or in its access to some special programs that don't exist on other platforms.

The way in which NCs can best be handled as thin clients is an open question. A visual display terminal is certainly thinner. Finally, an NC is likely to demand more accessible bandwidth than a corresponding PC or visual display terminal. This might cause problems in many of today's network environments, and might also lead to "constipated" servers.

Interestingly, some of the companies that are backing NC the most (Oracle, Sun, and IBM) have themselves faced difficulties in adapting to the age of the PC. Perhaps they see the NC concept as a chance to return to the "good-old centralized days," where the world could be divided into central computers and terminals, and the majority of software came bundled with computers (and hence was completely proprietary).

The final irony is that if a market for NCs really exists, Microsoft can potentially take over this market with Windows CE. Windows CE is based on well-known and recognized (proprietary) standards, which is not the case for its competition.

Can Microsoft Live Up To The Expectations Of The Outside World?

Microsoft is predicted to capture more than 90 percent of the computer market during 1998 with its Windows family: from the Windows terminal and Windows CE, to Windows 98, NT Workstation 5.0, and NT Server 5.0. This means that, lacking any serious unforeseen upheavals, Microsoft will dominate most of the computer world and the consumer electronics market.

The biggest "problem" Microsoft is likely to confront is how to continue growing at its previous rates. On July 17, 1997, Microsoft announced that its fiscal year, which ended on June 30, showed a total turnover of $11.36 billion, which was up by 31 percent compared to the previous year's result of $8.67 billion. Its net income equaled $3.45 billion, with earnings of $2.63 per share, up by 54 percent from the prior year.

Mike Brown, Chief Financial Officer at Microsoft, summed up the year as follows: "Microsoft finished a year with growth in both trade and profits driven by the success of Windows 95 and the Office applications." However, he went on to say, "Microsoft can look back on two fantastic years thanks to the success of its 32-bit products, but we anticipate that our growth in profits will slow down next year."

The reasons for this reduction in growth are simple: "Next year will be a seesaw for product turnover." Yet surprisingly, Mike Brown finished off by establishing that "no major product launches are planned." This is in line with a press release that Microsoft issued several months later: Windows 98 wouldn't be launched until the second quarter of 1998. So Windows 98 cannot contribute significantly to Microsoft's annual profit.

The Registrar of Restrictive Trade Practices, who is responsible for trade monopoly in the U.S., has in recent years repeatedly refused permission for Microsoft to buy IT enterprises that the Registrar believes might have a positive effect on the bottom line of the company. The U.S. Justice Department is constantly attacking Microsoft, and they seem remarkably interested in Microsoft's activities. The latest move by the authorities was legal action regarding the forced bundling of Internet Explorer with Windows as a prerequisite to purchasing Windows products.

The restrictions on Microsoft mean that it must develop growth by itself. It is forced to do so because it can't use its coffers, which currently hold approximately $9 billion, to purchase growth through acquisitions. Therefore, next year we likely will see a more moderate growth rate for Microsoft. This piece of news is not bound to give Bill Gates sleepless nights. According to *Forbes*, he is estimated to be the second-richest man in the world, with assets of approximately $36.4 billion.

Microsoft's Plans Until The Year 2000

Microsoft has produced a string of successful operating systems since the early 1990s, starting with Windows 3.1, followed by Windows 95, and now with Windows NT Server. Likewise, the huge demand for Microsoft Office has placed Microsoft in the top rank among software and operating system vendors.

Microsoft's continuous, massive display of innovation demonstrates that, unlike some other high-tech firms, it won't need to resort to cutbacks and downsizing any time soon. On the contrary, Microsoft's plans are extremely expansive, including large-scale sales promotions aimed at practically all areas of the computer trade.

Since Microsoft became a publicly traded company on the NASDAQ Stock Market in 1986, it has eclipsed General Motors as the top stock-capitalized company in the United States, with 22,232 employees and a $226 billion market capitalization. General Motors has 766,000 employees and a much lower market capitalization of $124 billion.

Nothing seems capable of stopping Microsoft's growth, which makes its plans for the future very interesting to computer users everywhere. Microsoft's dominant position in the computer industry warrants a discussion of how its products are likely to develop in the short and long terms.

In the short term, Microsoft likely will segment the server market and focus on penetrating the high-end portion of this market. This strategy requires that Microsoft increase fault tolerance and scalability for the NT platform, and that it handle the challenge of keeping the BackOffice Suite's future development ahead of competing Internet and intranet companies.

In the long term, Microsoft wants to establish Windows NT Server as the dominant operating system for handling clients, placing its closest competitors on the sidelines. To achieve such dominance, Microsoft must set up a convincing distributed architecture, with an ever-increasing integration of the Internet that is capable of handling IT environments of any size.

Sorry, But Which NT Do You Mean?

Explaining Windows NT in simple terms is not easy. What sort of entity is it? The answer is complex because many variations of Windows NT exist, each having different capabilities.

The variety of Windows NT Servers available has led to much confusion and frustration in the computer market. In fact, when Windows NT 4.0 was launched, Microsoft was attacked as being the "Evil Empire," and at that time, NT 4.0 was only the second of the four NT variations now available.

The emotional discussions surrounding the launch of Windows NT 4.0 resulted from Microsoft's decision to differentiate between the uses for the two Windows NT variations, NT Workstation and NT Server. Microsoft noticed that several businesses were using NT Workstation as a server, which was not its intended use. Consequently, Microsoft put a clause into its NT Workstation license agreement stating that a maximum of 10 clients could be connected to an NT Workstation-based computer at any one time. If a company using NT Workstation wants to serve more than 10 clients at the same time, it has to buy the more expensive NT Server.

Microsoft's tightening of its Workstation license agreement led to vehement media attacks against Microsoft, as well as attempts to prove that hardly any difference exists between NT Workstation and NT Server, making the difference in price unreasonable.

Microsoft's difference in prices for NT Workstation and NT Server is similar to a situation in which Intel established an artificial differentiation in price for two of its processors. The Intel 80486SX processor—quite a few of which were sold in the age of the 80486 processor—was actually an 80486 processor from which Intel had deliberately removed a portion of the chip, which caused the floating-point unit to stop functioning.

Microsoft recently realigned NT Server into two new products: *NT Server Enterprise* and *BackOffice Small Business Server*. This realignment has gone very smoothly, but the computing public has raised many questions, such as the following:

- Does the product differentiation make sense?

- Will customers accept it?

- Are the prices set at the right level?

- How do the NT Server products compare with those of the competitors?

Understanding Microsoft's Product Differentiation

Microsoft's recent differentiation of the Windows NT operating systems into four products makes foreseeing the future of the entire NT situation slightly more difficult. As of Microsoft's most recent changes, the following four variations of NT now exist:

- Windows NT Workstation

- Windows NT Server

- Windows NT Server Enterprise Edition

- BackOffice Small Business Server

Windows NT Workstation

NT Workstation is a scaled-down version of NT Server, which means that a few aspects have been altered in NT Workstation: application scheduling, priority, and related matters. NT Workstation does not contain the applications that are relevant for use only in servers. As previously stated, NT Workstation's license agreement limits to 10 the number of workstation computers that can be connected to NT Workstation at any one time.

NT Workstation and NT Server are very similar products, which Microsoft doesn't intend to change, because it makes developing new versions of NT easier, and it makes life easier within corporate IT departments, which need to master only one operating system.

A public "secret" of Microsoft is that it intends to split NT Workstation into two separate products at some point, probably in 1999 or 2000. One product will cover the low end of the market (currently covered by Windows 95/98), and the other product will continue to cover the high end of the market, to which the current version of NT Workstation is geared.

The Three Windows NT Servers

The server side to Windows NT is slightly more complicated than the client side. In the latter half of 1997, Microsoft began marketing two variations of Windows NT

Server, so a total of three different Microsoft server operating systems are now available to choose from. These are shown in Figure 2.1.

Understanding the three NT Server variations is not as difficult as you might expect. In fact, Microsoft's product differentiation makes a lot of sense, because it divides the server market into three categories: high-end users (NT Server Enterprise Edition), midlevel users (NT Server), and low-end users (BackOffice Small Business Server).

Windows NT Server Enterprise Edition

Microsoft's business strategy for Windows NT Server Enterprise Edition is to have it supply slightly more scalability and manageability than its "kid brother," Windows NT Server. NT Server Enterprise Edition is designed for use in the largest business environments and for special jobs (which means that Microsoft has fixed the price for NT Server Enterprise Edition 4.0 considerably higher than for NT Server).

The following five basic technical enhancements included in NT Server Enterprise Edition 4.0 constitute the major differences between it and NT Server 4.0:

- *Symmetric Multiprocessing (SMP) support of up to eight processors*—NT Server 4.0 supports a maximum of only four processors.

- *Microsoft Cluster Server* (previously known as *WolfPack*)—Provides for high availability (where one of several processors can fail and the server continues to run

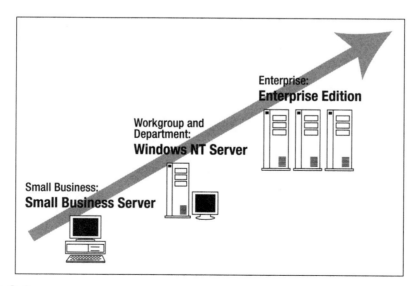

Figure 2.1
Windows NT Server 4.0 comes in three variations that cover essentially different market areas.

with no intervention from the administrator) in the current version, and clustering will soon be added to it.

- *Microsoft Transaction Server*—This is a special version designed for the Cluster Server.

- *Microsoft Message Queue Server*—This is a special version that sets no limits to the number of users that may be connected simultaneously. It operates with a gateway from Level 8 and is supposed to be used on the Cluster Server. Level 8 is a service that makes it possible to use queues from the IBM MQSeries product with Microsoft's own Message Queue Server. The Message Queue Server contains an intelligent routing service that can find the cheapest path to the network automatically, provided that various routes exist between the locations. Message Queue Server carries out automatic rerouting if a network segment is down.

- *Better RAM tuning of the memory consumption of the NT nucleus*—The potential RAM-application size of the NT nucleus is reduced from 2GB to 1GB, which means that applications get access to up to 3GB of RAM instead of the 2GB limit of NT Server 4.0.

Moreover, Microsoft apparently has removed some memory-leak problems from NT Server Enterprise Edition 4.0 that have occurred in NT Server 4.0. *Memory leaks* occur when not all the memory used by a given process or application is released after its completion. Memory leaks have been a source of irritation and some operational instability in NT Server 4.0. Therefore, many NT Server experts recommend choosing NT Server Enterprise Edition 4.0 for servers with more than 512MB of RAM.

> **Note:** Microsoft has also developed special Enterprise Edition versions for three BackOffice applications (SQL Server, Exchange Server, and Site Server). As the name Enterprise Edition indicates, these BackOffice applications are capable of utilizing the special facilities in NT Server Enterprise Edition.

Windows NT Server

Windows NT Server 4.0 is the familiar product that is popular today. It has not been changed by Microsoft. NT Server is geared toward medium to large companies that wish to have a secure and distributed business environment.

BackOffice Small Business Server 4.0

BackOffice Small Business Server 4.0 is a reduced variation of Microsoft's Windows NT Server. Small Business Server (SBS) can only support a maximum of 25 users at one time and is unable to handle any kind of trusts against other domains.

However, BackOffice SBS is more than just a reduced version of NT Server—Small Business Server contains the two most frequently used applications in the BackOffice program: Exchange Server and SQL Server. Small Business Server also includes two new applications: *Fax Server/Service* and *Modem Sharing Server.*

BackOffice Small Business Server has a very easy user interface, which includes the most commonly used objects and jobs, such as facilities to add new users, printer sharing, and fax handling. Microsoft stated in its first advertisements for SBS that it is considering including its *Hydra* product (see Chapter 1 for more information on Hydra) at a later time.

Small Business Server is a splendid example of how Microsoft is gaining not only a foothold among the world's small enterprises, but also within the emerging market for small servers in home offices. The market is attractive: The number of small businesses is steadily increasing globally, which likely will lead to a larger market turnover for small business servers than for large, network servers.

Microsoft's prospects in the small business market are further bolstered by the fact that the majority of small businesses haven't reached the same level of computerization as big companies, which means that a large opportunity should exist in this area. To give an idea of just how big the small company market is for Microsoft, a recent global poll showed that there were 70 million computers owned by small companies, which is more than double the 33 million computers that large companies have.

Predicting NT Server's Future

Most computer-market analysts believe that Microsoft has completed its plans for NT Server by splitting it into three variations. However, rumors are circulating in the computer industry that Microsoft intends to develop a fourth NT Server (to be called *Com Server,* or something similar) that will focus on the many NT communication technologies and introduce several new applications in this field. But Microsoft seems to have shelved any such plans for the moment. So, despite the lack of guarantees in areas governed by market mechanisms, the inclusion of the three NT Server variations in the release of Windows NT 5.0 seems to be a safe bet.

The most likely scenario is that businesses in the various market segments will choose whichever NT Server variation, with its built-in server applications, is intended for their segment. The choice and the splitting up of the built-in server applications relate more to the position on the market in regard to the competitors than anything else.

The Primary Target Areas: High-End Markets And Scalability

Windows NT Enterprise Edition 4.0 leaves no doubt that Microsoft intends to establish itself in the high-end, information technology arena. Not surprisingly, one of Microsoft's established goals is to establish Windows NT as a high-end alternative to the existing complex and powerful Unix solutions on minicomputers and mainframes.

With the appearance of NT Enterprise Edition and the related BackOffice Enterprise Edition, Microsoft has established the software foundation for access to the high-end market, where *scalability* is not only an empty marketing term, but also a word that potential customers must know well if they are considering high-end products.

Microsoft wants to be part of the high-end market, but paradoxically, it has announced that Windows NT 5.0 will not be supported by the RISC processors (PowerPC from IBM, MIPS from SGI, and so forth) on which NT 4.0 can run. Microsoft already stopped supporting the Intergraph Clipper chip, also RISC based, when it replaced NT 3.51 with NT 4.0. Windows NT 5.0 thus is limited to running on the Intel 80486 series of processors (including the Pentium) and the Digital Alpha processor family.

This is unfortunate. Perhaps future versions of Windows NT 5.0 will run on RISC processors, although no known plans exist. Regardless, the producers of PC servers that aren't already on the high end of the market, such as Compaq, have quickly followed Microsoft's Enterprise Editions with advertisements for their own servers.

A viable solution for your business requires more than just having the necessary software and hardware. Scalability is only a small part of the equation, because the solution must also have a very high level of reliability against system failure, and its dependability must be proven in practice.

Scalability Day

The impressive display that Microsoft presented on its "Scalability Day" in May 1997 caused the IT departments of many large companies to notice Windows NT. Scalability Day was a marketing exposition intended to demonstrate the power of Microsoft's tools to the public. Potential Enterprise Edition customers wanted to be reassured that other businesses had successfully implemented the software before they would purchase it for their own business.

Note: An instance that took place at Scalability Day provides a good example of the difference in perspective between Microsoft and the systems administrators who are responsible for the critical applications at companies. Bill Gates and numerous Microsoft partners demonstrated a banking system program that is designed to run ATMs (automated teller machines) capable of handling more than 1 billion transactions per day. One of the first questions from the audience was: "How many users at the same time can the system handle?" Microsoft didn't have available the data necessary to answer that question.

Most computer professionals who are familiar with Scalability Day regard it with mixed feelings, because the ATM solution and the other displays are simplified scenarios, tailored to sensibly scale a system that consists of many small, autonomous systems linked together on a network. Benchmarks of this kind are no longer convincing, because the simplest computer problems—creating sufficient throughput on high-end systems—have been solved.

Microsoft's demonstration of the ATM system (DebitCredit) is a particularly insightful example of what happens when marketing takes control over the IT department. DebitCredit may be the perfect benchmark to use to reach high figures on a system that lacks any facilities to parallelize or distribute the treatment of data. Microsoft's 1-billion-transaction system consists of 45 servers that work fairly independently of each other, which means that data isn't even collected in one single database, nor with any kind of automatic leveling of the load, nor with joint system administration and security. In short, Microsoft's ATM demonstration is of a system that no self-respecting bank would ever consider.

Very simple benchmarks, such as DebitCredit, are effectively pointless demonstrations. In the real, harsh world, transactions grow increasingly more complex, and are very seldom alike. The load and the number of users at any one time can cause violent fluctuations, yet the system must be tolerant of errors and function at top capacity for lengthy periods of time.

It's Not Just A Question Of Scalability

Windows NT Server's capability to perform mission-critical jobs still leaves a lot to be desired. The existing Unix and mainframe solutions have been performing better. For instance, the throughput tests carried out by SAP reveal that mainframes are still able to handle more users at one time—SAP's tests indicate approximately three times as many—than a network of NT Servers. According to Bernd Lober, who is responsible for Microsoft NT implementations at SAP, numerous NT Servers can handle a maximum of approximately 1,300 concurrent users, whereas an IBM S/390 can handle more than 3,000 users. These figures are based on 15-minute load tests, so the gap could easily prove to be more than twice as high.

Also, Windows NT hasn't been sufficiently tested yet with regard to fault tolerance. In mission-critical terms, the system must be able to be operational in a matter of seconds, no matter what error occurs. Moreover, NT's administrative tools still are lacking when compared with the tools offered by other mainframes.

Thus, Windows NT Server's success in the long term depends on more than scalability. NT Server must not only be able to perform 1 billion transactions in a day, but, most importantly, it must also be able to deliver constantly *reliable* transactions.

It is quite complicated to define precisely what is required of an operating system. For instance, Unix still hasn't been able to master the heaviest tasks, even though the most common Unix platforms can handle at least 16 processors (compared to NT's 8), which is an architecture that is capable of handling at least the same capacity as the current mainframes (which are several times more expensive). So far, Unix has gained a niche only for certain data-breaking tasks (notably data warehouses), whereas the majority of batch handling still belongs to the mainframe domain.

> **Note:**   Paul McGuckin, Vice Director for Server Research at the Gartner Group, recently stated in Datamation *magazine that he expects NT to reach the Unix level of scalability within the next five years. He anticipates that during 1999, NT will scale sufficiently well to be able to meet, and thus handle, more than 80 percent of what is required of application and database servers. The rest of the high-end market will continue to be dominated by mainframes and mainframe-like systems.*

According to a report from the Gartner Group, one NT server currently can support only 400 users connected simultaneously, whereas the best Unix solutions can handle approximately 1,500 users at the same time. The Gartner Group estimates that in 1999, NT will be able to service 1,200 users concurrently, while the maximum capacity of Unix will rise to 3,000 users. By comparison, a modern mainframe can handle 10,000 or more users concurrently.

Before NT Server can play a significant role in the high-end market, Microsoft must achieve the following tasks:

- Supply Cluster Server products with clustering support for more than two servers (the current product's limit).

- Improve SMP support so that the operating system is able to use many simultaneous processors. Supporting at least 12 processors and preferably 20 will make Microsoft competitive with similar processor configurations that are common on large businesses' operating systems. An operating system's capability to handle this number of processors is not sufficient—it must really be able to utilize them in parallel, so that the system is truly scalable.

- Improve the system tools for NT to the point that changing a number of configurations is possible without having to restart the whole operating process, which wastes valuable time and requires applications to be shut down temporarily.

- Make the most important applications for mission-critical use, such as database systems from Microsoft and other third-party developers, capable of using NT reliably and effectively.

- Make NT capable of supplying a far greater level of security for both the network and the server applications.

Likewise, industry observers recommend that Microsoft spend more time with companies such as IBM, NCR, Computer Associates, Digital, Tandem, and Compaq, because they have experience in developing high-end systems. This would help Microsoft address all the necessary details (to gain more credibility in the high-end market) and increase its knowledge and experience on NT and the market as a whole. A basic prerequisite of selling a mission-critical system is that the customer feel satisfied that a sufficient service and support apparatus stands behind the solution.

IBM And Microsoft: An Odd Couple

Although Microsoft makes an everyday effort to connect Windows NT Server with its BackOffice Server applications, businesses may not see the sense in using anything more than NT Server as a basis for their mission-critical solution.

Microsoft's present BackOffice solutions aren't unique with regard to scalability, and they are still quite new. Recently, IBM demonstrated a solution that is based on an NT Server similar to Microsoft's ATM banking system. This test showed that the IBM system was able to handle 14,000 transactions per second, or 1 billion transactions in 20 hours, aided by the IBM DB2 and the IBM Encina Server applications (which, incidentally, are much better known in larger companies).

Surprisingly, BackOffice has attracted a lot of attention, despite its lack of uniqueness or a clear market demand compared to the other NT variants. This is due, in part, to the fact that Microsoft has such a good grip on the market that most people—even seasoned IT professionals—automatically assume that Microsoft is the world's biggest software supplier. This is false: In terms of sales, Microsoft is a distant third (after IBM and Computer Associates). A large part of the turnover of IBM and CA comes from their sales of solutions for mainframes and minicomputers, which are significantly higher than for PC solutions. Microsoft is now moving in the same direction with its Enterprise Edition products.

With its NT products in position, the IBM marketing department has started spreading the NT message in the new market. One of IBM's most convincing slogans is that IBM and its Lotus division offer the biggest selection of NT applications (more than 100 applications are available). IBM also advertises that its solutions will never have problems with scalability and portability because IBM has server applications for many other operating system platforms.

IBM's declared goal is to be the leader in the market for NT personal computers and servers, applications, and middleware, as well as for service and support. Its goal is likely to be achieved before the end of 1998.

> **Note:** An April 1997 report from the Aberdeen Group states, in part: "IBM has recently started to publish a new strong NT-in-the-enterprise message that gives IBM's customers the liberty to choose the operating system and application environment that makes sense in solving a given task while IBM supplies the service and support that their customers need no matter what operating system environment they choose."

In 1997, for the first time ever, IBM created a prototype of a Microsoft operating system. This means, in the short run, that Microsoft will attract more attention from companies that use solutions from IBM and its equals. This also means, however, that Microsoft has a tough competitor in its own backyard, for the first time.

Several other software giants have recognized the full potential of Windows NT: SAP, Oracle, Baan, and PeopleSoft have ported their most important server applications to Windows NT. As stated in Chapter 1, NT Server and SAP have turned out to be an extremely successful combination.

The NT platform promises an uncertain but exciting future. Following the current trend, by the year 2000, NT Server may claim the largest number of server applications ever, which is a message that buyers and software developers should not overlook. In September 1997, Microsoft stated that more than 1,800 applications had been developed for NT Server, 350 of which are equipped with a BackOffice logo.

Microsoft Focuses On The Architecture

Parallel with its efforts to increase the number of server applications, Microsoft is working on making the NT platform even more suitable as the central component in a distributed environment. It is doing this by improving the distributed architecture of Windows NT.

The following list includes some of the most important aspects of an architecture:

- Modularity

- Openness and interoperability

- Scalability

- Manageability

- Internet/intranet support

- Support level among suppliers of third-party applications

- Customer understanding and demand that incoming components meet the architectural requirements

Until now, Microsoft's architecture has been pretty confusing, consisting of numerous acronyms that must be pieced together to understand its meaning. To add insult to injury, Microsoft has tended to create its own proprietary standards instead of following any de facto or de jure standards and embedding some of the architectural components into its products. Thus, Microsoft's architecture has been limited to a single platform (Windows NT) and has been usable only in organizations with a strategy centered around Microsoft.

Departure from this strategy is in sight at Microsoft. Most importantly, Microsoft's architecture is becoming more complete and thoroughly tested, while at the same time it is making a virtue of "selling" its new standards to third parties, who must then improve their own applications on other platforms (non-NT) to the level of Microsoft's standards.

The culmination of Microsoft's architectural efforts thus far came at the Professional Developer's Conference in late September 1997, where Microsoft launched Distributed interNet Applications Architecture (DNA) and COM+. The components of DNA are shown in Figure 2.2. Microsoft is marketing Windows DNA and COM+ as the new architectural frames for future, scalable, multilayered solutions to distributed data handling supplied via any network.

COM+ is a Web-prepared extension of COM (Component Object Model) that makes it possible to extend the Windows-based component technology to cover other component technologies and languages that are becoming increasingly popular on the Web. COM+, in effect, transforms the client/server applications to Web applications.

DNA is quite different; it is a three-layered model for developing the next generation of Windows applications, in which the application is divided into components for storage, program logic, and graphical presentation. DNA is, of course, closely integrated with the Active Directory, which handles identification, security, and connection

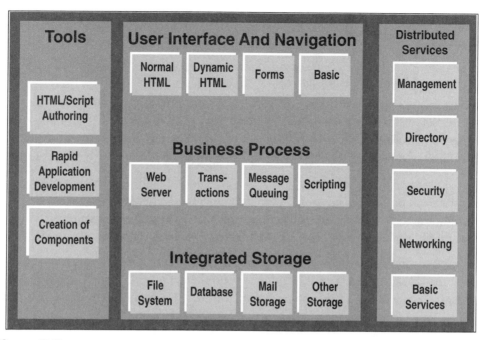

Figure 2.2
Microsoft DNA contains all the components necessary to establish a distributed IT environment.

of users, either to distributed applications or to components that can be stored anywhere on the network—regardless of whether it's a LAN or the ultimate WAN, the Internet. (For more about Active Directory, see Chapter 4.)

DNA is a consolidation of several existing Microsoft technologies. COM+ is also part of the DNA frame system.

Microsoft thinks that the development of applications for tomorrow's distributed environments will take place in the same environments as today. However, Microsoft doesn't spend much time discussing Java—Microsoft seems to ignore Java as a framework for distributed solutions. Instead, it focuses on Dynamic HTML as a solution to creating cross-platform applications. The same is true for DCOM's competitor, Common Object Request Broker Architecture (CORBA). Microsoft very likely will only start integrating Java or CORBA if the market forces it to do so.

What Do The Analysts Think?

The market research firm International Data Corporation (IDC) indicates that Microsoft sold approximately 1 million copies of NT Server in 1997, which is a significant increase compared to 732,000 copies sold in 1996 and 363,000 copies sold in 1995 (see Figure 2.3).

According to preliminary calculations from IDC, NT Server hasn't fully lived up to its great expectations. The sale of NT Server licenses has increased "only" by 80 percent in 1997, to 1.3 million units, which is a 39.8 percent market share. The sale of Unix server licenses rose by 10.8 percent to 717,000 units. NetWare and OS/2 registered a decline of 9.4 percent (900,000 server licenses) and 34 percent (226,000 server licenses), respectively.

Most analysts expect that Windows NT Server will soon squeeze Unix out of the market for small application solutions, so that, consequently, the growth rate of Unix will drop. Windows NT Server 5.0 will certainly be in an extremely strong position to meet the technological challenge from Unix with regard to slightly bigger solutions.

No comparison between the two competing operating systems exists when it comes to marketing. Whereas NT Server is a uniform product across all server platforms, Unix consists of many variations. Some of the best known Unix variations are IBM AIX, Sun

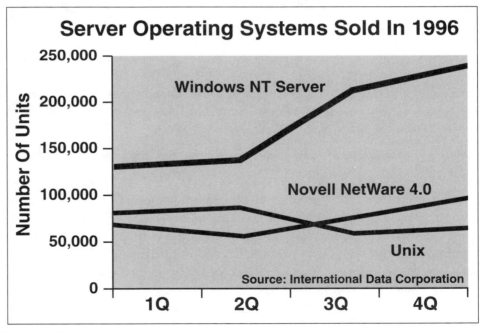

Figure 2.3
Windows NT Server seems to sell well, which is clear from its sales figures for the three most commonly used server systems. This information is taken from a slide in Bill Gates' presentation at the TechEd 97 Conference.

Calculating Market Share

Three different calculation methods exist to count market shares for servers: the number of server licenses, the number of client licenses, and the turnover generated. Operating systems that are used primarily for applications and/or in small firms have the advantage when regarding the number of server licenses. Operating systems that are common in large installations have the advantage when calculating the number of client licenses. The turnover generated tends to be the least fair calculation method (and hence, the one that is used the least), because the price derived tends to vary a lot among operating systems. Notice, moreover, that Microsoft prefers to speak of new sales, while its competitors prefer to speak of the total base installed. This is because Microsoft can't boast of a very large base of server products, and its competitors can't produce Microsoft's sales figures, but have been on the market longer and have sold more systems.

Solaris, Hewlett-Packard HP-UX, SNI Reliant Unix, SGI IRIX, and Linux. The fragmentation among Unix vendors causes their marketing messages to be extremely unclear, and results in a reduced number of applications available on a given Unix platform.

The latest figures indicate that NT is in the process of taking over the role previously held by NetWare. Although NetWare owned the market a few years ago, with an approximate 80 percent share, its share today is well below 50 percent.

Since 1995, the sale of NetWare server licenses has declined dramatically because a large portion of these licenses cover resale. This includes the immensely popular NetWare 3.1x operating system, which Novell is trying (unsuccessfully) to replace with NetWare 4.x. According to a Forrester Research report from August 1996, large companies no longer consider Novell a strategic supplier. They consider NetWare to be a "legacy" operating system, which is an operating system that is replaced at a company's first convenience. Although 90 percent of the IT bosses questioned said they currently have NetWare, only 48 percent said they expected this to be true in 1999.

The results of the Forrester Research report were repeated in research performed in Europe by IDC. IDC interviewed 500 companies in November and December of 1996. The results show that NT Server is gaining a strong foothold in Europe in the low-end (small business) market, and also has a certain influence in the somewhat higher end (large businesses). While the sales of NT Server increased, there was a related decline of NetWare and Unix sales in Europe.

Microsoft's launch of NT 5.0 definitely will increase the sale of NT Server. Bill Gates has said several times that NT 5.0 is the most important version of NT since the first version was introduced in 1993.

The market position of NT Workstation, however, is much weaker. IDC calculations show that approximately 2.2 million copies of NT Workstation have been sold since 1996, 30 percent less than what IDC expected. NT Server's toughest competitor was Windows 95, which IDC anticipated. Approximately 60 million units of Windows 95 have been sold since it was launched in August 1995. The market trend seems to have been more merciful to NT Workstation since IDC's report, as Microsoft announced last November that it has sold more than 11 million copies of NT Workstation.

Convincing the market to focus on NT Workstation in 1998 won't be easy for Microsoft because it plans to launch Windows 98 in the second quarter. But if NT Workstation does gain popularity, Windows NT 5.0's introduction will be even bigger.

What's In The Cards For The Future?

What will succeed NT 5.0? This is a very good question. Microsoft has wisely abstained from discussing in detail the future after Windows NT 5.0. This is a good example of Microsoft's professional attitude of handling the market. NT 5.0's launch will be more successful if Microsoft *doesn't* talk about the technologies and applications that it didn't have time to embed in NT 5.0. Microsoft has stated that, in the very short term, it plans to launch a Service Pack every three months for NT 5.0 and Windows 98. It also expects to introduce a few new facilities and applications.

We expect that some of the successor(s) to NT 5.0 will include:

- A 64-bit operating system

- Further improvement and simplification of the user interface

- Increased intelligence in the interaction of the user interface, so that the PC can automatically handle even more tasks for the user

- A focus on natural user interfaces that enable the user to speak to the PC and the PC to read aloud

- Complete elimination of the differences in interfaces with various types of communication (such as mapping drives for servers and using hypertext on the Web)

- Continued focus on the Zero-Administration Windows (ZAW) end goal: to establish the administrative-free client; ZAW is a new technology in NT 5.0 for improved software installation in Windows-based environments

- Automatic load balancing across large clusters

- Self-repairing network topologies

- Regular development of the distributed facilities and integration to the Internet

In 1999 or 2000, Microsoft most likely will be ready to introduce its so-called "Windows 2000" launch, consisting of all versions of Windows, based on the Windows NT nucleus.

Welcome To The Revolution—A Survey

Reading about Windows NT 5.0 on Microsoft's Web site or glancing at its specification sheet is sufficient to realize that Windows NT 5.0 is a complete revolution compared with its predecessors.

The Windows NT 5.0 revolution is found neither in the actual nucleus of the operating system nor in its user interface. The revolution consists of numerous highly important superstructures that remove the remnants of the LAN Manager heritage from the NT environment.

Some of the most important new features of NT 5.0 are the following:

- *Active Directory*—A directory service
- *Microsoft Management Console (MMC)*—A standardized and component-based umbrella for administration
- *Distributed File System (DFS)*—Makes establishing distributed file systems possible
- *Distributed COM (DCOM)*—Makes creating distributed applications possible
- *Active Directory Services Interface (ADSI)*—A standardized interface for all forms of directory services
- *Dynamic Domain Name Service (DDNS)*—Replaces the old WINS
- *Active Desktop*—A new and very Web-inspired Windows user interface
- *Win32 Driver Model (WDM)*—A new driver architecture

In addition to these features, many very important (although less conspicuous) features are included regarding the file system, network handling, and system security. Several of these new items alone are sufficient reason for every professional computer user to evaluate NT 5.0 more closely.

Underlying these new features is the previous version of Windows NT, because Microsoft has reused most of the existing NT nucleus. However, this reliance on NT 4.0 doesn't make Windows NT 5.0 any less revolutionary. To the contrary, I believe it bodes well for the stability of NT 5.0—and high stability is an absolute prerequisite for the operating system to be usable for servers.

In short, Windows NT 5.0 is a far bigger and better product than its predecessor, NT 4.0, which simply upgraded the user interface of the old Windows 3.x to look and feel like Windows 95. Bill Gates is right in his statement that "NT 5.0 is the most important version of NT since the first version."

This chapter provides an overview of all the features in Windows NT 5.0, and discusses the differences between NT Server and NT Workstation.

From NT 4.0 To NT 5.0

A discussion of Windows NT 5.0 is complicated by the fact that NT 5.0 will likely consist of four versions of NT, as briefly outlined in Chapter 2. Building on Chapter 2, this section provides a breakdown of the individual features of both NT Workstation 5.0 and NT Server 5.0. However, it is too early to predict how Microsoft will design the differences among the three different variations of NT Server (discussed in Chapter 2).

If you focus only on the underlying nucleus of the operating system, NT 4.0 and NT 5.0 are very similar. A big portion of the operating system program code in NT 4.0 is identical with the current beta version of NT 5.0 (other than corrections of errors and program components made in 5.0). In other words, NT 5.0 is essentially the same program code in Windows NT 4.0, up to and including Service Pack 4. The vast majority of the features that distinguish NT 5.0 from NT 4.0 are superstructures of the operating system.

Important New Features In NT Workstation 5.0

The applications included in NT Workstation 5.0 are a thorough improvement to the applications supplied with NT Workstation 4.0. Some NT Workstation 5.0 applications are available for NT Workstation 4.0, too, as "extras" (and are so noted in the following list). The following is a complete survey of the most important new features of NT Workstation 5.0:

- *Internet Explorer 4.0*—The latest version of Microsoft's popular Web browser. It offers the best possible integration with the OS. (Also available for NT Workstation 4.0.)

- *Personal Fax for Windows*—New version of the existing fax tools. The previous version is included in NT Workstation 4.0.

- *Direct X 5.0*—The latest version of Microsoft's collection of APIs, especially developed to meet the demands of the market for entertainment. DirectX 5.0 allegedly includes the latest DirectX-based games.

- *Asynchronous Transfer Mode (ATM) support*—Gives future applications the advantage of all the possibilities of ATM via the operating system.

- *Plug and Play*—Built-in support of Plug and Play, thus enabling NT to gain ground in the portable computer market.

- *Universal Bus (USB) support*—Capacity to connect many units to the computer's serial port. USB requires very little user knowledge, which is why it could prove to be extremely popular with end users.

- *IEEE 1394 support*—The new standard for high-velocity communication. Can deliver up to 10Mbps bandwidth.

- *Advanced Configuration and Power Interface (ACPI Power)*—Improved Power Management standard that is able to operate peripheral units far better than is possible with NT 4.0.

- *Windows Scripting Host*—Capability to carry out scripts from the user interface or command line. Scripting Host is supported by Visual Basic and Java scripts, and is a language-independent architecture that enables you to build script interpreters for other languages.

- *Task Scheduler*—New scheduling tools to replace the previous AT service.

- *Microsoft Management Console (MMC)*—A new umbrella for the operating tools, to ensure a uniform user interface among all system tools used in the NT environment, NT's own tools, and the system tools of other applications.

- *FAT32 support*—FAT32 is an improved version of the FAT (File Allocation Table) file system already used by the OSR (OEM Server Release) versions of Windows 95, as well as in Windows 98. The OSR is a newer version of Windows 95 that was released at the end of 1996.

- *NT File System (NTFS) improvements*—The new version of NTFS allegedly is faster and has many new facilities, such as disk-quota allocation for every user, file encryption, and the capability to add extra disk space to an NTFS volume—without having to restart the system.

- *Universal Disk Format (UDF)*—A new file system for handling DVD drives and CD media.

- *Defragmenting tools*—The built-in NT tools now can also defragment the disk, regardless of whether it is a FAT, FAT32, or NTFS file system.

- *NDIS 5.0 driver*—New network architecture that contains support for broadcasts and reservation of bandwidth.

- *Win32 Driver Model (WDM)*—The new driver architecture for 32-bit Windows, which will be used for new types of units. WDM drivers will also be used by Windows 98.

- *Smart Card support*—Microsoft imagines many situations in which the Smart Cards will be used in PCs, and they should also be compatible with various Network Computer standards.

- *Fibre Channel support*—Fibre Channel is a technology that makes reaching speeds of up to 1Gbps possible. This technology will primarily be used with storage media for servers.

- *64-Bit support*—Provides the capability to optimize the performance-related capacity of PCs that are based on the new 64-bit Alpha processors and the future Intel 64-bit processors. This technology will mostly be used with servers.

- *Intelligent Input/Output Architecture (I_2O) support*—I_2O provides the capability to remove part of the operating task of I/O units from the main processor (the CPU) and delegate it to other processors.

- *Multimedia Extensions (MMX) support*—As with Windows 98, NT 5.0 allegedly is geared to be used with the 57 extra MMX CPU instructions that follow the Intel format. MMX, a superstructure for the Pentium processor, improves performance with multimedia tasks via numerous special instructions. Intel's MMX and Pentium II processors, Advanced Micro Devices' K6, and Cyrix's 6x86MX all are furnished with the extra MMX set of instructions.

- *Simultaneous monitors*—The capability to connect up to four monitors that the operating system (and thus applications) regards as one monitor. This has fantastic possibilities, from improved database monitoring to "surround" video games.

- *Accelerated Graphics Port (AGP) support*—This is a new standard for 3D graphics that enables you to improve performance on "ordinary" computer systems.

Important New Features In NT Server 5.0

The next list contains the most important new features of NT Server 5.0. In addition to this list, NT Server 5.0 includes all the new features of NT Workstation 5.0 outlined in the preceding list, and many new administration tools that are based on the Microsoft

Management Console standard. The most important new NT Server 5.0 features are the following (features available for NT Server 4.0 as "extras" are so noted):

- *Active Directory*—Directory service that is capable of storing information for all the network objects in one place. This service will be good for users connecting remotely or at a new workstation, who will be able to have their familiar environment appear.

- *Dynamic DNS (DDNS)*—Replaces the present WINS (Windows Internet Naming Service) with a name index.

- *Distributed File System (DFS)*—Provides the capability to spread a file structure across several servers and, if desired, introduce fault tolerance by duplicating the same part of the file structure across several servers. This version is also compatible with NT Server 4.0.

- *Microsoft Installer*—A new technology for improved operation of the software installation in Windows-based environments (also covers the much-talked-about IntelliMirror technology). Maximum performance is attained only in conjunction with NT Workstation 5.0. The Microsoft Installer technology is the key to full implementation of ZAW (Microsoft's Zero Administration for Windows initiative).

- *Transaction Server*—Gives access to administer various program components far more effectively than the traditional transaction-based administration. (The latest version is also available for NT Server 4.0 as part of the Option Pack.)

- *Message Queue Server*—A messaging and queuing system that is Microsoft's attempt at ensuring reliable delivery of messages and data in a distributed environment. (The latest version is also available for NT Server 4.0 as part of the Option Pack.)

- *IIS*—The latest version of Microsoft's extremely successful Internet server that makes subscribing to FTP and HTTP services on the network easy. (The latest version is also available for NT Server 4.0 as part of the Option Pack.)

- *Index Server*—Provides the capability to index all the text and properties of various types of files, including HTML files. This provides quick and powerful text searching of documents. (The latest version is also available for NT Server 4.0 as part of the Option Pack.)

- *Cluster Server*—Microsoft's clustering solution, which currently contains only high-availability facilities. Cluster Server was previously known as WolfPack. It already is included as part of NT Server Enterprise Edition 4.0. NT Server 5.0 is likely to contain a newer version of Cluster Server that also has clustering support.

- *Kerberos authentication*—NT 5.0 introduces the Kerberos protocol for user authentication. So far, Kerberos is the strongest known security protocol for distributed environments.

- *Public Key Certificate Server*—Provides the capability to use public key authentication for domain accounts via SSL/TLS (Secure Sockets Layer/Transport Layer Security). SSL/TLS provide communications privacy over the Internet.

- *Quality of Service (QOS)*—Gives QOS-prepared applications access to reserve bandwidth and priority in the transmission of data.

- *Multiprotocol routing*—Provides the capability to use the server as a router on IP- and IPX-based networks. (Also comes in a version compatible with NT Server 4.0.)

- *IP security*—Makes it possible to encrypt data transmitted via the network.

Upgrading To NT 5.0

On several occasions, Microsoft has stressed that the installation routine of Windows NT 5.0 will make upgrading the following operating systems possible:

- Windows 3.1x

- Windows 95

- Windows NT 3.51

- Windows NT 4.0

Microsoft apparently is considering allowing users to upgrade to Windows NT 5.0 from Windows 98, too. Currently, no one is certain whether a Windows 98 upgrading route will be built into the first version of NT 5.0 or will come at a later date. The current beta version of NT 5.0 supports upgrades from Windows 95 and Windows NT 4.0, and the method is relatively simple.

The New User Interface

The biggest change in the interface for Windows NT Workstation 5.0 and Server 5.0 is actually an offshoot of Internet Explorer 4.0. Windows NT's user interface acts more like a Web browser than the previous Windows user interface (see Figure 3.1). Microsoft calls this more-Web-like user interface *Active Desktop*.

NT Active Desktop is similar to the Web in that single-clicking any given program icon opens that icon's corresponding program, and all clickable objects are now underlined. Also, an extra toolbar has been added to the taskbar located next to the Start button. The standard configuration of the toolbar in Windows NT 5.0 and

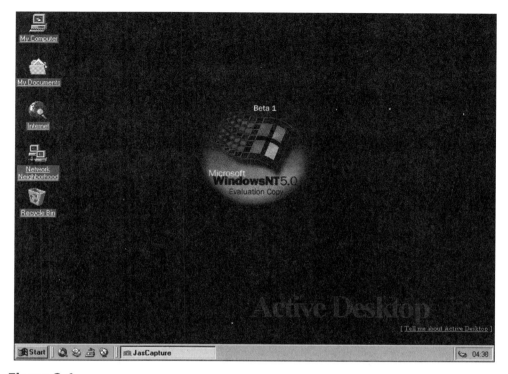

Figure 3.1
The Windows NT Workstation 5.0 Active Desktop. It may vary a bit, depending on a user's setup choices.

Windows 98 contains the Quick Launch Toolbar, which consists of four icons: Internet Explorer Web browser, Outlook Express, a clean Desktop (where all windows are minimized), and a list of available channels for the Active Channel service. As with ordinary toolbar buttons, you simply single-click an icon to open its corresponding program.

Microsoft has changed the standard background color of the beta version to black. The bottom of the screen is marked in a shade of gray that indicates you are working with Active Desktop. These two characteristics apply only to NT Workstation 5.0, because Active Desktop is not fully functioning in the current beta version of NT Server 5.0.

In short, the NT 5.0 desktop user interface differs completely from the desktop of NT 4.0. The only obvious similarities are the standard icons and the toolbar. Otherwise, the new NT desktop is identical with the Windows 98 desktop.

Don't be deceived by appearances: The underlying NT 5.0 user interface is identical to the underlying NT 4.0 user interface. The difference in appearance is due to Internet

Explorer 4.0, which introduces the user interface changes just mentioned. You also can remove all the user interface changes to return to the familiar NT 4.0 look.

If you want more information about the changes in appearance of the user interface, you'll have to read some literature regarding Internet Explorer 4.0 or Windows 98. This book focuses more on the other features of NT 5.0 because the appearance of the user interface can vary extensively.

The Big News: Active Directory

Active Directory is the big NT Server 5.0 news. It is Microsoft's offer of a scalable, hierarchical directory service that is capable of competing with Novell's NDS and Banyan's StreetTalk products.

The introduction of Active Directory may seem slightly contradictory to seasoned NT Server observers because Microsoft has insisted that NT Server 3.51 was launched with a directory service. Microsoft argued that NT Server 3.51 supplied one single login and that all users within the domain were replicated. The replication worked such that users were still able to be authenticated and have access to their network resources after their computers were moved to a different physical location (for example, a satellite office on the company network). When NT Server 4.0 was launched, Microsoft started consistently referring to this solution as a "directory service."

However, the two facilities just outlined are far from sufficient to create a directory service. A genuine directory also has the following properties:

- Storage of information on the environment in a distributed form

- Support for "white pages"-type searches (searching based on a certain attribute; for instance, a name or a telephone number) and "yellow pages"-type searches (searching based on fairly precise classifications; for example, all color printers or LaserJet printers on the second floor)

- The capability to spread login to the directory to also cover new applications and services

- The capability to remove dependency on physical locations

Like its competitors, Active Directory is very similar to the X.500 model, which defines the directory chart (how information is stored in the directory). Active Directory uses a scaled-down version of the X.500 chart, which consists of object classes and attributes. The structure of Active Directory is fairly simple, and few rules exist with regard to the most important objects, and which attributes a class or an object contains. For instance, a user interface can contain properties associated with only one user (for example, the email address and user profile).

Just like its competitors, Microsoft foresees its directory being extended with new objects that meet the special requirements and directory-prepared applications of the company. In Active Directory, this will be via Active Directory Services Interface (ADSI) or the Lightweight Directory Access Protocol (LDAP) C-API.

Domains

Typically, every Active Directory will contain a domain tree, and it will be possible to concatenate several domain trees. A *domain tree* is a hierarchical representation of the system in a treelike structure. This representation can take the form of either a single domain, or a tree of trees that represents multiple domains. The domain can be divided into organizational units (the OUS) that, likewise, can be organized in a tree-like structure.

If the msn.com domain is placed at the top level in Active Directory, you can open a number of underlying domains by names such as northamerica.msn.com, europe.msn.com, and asia.msn.com. These underlying domains also may include one or more domains underneath them. Each single domain, likewise, may contain several organizational units; for example, production.europe.msn.com, sales.europe.msn.com, and marketing.asia.msn.com.

Each NT Server 5.0 domain contains its own directory, which enables you to delegate more administrative privileges on a far more detailed level than ever before. Unlike the NT 4.0 architecture, you can delegate specific administrative rights of individual users, or groups of users, in NT Server 5.0.

Active Directory uses the Domain Name Service (DNS) protocol to localize instances of the directory and LDAP 3.0, so that they can be searched for in the directory. This means that TCP/IP has become the standard protocol of NT Server 5.0 in every sense, and what remains of the NetBIOS background in the shape of Windows Internet Naming Service (WINS) has been removed. To ensure backward-compatibility, NT 5.0 can still handle WINS and the other "older" net protocols, such as NetBEUI.

NT Server 5.0 domains use multimaster replication to ensure high access to the directory and help in distributing administration rights throughout the company. Multimaster replication means that each domain controller (DC) contains a master replica of the directory of the domain, and that all changes are automatically spread to all DC servers.

Multimaster replication eliminates the division of roles in the Primary Domain Controller (PDC) and Backup Domain Controller (BDC) that was used in NT Server 4.0. Because of its backward-compatibility, NT Server 5.0 can also act as a PDC or BDC, so that it can coexist with NT Server 4.0-based domain controllers. In that case, the NT Server 5.0 acting as a PDC/BDC will cause the multimaster replication to be switched off.

Transitive Trust Connections

One drawback of introducing Active Directory (compared with the existing domain-based solution) is that the new domains and domain trusts assume a far more complex form than is the case with NT 4.0. This is why NT Server 5.0 also enables you to automatically define transitive trust connections among domains, which is an immense administrative advantage compared to the previous versions of NT Server. A *transitive trust connection* means that, by defining a single trust connection between two domains, all domains situated under the two given domains may be configured to automatically inherit the defined trust.

Transitive trust removes the worst headaches of the domain methodology, without escaping it completely. Transitive trust is a great relief from NT 4.0, with which administrators have to define their own bidirectional (two-way) trust relationships between every single domain pair that trusts each other. For very big domains, this can lead to an absolute administrative nightmare.

Cisco is currently porting Active Directory to Unix, while simultaneously implementing Active Directory on Cisco's large and extensive line of network components. These two developments could turn out to be the key to making Active Directory a standard for directory services.

> **Note:** Active Directory is discussed in depth in Chapters 4, 10, 13, 14, and 15. Appendix A contains a short survey of NT 5.0's new tool for transmitting information from Novell NetWare-based installations (both bindery and NDS) to Active Directory.

Greatly Enhanced Manageability

NT 5.0 offers a lot of improvements in terms of handling the server and consumer environment. These improvements are due mostly to two innovations: Microsoft Management Console (MMC) and the technology of Microsoft Installer.

Microsoft Management Console

MMC is an umbrella of sorts for all kinds of tools used to administer the NT environment. MMC is nothing in itself, yet it shows signs of being of great importance in future administrative situations.

MMC is not a standalone administration tool; rather, it is a collection of all previous administration programs, tied together with a similar "look and feel" to that of Windows NT Explorer. Some of the more important features are the following (see Figure 3.2):

- MMC displays a graphical console that contains programs (known as *snap-ins*) that give access to administer certain parts of the NT environment.

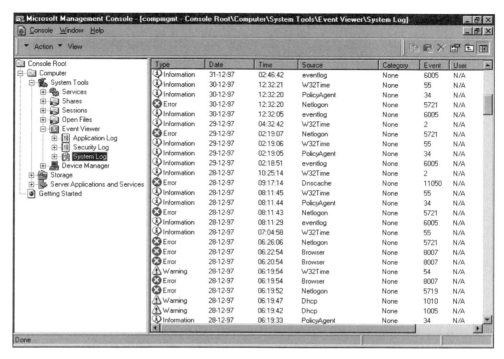

Figure 3.2
This example shows the standard configuration of the Computer Management MMC, in which the Computer Management snap-in and a chain to some Web-based documentation are fed into the computer.

- The various snap-ins are organized in a tree structure that contains all the tools and information that the administrator needs to perform a given task.

- The various windows in the console can display various parts of the tree structure, thus making it quite straightforward to perform a certain task.

Thus, administrators can perform all parts of a given administrative job from a single console instead of having to shift among different applications, dialog boxes, and locations on the network. You might as well get used to MMC, because Microsoft has announced that manufacturers of server applications that have the coveted BackOffice logo are going to supply snap-ins for MMC in the future (after NT 5.0 is on the market).

Microsoft Installer

Another very exciting feature in NT Server 5.0 is the Microsoft Installer technology (which covers the much-discussed IntelliMirroring concept). Microsoft Installer is a prerequisite for full implementation of the Microsoft Zero Administration for Windows initiative (ZAW).

The Microsoft Installer technology comprises the following features:

- A standard package format and a built-in installation service that handles installation, repairs, deinstallation, and tracing the dependence of certain components.

- Increased sturdiness in the capability to repair or reinstall applications and to roll back every transaction relating to the installation.

- "Just-in-time" installations, whereby future applications can be tailored to be installed when they are about to be used for the first time. The Microsoft Installer technology management API handles this task.

- Intelligent replication of user and application data between the user and the server, which enables redundancy in the storage of data. This is a great advantage to the administration (and reliability) of every single customer.

In addition to the Installer technology, other features that improve manageability are included in NT 5.0. For instance, NT 5.0 offers built-in support for scripts (via the Windows Scripting Host) written in Java or Visual Basic. Likewise, NT 5.0 is the most language-oriented Windows product that Microsoft has made so far. This feature will attract companies that cater to several language areas. NT 5.0 is thus "multilingual" with regard to APIs, tables of characters, keyboard layout, and so on. This makes developing applications that cover many different languages much easier.

Note: You can read more about the administration of users and servers in Chapters 7 and 8.

Ready For The Distributed Future

Windows NT 5.0 is the final piece in Microsoft's much-discussed Cairo jigsaw puzzle. *Cairo* is the code name for the distributed services that Microsoft has been promising Windows-based users since the early 1990s. Several of these services are already available for NT 4.0, such as the Windows 95 GUI, DCOM, and DFS.

Cairo's distributed services comprise the following:

- Distributed COM (DCOM, previously known as Network OLE or distributed OLE)

- Distributed File System (DFS)

- Active Directory

Distributed COM

DCOM actually arrived with Windows NT 4.0 in 1996. But taking advantage of DCOM wasn't possible until Active Directory appeared in NT 5.0, which is part of the reason you probably haven't heard very much about DCOM.

DCOM's technology enables software developers to establish component-based applications across the network. This means DCOM is Microsoft's extension of the COM object model (used for OLE/ActiveX) to cover the network.

DCOM is a standardized method of communicating with object-oriented programs placed on PCs other than your own. In other words, DCOM enables objects across the network to be used as if they were present locally, without any changes to the program code of the object. DCOM also enables all existing "well-mannered" ActiveX applications, such as OLE applications, to function across a network.

DCOM is not particularly usable without Active Directory, due to various fundamental problems. Without Active Directory, DCOM has to be operated via point-to-point communication from one machine designated as the OLE server of the client. This is complicated in terms of administration, scalability, and fault tolerance. Active Directory enables you to place the DCOM program components everywhere on the network, thus creating the necessary degree of scalability and error tolerance.

Distributed File System

The Microsoft Distributed File System (DFS) enables you to combine separate network-connected volumes for a single, logical network volume or share. Increased fault tolerance also is possible by duplicating the whole or parts of the given volume across two or more servers.

DFS is organized as a logical tree structure that is independent of physical restrictions. The DFS tree topology is automatically linked to the Active Directory, which enables you to establish the wanted degree of fault tolerance in the DFS solution.

Active Directory

With regard to the distributed world, you can communicate with Active Directory via Lightweight Directory Access Protocol (LDAP). Although the LDAP standard is not yet fully completed, it is the only real standard for communicating across various directory services, and it provides a safeguard against poor file-locking behavior.

Note: Chapter 5 discusses the distributed facilities of NT 5.0 in detail.

Scalability And Fault Tolerance

No matter where you look, NT 5.0 has some degree of increased scalability or fault tolerance compared with NT 4.0. The most immediate initiatives in this direction are Active Directory, DFS, Cluster Server, DCOM, and the new version of NTFS.

NT 5.0 contains various hardware-oriented features that quite clearly provide much more scalability and fault tolerance for the platform. Some of the most important features are Fibre Channel, 64-bit processor support, and I$_2$O.

Fibre Channel

Fibre Channel is a fairly new technology in PCs. It combines transport protocols (such as SCSI and TCP/IP) into one single technology that can reach a maximum speed of 1Gbps. Because of the extreme speed (and high prices), Fibre Channel will primarily be used in the storage and backup media of the future.

64-Bit Processor Support

NT 5.0 also is slated to support the Digital Alpha 64-bit processors in the initial release, and more 64-bit processors (such as Intel) in later NT 5 releases. 64-bit support means that the OS's upper limit for handling physical memory breaks the present 4GB limit, which the biggest NT Server solutions are about to overtake by increasing the theoretical maximum to 16,777,216 terabytes. At first, using RAM of up to 32GB will be possible only on the Digital Alpha-based computer, which is currently the only 64-bit processor platform that can handle Windows NT 5.0. Microsoft's close cooperation with Intel should indicate that Microsoft probably has already taken into account the next Intel generation of processors (the IA-64, code-named Merced), which will also be of the 64-bit type. Merced is expected to be available in late 1999, and is a cooperative effort between Intel and Hewlett-Packard. Whether the 32GB ceiling for consumption of RAM will continue to be a limit compared to the 64-bit processors is impossible to say presently.

I$_2$O

Windows NT 5.0 is also able to utilize the new I$_2$O (Intelligent Input/Output), which allows processing power going to I/O units to be separated from the main CPU and passed on to other processors dedicated to such jobs—thus achieving higher system performance and greater scalability. What's new here (offloading CPU cycles to other processors such as graphic accelerators has been around for awhile) is that this is for disk I/O, and no longer uses CPU interrupts to greatly reduce overhead. For example, many databases that are I/O-bound (the I/O has excessive contention) can use I$_2$O for improved throughput (over 50 percent improvement in some recent tests). Also, I$_2$O creates a common architecture across several devices and operating systems.

> **Note:** You can read more about the scalability and fault tolerance of NT 5.0 in Chapter 6.

Many New Features For The File System

The NT File System (NTFS) has undergone many changes, and some very necessary overhauls.

Windows NT 5.0 is furnished with the new FAT32 file system to ensure compatibility with the smaller Windows products (Windows 95 OSR versions and Windows 98). FAT32 is not compatible with the well-known FAT format (which Microsoft now calls FAT16), nor with all the programs and operating systems based on this illustrious file system. Reformatting the disk is the only way to go to FAT from FAT32. The FAT32 tradeoff for its incompatibility with FAT16 is that FAT32 is capable of establishing disk partitions of more than 2GB and using the space on the big disks more optimally (because of FAT32's smaller cluster sizes).

NTFS will always remain a far better and more advanced file system than FAT32. Therefore, using FAT32 in a pure NT environment is not recommended. Undoubtedly, Microsoft's focus on FAT32 is due to its similarity to FAT16, and that Windows NT 5.0 will be able to read Windows 98 files, which will be stored in the FAT32 format.

The biggest news in NTFS is Encrypting File System (EFS), which enables you to encrypt selected files and directories to protect them against unauthorized access by other users with access to the system.

NTFS also contains support for the junction points that enable you to integrate rooms or network-connected volume resources in the local file system. For instance, the C:\APPS directory can point to a directory on the file server. This facility removes the present limitation of 26 locally mapped volumes (which covers the letters A to Z), enabling construction of more-complex, but also more logical, volume structures.

Other big news in NTFS 5.0 is that administrators are now able to allocate disk quotas on the NTFS volumes for individual users or to extend a volume with unallocated disk space—all without having to restart the PC. NTFS 5.0 has built-in *Distributed Link Tracking*, which maintains shortcuts when files are moved from one volume to another computer.

> **Note:** NT's file handlers (and NTFS 5.0 in particular) are described more thoroughly in Chapter 16.

Even More Focus On Network Communication

Much has happened to network communication in Windows NT 5.0, too. NT 5.0 offers a new version of the Network Device Interface Specification (NDIS) network architecture, which also has Asynchronous Transfer Mode (ATM), Quality of Service (QOS), and cordless WAN as part of its new functionality. NDIS, created by Microsoft and 3Com, enables a Network Interface Card to support multiple network protocols on a network.

Furthermore, the TCP/IP stack in NT 5.0 offers support for Winsock 2, IP multicast, fast transmit and fast recovery, detection of conflicts in address allocation, long time-out intervals, and automatic address allocation. This will make TCP/IP, which is one of the most popular communication protocols in the world, compatible with more NT application environments, and will make NT 5.0 a much more robust environment.

Winsock 2 is an interface that is independent of protocols for network applications. It contains support for a variety of network services, such as realtime multimedia. By means of the same socket principle that BSD Unix uses, Winsock 2, as with the previous versions, prepares applications for network access to practically any transport protocol, not just TCP/IP. The features in Winsock 2 include name resolution that is independent of protocol, multicast and multipoint transmission, and QOS.

Another feature in NT 5.0's IP stack is the proposed Internet standard, Resource Reservation Protocol (RSVP), which is intended to introduce QOS support. RSVP books network resources, and can handle reservations to unicast (one-to-one communication) and multicast (one-to-many communication) applications, where the receiver is responsible for making reservations. All reservations are maintained in a "soft state" on the routers that the network communication passes across.

NT 5.0's DNS has become dynamic, and is now called Dynamic DNS (DDNS). This means that you can update single rows in the DNS table, without having to re-feed the entire DNS database. This keeps TCP/IP information up to date with all kinds of administrative complexities. DDNS thus is intended to replace the existing WINS service, which has been kept to maintain backward-compatibility.

The shift from WINS to DDNS has caused certain changes in the Dynamic Host Configuration Protocol (DHCP) server. The DHCP server is still handled by a separate service, yet it enables you to benefit from some of NT 5.0's new facilities, notably the location-independence of Active Directory. DHCP servers assign dynamic IP addresses to computers on a network.

Other improvements of NT 5.0 are the standardized ATM interface, Telephony API 3.0 (TAPI), and infrared communication. Also, the Enhanced Multilink Channel Aggregation (EMCA) enables you to dedicate several ISDN channels on a Basic Rate Interface (BRI) connection. The net result, of course, is higher bandwidth.

Note: *All information immediately relevant to network handling is discussed in Chapters 9 and 12. Other chapters indirectly contain information necessary to understand how NT 5.0 acts on a network.*

A Critical Priority: Security

Microsoft obviously has learned from past experience regarding security. Ever since Microsoft started the design of NT Server 5.0, the focus on security has been more intense than ever before.

The primary authentication mechanism in Active Directory is Kerberos Version 5, which is generally recognized as the most reliable authentication method for distributed environments. Windows NT Server 5.0 is backward-compatible with the old LAN Manager authentication methodology (also known as NTLM), which leaves a lot to be desired in terms of security. NT Server 5.0 is also built to support other possible authentication mechanisms as alternatives to Kerberos.

NT Server 5.0 also contains a Microsoft Certificate Server for issuing, renewing, and canceling digital certificates. *Digital certificates* are used for public-key encryption applications, notably server and user authentication in connection with Secure Sockets Layer (SSL) or Private Communication Technology (PCT) protocols.

Administrators are given the tools needed to map digital certificates for user accounts in the directory, which gives NT Server 5.0 a tangible advantage over all the existing network operating systems. This ensures a consistently high degree of security for exchanging information via the Internet and between any two machines.

NT 5.0 also enables administrators to establish various levels of security at the communications level (given that communication takes place with the TCP/IP protocol) via IP Security Management. Thus, NT 5.0 Server can encrypt whole, or parts of, communications between computers, which—together with the other security mechanisms in NT 5.0—certainly provides an incredibly high degree of security against unauthorized persons.

Support for *Smart Cards,* small, credit-card-like plastic cards, is one of the least known features on the hardware scene. Smart Cards may be of great importance for security in the future, as Microsoft already predicts. For instance, Smart Cards potentially will be used to ensure increased security for logging on, reading, and sending messages during video conferences, shopping, and many other tasks.

Note: *The many new security concepts in NT 5.0 are discussed in Chapter 11.*

Other Advanced Technologies

Windows NT 5.0 includes several new forms of hardware support.

Plug And Play

NT has finally been equipped with full Plug and Play support via the Advanced Configuration and Power Interface (ACPI) standard, which brings the NT operating system on par with Windows 95/Windows 98. In practical terms, this means NT can now be installed on lightweight portable computers or stationary PCs, and makes adding and removing hardware configurations easier. Furthermore, handling of PC Card/PCMCIA has been improved: You now can insert PC Cards and have them approved on-the-fly by the operating system.

ACPI

Like Windows 98, Windows NT 5.0 offers built-in support of ACPI, which is a greatly enhanced power-management standard (compared with the earlier APM Standard Power Management) devised by Intel, Microsoft, and Toshiba. Support has also been introduced via Microsoft's OnNow Design Initiative, which enables a PC to be on standby (dormant) even if it appears to be switched off. The computer is ready for use seconds after the user presses the on/off button. (A PC can also be activated immediately by a remote telephone call under the OnNow Design Initiative.)

Importantly, NT 5.0 does not support APM and thus requires ACP-prepared systems to supply any kind of power management.

Universal Bus

Universal Bus (USB) is similar to the serial port. A USB port has the following four clear advantages over a traditional serial port:

- It is capable of working with up to 12Mbps, whereas the traditional serial ports can handle a maximum of 115.2Kbps. USB is also equipped with a special low-velocity bus that has a transmission speed of 1.5Mbps.

- It supports connecting up to 127 units on each port. Each unit is connected to the USB port in the same way, irrespective of whether the unit is the first or number 127. As previously stated, it is not yet possible to add more than one unit to a traditional serial port.

- A USB port provides access to electrical current. This gives vendors of peripheral units for the serial port the opportunity to remove all extra sockets from the peripheral unit, which is nice for consumers, because the result is a drop in electricity consumption.

- All USB units attempt to notify the operating system of their presence and the type of driver they require, so that the configuration can be completed without user interaction.

USB combines the best facilities in the SCSI architecture with a far more advanced Plug and Play standard than the existing one (which didn't turn out to be very capable of "thinking for itself" or to be as sturdy as anticipated). If Windows NT 5.0 already has access to the necessary driver for the USB unit, then all setups will be automatic and immediate, without even having to restart the computer.

IEEE 1394

The IEEE 1394 bus standard (also known as FireWire) is very similar to the USB standard from the user's point of view. The only two differences between USB and IEEE 1394 are the bus speed and the theoretical number of connected units.

While USB can handle speeds of up to 12Mbps (roughly the same speed as an enhanced parallel port), IEEE 1394 can supply a vastly more impressive bandwidth of 100, 200, or even 400Mbps (depending on the units connected). Currently, an even faster version of IEEE 1394 is being tested (1394.B) that allegedly can reach a speed of 800Mbps or 1Gbps!

Theoretically, up to 127 peripheral units can be set up with USB, whereas IEEE 1394 is limited, theoretically, to 63. Neither figure is likely to be reached by even the most demanding solutions (for the time being).

DVD

DVD discs are fairly identical in size and appearance to existing CD-ROMs. However, DVDs' storage capacity of 4.7GB is markedly greater than the approximate 600MB of CD-ROMs. Future versions of DVD are expected to enhance this capacity still further, to 17GB, by using both sides of the disc and by placing two layers of data on both sides. Reading a CD-ROM from a DVD drive is possible, but you need to have a DVD-2 drive if you want to read home-burned discs (CD-R discs).

AGP

Windows NT 5.0 supports the standard Accelerated Graphics Port (AGP), which will soon establish itself as the dominant standard for 3D graphics accelerators. AGP's dominance will occur because it is far faster than the present architectures, and Intel strongly advocates the AGP standard. Tests show that AGP is four times faster than the traditional PCI bus.

AGP is a more productive architecture primarily because it has high-speed access to surface textures and other graphical surfaces in the normal RAM of a PC. This higher speed is attained by allowing direct access to system memory, rather than loading the textures into local video memory. When used with the Pentium II processor, the texture data is accessed in system memory by the graphics chip while the Pentium II is doing other activities. Likewise, AGP has some special facilities that boost productivity, enabling much faster reading and writing to these surfaces than previously feasible. The AGP bus operates at 66MHz, and uses pipelining and 2X data transmission.

WDM

Windows NT 5.0 offers a completely new driver architecture: WDM (Win32 Driver Model). WDM is also newly implemented in Windows 98, and Microsoft promises that WDM will be used in other Windows operating systems in the future. WDM is an important new driver architecture because it relieves one of the biggest support nightmares for Microsoft: drivers written by third-party developers that have access to fundamental kernel services. These drivers are a frequent source of instability in Microsoft operating systems. The WDM, which has already been partially implemented in Win95, is an attempt to reduce this instability.

WDM may be capable of cutting by 50 percent the cost that hardware manufacturers incur when developing drivers for Windows. WDM's driver model is based on a class/minidriver structure, bringing about a modular and expansive architecture that makes developing new drivers easier.

The WDM driver classes in Windows NT 5.0 cover the following types of units:

- Still picture units (such as cameras, scanners, and videocapture), multimedia units (such as MPEG decoders, videocapture, sound, and DVD recorders), and broadcast architecture.

- Various in-data units. At first, this will include only USB units that are covered by the Human Interface Devices (HID) specification, which includes keyboards, mice, pointing units, and many types of game controls. Due to the nature of USB, you will be able to use multiple keyboards or mice simultaneously.

- The basic types of USB units (hubs and controllers), loudspeakers, and the HID units listed in the preceding bullet.

- The basic types of IEEE 1394 units (controllers).

Presently, no WDM driver classes are available for mainstream PC units (such as graphics cards and in-data units connected to non-USB ports, which comprises practically all existing keyboards, joysticks, and mice).

More New Server Applications

Windows NT 5.0 currently doesn't offer anything new in the area of add-on applications. The current beta version only contains Internet Information Server 4.0, which includes Index Server, Certificate Server, and Transaction Server.

The final version of NT 5.0 is expected to contain two additional add-on applications—Transaction Server and Message Queue Server—which will make the platform considerably more qualified to handle distributed environments.

Note: *Chapter 18 focuses on the independent server applications included with NT Server 5.0. Chapter 19 presents an in-depth discussion of NT 5.0's influence on the development of Microsoft BackOffice applications and the increasing number of server applications from third-party suppliers.*

NT Workstation 5.0 Vs. Windows 98

Microsoft claims that the division between the different versions of Windows is really quite simple to understand. Microsoft views the Windows line of products as follows:

- Windows 95 is the most accessible 32-bit operating system.

- Windows 98 is an evolutionary upgrade of Windows 95. In the future, this version of Windows will be the most accessible 32-bit operating system. It will make daily computer work easier, faster, and more reliable, and will be fully integrated with the Internet.

- Windows NT Workstation 4.0 currently is the most powerful 32-bit operating system, developed with a focus on reliability, manageability, security, network use, and productivity.

- Windows NT Workstation 5.0 will be a fundamental upgrade of all versions of Windows. NT Workstation 5.0 will be the most "exclusive" 32-bit operating system for company use.

But the Windows world is not that simple, and Microsoft's staff readily admits this, when pressed. In fact, in July 1997, following the preceding "simple" explanation by Microsoft of its Windows product line, its Vice-CEO for Platforms and Applications, Paul Maritz, stated: "We admit that company users have a large breadth in what they require of their computers. We expect to see customers start a mix of Windows-based systems tailored for the specific user needs and system requirements."

In short, a sensible computer user or IT department can't choose its next operating system based on Microsoft's simple version of reality. They have to consider very carefully whether they want to choose Windows 98, NT Workstation 5.0, or perhaps a combination of both operating systems.

Ultimately, you have to decide which OS is best for your situation. However, by late 1999, you should change to either Windows 98 or NT Workstation 5.0—if you want to stay up to date (and be on an OS platform for which new programs are being developed).

The new operating systems will make demands on your PC that are even greater than the demands of your current OS. It just isn't feasible to set up Windows 98 or NT Workstation 5.0 on a PC with less than Pentium 60MHz, 32MB RAM, and a fairly fast SuperVGA graphics card (preferably of the accelerated type). Also note that NT Workstation 5.0 generally has lower performance than Windows 98 when using the same hardware, but that the opposite is true if the computer has more than 32MB RAM and/or a Pentium Pro processor. On the other hand, NT Workstation 5.0, like its predecessor, offers poorer compatibility with older hardware and software products, due to the more limited number of NT drivers.

Whether you choose Windows 98 or NT Workstation 5.0 depends largely on your expectations. Windows 98 undoubtedly is an evolutionary product. However, the designers of Windows 98 have actually limited themselves technologically to maintain compatibility with the many thousands of applications for DOS and Windows.

So, if you are looking for an uncompromisingly designed 32-bit operating system for PCs, buy NT Workstation 5.0. As previously stated, Microsoft foresees a future dominated by NT. Windows 98 is just an intermediate station along the way.

Table 3.1 summarizes the most important differences and similarities between NT Workstation 5.0 and Windows 98.

In short, if you are looking for a good, deliberate upgrade from Windows 95 or Windows 3.11 for a company that is limited to requiring high backward-compatibility with DOS/16-bit Windows or many fairly small PCs, Windows 98 is your best choice.

If you want optimum results with regard to operating and managing an NT Server-based environment, or you just need to implement the most productive and scalable operating system on the company's computers, you should concentrate on NT Workstation 5.0.

I have difficulty understanding why a company would choose the "middle course" and use a combination of Windows 98 and NT Workstation 5.0, which Microsoft has recommended as an alternative. (For instance, using Windows 98 for jobs that require backward-compatibility and NT Workstation 5.0 for all other jobs, which spreads out two operating systems across many users in the same company.) This

Table 3.1 A comparison of NT Workstation 5.0 and Windows 98.

Facility	Windows NT Workstation 5.0	Windows 98
Ideal size of RAM	32MB RAM or more	16MB RAM or more
Estimated consumption of hard disk	At least 120MB	At least 80MB
Processor type	80486 or higher, or Digital Alpha	80486 or higher
SMP support	Yes	No
Win32 pre-emptive multitasking	Yes	Yes
Win16 pre-emptive multitasking	Yes	No
Compatibility with MS-DOS	Reasonable	Extremely high
File systems	NTFS, FAT32, and FAT	FAT32 and FAT
ACPI Support	Yes	Yes
APM Support	No	Yes
DCOM Support	Yes	Yes
DirectX Support	Yes	Yes
DVD Support	Yes	Yes
MMX Support	Yes	Yes
Plug and Play Support	Yes	Yes
USB Support	Yes	Yes
WDM Support	Yes	Yes
Active Desktop	Yes	Yes
Automatic installation of applications via NT Server 5.0	Yes	No
Possibility of encrypting the whole or parts of the file system	Yes	No

"nondecision" will result in an unpleasant experience when attempting to implement and administer two new and different operating systems.

For most companies, keeping the existing PC operating systems and choosing either Windows 98 or NT Workstation 5.0 (not both) for all future PCs (and any existing PCs that can handle it) is probably simpler and cheaper.

If your company still uses 16-bit Windows, the time to change has arrived. Practically all independent software developers have already "forgotten" Windows 3.1, and Microsoft is pressing PC producers to drop Windows 3.1 from their products. Microsoft has notified PC producers that if they continue to preload Windows 3.1 in PCs, they (not Microsoft) will be responsible for supporting the operating system.

More Benefits Than Shortcomings

For unknown reasons (most likely because the software developers still haven't finished moving the functionality from the drawing board into the real world), Microsoft has excluded a few of the necessary production functions in the current beta version. This fact, by definition, ought to make the current beta version into an alpha version.

 ### Alpha Vs. Beta

Alpha testing takes place at an early stage in developing a program, when the software supplier hasn't decided exactly how the program should look or precisely what it should contain, but the program is developed enough to be used by noncompany users/developers.

Beta testing takes place when the software supplier judges that so few bugs remain in the program that it is ready for the final test before being released for sale.

In recent years, practically all software suppliers have ceased to use the expression alpha test, for marketing reasons. Instead, test versions are dubbed beta version as soon as they can be handled by third-party users, and right up to their release.

Some facts about NT 5.0 remain obscure, due to many shortcomings in the current beta version. However, this doesn't hinder an overall understanding of the product.

The following list sets forth the most important shortcomings regarding the beta version of NT 5.0, in order of priority:

1. Part of the Microsoft Installer technology is missing.

2. A few vital details still need to be in place before Active Directory is ready to be implemented in a greater environment.

3. DFS does not contain replication facilities.

4. A few administration tools haven't yet been converted to MMC snap-ins.

5. Active Desktop is active only in NT Workstation 5.0 (not in NT Server 5.0).

6. NT 5.0's built-in Internet Explorer 4.0 may not be included in the production version. Public Preview 2 will most likely be in the final version of NT 5.0.

7. The Disk Defragmentation tool hasn't yet been equipped with a graphical user interface.

8. Personal Fax for Windows is missing.

9. Message Queue Server is missing.

10. PC Card handling still leaves a lot to be desired.

11. NT 5.0 still has problems handling FAT32 drives, especially with regard to the installation.

12. Upgrading to NT 5.0 is impossible if Internet Explorer 4.0 is installed on the previous NT version.

13. Support of several simultaneous monitors hasn't been implemented yet.

14. Smart Card handling doesn't make it possible to execute logons.

Apart from this list, numerous other minor or irrelevant details were left out of NT 5.0 beta 1, as Microsoft ran out of time to bring them into the environment. The list of these minor bugs is too extensive to include here.

Microsoft realizes that NT 5.0 beta 1 isn't completely ready, which is why it has been submitted only to software developers thus far. When beta 1 was released at the Professional Developer's Conference, Microsoft made very clear that beta 1 could be used only to develop software and for basic testing, whereas beta 2 allegedly will be ready to use for small pilot projects with users.

The number of shortcomings still doesn't seem very alarming from a purely architectural perspective. The product certainly isn't ready to be implemented for purposes other than testing, because the program code hasn't been tested sufficiently, and a few important components are missing. Nevertheless, NT 5.0 beta 1 provides a fairly complete picture of how NT 5.0 works. I am quite convinced that, by reading this book, you won't miss any vital points regarding NT 5.0—not even after NT 5.0 is in the stores.

My experience from studying the testing of Microsoft's latest Windows operating systems (Windows 95, Windows NT 4.0, and Windows 98) indicates unambiguously that few changes—if any—in functionality will occur after the early beta phase. Experience does show, however, that you can never be absolutely sure of the launch date, because Microsoft changes its plans continuously. It is, after all, geared to the market.

Directory Services:
A Whole New World

Imagine having to keep track of the names, telephone numbers, and addresses of several hundred or several thousand people—without a telephone directory. This is an everyday task for many network administrators because they use a network system without directory services. The capability of directory services to organize a network is one of the primary reasons why directory services have been a big hit with network administrators over the last 10 years.

Despite general agreement that directory services can save a lot of money in working expenses, very few companies that use Microsoft operating systems use directory services, because they are available only with Novell NetWare/IntraNetWare 4.x, Banyan VINES, IBM Warp Server with Directory & Security Server (as an extra package), and Windows NT Server with ENS Services from Banyan (as an extra package). This will be changing, because Windows NT 5.0 supports Active Directory 5.0 (which will be described in detail throughout this chapter).

Much confusion exists regarding what *directory services* truly are. The goal of this chapter is to eliminate any such confusion, as well as to provide a fairly comprehensive explanation of the various directory services currently or soon to be available.

Why Directory Services?

Studies of working expenses for data management always seem to claim that directory services can save the IT budget a lot of money. Well, those studies are right.

Imagine a typical company with 200 users. This company has more than 500 user accounts that need to be maintained on various servers and services. These accounts are spread out, with 200 users who share file and printer services, 200 users of email, and numerous other users of database systems and other specialized systems.

This company's network administrators undoubtedly dream of a simpler way of handling users and their data. Who wouldn't want to escape all the overlapping work of handling employees, services, and data? But their dreams often remain unfulfilled in the real world, in which users typically are connected to several servers and the environment is filled with fragmented and duplicated data.

Directory services enable you to place all such information under just one structure. A directory service provides universal access to all computer resources, with a user account for each user, irrespective of the number of servers and services that each user needs at their disposal.

Currently, all information and data is saved in a simple directory that is associated with a specific application. This directory often is called a *name service,* to avoid any confusion with true directory services. Thus, the term *name service* is used in this book, too.

A name service can be either one-dimensional (1D), two-dimensional (2D), or three-dimensional (3D). A *1D name service* means that a user account must be set up for every server to which the user has access (see Figure 4.1). A *2D name service* means (in principle) that users are set up in only one place (see Figure 4.2). However, this method has many limits with regard to both the administrator and users, especially in network configurations with multiple name servers. Thus, a 2D name service is

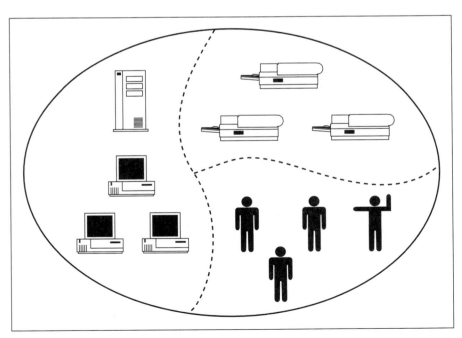

Figure 4.1
Novell NetWare 2.x and 3.x Bindery are examples of typical 1D name services.

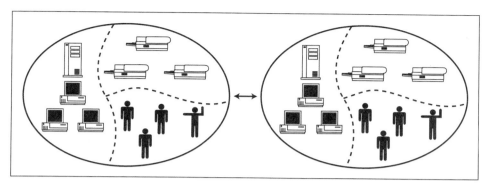

Figure 4.2
Microsoft has taken various initiatives with NT Server 4.0, such as expanding a 1D name directory to 2D.

not the most flexible or user-friendly solution. A *3D name service* enables a user to log on to the network from one place, and have universal access to all computer resources for which they have permission. (The same concept also applies to network administrators.) 3D name services are true directory services, and thus are the best name service for network use (see Figure 4.3).

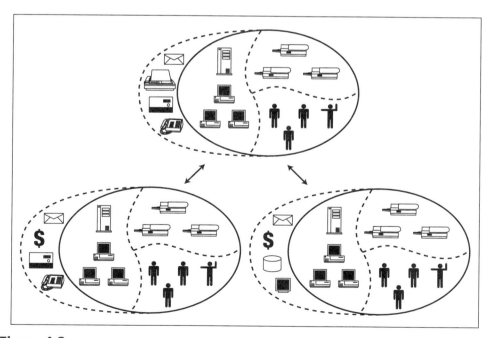

Figure 4.3
The only real choice, both in practical and theoretical terms, is a genuine directory service, which must be 3D.

Practically all server applications—email, databases, network administration tools, and so on—are based on their own name services. This results in increased working expenses for every server application that is added, as the number of users administered is inversely proportional to the number of software systems. To this can be added a directly proportional increase in expenses to solve error situations, because users will be more confused due to the many different user names and/or passwords.

Understanding Directory Services

The philosophy underlying directory services is directly opposite to the philosophy of a name service. The ideal directory service is able to link more users with particular resources on the network. Such a directory service can function as a network administration tool for the network administrator, and is equivalent to a phone book for all users at any one time. A directory service is the tool that connects the directories of various applications across the network—from the PC to the mainframe—and then out to the whole world via the Internet.

A very short (and precise) definition of *directory service* is a physically distributed, logically centralized storage place for data that is used to administer the entire computer environment.

A directory service must have, at a minimum, the following properties:

- *The user should have access to all the services, resources, and applications that they are authorized to use through a single logon.* This requires a certain degree of openness in the solution to the directory service. Likewise, for the environment to be successful, producers of server applications must provide directory service support for their applications.

- *All information on the computer environment as a whole—including any active network components—should be kept in a distributed form.* The information will be replicated among several servers, so a user or service that needs access to the directories can fetch this information from a relatively local server.

- *Data replication, to ensure overall system consistency for all users.* All changes carried out on one part of the directory must be spread to everybody on the network, to ensure that the information in the directory is the same regardless of where you retrieve it from.

- *It should support white-pages-type searches and yellow-pages-type searches.* White-pages-type searches are on the basis of a certain attribute, such as a name or telephone number. Yellow-pages searching is on the basis of fairly precise classifications, such as all color printers or LaserJet printers on the second floor.

- *The possibility of removing dependence on physical locations in conjunction with the administration of the computer environment.* This means that the administrative tools no longer need to be centrally located and administered. For instance, the responsibility for administering certain areas of the directory can be partially or wholly delegated.

The planned tasks of Microsoft's Active Directory are outlined in Figure 4.4.

X.500

The attempts by various software producers to create a directory all have one common denominator: X.500.

The X.500 specification is a set of protocols that the International Telecommunications Union (ITU) and International Standards Organization (ISO) have approved as formal standards for defining what ensures access to, distribution of, and administration of the information in the directory.

As with several other standards that have been set by international organizations in the past (such as with the standard for the OSI network protocol), X.500 has turned out to be a paper tiger. In its attempts to create a directory service that truly meets all the demands that reasonably can be made on it, the ITU and ISO ended up with a specification so complex and compressed that no vendor can precisely meet it, although many attempts have been made in the last decade. Moreover, the complexity of X.500 means that the various implementations of X.500 suffer by being mutually incompatible and having incredibly poor output.

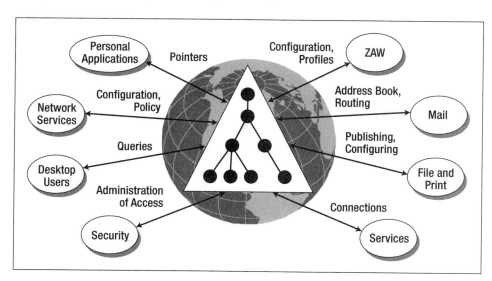

Figure 4.4
Microsoft has great expectations regarding the tasks Active Directory can be used for.

But X.500 is based on very careful consideration. Therefore, all the existing directory services are modeled on the basic features of the X.500 specification. Every producer has adapted features from the X.500 specification that they think are relevant for them. They quickly realized that the overall structure of the X.500 directory is extremely sensible, and thus have adopted it. The hierarchical object-oriented structure of X.500 resembles a tree that is turned upside down, with a root at the top and branches that hang down (see Figure 4.5).

The structure of the X.500 specification means that the tree's objects will always be unique when the name and location are combined. The objects in the tree that are variable by nature are known as *container objects*, while the rest are known as *non-container objects*. Container objects are basically utilities used to contain a variety of other objects, and are popular in C++ and other object-oriented programs. Non-container objects are like constants, such as sequences.

Most directory services have several different types of container objects. The X.500 standard has the following container objects:

- Os (Organization)
- OUs (Organizational Units)
- Country
- Locality

Os can be used only on the highest level in the tree, whereas OUs can contain other OUs.

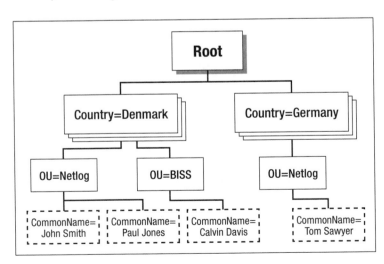

Figure 4.5
The overall structure of an X.500 directory, which is used by all current directory services.

Among the noncontainer objects are the following:

- Instance users
- Groups
- Aliases
- Servers
- Volumes
- Computers
- Print servers
- Print queues
- Printers

A good directory service will give applications and administrators the capability to add new object types, as needed.

A distinction exists between objects with ramifications and those without ramifications so that underlying objects can inherit properties, which enables the directory service to be extended in a safe and uniform manner. X.500's tree structure ensures that a safe collating sequence for a given object can always be identified. This is immensely important when deciding which properties every object should have.

Not A True Client/Server Without Directory Services

In addition to directory services being a prerequisite for cutting daily network expenses, they are also the "missing link" for client/server and true distributed data processing. Directory services enable users to access an application regardless of where it is placed, and they enable administrators to move data and services everywhere on the network, at their own discretion, without bothering users—and without users ever noticing the movement.

But, just as establishing a global telephone directory is difficult to imagine (which may actually be a more practical task than gathering data from all computer systems in a directory service), the technology of directory services is still in an embryonic state. The technology has come a long way from the first tentative efforts to enable administration of all resources on any existing computer platform, but the tremendous speed with which the Internet is expanding makes establishing something resembling a global telephone directory absolutely necessary. As the

Internet is rapidly turning into an electronic version of an old-fashioned market-place in which output is sold (including working capacity), the urgency is increasing to set up a single, albeit very flexible, storage place in which information can easily be found. Directory services is the technology that can provide that storage place.

The expanding Internet has made computer market heavyweights far more interested in directory services than they used to be. This new interest is due to the realization that directory services will be one of the cornerstones for future network computing. From a purely tactical, technological perspective, directory services will be one of the most strategic technologies ever created, due to the potential impact of the Internet (and intranets).

Professional IT users are also moving toward directory services. Whereas network administrators have historically shown more interest in directory services (because they have had success using them), many other IT professionals are now realizing the potential of directory services.

Network administrators are the pioneers of directory services, partially because the network area was hit hardest by soaring expenses in the 1980s and 1990s, causing administrators to find cost-effective network solutions, but primarily because the most popular network system, Novell NetWare, is among the pioneers of directory services. Also, the slightly larger networks have been fighting hard against various forms of less-than-optimal user account management methods. Additionally, the types of services and servers are increasing and becoming ever more complex.

Directory services have many uses beyond the administration of networks. The primary point of directory services is to create universal access to all resources—so that users can log on to the network to gain access to resources, instead of having to log on to a particular server, or group of servers, to find particular resources (as is often required today).

The directory service that proves to be superior in the market will be guaranteed not only control over one of the most vital technologies of the future, but also a large license income. This is the primary reason why directory services are of such great interest to Microsoft, IBM, Cisco, Sun, Banyan, Netscape, Novell, and others.

The Recent History Of Directory Services

Currently, only two directory services from traditional suppliers of network operating systems have successfully established themselves on the PC-based market: Banyan Systems' StreetTalk and Novell's NetWare Directory Service (NDS). Despite the lack of competition, the sales figures for these two directory services have been far from encouraging from a marketing standpoint.

Banyan has sold its StreetTalk directory service for more than 10 years as part of its VINES network OS. Novell entered the market more than five years ago with NDS, which is an integral part of the NetWare 4 network OS.

A few years ago, IBM launched a directory service platform for its Warp Server OS. Initially, IBM stated that it would install its directory services in the next version of Warp Server. However, for unknown reasons, the technology came in an extra package called Directory & Security Server, which has practically disappeared in IBM's marketing. So, not only does IBM Warp Server have a limited market share, IBM sold only a few copies of the Directory & Security Server package.

IBM's directory service is based on the Open Software Foundation's (OSF) large-scale Distributed Computing Environment (DCE) specification, which is supported by Digital and Sun in a similar, half-hearted way as IBM. From its tentative start with directory services, IBM has gone to a ubiquitous message that the OSF specification ought to be implemented on all IBM server platforms, from PCs right up to mainframes. IBM would then use the OSF specification to provide improved integration among its many operating system platforms. IBM foresees doing the same for its many service applications in the future. However, these ideas haven't progressed any further than the drawing board with Warp Server and AIX.

In disregard of IBM's message, other producers (such as ICL) have chosen to concentrate on X.500-based products. After several years of confusion, X.500 stands the best chance as a gateway technology among various directory services, rather than a solution in itself. Since the appearance of the Lightweight Directory Access Protocol (LDAP) standard, many indicators doom X.500 to a technological graveyard, together with other similar ISO initiatives. But the hierarchical structure of X.500 remains, along with the essence of the X.500 specification.

In addition, X.500 lives on through the LDAP standard. LDAP is designed to give network clients the chance to inquire about, and handle, the information available from a directory service. The LDAP protocol was originally designed as a simple version of the X.500 specification (Directory Access Protocol), which gave access to the X.500-based directory services via the TCP/IP protocol. LDAP is so attractive because it has implemented all of the important X.500 DAP facilities in a way that ensures much higher productivity. LDAP is quietly moving away from its origins, because it is now used for all kinds of directory services, and people want to expand LDAP from being capable of handling only client inquiries to also handling server-to-server communication among different directory services.

Not long ago, Netscape appeared on the server stage with its Directory Server, which attracted much attention, mostly because Directory Server is designed substantially by the same design team that developed the LDAP standard. Netscape's aim for Directory Server, however, is to attract company clients to its server software and other products, rather than to attempt to establish Directory Server as a competitor to the directory services that already exist.

Microsoft's Active Directory

Finally, after a lot of fanfare, Microsoft has entered the market by launching NT 5.0, which contains the Active Directory directory service. NT Server's success appears to be Microsoft's best bet for Active Directory becoming the most popular directory service, as NT Server's market share keeps increasing. Furthermore, NT Server has wide support among developers of server applications, and Microsoft has recently entered an agreement with Cisco under which Cisco will use Active Server to handle its network components.

Undoubtedly, Active Directory's biggest boost is simply the fact that it has become a reality with the beta release of NT 5.0, which may also guarantee that NT Server isn't ignored for lack of a directory service. The Banyan and Novell directory services won't be able to reach too many more users before NT 5.0 is available in stores.

At this early stage, comparing the number of NT Servers installed with the corresponding number of Banyan VINES servers and NetWare/IntraNetWare 4.x servers doesn't indicate whether the two upstarts stand a chance of keeping Microsoft from becoming entrenched in the directory service area. The market is still very young, so choosing winners and losers is impossible in what promises to be the most strategic technology of the future. Since LDAP has appeared, several directory services will likely dominate the market, rather than just one.

It's All In Your Point Of View

The sudden focus on directory services from all sides of the market also tends to confuse the area, because leading vendors have completely opposite interests and points of view. For example, a serious dividing line is the question of whether a directory service is a network operating system or a server operating system. The following points explain the differences between these two systems:

- *Network operating systems*—Optimized for the fairly simple file and print services and the more-advanced directory services. Network operating systems are not very good at handling server applications.

- *Server operating systems*—Designed primarily for handling applications on the server; for example, database systems, groupware applications, Internet server applications, and special applications. Administering files and printers is just one of the many services offered by server operating systems.

Novell NetWare and Banyan VINES are network operating systems, whereas Windows NT 4.0 Server, IBM Warp Server, and the Unix implementations are server operating systems. Other server operating systems include big systems such as OS/400, MVS (Multiple Virtual Storage; the operating system for old IBM mainframes since 1974), and other well-known operating systems for host sites. A lot of extensions aimed at the PC environments have been added to the PC operating systems in recent years. The big systems (MVS and the like) have other configurations, as they are geared toward batch jobs, handling terminals, and other similar situations. Their common denominators are great for the handling of CPUs, but are moderate in their I/O handling.

These differences mean that the suppliers who take a network operating system approach have to do a lot of work to spread the concept of their directory services to other platforms. They constantly have to try to convince buyers that their platform is still the best, and they often target the providers of the most important company applications to persuade them to use their directory services APIs.

The system requirements of network servers and application servers are very different, as shown in Table 4.1. Application servers tend to demand more in terms of processors and RAM, and require some scalability by clustering and/or symmetric multiprocessing (SMP). The demands of network servers tend to be more bandwidth-oriented, which is why they need the capability of direct pass-through of data from the network card to the RAM and hard disks.

A network operating system is used to supply the basic output on the network, namely the file and print services, and possibly a log consisting of basic directory services. A server operating system, on the other hand, typically is oriented toward handling

Table 4.1 *The system requirements for network servers and application servers.*

	Network Servers	Application Servers
CPU	low	high
Internal bandwidth	high	moderate
Hard disk space	high	moderate
Internal card space	high	low
Size of RAM	moderate	high
Clustering	low	high
SMP	low	high
High uptime/fault tolerance	high	high

Table 4.2 *The relative amount of tasks handled by network and server operating system.*

Task	Network Operating System	Server Operating System
File services	high	low
Print services	high	low
Multitasking	high	high
Crash protection (pre-emptive multitasking)	low	high
Multithreading	low	high
Login operating/Directory services	high	low
Administration of users	high	moderate
Choice of applications	low	high

applications in a controlled and efficient manner. Table 4.2 shows a comparison of the tasks handled by network and server operating systems.

Novell's and Banyan's network operating systems are representative of the heavy pressure that network operating systems have endured in recent years. Not only must they constantly compete with each other (as well as other companies), they must also convince customers that operating with two different operating systems for the servers is worthwhile: one OS to handle basic network services and another OS to handle server applications.

Novell's and Banyan's task of convincing application developers to develop programs for their network operating systems has proven to be a gigantic one, because the developers have only the following two choices:

- Develop their server applications to be handled by an operating system that actually is not very well suited to handle applications. This is because it is designed for maximum speed in handling the traditional network jobs, such as file, print, and directory tasks.

- Develop an extra program, coded more closely to the network operating system. It builds a type of directory service on their preferred server platforms, as the server platforms don't provide any kind of ready access to the directory services.

Novell's and Banyan's job of persuading developers to support their products is further hindered by the fact that neither of the two "mature" directory services have been able to demonstrate convincing results regarding market share. (The applications developers are hoping integration of directory services will take place.)

Novell NLM (NetWare Loadable Modules) generally is not considered a very good environment in which to handle applications. Despite many promises, Novell has never succeeded in manufacturing a sensible, development-innovative environment. Had Novell succeeded in making such an environment, it may have changed the general unwillingness to use NLM.

Novell has announced that, in the future, NLM will be replaced by Java in IntraNetWare. This seems very sensible, considering NLM's lack of success. The substitution of Java won't occur for quite a while, and may not solve the problems anyway, because Java currently has many shortcomings, including bad performance. Novell only recently decided to have its directory services ported to platforms other than NetWare. These efforts are still at a relatively early stage. Thus, no easy solution currently exists for how applications are going to make a given directory service communicate on a given server platform.

The market players that are based on a server OS (for example, IBM, Microsoft, and all Unix suppliers) have considerably easier circumstances, and are confident that buyers will view the server OS platform as the best. These companies are able to tell applications vendors in a fairly straightforward manner—depending on their respective market positions—that the vendors have to integrate their applications with their directory service API if they want to use the server operating system correctly. A server OS producer can even make integration a prerequisite for an application developer to be granted the use of that OS producer's logo on the market, which is almost vital for an application's success. The superior bargaining position of the server OS producers has made maintaining a consistent platform message to the market easier for those producers.

Windows NT Server is selling well on the market. Sales of Unix servers is more moderate, which shows that the market is shifting. The market shift is partly a result of IT departments constantly seeking to reduce the number of different operating system platforms within their departments, which is generally accepted as a sure way of avoiding further increases in operating expenses. Once they purchased NT Servers, they did not always wish to add Unix servers into their environment.

The basic precondition underlying the market shift is the changing performance of the server operating systems and network operating systems for handling traditional jobs (file, print, and directory handling). Whereas network operating systems previously (in the 1980s and the first half of the 1990s) had the advantage in this area, the difference has shrunk considerably because of the enormous growth in the horsepower of the servers. Currently, the margin of difference between the two platforms is so small that choosing a network OS based on the assumption that it handles traditional tasks better is not a valid reason.

The market tendencies in recent years show that server operating systems have some very clear advantages over network operating systems. But not until one or more producers of server operating systems decide to concentrate more on establishing a position for directory services can a prediction be made regarding which type of operating system will prevail in the future.

Is Porting The Key To Success For Directory Services?

None of the present directory service solutions have been able to fully meet the expectations of having one common storage place for all the information of a computer environment.

But this doesn't mean that businesses that have implemented one of the present directory service solutions haven't benefited from it. All investigations regarding the matter have shown that these businesses have reduced their operating costs, compared with companies that use name services only. The reduction in operating expenses is closely tied to the size, complexity, and division of labor in a particular business. Small businesses with a simple organizational structure and one central IT department will only save a little (or nothing) by implementing a directory service. Big companies with a complicated organizational structure and a decentralized IT group will save a lot by implementing a directory service.

Directory services are a great advantage in handling traditional network services, but tend to be limited for this purpose because very few providers of service applications have integrated their products with one or more of the existing directory service solutions. Also, most companies still operate with more than one operating system platform for the servers, and typically can't agree on one single directory service solution.

NDS

Despite a poor beginning, Novell NDS's figures show that it is doing well among OS platforms (other than Novell's own NetWare and IntraNetWare). Apart from having designed a porting of NDS for Windows NT 4.0 Server (NDS for NT), Novell has entered into agreements with Hewlett-Packard, Sun, and SCO to build NDS support into their Unix operating systems.

In July 1997, Novell experienced a slight breakthrough by reaching an agreement with IBM that NDS would be ported for IBM mainframes and AIX (Advanced Interactive Executive) systems. This was quite a surprising step—albeit a positive one—because IBM had hitherto focused on a DCE-based directory service solution. However, IBM apparently is now considering changing course to NDS, although it argues that NDS porting is just "supplementary" to its own original DCE solution. IBM's explanation deserves credit, because DCE has had limited success, and it leaves open the possibility for customers to choose either NDS or DCE. IBM doesn't have any great marketing impetus to support NDS, because far too few companies have implemented NDS.

Currently, NDS is ported, or is going to be ported, to the following operating systems:

- SCO UnixWare

- Hewlett-Packard HP-UX

- Caldera OpenLinux

- Sun Solaris

- Fujitsu DS/90

- IBM AIX, OS/400, and MVS systems

However, implementing Novell NDS is currently possible only on networks that have a certain number of NetWare/IntraNet 4.x servers. The current porting to other platforms presupposes that integration is toward NetWare or IntraNetWare servers. Novell has promised that an NT 5.0 version of NDS is being developed, which (like NDS for NT 4.0) means that having NetWare or IntraNetWare servers won't be necessary.

On the application side, integration to NDS is available only in Novell's own server applications, comprising the GroupWise groupware system, the administrative tool ManageWise, the firewall BorderManager, and the Web Server, together with a few other server applications from third-party providers. The following is a list of fairly well-known applications from third-party providers that are NDS-prepared:

- Attachmate EXTRA!

- Cheyenne ARCserve, FAXserve, and InocuLAN

- HP JetAdmin

- IBM TIME 10

- Intel LANDesk Management Suite

- Legato NetWorker

- Lexmark MarkVision

- Lotus Notes, Domino, and cc:Mail

- McAfee Service Desk and SaberTools

- ON Technology DaVinci eMAIL

- Oracle7 and Oracle8

- PC Docs

- Seagate Backup Exec and Desktop Management Suite

- Sybase Open Server and SQL Server

- Watcom C/C++ and FORTRAN77

Of course, this list isn't enough to impress would-be NDS buyers, so Novell is now trying more than ever to spread NDS to some of the most important server applications and other OS platforms.

Most analysts predict that Novell's chances of success are slim regarding server applications, because the still-nonexistent Microsoft Active Directory has already won, by far, the most acceptance among application developers. Already, 250 application developers have expressed their support for Active Directory. NDS still lacks a stable OS platform to handle big server applications. Novell might have had this in mind when it announced that NDS would be completely ported to Windows.

StreetTalk

Banyan has made its StreetTalk service available for other platforms via the following products:

- ENS for NetWare

- ENS for AIX

- ENS for Solaris

- ENS for HP-UX

- ENS for SCO-Unix

- StreetTalk for Windows NT

Judging by the low level of information on ENS for the different variations of Unix, Banyan's interest in these products must be viewed as doubtful.

However, StreetTalk for Windows NT doesn't presuppose that VINES servers are present on the network in order to function—StreetTalk for NT is based on the Universal StreetTalk product, which (in 1995) Banyan promised to make available to all producers who want to build in support of the StreetTalk protocol.

Unfortunately, Banyan's hopes that Universal StreetTalk might attract more application developers to StreetTalk have been dashed. StreetTalk doesn't seem to have gained much support with some of the popular server applications, and Banyan isn't concentrating on StreetTalk on its company literature. Thus, interest in StreetTalk is unlikely to increase. The following producers of server applications are mentioned on Banyan's Web site as "partners": Attachmate, Legato, Oracle, Powersoft, and SAP. The only server application actually cited on Banyan's Web site as being capable of utilizing StreetTalk is Banyan's own mail system, Intelligent Messaging.

Active Directory

Although Microsoft has been relatively slow in deciding which direction it wants to take regarding directory services, it has recently chosen to go its own separate way: Microsoft wants to deliver its directory service (Active Directory) only for NT Server 5.0. So far, Active Directory clients are planned only for Windows 95 and NT Workstation.

However, Cisco recently entered into an agreement with Microsoft that gives Cisco the chance to port Active Directory to Cisco's own IOS operating system, which is used by the majority of its active network components and Unix. Cisco hasn't announced which Unix variants it intends to port Active Directory to, but they have promised that it will be available for the most popular Unix flavors. Whichever variants it chooses, Active Directory's market share and supporting application development will surely get a boost.

Microsoft has also developed its own directory services API, dubbed Active Directory Services Interface (ADSI). The idea of ADSI is to enable program developers to write one single API. This API then has access to practically any directory service. ADSI is Microsoft's not-too-hidden "Trojan Horse," which should lure application developers farther away from writing directly to NDS or StreetTalk. Microsoft's competition hasn't failed to respond: Novell and Sun are defining a competing Java-based API called Java Naming and Directory Interface (JNDI), which will compete directly with ADSI.

At the same time, Microsoft has made a smart move that none of its competitors have been able to match so far: Microsoft is aiming at the evident alternative to openness—standardization. In Microsoft's opinion, directory services must be implemented through harsh standardization, combined with the use of the LDAP standard for handling other platforms, particularly the Internet.

As stated earlier, Active Directory shows signs of having a great advantage with respect to application support, compared to what competitors are offering. Microsoft already can boast of having a list of about 250 application developers. Among them are producers of practically all the popular server applications available today that support Active Directory. But then again, application developers don't have much choice—sooner or later, Microsoft undoubtedly will make integration of Active Directory compulsory for an application to receive the prestigious BackOffice logo.

Despite Microsoft's Active Directory solution being very late to market (compared with its competitors from Banyan and Novell), all analysts agree that it isn't too late. In fact, the majority of analysts believe that Active Directory stands a real chance of outpacing its competition, because very few companies have managed to implement a truly integrated directory service solution. The good growth rate of server applications and servers based on NT Server makes Active Directory a real threat.

Know Your LDAP!

Sure signs that competing companies are trying to outdo each other in their standardization attempts are the fact that today's solutions are available only to a limited number of computer platforms, and the fact that application developers have shown very little interest in integrating directory service. Strict standardization is the only alternative for an environment with just a single or a few operating systems and server applications, which is unacceptable for most companies.

Most companies' standardization attempts will focus on LDAP, including heavyweights such as Netscape, Sun, Microsoft, and Cisco, which is one reason why LDAP is expected to be the future gateway standard for directory services. Users of directory services should start to receive more than just marketing platitudes as a result of this growing competition at standardization.

LDAP's popularity also means that the battle will move to the LDAP workgroup. Microsoft has been very active, at a very early stage, regarding LDAP, which is one reason why Microsoft has come up with its smart solution: full access to Active Directory via LDAP. Novell recently expressed interest in raising NDS to an Internet Engineering Task Force (IETF) standard, equal with LDAP, or at least in putting some clear NDS imprint on the LDAP standard. Novell wants to establish NDS technologies as a basis for replication, which is very weak in LDAP 3 and nonexistent in LDAP 2 (currently the most popular version of LDAP). The replication model in LDAP 3 is master-slave, which means that the entire directory service database is replicated every time a change has occurred—a very primitive form of replication that isn't practical for wide area networks (WANs).

Novell has a clear incentive for making NDS a standard: OS and server application manufacturers will be more interested in having built-in NDS support if it is granted standardization. One drawback for Novell is that raising the whole or parts of NDS to standardization level could be incredibly costly. At a minimum, Novell would have to give up several of its patents, which are some of the crown jewels of Novell. This is a primary reason why reaching a compromise is doubtful, in addition to the fact that Cisco and Microsoft are jointly promoting another replication model.

The Solutions Aren't As Similar As They May Seem

While Novell and Banyan are very aggressive advocates for, and the biggest suppliers of, directory services for the PC environment, Microsoft is just beginning its conquest of this market. Consequently, the three companies are beginning to send confusing signals.

Novell, Banyan, and Microsoft have trouble discussing a standard for directory services because they each have chosen to attack the matter somewhat differently. Even if all the vendors of directory services focus on the X.500 standard, their implementations are significantly different. The framework of this book isn't intended to provide a lengthy, in-depth discussion of the three directory services. Instead, some of the most significant properties of the three directory service implementations are discussed in the following pages.

NDS

NDS's biggest advantage is that it currently has the biggest client base, with the broadest support on the market. An important fact regarding the implementation of NDS is that it may be necessary to divide the tree into several separate segments (called *partitions* in NDS jargon), depending on the density of traffic and the total number of objects in the database of each server.

NDS trees ideally must not have groups of more than 500 users, or partitions and contexts (in other words, the branches of the tree) with more than 1,500 users. NDS trees easily can have many thousands of users, but the tree must not be too flat. Ideally, an NDS tree is triangular in form.

NDS's most pronounced Achilles' heel is that finding objects in the directory can be extremely difficult, because NDS lacks integrated search tools for users. An administrator can even inadvertently make finding objects much more difficult, by defining deep trees. Also, the NDS tree structure is difficult to alter after it has been established, although this has improved in recent years. Likewise, the overall chart of the trees needs to be the same everywhere in each individual tree, so that all trees can be kept in sync with each other. The inheritance of the chart means that the entire organization must agree upon the structure and content of the name system. This can cause much frustration in bigger companies that have a decentralized structure, because two trees that are merging into one tree must necessarily merge into the same chart.

Finally, replication must be configured for each partition, and a plan must be drawn that ensures the clocks in all servers are always completely synchronized, which might further complicate the administration of the environment.

To avoid excess consumption of bandwidth (due to directory notice), at least one NetWare or IntraNetWare-based server is required on every WAN location within the organization, because the other server platforms currently only integrate into a separate NDS database. To date, none of the server platforms contain an NDS database.

StreetTalk

StreetTalk's greatest advantage is that it is the oldest directory service of the three, which means that it is past the bugs of early development. Furthermore, StreetTalk is equipped with some incredibly strong and flexible search facilities, plus some good possibilities for defining and locating aliases or nicknames. Users should be able to find the object they are looking for on the first attempt with StreetTalk.

StreetTalk is probably the most flexible and easily accessible directory service of the three. For instance, it gives access to multilevel replication, an enormous relief in megasized environments. Yet StreetTalk has the reputation of being the slowest directory service and consuming the most bandwidth.

StreetTalk's biggest limitation, quite clearly, is that it supports only level-level names, which means objects can be members only of a group or an organization that is placed at the root of the tree. This limitation isn't much of an organizational problem for anyone other than the biggest and most advanced companies. By comparison, NDS and Active Directory both make "infinite" tree depth possible, which makes their structures perfect for any type of organization, regardless of size.

Active Directory

Ironically, because Active Directory isn't yet available, the tendency is to attribute a lot of optimistic properties to it that the other two directory services don't possess.

One of Active Directory's real advantages is that Microsoft is working to ensure that replacing NT domains with Active Directory will be practical. The domain concept remains present, and has merely been aligned for use in a directory tree. Microsoft's foresight will enable NT 5.0 to be implemented immediately on a network in which old versions of NT Server are still in use.

Another advantage of Active Directory is that it is widely based on standards that already exist (DNS, LDAP, and Kerberos), enabling an administrator to use an individual chart for every domain in the directory tree.

The main drawback of Active Directory is due to Microsoft's concentration on backward-compatibility, resulting in the trust concept and part of the "domain world" of ideas sticking with Active Directory. However, Active Directory is equipped with *transitive trusts* (trusts inherited throughout the entire structure), which significantly reduces the disadvantages of maintaining backward-compatibility with the trust concept.

Another drawback of Active Directory is that administrators still must allocate file and print rights via groups rather than according to the directory tree. Moreover, and somewhat surprisingly, delegating administrative rights to individual objects or groups of objects isn't possible with Active Directory, but instead, an organizational unit (OU) must be the least delegated object. Finally, handling resources globally with Active Directory is impossible.

Active Directory undoubtedly is hiding other drawbacks that haven't surfaced yet, as the product still is in its early stages.

Some Words Of Warning

Not everybody is able to design an efficient and sensible directory. A directory designer needs an in-depth understanding of a directory service's technology, as well as sufficient experience in modeling in the real world.

Mistakes can be fatal. A wrong tree design can mean that the stability and productivity of the network environment is drastically reduced—just as if the network itself had been incorrectly designed. With regard to the design, you must pay special attention to how the replication and the conditions of replication are configured. For example, you need to configure how long it takes until objects are allowed to be used, or when objects should be removed from the tree. You must also pay attention to whether the directory tree is based on the organizational plan or the geography of the company.

It Takes Time

Despite general agreement that a directory service is the only solution to the ever-increasing pile of data on company networks, only a few companies have implemented directory services.

Why is this so? Most analysts point out that realizing the advantages of directory services is very difficult without actually implementing them. Likewise, a shift from name services to a global directory service is such a monumental change that most IT sections instinctively draw back.

But directory services are here to stay. They will be part of the everyday life of the network administrator beyond 2000. It is still too early to predict which directory service(s) will be favored by companies, and due to the many diverse approaches to directory services, some common denominator likely will be needed among the various directory services (unless one directory service dominates the market). I don't think this is likely to happen in the short or intermediate term, as a change of server platforms is very painful to implement. LDAP could very well become this helpful common denominator.

The struggle among the various directory services likely won't focus on technological qualities and standards, but on something as simple as the number of platforms and applications that a given directory service can handle. This is the only way in which directory services can really help a business save money on working expenses. And, amazingly, Microsoft Active Directory apparently is well on its way to having such a money-saving advantage—even before it is released—because application developers and Cisco, Microsoft's collaborator on Active Directory, very strongly support it.

Introducing The Tools For The Distributed World Of The Future

Recently, high-ranking Microsoft representatives have been asking the same question: Is the era of the personal computer over?

Not surprisingly, the answer from the Microsoft people has been a resounding "No." They argue that the market for common consumer electronic units, such as telephones, radios, and TVs, was only close to the saturation point when more than 80 percent of the population had them. The PC market has not even come close to this level of saturation in America, let alone the world. So the PC still has a fairly long lifetime.

Yet Microsoft believes that the PC is undergoing a lot of changes. It is moving away from the current monolithic model for clients and servers, which has been the standard since the computer was born, to the *distributed data-processing* model, in which the system consists of several different and physically separated components, in terms of both hardware and software. Microsoft regards distributed data processing as a logical continuation of the current trend. Likewise, distributed data processing is an attractive solution as businesses achieve greater flexibility in their use of information technology. Distributed data processing enables a business to move entire or partial applications among servers and clients on the network, without having to change the setup of the systems that use the given applications.

The fact that Microsoft is now talking about distributed data processing is not a coincidence. As many people know, Microsoft has been considering several technologies for distributed data processing since 1991 (developed under the code name Cairo). Windows NT 5.0 is the final piece to Microsoft's much-discussed Cairo jigsaw puzzle, which is why Microsoft is now eager to praise distributed IT environments.

Currently, the family of Cairo technologies in NT 5.0 consists of Distributed COM, (DCOM, previously dubbed Network OLE), Distributed File System (DFS), and Active Directory. This means that, on paper, NT 5.0 does not appear to be much more of a Cairo-like product than its predecessor. Observers of the evolution of NT know that DCOM and DFS actually appeared with NT 4.0 in 1996.

Although Microsoft and others have not made a lot of fuss over DCOM and DFS, distributed data processing is one of the areas that undoubtedly will be very much in the limelight when NT 5.0 is first released. Active Directory and some new helpful facilities (Microsoft Transaction Server and Microsoft Message Queue Server) provide the functionality necessary to implement the theories underlying distributed IT environments.

Objects Are The Basis Of The Distributed World

Before moving further into the distributed world, some definitions need to be clarified. *Distributed data processing*, in simple terms, enables a business to eliminate the necessity of placing an application in one specific physical location. In a *distributed environment*, the entire application, or parts thereof, are spread across several computers—up to the whole network—as the need arises.

Of course, this distributed architecture can be achieved for an application only if that application can be divided into several mutually independent components. Object orientation is one way to accomplish this division, and thus may be regarded as a natural prerequisite for distributed data processing (which is why Microsoft has focused so much attention on object orientation in recent years).

When Microsoft talks about distributed data processing, it often refers to *distributed objects*. Distributed objects enable systems administrators to spread application components (such as software agents, remote procedures, and other objects) evenly over the entire network, making the components immediately accessible to all other object components, regardless of whether they are used on clients or servers.

The client/server terminology will be a relic of the past after distributed objects introduce this wider and more minute spreading of functions and data. In theory, using middleware to gain access to data won't be necessary with distributed objects (as is the case with the client/server architecture). In the distributed future, middleware will take the form of more-generic and flexible program components, united in solving every single task. For instance, if a client needs to access data, it can send a short message via a slow WAN attachment to an intermediate object, which, in turn, can send a more extensive message to either a Remote Procedure Call (RPC) mechanism, a distributed TP monitor, several new intermediate objects, or—as a fourth possibility—obtain the required data locally.

Microsoft and its competitors have been in sharp competition for several years over the standardization of object technology, because distributed objects are the foundation of distributed data processing. Average users typically have experienced this struggle over standardization of object technology only in the form of the standard for compound documents. However, the struggle involves something much more important: the standardization of the components necessary for distributed data processing.

Compound Documents

Compound documents are formed by embedding parts of a document from one application in a document from another application. An example of a compound document is when you insert an Excel spreadsheet into a Word document, so that you can revert to, and make changes in, the original Excel spreadsheet by double-clicking the embedded spreadsheet. Most users of Windows use Object Linking and Embedding (OLE) in everyday life when they cut and paste objects among various applications via the Paste Special facilities available under the Edit menu in most Windows applications.

The struggle over the standardization of compound documents was won by Microsoft's OLE without much challenge. OLE was so well established on the market by the time OpenDoc (the much-delayed alternative standard) appeared, that OpenDoc never had a chance. When OpenDoc was finally ready, the majority of Windows users were already using OLE in their everyday lives, without giving it much thought, and so OpenDoc was too late.

OLE's overwhelming success means that, as the only player on the market, Microsoft has a real base to work from in the objects area. Numerous application-development tools already exist for OLE, as well as a multitude of OLE-based components. These components are also known as *ActiveX controls*, *OCXs* (OLE Components), or *OLE controls*.

Like OLE, ActiveX is based on Microsoft's object-oriented model, called the *Component Object Model* (COM). COM is Microsoft's foundation for the distributed objects of the future. COM is part of the *really* interesting struggle: the struggle over the *Object Request Brokers* (ORBs), the technology that makes sharing objects across the network possible.

ORBs serve as a kind of control center for translating information among separate applications. An ORB sends inquiries from clients to and from server components that are placed either locally or on a remote system. The clients communicate with the server components via an interface that stores the initialization methods and available functions of the server components. These interfaces are defined in the *Interface Definition Language* (IDL).

COM Vs. CORBA

The fight for the distributed object standard has been clearly marked from the very start. On one side of the ring is Microsoft's COM, and on the other side is the *Object Management Group* (OMG), an interest group of more than 700 suppliers of object-oriented tools that created the *Common Object Request Broker Architecture* (CORBA) standard. On the fringes are some companies that are already working on slightly different ORB standards, but they don't stand a chance of establishing themselves as huge contenders on the market. For example, Distributed System Object Model (DSOM) is IBM's facility for OpenDoc. DSOM has nearly identical characteristics to Microsoft's DCOM, which is the facility for OLE.

All odds have been against Microsoft's COM from the start. Practically all the manufacturers of operating systems and application software—except Microsoft—supported CORBA from its early stages. However, despite all the good intentions, CORBA has not been able to leverage its great support and greater technological might to keep COM out of the market.

Consequently, Microsoft has had time to work at refining COM, so that—technically speaking—COM is no longer inferior to CORBA, although comparing CORBA and COM is difficult: ActiveX and DCOM form an integrated, coherent development environment, whereas CORBA is a collection of specifications, developed by many software developers, which gives CORBA a certain liberty in translation and implementation (and thus less cohesion). This means, for instance, that whereas CORBA always calls for the use of IDL to specify interfaces and inheritance for objects, DCOM supports the use of a binary interface standard directly through aggregation. DCOM can also support IDL through the COM-to-CORBA inter-networking specification.

However, CORBA is not dead—the majority of Microsoft's competitors (for example, Digital, Hewlett-Packard, IBM, and Sun Microsystems) continue to support CORBA, thus making it available for most modern computer platforms. Until about a year ago, the CORBA implementations by various providers lacked compatibility, due to the lack of a communication standard among the CORBA network applications. However, the CORBA 2.0 General Inter-ORB protocol has filled this void. This protocol has been adapted to TCP/IP networks in the form of the *Internet Inter-ORB Protocol* (IIOP), which recently was given an exciting boost by Internet giant Netscape's decision to concentrate on IIOP for interprocess communication among distributed objects on the Web.

Of the two choices available on the ORB market, CORBA typically is the preferred choice when spanning several operating system platforms, whereas COM clearly is the preferred choice for Windows environments. Since COM's appearance, Microsoft has refined its solution so much that technological differences no longer exist between the two ORBs. Also, one of Microsoft's partners, Software AG, has introduced various COM portings on numerous Unix platforms. Software AG has several portings under way within the Unix area for the most widespread mini- and mainframe platforms.

Java

Parallel with the ORB struggle, a mass of criticism has concentrated on a completely new dark horse called *Java*. Java challenges ActiveX controls, and has been much better than OpenDoc at taking a stand against the Microsoft standards.

Microsoft certainly is following Java's developments very closely. In fact, Microsoft already has a license to use Java and has embedded Java support in its Internet Explorer browser. This has resulted in litigation between Sun and Microsoft regarding whether Microsoft's implementation of Java complies with Sun's licensing agreement.

Microsoft's declared goal is to supply the Java VM with the highest possible yield to the Windows environment, to supply strong Java development tools, and to optimize the integration to Java from ActiveX. This sums up Microsoft's intentions, but it might be forced to place Java more centrally in its future strategies. However, as long as Microsoft is able to maintain the present focus on ActiveX among the majority of Windows program developers, it will not be interested in anything but COM (in the form of DCOM or COM+) when discussing distributed objects.

Microsoft DNA—The New Miracle Cure?

When it comes to object standards, Microsoft is so self-assured of its position in the market that it has started indoctrinating independent program manufacturers to the concept of distributed data processing.

Java Vs. ActiveX

Parallel with the fight surrounding ORBs, a struggle has started in the market for components to tackle Internet and intranet applications. This struggle is between Java and ActiveX.

However, these two solutions are very different technologically, which may decide their respective futures. ActiveX is specially built for Windows environments, whereas Java is independent of the operating system. Java can run on Windows, Macintosh, and various Unix environments, among a few others.

The difference in ActiveX and Java is very clear in the way they operate. ActiveX components are compiled for the Windows environment and written with Windows-based development tools, such as Microsoft Visual C++ and Visual Basic. When an ActiveX object is retrieved for use, it is compiled and ready to operate. ActiveX controls can benefit from programs and data that are stored on the same client. There could, for instance, be an ActiveX control that is responsible for finding and installing updates in the Windows 98 Update Manager solution. ActiveX components may also be used as application servers via DCOM.

The fact that ActiveX operates as an independent program, thus enabling the use of existing programs on the given computer, correlates to a greater weakness in its security. This greater weakness is due to the fact that no restrictions exist as to how an ActiveX control behaves. For example, ActiveX allows free access to change the operating system, such as deleting files or installing viruses. Moreover, ActiveX depends on a platform, as does any other form of compiled code that interacts with the operating system.

Java, on the other hand, is an interpreted language. When a Java application is designed, it is translated from the Java language to a pseudocode, instead of a machine code. This means that when the Java component is started, the Java code is interpreted on the client system within a Virtual Machine (VM). Such Virtual Machines are written and optimized for every single operating system that Java runs on.

Applications written in Java thus can be operated without modification on all the computer platforms for which Virtual Machines have been developed, which includes practically all modern operating systems. The VM is a kind of buffer layer between the Java code and the operating system, which removes the security risks associated with ActiveX.

The darker side of Java's platform-independence is that the standard interface elements of the OS (for example, key buttons and scrollbars) are not available for Java applications. This means that application manufacturers have to construct their own interface elements. Sun is trying to standardize the user interface elements toward the normal elements of the OS by embedding support of the most common elements in the Java Class Libraries. Another downside is that an interpreted language like Java is, by definition, considerably slower than a computer language, in which the program code is translated into a machine code in advance.

The first clear opportunity for loyal Microsoft supporters to think and speak about distributed data processing was at the Professional Developer's Conference, held in late September 1997. At this conference, Microsoft launched its *Distributed interNet Applications* (DNA) architecture and COM+.

COM+ is a Web-enabled extension of COM, which enables you to extend the Windows component technology to cover the new component technologies and languages coming from the Web. COM+ is intended to reshape today's client/server applications into Web applications, thus ensuring that current Windows applications, if necessary, can be drawn into the age of the Internet, while simultaneously ensuring that Windows survives in the age of the Web.

DNA is a three-layer model for developing the next generation of Windows applications, in which the application is split into components for storage, program logic, and graphical presentation. DNA is closely integrated with Active Directory, which handles the identification, security, and attachment of users to distributed applications or components. These applications can be stored anywhere on the network, regardless of whether that network is a local area network (LAN) or the ultimate wide area network (WAN): the Internet.

DNA, roughly speaking, is just a consolidation of various existing technologies by Microsoft, and COM+ is one of the most important pieces in the DNA architecture. With its usual modesty, Microsoft describes DNA and COM+ as the new architecture of the future—scalable multilayer solutions for distributed data processing that any network can supply.

Application developers undoubtedly already know that they will have to construct future applications based on these two standards. Among others, SAP, Baan, PeopleSoft, and Computer Associates have already indicated that their future generations of applications will be designed on the basis of DNA and COM+.

Microsoft emphasizes that DNA and COM+ are based on a selection of acknowledged standards. It makes this assertion because DNA uses a series of current HTML standards, and Microsoft is in the process of porting Internet Explorer to numerous Unix platforms and to the Macintosh. Simultaneously, Microsoft is having COM ported onto Unix, Multiple Virtual Storage (MVS) the operating system for old IBM mainframes since 1974, and Macintosh, through its partners.

What Is DNA?

Microsoft defines DNA as an architectural framework with which to construct modern, scalable, multilayered, distributed data-processing solutions supplied over any network.

The slightly more detailed objective for Windows DNA is to establish an environment in which to develop applications based on the Windows platform, and in which to unite and integrate the personal computer with the Internet. Windows DNA integrates these two worlds by making a series of demands regarding which core services should be present in the operating systems. This ensures that PCs are able to communicate and cooperate just as well across the network of the company as with any kind of public network.

The whole idea of Windows DNA, therefore, is to establish a uniform procedure with which to integrate the Web and client/server data-processing models. Through DNA, Microsoft hopes that many new software solutions will be developed that are easy to integrate with users' existing investments in PCs, minicomputers, or mainframes, yet at the same time, enable users to benefit from new Internet technologies.

Windows DNA covers all levels of a modern distributed application, from user interface and navigation to business procedures and storage. Windows DNA presupposes that program developers will use the application services from the Windows platform. Generally, the services are through COM. Note that the current Windows DNA does not readily replace COM+, which was launched alongside DNA. Figure 5.1 shows the various components of Microsoft DNA.

Windows DNA consists of a series of open Internet standards and various well-defined proprietary Microsoft interfaces. The standards that currently form Windows DNA are shown in Tables 5.1 and 5.2. Windows DNA consists of the application services listed in Table 5.1 and the infrastructure services listed in Table 5.2.

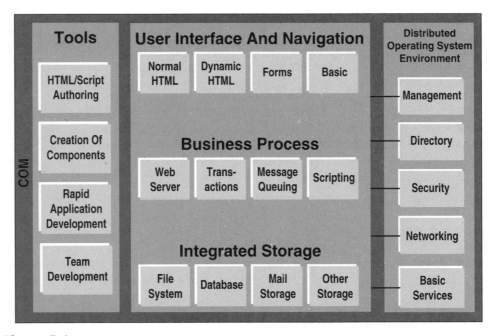

Figure 5.1
Microsoft DNA consists of various components that are all mutually integrated and tied together via COM+.

Table 5.1 *The application services included in Windows DNA.*

Application Service	Interface Or Technology	Corresponding Microsoft Product Or Component
Web server	HTML	Internet Information Server
Web browser	HTML	Internet Explorer
Scripting	VBScript, JavaScript, Dynamic HTML	Internet Explorer and Windows Scripting Host
Transaction service	OLE transactions	Transaction Server
Message queue service	Falcon API	Message Queue Server
Database	ODBC, OLE DB (OLE database)	SQL Server
Mail, Calendar, and so on	MAPI, POP3	Outlook and Exchange Server
Java Virtual Machine	Java	Microsoft Java Virtual Machine
Universal access to data	ADO, OLE DB, ODBC	Several products

Table 5.2 *The infrastructure services included in Windows DNA.*

Infrastructure Service	Interface Or Technology	Corresponding Microsoft Product Or Component
Directory	Active Directory Services Interface	Active Directory
Security	Secure Sockets Layer	Internet Explorer and Windows NT Server
Network handling	TCP/IP, pipes, Winsock, and so on	The entire Windows family
File and print	Server Message Block (SMB)	The entire Windows family
Components	COM, DCOM, ActiveX	The entire Windows family

Microsoft divides Windows DNA into a set of distributed application services, distributed infrastructure components, and common interfaces. This division operates in a multilayered environment in which COM and other standard protocols act as the glue among the application layers (see Figure 5.2).

An important fact to note is that Windows NT 5.0 contains the full implementation of Windows DNA for both clients and servers.

Focus On COM+

One key to Windows DNA is that it provides a vast choice of fairly easy-to-use integrated services for program developers to create and use software components and applications. These system services are supplied via COM. In the future, a much

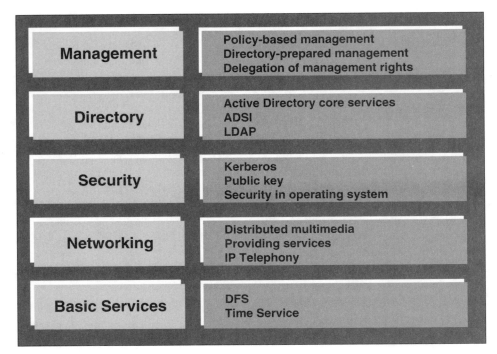

Management	Policy-based management Directory-prepared management Delegation of management rights
Directory	Active Directory core services ADSI LDAP
Security	Kerberos Public key Security in operating system
Networking	Distributed multimedia Providing services IP Telephony
Basic Services	DFS Time Service

Figure 5.2
NT 5.0 is equipped with numerous distributed facilities.

wider range of services will be supplied via COM's successor, COM+, which hopefully will make designing new applications much easier for developers.

COM and COM+ are mainly of interest to program developers, which is why Microsoft emphasizes that COM and COM+ are independent of a particular computer language, enabling Java, C++, Visual Basic, and other COM-related programs to use COM. Microsoft also stresses that components already exist that open COM objects to the world of CORBA.

COM+, an extension of COM, consists of an improved component environment that offers a simpler and sturdier model for registration, installation, and versioning of components, which will make using and handling the COM technology easier. Several other COM+ features support the development of component-based distributed applications. Some of these features include improved security facilities, support of transactions, improved inherited properties, and asynchronous messaging facilities. With regard to messaging facilities, COM+ and several of Microsoft Message Queue Server's services use objects, which makes constructing applications with asynchronous interfaces a straightforward process.

Probably the most important feature of distributed applications is the new *interception mechanism*, which enables components to dynamically route their functionality in order to call several different services when handling the program code (instead of being connected in advance to one single service). Interceptors thus can receive and treat events related to establishment, handling errors, call-off, and deletion of instances.

Interceptors supply the mechanism necessary to implement transactions and system surveillance. COM+ uses interceptors when establishing access to data and other distributed services.

One of the great advantages of the interception mechanism is the way in which the components are treated: You just place some attributes in the given class, which might, for example, be from a traditional development environment. No more new APIs exist to learn, and no complex code precludes program developers from writing the application logic. Instead, just a few attributes must be indicated.

From COM To DCOM

DCOM (Distributed COM, previously called Network OLE or Distributed OLE) is a sort of object-based bus that was built to enable communication among components across processors and computers. DCOM thus supports the establishment of distributed applications that communicate with other components, and that use distributed Windows platform services across the network.

DCOM makes network communication transparent for the components, so that communication among the components appears precisely the same to users, regardless of whether the given component or service is situated somewhere on the network or on the user's local machine.

DCOM expands Microsoft's COM concept to also cover network functions. As such, DCOM is a basic prerequisite for obtaining distributed functionality in the ActiveX environment, while simultaneously enabling all existing "well-behaved" OLE applications to immediately function across the network.

The greatest advantage of DCOM is also inherited from COM: numerous very strong development tools and a vast number of commercially available ActiveX components.

DCOM is based on the Open Software Foundation (OSF) Distributed Computing Environment—Remote Procedure Call (DCE-RPC) protocol, which is independent of the underlying communication protocols.

The philosophy underlying DCOM calls all applications *objects*. In the DCOM environment, client applications can communicate with the various objects only through interfaces that contain a number of pointers for the functions available in a given object. The interfaces are the key to DCOM (and COM). The components themselves are just implementations of programming interfaces. A given component can be removed and replaced with another component if the new component is supported by the same interface.

DCOM supports *interface inheritance*, which means that one interface can be imported from another interface, but the imported interface cannot inherit the components accessible underneath the original interface. DCOM makes reusing existing components possible by transferring the interface pointers of other objects to the original objects.

Every object must be registered on the local machine in order for the client to find the object via its *Globally Unique Identifier* (GUID) in the registration database. DCOM uses the Windows NT security system and, as such, supplies the *Access Control List* (ACL) that contains the users and the access rights of the groups for the various components. These lists may be configured via either the DCOM configuration tool or a direct call to the NT security functions.

DCOM is not in itself a solution to two of the most fundamental problems in a distributed world: How do you find the objects you want, and how do you keep the necessary level of security for those objects? This requires an efficient and flexible distributed name service. Microsoft offers Active Directory (discussed in Chapter 4) as this service, which is part of NT Server 5.0.

Moreover, DCOM contains no fault tolerance or load balancing. Microsoft anticipates that its Transaction Server will handle these two decisive functions in large IT environments.

Microsoft is busy gearing the two central DCOM products to incorporate error tolerance and load balancing. As already mentioned, Windows NT Server will be equipped with the necessary infrastructure for handling DCOM efficiently (mainly through Active Directory), whereas Microsoft Transaction Server is based on COM and uses DCOM to handle communication among components across the network.

DCOM has long been expected to have great future potential. With Windows NT Server 5.0 (which will also contain Transaction Server), DCOM's great potential may finally be implemented. NT Server 5.0 and DCOM contain the services necessary to handle a truly distributed environment. As DCOM's potential becomes demonstrable through its implementation, program developers will surely follow with a series of new and exciting DCOM-prepared applications.

In fact, the announcements for DCOM-prepared applications are already beginning to appear. Some rather exciting news about DCOM is that the SAP DCOM Component Connector will enable administrators to mix SAP R/3 objects with other COM objects across the network, while simultaneously maintaining a sufficient security level via the distributed security service of Transaction Server, which is integrated with NT's security. The SAP DCOM Component Connector is part of the Business Framework family of products, which SAP promises to deliver at the same time as R/3 version 4.0.

DFS And Other Initiatives For Distributed Storage

COM+, DCOM, Active Directory, and Transaction Server are not enough to create the necessary infrastructure for a true distributed environment, because one important component is missing: storage.

Microsoft offers three vital technologies for storage: Distributed File System, junction points, and OLE DB. All three technologies are pretty new and relatively unknown to most computer professionals.

Distributed File System

Distributed File System (DFS) is probably the best known of the three technologies because it currently is part of Windows NT Server 4.0. DFS provides the capability to create distributed file systems that spread across several servers. The distributed file system appears as a single, coherent tree structure, even if it spreads over volumes placed on many different servers.

DFS's advantage is that users don't need to know the name of the server on which the information is stored. The user sees the many servers as one server.

Another equally exciting aspect of DFS is that it provides the capacity to place the same parts of the directory tree on several servers. This is a safeguard against server breakdown, because if one server crashes, another server has a copy of the directory tree.

In the current version of DFS, the duplication capability is limited to static data, because DFS is not equipped with any functions to spread around changes in the files on the particular server. Also, the root for the DFS tree can be placed only on one server, which constitutes a critical, single point of failure for the whole tree. Moreover, DFS is not compatible with Microsoft Cluster Server (previously known as WolfPack). These limitations have been removed in Windows NT Server 5.0, which makes the DFS technology such an exciting tool with which to solve many different file-bound tasks that require maximum accessibility and the possibility of splitting the load across several servers.

For a change, DFS is not restricted to NT-based servers. The only requirement is that the root for the given DFS tree must be placed on a Windows NT Server 4.0 or 5.0 that is equipped with the DFS server software. All the underlying volumes in the DFS tree can be placed on any type of Microsoft server or other types of servers for which an NT-based client exists—this includes any version of NT Server and NT Workstation, NetWare, Windows 95 and 98, Windows for Workgroups, LAN Manager, and Network File System (NFS), which is used to share files over a network in Windows 3.x, Solaris, and other operating systems.

However, handling DFS trees on a PC is possible only if the PC is equipped with a DFS client. DFS clients are available only for NT Workstation 4.0/5.0 and Windows 95/98. Figure 5.3 shows the DFS Administrator. You can read about DFS in more depth in Chapter 17.

Junction Points

In NT 5.0, NT File System (NTFS) introduces a new facility called *junction point*, a tool to link together volumes across several servers (just as linking is done with DFS). NTFS junction points contain only a fraction of the DFS functionality, and don't include load balancing, introduction of fault tolerance, integration with file systems other than NTFS 5.0, or information retrieval from Active Directory.

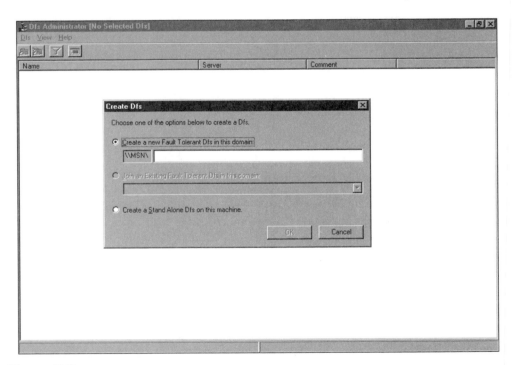

Figure 5.3
DFS has become a far more integrated part of the new NT Server, and all the basic limitations of DFS have been removed.

But NTFS junction points are an excellent way to link many different volumes in the same directory tree, especially in situations in which using a DFS-based client is possible.

OLE DB

The aim of OLE DB (database) is to provide universal access to all forms of data in a COM environment, irrespective of data type and location. OLE DB is a component technology in which the data sources are made accessible via interfaces, thus reflecting the functionality of the underlying data source. For instance, OLE DB enables you to build new components on top of these interfaces, and to create sturdier data models.

A given OLE DB data source provides an interface for one or more kinds of data. Such data sources have different functionality, and Microsoft has spent a lot of time ensuring that the functions the data sources can offer are not limited. Thus, many different kinds of advanced facilities can be accessed beyond the basic interface, which typically consists of simple tabular data.

OLE DB thus complements the well-known ODBC API, which gives universal access to SQL-based databases. Databases are just one of many possible data sources in OLE DB—Microsoft potentially could completely replace ODBC with OLE DB.

> **Note:** So far, Microsoft hasn't promoted OLE File System (OFS) very much. This is noteworthy because Microsoft previously described OFS as being the final point in the series of OLE extensions, as well as one of the main attractions of Cairo. The principle underlying OFS is that OLE files should be capable of being stored in the same way as other kinds of files, thus enabling true client/server handling of OLE components. OFS's OLE files thus replace the peer-to-peer principle in the current Windows file systems, such as FAT, VFAT, and NTFS. However, OFS apparently is still too far from being ready to be included in the initial release of NT 5.0.

Transactions And Message Queuing

Most people will be surprised that Windows NT Server 5.0 also includes Transaction Server and Message Queuing Server as its implementation of a transaction monitor and message queue system, respectively.

Upon closer study, Microsoft's inclusion of these two products is actually quite logical. Establishing a large, homogeneous distributed IT environment is seldom possible, because the risk that parts of the installation won't be accessible in a given time interval rises dramatically in proportion with the number of servers. Likewise, as the number of servers that exist in a transaction/message system increases, so increases the risk that one computer involved in carrying out a certain transaction won't be able to complete its part of the job, because more potential points of failure exist.

Message queue systems and transaction monitors are built specifically to handle these two risks in a manner that ensures consistency and transparency are not compromised, which is a prerequisite for establishing a distributed IT environment.

Transaction Server

Microsoft Transaction Server is a component-based transaction treatment system for developing, implementing, and handling high-performance, scalable, and robust server applications. Transaction Server might even be expanded to cover the Internet in the future.

The main task of Transaction Server, like any other system for transaction treatment, is to ensure that a given number of operations are all performed correctly, and if not performed correctly, to so indicate by rolling back to the situation prior to the change in operations.

The aim of Transaction Server is both to simplify the development of applications and to ensure the integration of data. Transaction Server defines a software model for developing distributed component-based applications. It also provides a runtime infrastructure for implementing and handling such applications.

Transaction Server is designed to work with any type of resource-handling application, including databases, file systems, and picture stores supported by a transaction-based, two-phase commit protocol. The two-phase commit protocol ensures that a transaction is consistent among several servers. For example, if a network failure occurs in just 1 of 30 servers during a distributed transaction, the transaction is rolled back on all servers. The two-phase commit protocol enables businesses to build onto existing investments in Unix-, mini-, and mainframe-based data stores after Transaction Server is introduced.

Message Queue Server

Message Queue Server enables applications to communicate across heterogeneous networks and systems that are temporarily shut down. The applications send their messages to Message Queue Server, which places the messages in special queues that repeatedly attempt to deliver the messages to other applications—until the receiver systems become available, at which time the messages are delivered.

Message Queue Server provides the security that messages are delivered as soon as possible. Likewise, the routing of the messages is more efficient, and different messages may be assigned different delivery priorities.

The bigger a distributed IT environment is, the stronger the need for safe message delivery, and hence, the more beneficial Message Queue Server becomes to that IT environment. Message Queue Server can also be a prerequisite for efficient operations of heterogeneous IT environments, or IT environments consisting of numerous geographically separated sections linked with unstable lines.

Microsoft's Strategy For Distributed IT Environments

To an outsider, Microsoft's strategy for distributed data processing seems pretty confusing. For some reason, Microsoft has never felt the need to explain its actions in an educational manner. This is unfortunate—of all the manufacturers on the market, Microsoft's strategy is one of the easiest to understand, because it focuses only on COM/DCOM and the Windows platform.

The core of Microsoft's strategy is that it wants to integrate all of the following facilities necessary to establish a distributed IT environment on one single platform, Windows NT Server:

- Web server (Internet Information Server)

- A scalable ORB (COM/DCOM)

- Transaction handling (Transaction Server)

- Message-oriented middleware (Message Queue Server)

- Distributed security (Kerberos)

- Directory services (Active Directory and LDAP)

- Network handling (TCP/IP, DNS, and so forth)

Microsoft's strategy is almost the opposite of its competitors, who want to divide into layers and separate the necessary middleware into various bits and pieces, whereby all these application services are placed on top of the operating system. This procedure of other software manufacturers is quite openly against the methodology of Microsoft, which is completely proprietary (forcing consumers basically to choose or not choose the entire package).

Yet the open procedure offered by Microsoft's competition suffers from some clear shortcomings, which seasoned computer specialists have seen far too often. The biggest shortcomings are that each application service has to gain a foothold as a standard independently, and each service has to be purchased separately. This increases the risk of incompatibility among the various services.

The computer market may, justifiably, be very tired of the increasing incompatibility—and hence increased complexity—in existing IT environments. Or, perhaps the market feels that common sense dictates the implementation of Microsoft's latest products (such as Windows NT Server, with all of its built-in services) and standards, rather than having to consider individually the many different alternatives. The future will tell which way the market chooses to go.

Better Scalability And Fault Tolerance

Microsoft has set several goals for itself with the next version of Windows NT. One of these goals is to increase scalability and fault tolerance on the NT platform to the level where a business can safely depend on NT as the basis for its mission-critical systems. This is a smart goal for Microsoft. After all, the PC platform hasn't managed to gain much of a foothold in this end of the mission-critical business market. The market today is completely dominated by minicomputers, mainframes, and Unix systems.

Other than a few computer manufacturers that are using Intel processors as a basis in some of their very powerful mainframe or supercomputer-class solutions, no instances of large-scale business implementations exist that are based on PC systems.

NT has been roughly handled by many of the market trendsetters. For instance, Jon C.A. DeKeles, Technical Director at ZDNet AnchorDesk, has said that Windows NT is furnished with some very tangible limitations, both physically and functionally: "Despite its progress, despite all its recent design wins, Windows NT isn't suitable for all applications." He adds that, right now, "...it's not the best answer to mission-critical applications (the ones that can't take a crash). Or for highly scaled applications (those that start small but eventually grow very, very big)."

The lack of any tangible evidence that a PC platform can handle mission-critical business applications and the skepticism of industry analysts regarding that proposition are two major reasons why very few business-computer buyers have chosen the PC platform to handle the central tasks in their businesses. Microsoft is trying to overcome the insecurity regarding the PC platform as a business solution by launching Windows NT 5.0; likewise, Microsoft has already attempted to respond as quickly as possible to this situation through its recent implementation of Enterprise Edition on Windows NT Server 4.0.

A brief look at NT's history shows that Microsoft has been targeting the market for business-critical solutions since early in the development of NT. The next several sections give a history of Microsoft's Windows NT from a business viewpoint.

A Brief History

The first version of Windows NT Server was ready in 1993, and the public already showed great interest in the operating system, due to both Microsoft's sales drive and the personal reputation of the lead designer of the NT operating system, Dave Cutler. Mr. Cutler came to Microsoft from Digital Equipment Corporation, where he held a top post in shaping the much-praised OpenVMS (Virtual Memory System), a DEC VAX/Alpha operating system, for handling many critical business applications.

Thus, Microsoft's new operating system, Windows NT, was developed from its inception with a focus on handling the most critical business problems, and being a real competitor to AS/400, mainframes, and Unix servers. However, Microsoft has experienced quite a bit of difficulty in making Windows NT Server an attractive solution for handling the most critical computer tasks.

Whereas Microsoft obviously aimed at having NT break through on the mass market, in terms of volume, it had its sights on the high-end market long before it started to conquer a solid clientele. Mike Nash, head of the Products Division of Microsoft Business Systems, said to *InfoWorld* in November 1995: "I guess our focus is on providing solutions for customers so they can begin using our products in more parts of their business." This statement came very shortly after Microsoft took over Network Managers and Netwise, from whom it gained the necessary know-how on network management, Remote Procedure Calls (RPCs), and distributed handling of transactions. Microsoft also entered into cooperative agreements with Software AG and Digital.

Despite Microsoft's good intentions, most industry observers agreed that Windows NT had a ways to go before it was ready to be rolled into the most sacred computer rooms, because it lacked basic fault tolerance and scalability.

The skepticism continues, even after Microsoft's Scalability Day in May 1997. In the real world, *scalability* means putting a lot of servers together and performing simple uniform transactions, which was the goal of Microsoft's demonstrations on Scalability Day. However, businesses were not fully convinced that they should use the demonstrated NT 4.0 Servers for their mission-critical applications, as other server operating systems were still more scalable.

Moreover, Microsoft has had difficulty convincing most of its competitors (including IBM) that they ought to port their business-critical applications to Windows NT. The historical tension between Microsoft and IBM has been particularly hurtful, as IBM firmly holds the largest base of mission-critical solutions on the market.

Microsoft has also borne quite a lot of self-created setbacks en route toward an operating system sufficiently stable to carry mission-critical applications. Certainly one of the worst blows to NT had to do with Microsoft's handling and launching of Service Packs. In late December 1996, Microsoft introduced Service Pack 2, which soon turned out to be so full of bugs that just a few weeks later, Microsoft was forced to send out corrections concerning two of the worst errors (incompatibility with antivirus programs and problems with RAS Multilink).

In an attempt to avoid further loss of prestige, Microsoft felt compelled to introduce a thorough test program for its Service Packs shortly thereafter. This test program seems to have improved matters significantly, because no major problems have been reported with Service Pack 3.

Now that we've taken a brief look at some of the obstacles NT is facing in establishing itself as a mission-critical business solution, capable of competing with minicomputers, mainframes, and Unix systems, the rest of this chapter discusses the prerequisites for a system to be considered capable of handling mission-critical business tasks, and whether Windows NT 5.0 fulfills those prerequisites.

The First Prerequisite: Fault Tolerance

Fault tolerance is the absolute prerequisite for business-computer buyers to show even remote interest in NT 5.0 while shopping for new servers. NT 5.0 must demonstrate sufficient reliability in its degree of fault tolerance (known by some in the industry as *error tolerance*).

So far, all versions of Windows NT Server have offered the following facilities for fault tolerance:

- *Security against application errors that make the entire operating system crash.* Microsoft has taken measures to prevent such catastrophes by including preemptive multitasking and by placing the applications in a protected memory.

- *Security against loss of data.* Loss of data is counteracted via the file system, NTFS, which is designed to ensure the best possible re- establishment of data and files in instances of fatal crashes. NT also offers *Redundant Array of Inexpensive Disks*

(RAID) software, with the possibility for disk mirroring and disk striping with parity. RAID is a popular implementation in Unix and other operating systems, and can improve both data security and performance in reading from disks in parallel.

- *Security against power loss.* Windows NT has built-in support of UPS, which enables the administrator to shut down the system properly in case of a power outage.

- *Security against single-point-of-failures around the logon server.* The possibility of establishing *Backup Domain Controllers* (BDCs) ensures that users can always log into the environment, irrespective of whether a particular server is down.

Computer professionals who have worked with systems that require high uptime know that the facilities in the preceding list are far from sufficient to establish error-tolerant systems for handling applications. Quite commonly, businesses that depend a lot on their computer systems (such as nuclear facilities, airline reservations, Las Vegas casinos, and so forth) require uptimes of 99.9 percent or more.

An uptime of 99.9 percent or 99.99 percent may seem demanding, yet it isn't. A guaranteed uptime of 98 to 99 percent permits approximately three to seven days of downtime per year, and a guaranteed uptime of 99.9 to 99.99 percent permits approximately one to nine hours per year of downtime. Imagine a situation in which an airline must stop working for a week because of computer problems, or a bank or hospital suddenly has to close for eight hours.

At best, a guaranteed uptime of 99.9 percent is possible with one server handling business over a five-year period. But this makes certain demands on the operating environment that aren't quite realistic. Experience tells us that many situations arise in which *planned* stoppages are necessary, such as for the installation of new software versions and servicing of hardware. However, a guaranteed uptime of 99.9 percent doesn't provide enough time and space for some of the *unplanned* stoppages.

In a business-critical context, spreading an application across more than one server fairly automatically is necessary, which is exactly why users of NT have awaited Microsoft Cluster Server (previously known as *WolfPack*) with great excitement. Cluster Server is the first actual standard for Windows NT that enables two or more servers to perform the same task concurrently.

The current version of Cluster Server (which is part of Windows NT Server Enterprise Edition 4.0), shown in Figure 6.1, makes sharing one application across two servers possible. This can only be a "cold" share of applications, in which one of the two servers remains up and running, untouched, if the other is down. Yet, even if this functionality seems rudimentary, it is a prerequisite for using NT Server for critical

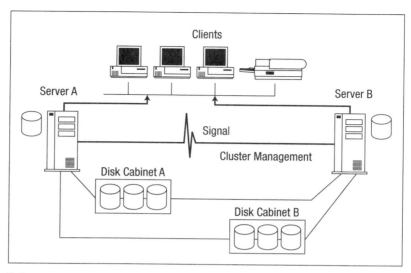

Figure 6.1
The cluster architecture under the current version of Microsoft Cluster Server.

applications. For example, this functionality enables an administrator to take one server offline, without affecting users very much. Theoretically, the only downtime involved in taking one of the servers offline is the time it takes to start all the server processes on the backup server, which is only a few minutes.

Also note that the disks must be placed in one or more separate cabinets, which requires you to think twice before buying high-end servers with internal space for a vast number of disks.

For Cluster Server to be successful commercially, it still needs to demonstrate stability over a long period of time and the capability to always function according to its intended use. Cluster Server most likely will be capable of demonstrating these attributes, because Microsoft is being helped by Tandem and Digital, who have a lot of experience with these exact types of fault-tolerant solutions.

Clustering For Improved Fault Tolerance

Marked differences exist between the demands put on a server when it must work with a network operating system and when it must work with a server operating system. Whereas scalability is practically a nonexistent factor for network servers, it is crucial when choosing an application server.

Whereas PC producers have refined their efforts (mainly concerning maximum bandwidth among the network interface board, the RAM, and the hard disks) toward the perfect network server over several years, the application servers are still a fairly new phenomenon for the manufacturers of PC servers. The potential buyers of the PC-based application servers are more or less in the same situation.

Scalability can take two different forms: SMP and clustering.

Symmetric multiprocessing (SMP) attempts to increase server performance by adding more processors. Ideally, the SMP server will provide an improvement in performance linearly with the number of processors that are added onto the system.

SMP makes demands on the server's capability to provide the necessary bandwidth for the given number of processors, and its efficiency in sharing tasks among the processors. Likewise, SMP makes great demands on the capability of the overall operating system to divide the tasks into small, independent parts, so that numerous jobs on the processors are not temporarily suspended.

Clustering is a fairly new principle that attempts to increase the reliability and accessibility of the server while simultaneously scaling productivity. Tandem and Digital were the first to use clustering in an attempt to enhance reliability and accessibility. They use an extra system of servers that are capable of providing "warm" backup for another server, so that the backup server can take over if the first system malfunctions.

The Gartner Group has defined three levels of clustering that makes classifying a clustering setup fairly easy:

- *Level 1*—Enables servers to share data across a common disk system. In this instance, a copy of the operating system is handled on every machine, but the servers are not really aware of each other. This enables one machine to step in as backup for another. Calling this high availability may be misleading, but many people are already dubbing this clustering, a fact that the Gartner Group takes into account.

- *Level 2*—Enables two servers to be sufficiently aware of each other that they are capable of using the same data at the same time, which enhances productivity and enables one server to take over immediately if the other server malfunctions. Currently, Level 2 is being applied on the application level in some database systems, yet the challenge remains to build Level 2 into the underlying operating system.

- *Level 3*—Means that the operating system is fully coordinated across several servers, enabling a job to be timetabled and coordinated across several servers. The operating system, the server, and the applications must be designed to cluster, just as with SMP, if the environment is to work according to its purpose.

The current version of Microsoft Cluster Server is only able to do clustering at Level 1. Not until the next version of Cluster Server (which will be in NT 5.0) will it be brought up to Level 2. Nothing has yet been reported regarding when (if ever) Microsoft anticipates reaching the highest clustering level.

NT 5.0 also addresses two areas that are always mentioned in connection with reliability: ready access to a set of very efficient administration tools, and the capability to dynamically alter as much as possible on the operating system, without requiring a cold restart. Cold restarts are bad for business solutions, as applications become unavailable temporarily. Some operating system parameters currently may be changed without requiring a cold restart, and the more that Microsoft improves in this area, the more popular the NT operating system will become in business environments. Microsoft promises that NT 5.0 will contain considerably more ability for dynamic restarts than NT 4.0, but so far, I have found big improvements only in terms of handling the files with NTFS. You can read more about the many new administrative tools of NT 5.0 in Chapter 7.

As previously mentioned, to be commercially successful, NT also has to prove its worth over a long time period as a mission-critical solution.

Anybody who works with operating systems that cater to a vast number of users with very different demands for data processing knows from experience that these demands can lead to system stress and can result in system slowdowns with too much overhead. This type of error is the most difficult to trace, because the error may be related to a very special load pattern, instability in the hardware, or timing conflicts among the input software components, operating system, database, transaction monitor, or other middleware (or the error may be related to one of many other problems).

However, even if version 5.0 introduces a series of new facilities and, hence, a lot of new program lines that potentially may be defective (which may slightly delay the testing time), time is favorably disposed to NT, because—as far as I can tell—the foundation of NT 5.0 is completely identical to NT 4.0. At most, NT's success is a question of whether a given program component, or the whole operating system, comes crashing down. The only suspect that could endanger the reputation of NT is Internet Explorer 4.0, which introduces the Active Desktop user interface. If Active Desktop crashes, the operator is prevented from connecting with the system on the local server. I hope very much that Microsoft tests Active Desktop much more thoroughly than it tested Internet Explorer 4.0 before it was launched, because it has since displayed many defects.

The Second Prerequisite: Scalability

Since the mission-critical applications are the very backbone of the company, the operating system, together with the underlying hardware platform, requires a reasonable degree of scalability to avoid being a hostage of an expensive and risky change of platform if a higher system performance is required.

Scalability has been one of the traditional weaknesses of NT so far. Even if NT offers SMP support, computer professionals generally know that Windows NT Server actually can't be scaled across four processors.

NCR (National Cash Register—the 110-year-old company that is now the largest massively parallel data warehouse supplier) performed numerous benchmark tests shortly after the release of NT Server 4.0. They revealed that an extension from four to eight processors generated an improved productivity of only about 33 percent, significantly short of the expected 50 percent improvement.

Regarding NT's limitation of only scaling up to four processors, Microsoft has a good excuse: Up until quite recently, a conventional Intel-based, high-end server could scale, at most, four processors. Despite a few specially designed PC servers with room for more than four processors, the interest for more than four processors has been so low that IBM, Compaq, and HP haven't even bothered with this market. So, Microsoft's decision not to invest in making NT scale more than four processors is quite understandable. Yet this excuse is becoming invalid, because Intel and the largest server manufacturers are now putting out a lot of effort (and money, through Intel's purchase of the multiprocessor server company Corollary in October 1997) designing standard components for the Pentium Pro-based systems that support up to eight processors.

How Scalable Is Scalability?

Measuring scalability of a given system is difficult, because the results depend on the type of applications that are measured. A big difference may exist in the amount of mutually dependent data handled on various processors.

Despite mainframes being the oldest technology, most analysts feel that mainframes are quickly losing their market position. IBM maintains that it has achieved close to complete linear scalability in its 10-track CMOS/MVS mainframes and its Parallel Sysplex, right up to the theoretical maximum of 32 systems. Yet many analysts believe that scalability on a 10-track SMP mainframe is only approximately 85 percent of full linearity with a selection of typical mainframe applications. The difference of what occurred and what was expected was due to system and programming overhead, preventing the full scalability. These analysts have not provided feedback on the scalability of Parallel Sysplex.

Things are more straightforward regarding Unix-based SMP systems. Here, scalability varies greatly depending on the precise SMP implementation; yet, in the worst scenario, productivity is at least 60 to 70 percent of full linearity when more than 10 to 12 processors are added on. Normally, productivity ought to be at least 85 percent.

Clustering suffers the same limitations as SMPs. Yet they are different in technical terms because the connection between the systems tends to be slower with clustering than with SMP.

No matter how you look at the issue, practical scalability is closely related to how the software and hardware was designed to scale. Mainframes tend to offer better scalability than Unix because of the vast experience mainframe designers can draw upon regarding applications on such systems. Nevertheless, the biggest manufacturers of database systems—Oracle, IBM, Sybase, and Informix—can profit from their experience with mainframes when they attempt to improve their Unix-based parallel RDMS products.

Microsoft now is working at providing increased scalability on all fronts. NT Server Enterprise Edition 4.0 can be scaled to eight processors and contains a 4GB RAM-tuning feature, which makes reallocating memory possible in the NT 4GB address space, so that some of the 2GB RAM reserved for the operating system may instead be used for applications. 4GB tuning frees up to 3GB RAM to handle applications, which is a 50 percent increase over NT Server 4.0.

Any prediction would be premature regarding whether eight processors and 4GB RAM tuning in Enterprise Edition 4.0 will provide a solution to scalability. Generally, improvements in productivity per extra processor decrease with the number of processors within the system. So, exactly how much extra performance can be gained by adding four processors, and perhaps increasing the available RAM from 2GB to 3GB, still needs to be sufficiently clarified with application benchmark tests in an NT 5.0 environment.

Microsoft is also working on the next version of Cluster Server, which is planned to contain actual clustering facilities equaling Level 2 under the Gartner Group model. Just what clustering facilities the next version of Cluster Server can offer, and what is required of the applications, is still unclear. Microsoft has stated on many occasions that NT Server 5.0 will be able to cluster 4 servers upon its release and, within a year, cluster up to 16 servers. NT Server 4.0 currently is capable of clustering only 2 servers. Apparently, we won't have to wait too long for this claim to be confirmed or denied—the next version of Cluster Server is supposed to be ready for delivery in the second half of 1998.

Windows NT 5.0 also introduces some new facilities that may enhance the scalability of the NT platform. The I_2O hardware architecture enables administrators to move part of the workload of handling I/O from the main processor to dedicated processors—thereby increasing the total productivity of the system—and 64-bit servers. Also, several small adjustments have been made to the file system and memory handling, which also contributes significantly to enhancing the performance of the system.

Yet, before the forecasts for scalability on the NT platform begin to sound too convincing, remember that the applications must be designed to take advantage of these facilities for the facilities to have any effect. Otherwise, most processors will not cluster well, despite the possibility of larger RAM memory or the extension of servers to genuine clustering, because the application would run on one server, instead of splitting its processing among the many clustered servers. Rewriting an application that is designed to be handled on one or two processors (such as for Windows NT 4.0) to benefit from multiple processors is a major task, because the application needs to be divided into many coordinated processors. This sometimes works contrary to the way in which the programming of the application was originally intended.

However, you should not be completely deterred by these problems. Although current products will not scale well, there is hope that some applications soon will. Microsoft has already designed special Enterprise Editions for part of its BackOffice applications, and many third-party manufacturers are also focusing on utilizing the new clustering facilities. The new possibilities for attaining higher levels of performance should not surprise manufacturers of mission-critical applications, because the technologies previously mentioned (except possibly I_2O) are already being used on several other complex operating system platforms.

The Third Prerequisite: Better Utilization Of Common Server Hardware

Beyond meeting the demand for scalability and fault tolerance, the buyers of mission-critical systems want the latest innovations in server hardware to be given top priority.

In this respect, they have something to look forward to with Windows NT Server 5.0. At long last, NT Server has been equipped with network handling that supports ATM, as well as the I_2O architecture and 64-bit processors.

Furthermore, NT Server 5.0 is designed to utilize the latest Fibre Channel standard, which many professionals have high hopes for. Fibre Channel increases the theoretical transmission speed between storage units, from the Ultrawide SCSI present maximum transmission speed of 40Mbps (megabits per second) to between 100 and 400Mbps.

As the name indicates, Fibre Channel is based on optical fibers, which can overcome the tight restrictions on distance that prevail in copper-based SCSI solutions. Fibre

Channel should be more fault tolerant than SCSI, because Fibre Channel is based on a ring structure rather than the current bus structure used by SCSI. Also, Fibre Channel can be made hot-pluggable (also known as *hot-swappable*), which means that peripherals can be added to or removed from a computer, and the operating system automatically recognizes the change. This is available with the new USB, the new IEEE 1394, and the familiar PCMCIA. Furthermore, Fibre Channel offers nice scalability with its support of up to 128 attached units.

According to Microsoft, NT 5.0 contains a lot of small, but perceptible improvements with regard to file handling (storage management and the file system itself), memory handling, and the network and communication infrastructure.

The major changes within storage management are the following:

- Online disk volume management (also contains improved performance)

- Windows NT Media Services (NTMS) (support of large, offline storage units)

- Enhanced backup and recovery

- Hierarchical storage management (HSM)

- Remote storage management (RSM)

- Defragmentation tools

The NTFS improvements consist of the following:

- Disk quotas per user for every volume (now users may be limited on one volume, yet unlimited on others)

- Sparse files (enables deallocating from the starting point of the file)

- Dynamic increases of the file system, without having to reboot the server or take the file system offline

- Compressed I/O readings, which reduces traffic and backup times on the network

NT 5.0 has Plug and Play and power management support. While a discussion of power management on a high-end server may not be too relevant, the Plug and Play draft should be of interest. Plug and Play is just as attractive with regard to servers as it is to clients, because the idea of Plug and Play for both servers and clients is to avoid—as much as possible—having to shut down the server after changes are made. Undoubtedly, in many instances, connecting units via the USB, FireWire, or a hot-plug PCI bus, which the system automatically recognizes in the Plug and Play architecture, is a big advantage. Note, moreover, that the Windows NT 5.0 Plug and Play system presupposes that a given unit meets the ACPI standard.

The Fourth Prerequisite: Access To Existing Company Applications

NT Server's impressive facilities for accomplishing mission-critical tasks are not of much use if the most common applications are not available on the NT platform.

Strangely enough, the ultraconservative SAP (a large German software company) has ensured that its applications will work on the NT platform from early on. Nearly all the other well-known NT Server applications have appeared within the last two years.

A steady stream of new server applications has appeared over the past 18 months. When Microsoft last provided an official estimate of the number of available server applications for Windows NT (during Paul Maritz' presentation at the Professional Developer's Conference in September 1997), the figure was 1,800 applications, of which 350 applications carried the BackOffice logo.

Recently, Windows NT Server achieved a significant breakthrough in handling mission-critical applications when IBM suddenly decided to support the development of NT applications, after having criticized Microsoft in general and NT in particular. IBM's decision likely was prompted by fear of being left in the technological graveyard. Despite IBM's many attempts to mar the popularity of NT, even the staunchest IBM supporters couldn't ignore the fine sales figures posted by NT.

When IBM changes its strategy, things move fast. In the autumn of 1997, IBM announced that the number of NT applications from IBM and its recently purchased Lotus division had exceeded 100 products, which is the largest selection of NT applications on the market from one single supplier. Included among the 100 applications are the following popular IBM server applications:

- *DB2*—IBM's relational database server

- *CICS/Transaction Server*—Customer Information Control System; provides transaction processing

- *MQSeries*—Message queuing middleware solution that coordinates database and message transactions

- *Lotus Notes*—The first-ever fully featured groupware solution with a replication model; it supports distributed databases of documents such as emails and Word files

- *Communications Server*—Integrates a company's computers with the Internet, intranets, and extranets

- *ADSM*—ADSTAR Distributed Storage Manager; this product fills tapes more efficiently with compression, scheduling, and incremental backups

- *TME 10 NetView*—IBM's network management product that gives managers network information and can page employees if there are problems; it also binds 3Com, Cisco, Bay Networks, and other networking products in a cross-platform solution

Many IBM clients and the IT industry are responding to the new signals from IBM regarding its support for NT. For instance, the Aberdeen Group has the following to say about IBM's NT strategy in their article "Moving NT Upscale with Enterprise-grade Solutions, Middleware, and Services" in April 1997:

"The political, philosophical, and technological battles between Microsoft (with its NT operating environment) and IBM (with OS/2, OS/400, AIX, and MVS) have ended—and a surprise winner has been declared: the business information-technology customer. IBM has just stepped forward with a powerful new public NT-in-the-business message—one that gives IBM customers the freedom to choose whichever operating system and application environment makes the most sense to accomplish their application tasks. IBM is doing this while also providing the service and support that its customers require, irrespective of the operating environment they choose.

"This announcement represents a major and long-awaited shift in IBM's public position. IBM has refocused on customer requirements—and has placed particular emphasis on delivering the products, services, and support that its customers need to move to NT as a business solution. In fact, IBM will add value to the NT operating environment by ensuring that IBM's key business applications, relational databases, systems management tools, and underlying middleware products are optimized to run on business-strength NT desktops and servers."

IBM's competitors are not wasting any time getting into the ever-more lucrative NT market. The NT versions of Oracle Parallel Server and Tandem NonStop—which both utilize the proprietary clustering solutions of their respective database systems and combine that with NT's clustering capabilities—show a great willingness to draw the NT technologies right to the limit.

The Fifth Prerequisite: Strong Technical Support

The last prerequisite for NT Server to gain a foothold in the business market for handling mission-critical tasks is for Microsoft to provide strong server support services.

Microsoft set up Microsoft Consulting Services (MCS) because business-computer buyers were dissatisfied with Microsoft's previous support level. Microsoft Consulting Services supplies planning, design, and administration to businesses. Microsoft's goal is to staff MCS with consultants who have at least 4 to 5 years of experience, are Microsoft product experts (although some have experience only with IT management), and train at least 120 hours per year.

Microsoft points out that MCS is not intended to replace other consultants, but that they should complement one another. Recently, we have heard of many companies that employ Microsoft-trained consultants who are dissatisfied with MCS, claiming it has stolen part of their lucrative, major consulting assignments.

Microsoft already has one of the most well-esteemed service and support organizations in the world, and it has a lot of experience dealing with large-company purchasers who want to buy Windows and Office products. This, in itself, does not guarantee the attention that big businesses demand for solving problems regarding servers. This is why Microsoft has created a new support program—Premier Support—for the largest businesses. Companies with more than 2,500 clients can buy yearly support contracts for a minimum of $40,000. The most important item in this contract is technical support 24 hours a day, 7 days a week when the server is down or similar catastrophes occur. Furthermore, a specially appointed Technical Account manager ensures that the client is satisfied with the services provided. This support typically is over the telephone, but now Microsoft offers support staff for remote diagnostics.

Apparently, Microsoft is getting a good grasp of what is required regarding service and support of its products for mission-critical solutions. Microsoft is also backed by several other support organizations worldwide (the Digital division of Compaq, Hewlett-Packard, and NCR) and more than 10,000 third-party suppliers.

Many other companies are competing to enter the lucrative support market. Just recently, IBM entered the market with its Global Services support organization. Microsoft probably doesn't mind this development, as Global Services happens to be the world's largest integrator of systems, so Microsoft can benefit from the sales generated from the integration of Microsoft products. And IBM already has a solid foundation in the IT departments of major businesses.

The Aberdeen Group states that IBM Global Services already has more than 1,200 NT-trained support staff beyond its more than 100,000 employees in 159 countries worldwide. IBM's declared goal is to drastically increase the number of staff members with an in-depth knowledge of NT so that it can be the world's largest supplier of professional services and support for NT by late 1998.

Regardless of whether large businesses are satisfied with the service and support available for Windows NT, Microsoft is struggling with a big, unsolved problem: providing enough computer professionals with an in-depth knowledge of Microsoft's products.

Although many educational facilities have appeared globally in recent years, Microsoft is very short of highly qualified product experts everywhere in the world. Microsoft acknowledges the existence of an overall lack of computer experts with sufficient experience and basic skills, which it gauges through its certification program. This program enables a person to become a Microsoft Certified Professional by passing a test in a specific product area, or to become a Microsoft Certified Solution Developer or Microsoft Certified Systems Engineer by completing various tests in a particular area. The number of Certified Professionals is growing by leaps and bounds, but so are the available jobs. This work shortage is not just for Microsoft; the entire computer industry is facing a severe worker shortage worldwide. In America, the number of computer degree students is actually declining, so the shortage should continue for some time.

The Success Of NT 5.0 In The Future

Microsoft has already been victorious in its struggle to win the back office of the company. But it has also experienced many setbacks.

Analyses show that Microsoft still has some more battles to fight to convert all the skeptics. But things are looking up: The questions asked of analysts today tend to be when—rather than if—they expect Microsoft will be fitted for the drawing room in mission-critical terms.

The latest predictions by industry analysts in the computer magazine *Datamation* (October 1997) estimate that NT will take five to nine years to establish itself as a solution to business-critical applications. I doubt that it will take that long when I look back on the history of Microsoft: Five years seems like an eternity for its style of business. Yet, predicting how things will turn out is extremely difficult, because nothing else in the computer industry resembles NT's situation.

If all the new facilities and functions of Windows NT Server 5.0 work according to plan, Microsoft should be able to change the first NT technical question from "Can it take the pressure?" to "Is it sufficiently strong to be used in business-critical applications?"

We will not know until well into 1999 whether NT 5.0 is sufficiently robust (assuming, of course, that NT 5.0 is released near the beginning of 1999. Robustness is impossible to clarify in a test environment—this will be decided when NT 5.0 enters the operational environments globally.

If NT passes the test of sturdiness quickly, and the purchasers and independent software developers accept Microsoft Cluster Server as the clustering standard for NT, then NT's breakthrough for mission-critical solutions could be as soon as the year 2000. This assumes that the present gap between the cost for software and hardware for NT and Unix platforms, respectively, remains constant. However, this is unlikely, because Unix suppliers realize that Windows NT has started to win market share from them.

Easier Server Administration

As stated in previous chapters, Windows NT 5.0 has many new functions, several of which are intended to meet higher levels of scalability and fault tolerance in the IT environment as a whole, and the administration of network PC clients in particular.

More fault tolerance (and scalability) may, in certain instances, be greatly advantageous to server administrators, but the improved facilities with which to administer clients do not always give a server administrator any real new management benefits. This, together with the fact that NT 5.0 has combined with many new technologies (for example, Transaction Server, Active Directory, Message Queue Server, Routing Service, NT File System junction point, and a much-enhanced version of Distributed File System), which are all extremely relevant in a modern server environment, might indicate that the server administrator will have more tasks to do in the future.

Fortunately, this isn't entirely true. Microsoft hasn't publicized it too much, but as far as administration tools are concerned, the all-important new feature is Microsoft Management Console, or MMC.

Beta 1 of NT has many of the old administration tools, which reportedly is a temporary arrangement, as the new MMC tools can't yet replace the old tools. You can find all the other NT 4.0 administration tools that aren't included in the NT 5.0 beta 1 release on the Microsoft Web site (**ntbeta.microsoft.com/support/updates.asp**), which is a bit odd, because although Microsoft has repeatedly stated that it is concentrating 100 percent on MMC, it doesn't include all of these tools in the beta 1 release.

So, for the time being, only Microsoft knows whether it will force a shift to the MMC-based tools by including only these tools in NT 5.0, or if it will keep all the old NT 4.0 tools, to make the transition to NT 5.0 as smooth as possible. Including the old NT 4.0 tools will meet the demand for uniform administration in environments with mixed

NT server versions. Regardless, this decision should be easy for Microsoft, because all the current NT 4.0 tools also function with NT 5.0.

In addition to MMC, several other administrative "bright spots" appear in NT 5.0. NT 5.0 is not just a pile of new server technologies and an expansion of the many existing technologies, it also has a lot of features that Microsoft expects will be helpful for the administration of networked environments. These new NT Server features and the capabilities they offer are the focus of this chapter.

Administration In The Windows NT Environment

One of the overall goals of Microsoft for 1998 is to reduce running expenses (typically enumerated in the so-called TCO—total cost of ownership) in Windows environments. This goal is clear from its ongoing work in Windows NT 5.0 and Windows 98.

Microsoft's initiatives to reduce running expenses are dubbed *Zero Administration for Windows*, abbreviated as *ZAW*. Microsoft ZAW is a collection of many different technologies, the overall goal of which is to establish an effective infrastructure for management (in other words, administration and monitoring) of the Windows environment, thereby reducing TCO for the total IT environment.

ZAW previously has been mentioned only in discussions about Microsoft's future client strategies. However, ZAW also caters to servers, as Microsoft believes that NT Server generally is being used on servers in businesses that use Windows 98 or NT Workstation on clients.

An additional reason Microsoft believes ZAW should necessarily cover both servers and clients is that, in IT environments, the administrative tasks become far more difficult to solve when all the components in the environment are thoroughly mixed. In a distributed environment, dividing the administration of the IT environment into the three traditional parts—systems management, network management, and client management—gets very complicated.

To achieve a reduction in the distributed IT environments of the future, administrative tasks for the whole IT environment must be considered as much as possible. This makes the challenge all the more exciting.

The collection of server-side ZAW technologies currently consist of the following:

- Microsoft Management Console (MMC)
- Windows Management Instrumentation (WMI)

- Web-Based Enterprise Management (WBEM)

- Systems Management Server (SMS)

- Numerous different techniques for improved client operation, including policy-based management

This chapter delves into MMC, WMI, and WBEM first, because these ZAW technologies are of primary interest to server administrators. The last two ZAW technologies listed, SMS and client-based techniques, are mainly of interest to PC client administrators, and are discussed in the next chapter.

Very Different, But Fundamentally Alike

Windows NT Server 5.0 is not revolutionary in terms of its fundamental handling of file and system rights on the server. The allocation of rights to printers and files is carried out in precisely the same way as previous versions of NT.

The fundamental components in the allocation of rights are still the Security Descriptors (SDs) and the Access Control Lists (ACLs), which means that, even if users are listed in the hierarchically designed Active Directory, allocating or removing particular rights is possible only for users or groups.

This fact is a bit surprising, because Active Directory introduces a new hierarchical way in which to structure users, and it can be used advantageously to allocate rights. For instance, users often are placed in a specific organizational unit (for example, marketing or production) and have a vast number of rights in common with others in that unit. These common rights could be neatly and efficiently expressed—if NT enabled administrators to use these organizational units when allocating rights. However, this hasn't been implemented.

Microsoft must brace itself for criticism in this respect, because its two biggest competitors, Novell's NDS and Banyan's StreetTalk, both see the possibilities of exploiting Microsoft's lack of support for organizational unit allocation. Novell's NDS and Banyan's StreetTalk both support allocation by organizational unit.

Microsoft Management Console

A virtual revolution has started in the more tangible parts of server administration—the actual tools with which to carry out the administrative tasks.

In the beta version of NT Server 5.0, the user interface and behavior of most of the administrative tools have changed from NT Server 4.0, because Microsoft decided, as part of ZAW, that NT 5.0's administrative tools need to be made far more similar to each other than in previous versions of NT.

The standardization of the administrative tools takes place via the completely new Microsoft Management Console. MMC is not a new administrative application, but rather a kind of passive user interface for handling management applications.

MMC's user interface looks very much like Windows Explorer (as shown in Figure 7.1), with the screen split into two windows (also called the *namespace*). The left window (also known as the *scope pane*) shows all the network objects in a hierarchical tree, while the right window (also called the *results pane*) shows the contents of the object currently being highlighted in the left window. This is very similar to the division in Windows Explorer, in which drives and directories appear to the left, and files and underlying directories appear to the right.

MMC is designed to ensure the same look and feel as Windows Explorer, but with maximum openness. As previously stated, MMC itself is nothing more than a shell that is used to present other tools. These tools (which may also include other NT 5.0 tools) are snap-ins that users can freely add and remove from a particular console,

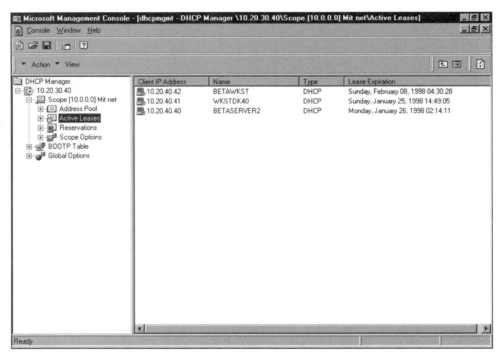

Figure 7.1
The new MMC-based DHCP Manager.

thereby creating an administration tool that exactly suits administrative demands. After the ideal console is put together, it can be redistributed to other departments that have the same demands, thus enabling a company's consoles to have a standardized appearance across the entire company.

Just What Precisely Is MMC?

MMC (previously known under the code name *Slate*) is a frame system that is designed to show administrative information. MMC acts as a host system for all administrative tools that are built as snap-ins. These MMC snap-ins can be designed by either Microsoft or third-party manufacturers.

MMC does not contain any management facilities, but it provides a common environment for snap-ins. All the administrative functions of MMC must be provided by these snap-ins. The MMC environment ensures that the various snap-ins perform in a manner that is as integrated and similar as possible.

Snap-in software constitutes the smallest atomic unit in the console (the window that handles the MMC software) and contains some management functions. Snap-ins are purely technical OLE server processes or applications. Snap-ins can function independently of one another or act as extensions of functionality in other snap-ins.

A *standalone snap-in* provides functionality even if it is read into a console that doesn't contain other snap-ins. A standalone snap-in isn't necessarily alone, however, because several standalone snap-ins can run simultaneously on the same console.

An *extension snap-in* provides functionality only when it is called by another snap-in. Extension snap-ins typically add one or more objects to the namespace (refer to Figure 7.1), or just extend the existing objects with new menus, toolbars, property pages, wizards, or Help.

The next level in MMC is the console and its tools (see Figure 7.2). The graphical display of the management software is called the *console*. The word *tool* refers to the MMC snap-ins that supply the functionality accessible via the console. Sometimes the tools are also called *documents*.

The console can contain one or more snap-ins (tools). The installation of tools can be saved in a Management Saved Console (MSC) file, which the administrator can then open later, or send to another administrator, who can open the file and thus re-create immediately the customized setup of the console.

Several MMC consoles may be handled simultaneously on the same computer. However, each console requires its own copy of MMC.

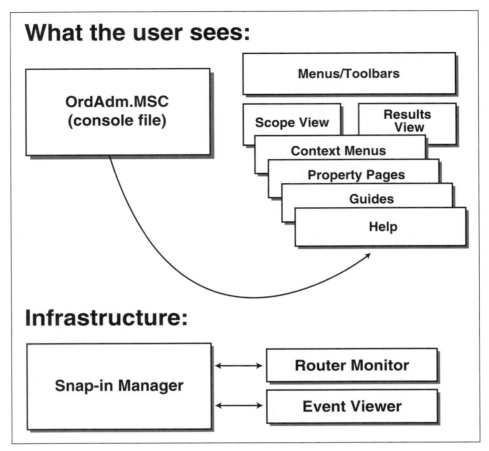

Figure 7.2
In theory, MMC looks like this. The user interface elements in each MMC console communicate with the snap-ins via the MMC Snap-in Manager. The snap-in designer is the only person who comes in direct contact with the Snap-in Manager.

When an MMC console is activated, one or more snap-ins are initialized. These snap-ins jointly constitute the namespace of the console (the sorted collection of elements that appears in the scope pane, or left side of the screen). The namespace is the master tree, stating what the console is capable of doing, and thus is comparable to the tree hierarchy of files and directories on a hard disk.

Any further panes in the MMC console are just other displays of the namespace, similar to having several instances of the Windows Explorer activated, all pointing to the same hard disk. In other words, every display can have its root in a different part of the tree, yet all point to the same fundamental data source, which ensures consistency of the environment.

When working in MMC, you can combine as many different snap-ins as required and thus create some administrative user interfaces that are tailored to handle the particular management tasks that you encounter in your business environment.

MMC is a full management solution, provided that the necessary MMC snap-ins are present within the system. MMC also has the inherent potential of being used inside an existing management system along the lines of HP's OpenView, and MMC can start other management systems. Thus, MMC can be called like any other Windows program, and shortcuts can be created to executable files, scripts, or URLs (Web addresses) from the MMC console.

Because NT-based consoles exist for the most common management systems, you can use MMC to administer Windows clients by making a call to a given MMC tool when the user wants to take a closer look at a specific Windows object. Alternatively, you can expect that several of the management systems will design consoles that take the form of MMC snap-ins. Microsoft has already announced that the future design tendency for the Microsoft SMS product will be to move part of the functionality over to the MMC environment via one or more snap-ins.

Contrary to other management consoles, MMC stipulates only the look-and-feel and compatibility prerequisites for snap-ins. How each snap-in actually carries out its tasks is left entirely to its designers. So, MMC does not depend on any protocols or repositories. The responsibility for these choices, and many others, remain with the snap-in designers, and not Microsoft.

Establishing setups that precisely match job assignments for various administrators can be accomplished with MMC, because it removes the differences in user interfaces among the administrative tools, while also providing the capability to design tailored views.

As Microsoft puts it, MMC is the result of Microsoft's effort to create better tools to administer Windows. The Windows-administration development team defined a common host for many of its own tools. The MMC project's initial goal was to support simplified administration through integration, delegation, task orientation, and overall interface simplification—all key customer concerns. As Microsoft addressed that goal, it increased the project's scope to include all Microsoft administration tools, and to offer this generalized management framework to its many independent software vendors (ISVs). MMC is a core part of Microsoft's future management strategy. Most Microsoft development groups will probably use MMC for future management applications.

To simplify the control panel, Microsoft is considering making the administration-oriented control panel applications, such as Devices and Services, MMC snap-ins. This means that these applications would be supplied with remote administrative support, enabling the system to be monitored and modified through alternate locations.

Microsoft continuously evaluates how to benefit best from the Internet technologies for management applications. Consequently, MMC snap-ins can perform tasks immediately via URL calls (and thus carry out tasks from an HTML user interface via Java and ActiveX) or ActiveX controls. Microsoft would like these facilities to be used to create a series of very simple user interfaces (known as TaskPads) for less-experienced administrators, similar to Administrative Wizards in NT 4.0. TaskPads don't exist in beta 1 of NT 5.0, so administrators still await some very simple user interfaces for daily management tasks.

Microsoft's long-term goal is for much of the MMC user interface to be based on Internet technologies. However, Microsoft believes that the Internet technologies aren't yet sufficiently mature to handle more-complex management tasks, as restrictions still exist on current user interfaces. Microsoft states that MMC is designed with the capability of being converted to HTML pages, without too many problems.

Note: MMC isn't limited to the new version of NT—MMC can also operate on Windows 95, Windows 98, and NT 4.0.

The MMC User Interface

As previously stated, the MMC console is the focal point for administrators. The MMC console is a Windows-based *Multiple Document Interface* (MDI)—a solution that enables more than one pane to be open simultaneously. The MMC console enables you to view one or more snap-ins, which contain the actual management tools.

The MMC console user interface very much resembles Windows Explorer's interface. The only difference is that more than one pane can be open within a console in MMC.

At a minimum, the MMC console pane contains a master menu and a toolbar (refer to Figure 7.3). The master menu contains the functions typically found in an MDI parent: functions with which to administer files, windows (including facilities to add and delete snap-ins), and Help screens. The MDI children's windows consist of two or three different components (also shown in Figure 7.3), including a command bar, the scope pane to the left, and the results pane to the right.

The command bar contains menus and buttons. Usually, access to at least two pop-up menus (Action and View) is provided. The Action menu contains a context-sensitive list of the actions possible for the chosen element. The View menu allows you to change the view in the right pane (the choices are Large, Small, List, Detail, or Web, which are just like the choices in Windows Explorer). The number of buttons on the command bar depends on the context.

The scope pane contains a tree hierarchy that shows the namespace of the tool, which is an inventory of the accessible elements in a tree structure. Each of these elements consti-

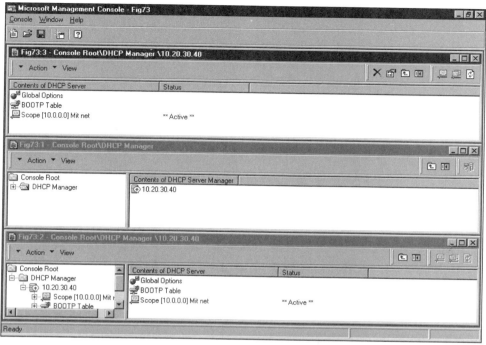

Figure 7.3

An example of a customized MMC console containing only one snap-in (DHCP Manager). Because MMC is an MDI application, several panes can be created—this example has panes that show three different views.

tutes an administrative object, a task, or a view. You can choose not to view the left pane in the Action menu (as shown in the topmost MDI children's window in Figure 7.3).

The results pane shows the associated details of the element that is chosen in the left pane. Often, the results pane shows a list of one directory's content, but sometimes it shows graphic images of varying complexity.

Depending on your requirements, the setup of the MMC user interface may vary from the advanced to the extremely simple (which might simply be a graphical point-and-click user interface). The extremely simple setup may be an HTML page or an ActiveX control snap-in in the MMC console. NT 5.0 beta 1 does not contain any simple snap-ins worth mentioning.

Adding and deleting snap-ins for a console is quite simple, which enables tailored solutions to be created that perfectly match the job situation of every administrator (see Figure 7.4). An experienced administrator may design more-limited MMC consoles, so that it is not as easy to make a catastrophic mistake by accidentally deleting a snap-in. The simple MMC console shown in Figure 7.5 took only one minute to design.

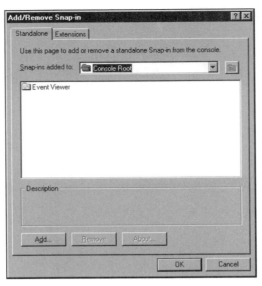

Figure 7.4
Adding one or more snap-ins to a console is actually quite simple.

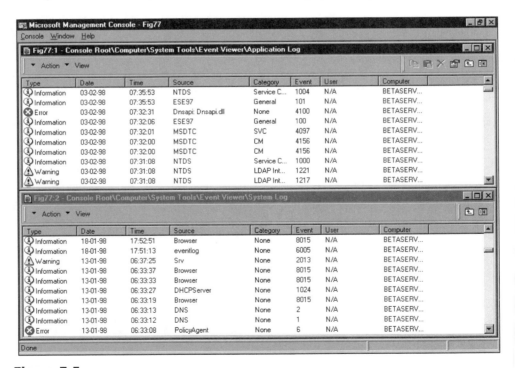

Figure 7.5
Designing tailored MMC consoles is incredibly easy—this console contains the two most common server logs.

Microsoft has made a special effort to ensure that the console is as manageable as possible, without limiting too tightly the powerful capabilities of the user interface, which would seriously damage carrying out daily routine tasks. Microsoft displayed incredible ingenuity by splitting the administrator pane into two parts that resemble the extremely user-friendly Windows Explorer interface. This means that collecting several snap-ins in the same console is fairly simple, because the tree hierarchy in the left pane simply expands.

Getting used to the MMC console takes a while, even though it is designed according to the same principles as Windows Explorer, which most administrators are familiar with from using Windows 95 or NT 4.0. But after some initial confusion, MMC proves to be a surprisingly great step forward compared to the current fragmented collection of tools (see Figure 7.6).

The MMC structure enables you to extend the functionality around one or more types of elements. Rather than adding new snap-ins, this can be accomplished via the extension snap-ins, which actually disappear into the user interface when they are added to the console. A particular extension snap-in's functionality is added to the

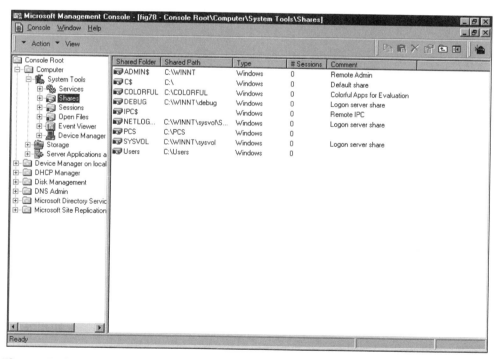

Figure 7.6

The MMC console is capable of powerful expression, without making things too complicated. This figure shows the most vital MMC snap-ins—all in one console.

context-sensitive menus (with certain limitations, of course, meaning that the snap-in's functionality may instead take the form of a standalone snap-in).

MMC's Future

I have no doubts that the new MMC will be a hit once NT 5.0 is publicly available. And it seems Microsoft realizes that it is on to something good, because it has promised that all existing NT management applications (all tools placed in the Administrative submenu of NT 4.0, as shown in Figure 7.7) will be replaced by MMC snap-ins that have at least the same functionality as the existing tools. Microsoft has not indicated in which release of NT 5.0 this will occur.

Beta 1 of NT 5.0 demonstrates that some work still remains before Microsoft reaches its goal regarding snap-ins. The special submenu—NT 4.0 Administrative Tools—still contains the following tools:

- Administrative Wizards

- Backup

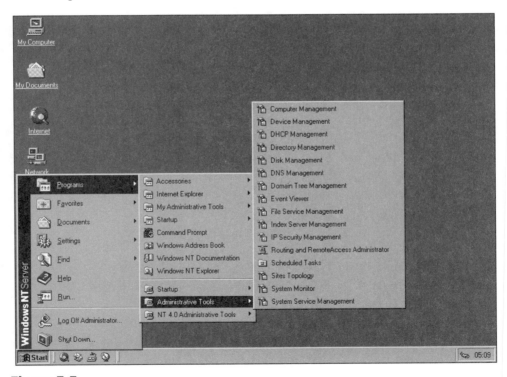

Figure 7.7
The MMC-based tools are located in the Programs menu under Administrative Tools, as in NT 4.0.

- DFS Administrator

- DHCP Manager

- License Manager

- Performance Monitor

- Remote Access Admin

- Server Manager

- System Policy Editor

- User Manager for Domains

- Windows NT Diagnostics

NT 5.0 still contains these tools, because the current MMC snap-ins do not entirely replace their functionality. Table 7.1 shows a summary of all the snap-ins that are available after NT 5.0 beta 1 is installed. Additional snap-ins are available for IIS and its underlying components. Although the number of snap-ins is impressive, a few details still need to fall in place before the MMC is able to fully replace the current management applications. Note that Table 7.1 describes the accessible snap-ins, which do not always correspond with the predefined MMC tools available from the Administrative Tools menu.

Table 7.1 *The MMC snap-ins for NT 5.0 beta 1 release.*

MMC Snap-in	Description	Also In NT Workstation 5.0
Computer Management	Contains the majority of functions for administering a single computer	Yes
Device Manager	Contains all information on the hardware units installed on the system	Yes
DHCP Manager	DHCP administration	No
Directory Service Migration Tool	Help tool for migration from Novell NDS to Active Directory	No
Disk Management	Disk administration	Yes
DNS Management	DNS administration	No
Event Viewer	Access to the three event logs	Yes
File Service Management	Contains vital information on file service (i.e., words, shares, sessions, and open files)	Yes
Folder	Establishes a directory in a specified place in the tree hierarchy	Yes

(continued)

Table 7.1 *The MMC snap-ins for NT 5.0 beta 1 release (continued).*

MMC Snap-in	Description	Also In NT Workstation 5.0
General Control	Capability to add an ActiveX control at a specified place in the tree hierarchy	Yes
Group Policy Editor	Administration of group policies	Yes
Index Server Management	Index Server administration	Yes
IP Security Management	Administration of the encryption possibilities on the IP level	Yes
Link To Web Address	Enables adding a binding to a URL at a specified place in the tree hierarchy	Yes
Media Services Management	Administration of new operation of the backup units that are media oriented rather than drive oriented	Yes
Microsoft Directory Service Manager	Administration of the Active Directory service	Yes
Microsoft Domain Tree Manager	Administration of the Active Directory domain tree	Yes
Microsoft Site Replication Manager	Administration of the replication setup	Yes
Monitoring Control	Adds monitor control that is used in System Monitor console, accessible from Administrative Tools menu	Yes
Schema Management	Gives access to schema for Active Directory service	No
System Service Management	Administration of the system services	Yes

Table 7.2 shows the tools that Microsoft considers to be right for carrying out the necessary administrative routines. Some of this information may change if Microsoft achieves its goal of having all existing management applications replaced with new MMC snap-ins.

As the two tables indicate, the Computer Management and Directory Management MMC tools are far more important than the other tools.

Computer Management Tool

Computer Management is intended to be the system administrator's primary computer-centered configuration tool. Computer Management provides access to the majority of things on a computer that an administrator needs to address in the daily

Table 7.2 *The management tools not yet included in MMC.*

Overall Task	Specific Task	NT 5.0 Tool	NT 4.0 Tool
Administration of Active Directory	Administration of domain trust relationships	Domain Tree Manage-MMC tool, accessible from the Administrative Tools menu. On the shortcut menu for the domain,select Properties|Trusts tab.	User Manager for Domains
	Administration of objects	Directory Management MMC tool, available from the Administrative Tools Menu.	Doesn't exist
	Administration of sites topology and replication	Sites Topology MMC tool, accessible from the Administrative Tools menu.	Doesn't exist
	Incorporation of a domain in the domain tree hierarchy	Domain Controller Promotion Wizard (dcpromo.exe, placed in the Win32 directory).	Doesn't exist
	View and adjustment of directory schema	Schema Management snap-in. To access snap-in, start the MMC, go to Console|Add/Remove Snap-in, and select it from the list.	Doesn't exist
Administration of users and groups	Adding logon scripts	Group Policy Editor snap-in. To access snap-in, start the MMC, go to Console|Add/Remove Snap-in, and select it from the list.	User Manager for Domains
	Administration of user accounts and groups	Directory Management MMC tool, accessible from Administrative Tools menu.	User Manager for Domains
	Delegating administrative privileges	Directory Management MMC tool, accessible from the Administrative Tools menu.	Doesn't exist

(continued)

Table 7.2   *The management tools not yet included in MMC (continued).*

Overall Task	Specific Task	NT 5.0 Tool	NT 4.0 Tool
Administration of security	Administration and monitoring of overall security	Security Configuration Editor snap-in. To access snap-in, start the MMC, go to Console|Add/Remove Snap-in, and select it from the list.	Doesn't exist
	Configuration of computer security policy for a stand-alone computer	Directory Management MMC tool, accessible from the Administrative Tools menu. On the short-cut menu, select Properties|Change under the Computer Security Policy heading on the General tab.	System Policy Editor
	Configuration of computer security policy for all computers in the domain	Directory Management MMC tool, accessible from the Administrative Tools menu. On the short-cut menu for the domain, select Properties|General| Computer Security Policy| Policy or Edit.	System Policy Editor
	Configuration of security policy for the domain	Directory Management MMC tool, accessible from Administrative Tools menu. On the shortcut menu for the domain, select Properties|Edit under the Domain Security Policy heading on the General tab.	User Manager for Domains
	Mapping of key certificates for user and group accounts	Directory Management MMC tool, accessible from the Administrative Tools menu. On the short-cut menu, select Properties|Name Mappings.	Doesn't exist
	Setup of permissions, auditing, and ownership for shares	File Service Management MMC tool, accessible from the Administrative Tools menu.	My Computer or Windows NT Explorer

(continued)

Table 7.2 *The management tools not yet included in MMC (continued).*

Overall Task	Specific Task	NT 5.0 Tool	NT 4.0 Tool
	Setup of permissions, auditing, and ownership for users, groups, and other directory objects	Directory Management MMC tool, accessible from Administrative Tools menu. On the shortcut menu for the object, select Properties|Security tab.	Doesn't exist
Administration of servers and resources	Administration of computers in the domain	Directory Management MMC tool, accessible from the Administrative Tools menu.	Server Manager
	Administration of disk storage and data security	Disk Management MMC tool, accessible from the Administrative Tools menu.	Disk Administrator
	Administration of server attachments and open files	Computer Management MMC tool, accessible from the Administrative Tools menu.	Server Manager
	Administration of shared volumes, directories, and files on a server	File Server Management MMC tool, accessible from the Administrative Tools menu.	Server Manager
	Monitoring of limitation of disk space available for individual users	Via the standalone Disk Quotas application, accessible from the Quota tab, which is among the properties for the NTFS volume. Select Properties on the shortcut menu for the NTFS volume in NT Explorer or My Computer.	Doesn't exist
	Publication of shares as volumes in the Active Directory	Directory Management MMC tool, accessible from the Administrative Tools menu. Choose the container, and then select New|Volume.	Doesn't exist

(continued)

Table 7.2   The management tools not yet included in MMC (continued).

Overall Task	Specific Task	NT 5.0 Tool	NT 4.0 Tool
Installation and administration of hardware and software	Addition and configuration of Gateway service for NetWare	Under Clients tab in the Network application of the Control Panel.	Under Services tab in the Network application of the Control Panel
	Addition and configuration of Internet card	The Hardware Wizard application of the Control Panel.	Network application of the Control Panel
	Addition and configuration of most network services	The Control Panel's Add/Remove Programs application on the Windows NT Setup tab. Select Networking Options|Details.	The Network application of the Control Panel
	Addition of hardware units	The Hardware Wizard application of the Control Panel.	Various Control Panel applications
	Configuration of hardware units	Device Management MMC tool, accessible from the Administrative Tools menu.	Device application of the Control Panel
Miscellaneous	Administration of services	System Service Management MMC tool, accessible from the Administrative Tools menu.	Services application of the Control Panel
	Configuration of Admission Control Services	Under Services tab in the Network application of the Control Panel.	Doesn't exist
	Configuration of IP security	IP Security Management snap-in.	Doesn't exist
	Monitoring of performance counts	System Monitor MMC tool, accessible from the Administrative Tools menu.	Performance Monitor
	Running of VBScript and JScript scripts	Windows Scripting Host. Can be called, for example, by writing the following: wscript [parameters] [name of script] [script parameters].	Doesn't exist

operation of the IT environment. This tool may be used to monitor any NT 5.0-based computer from any other NT 5.0-based computer on the network. The Computer Management tool does not distinguish between servers and clients, as long as the operating system is NT 5.0 and the user has the security privileges required.

Computer Management contains four different trees: System Tools, Storage, Server Applications and Services, and Getting Started (see Figure 7.8).

The System Tools tree provides access to the tools that are available in a specific computer. System Tools contains the following snap-ins: Services, Shares, Sessions, Open Files, Event Viewer, and Device Manager.

The Storage tree contains all the snap-ins with regard to disks; for example, Disk Management and Media Services Management. The Storage tree is empty in NT 5.0 beta 1.

The Server Applications and Services tree is reserved for optional snap-ins installed onto the system, or snap-ins found only for servers (such as DNS, DHCP, WINS, and BackOffice applications).

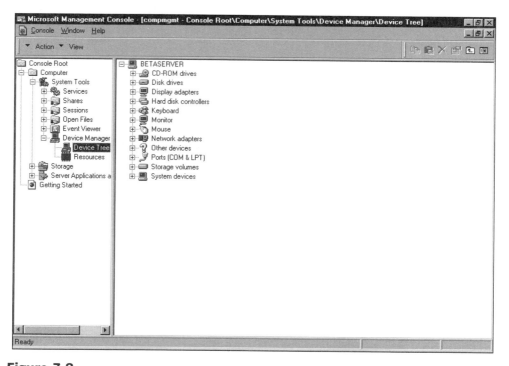

Figure 7.8
The Computer Management and Directory Management MMC tools stand apart. This figure shows the Computer Management tool.

The Getting Started tree is reminiscent of an early TaskPad for the Computer Management tool. It consists of a few simple HTML pages that end up calling a particular program. Getting Started gives ready access to online documentation (organized in beta 1 into "Quick Start," "Storage," and "Troubleshooting" help screens), wizards to add and remove hardware units and applications, the built-in backup program, and integrity checks of the disk. Microsoft intends to move the Getting Started function as a choice under the View menu, before NT 5.0 is released.

Directory Management Tool

The Directory Management tool, shown in Figure 7.9, gives access to the most frequently used parts of the directory. This includes a view of all directory objects in the given Active Directory domains, and the possibility to create new objects or remove some of the existing ones. Somewhat surprisingly, Directory Management is also accessible from NT Workstation 5.0-based PCs, provided that the user has one of the necessary security privileges.

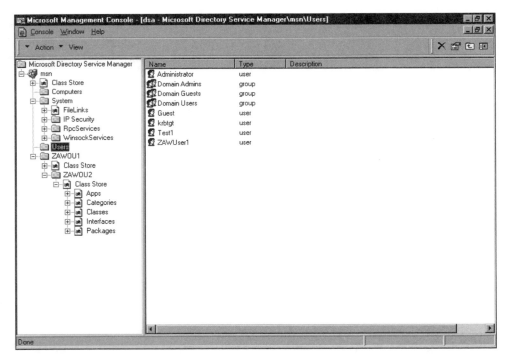

Figure 7.9
Directory Management is MMC's other outstanding tool.

The Directory Management tool is split into three different trees: Computers, System, and Users. The Computers tree contains a list of all the computers that are a part of the domain (in other words, all NT-based PCs), while the System tree contains all the system-specific services (for example, RPCs, Winsock, and IP security). The Users tree contains all the user-specific information (for example, users, groups, and print queues).

The number of snap-ins that will be added to MMC before NT 5.0 is released into production is still impossible to estimate. At the Professional Developer's Conference in September 1997, Microsoft promised that the following extra snap-ins would be added in beta 2 of NT 5.0:

- DFS
- Local user and group management
- Local security management
- Remote storage
- WINS
- Router

Additionally, TaskPads will be added, which don't exist in the current NT 5.0 beta 1.

Microsoft has also promised MMC snap-ins for the following products:

- System Management Server Opal (in which the main part of the product consists of MMC snap-ins)
- SQL Server 7.0
- Exchange Platinum
- Olympus
- BackOffice 5.0 version of SNA

Microsoft Transaction Server, SMTP, and NNTP snap-ins will be added in the accompanying Internet Information Server 4.0, for administering the IIS.

Many of the third-party manufacturers reportedly have started creating MMC snap-ins for their products, partially because Microsoft announced that support for Windows NT 5.0 is a prerequisite for obtaining the much-coveted BackOffice logo.

Web-Based Enterprise Management (WBEM)

One of Microsoft's other initiatives within the ZAW family is Web-Based Enterprise Management (WBEM). WBEM, shown in Figure 7.10, was launched in July 1996 with the backing of BMC Software, Cisco, Compaq, Intel, and Microsoft. Today, more than 75 vendors of hardware and software have stated that they support WBEM. (See **wbem.freerange.com** for an in-depth analysis of this topic.)

WBEM is an attempt to create a wide selection of standards for using the traditional Web technologies to administer systems and networks from large, management-framework systems—similar to HP's OpenView, TME 10, and CA Unicenter. WBEM defines a series of schemas and protocols with which to achieve this goal. Parts of these definitions have already been ratified by the Desktop Management Task Force (DMTF) through the Common Information Model (CIM).

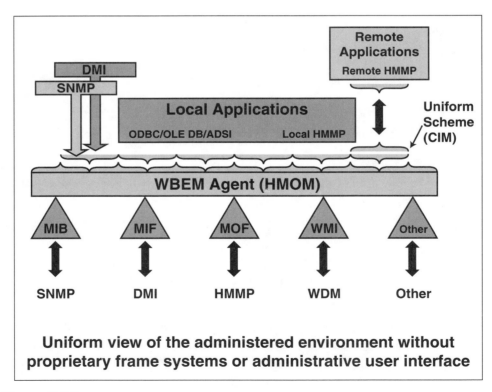

Figure 7.10
Microsoft WBEM's layer in the information management hierarchy for local applications.

A taskforce representing several manufacturers have designed the WBEM technologies, and WBEM is intended to be independent of manufacturers, protocols, and management standards. This may sound plausible, but it is a radical break with the current state of affairs, in which Simple Network Management Protocol (SNMP), Desktop Management Interface (DMI), and Common Management Information Protocol (CMIP) are closely linked to network management, desktop management, and telecom management, respectively. Another management standard, dubbed Hypermedia Management Protocol (HMMP), has recently emerged in connection with the Web.

WBEM and MMC thus are complementary entities. Whereas MMC provides administrators an integrated, task-based management user interface, WBEM defines the mechanisms necessary to model the systems to be administered. MMC is a technology that is specific for Windows, whereas WBEM is independent of platforms, and hence is able to model the entire system, from the network, across the computers attached to it (including non-Windows-based computers), up to the applications operated in the environment. MMC is independent of WBEM, yet WBEM can give each snap-in a consistent method for accessing the components in the IT environment, and WBEM can understand the relationships among the individual components.

WBEM is designed on the basis that a single management methodology can provide the solution to present and future management problems. This methodology is founded on a task-oriented view of the world and presupposes the need to have the management system consist of several tools that interact. This required specification leads to object orientation, and the basic structure and draft of WBEM is based on the object-oriented paradigm.

WBEM rests on a uniform model, which, together with the usual selection of object-oriented functions, makes defining a common object-oriented schema possible. The standard schema constitutes a common framework—a fundamental topology regarding classifications and facts. It also contains a fundamental selection of classes, which establishes a common frame of reference with which to describe the environment to be administered. The schema can be presented in different ways, such as a selection of HTML pages.

The key elements in the standard schema are classes, properties, and methods. The schema is also supported by events and associations as types of classes, and references as types of property.

Each component in the management environment is called a *managed object*. Properties, attributes, and other particulars covering a managed object are stored in classes. These classes are organized in hierarchies with regard to association and heritage, all grouped according to fields of interest, such as network, applications, and systems.

Each field of interest represents a *schema*, which is a partial amount of the information accessible on the administered environment. The schemas will gradually develop, and extensions to schemas can readily be added. For example, you can add new classes and properties that are currently not part of any other schema.

The WBEM consists of two elements: provider applications and client applications. *Provider applications* provide information on any special facilities in one or more units being administered; *client applications* are the software that use WBEM.

WBEM is a spectrum of technologies that is designed to improve the management situation, and as such, will not become a Microsoft product. Judged by statements thus far from Microsoft regarding management framework systems, it currently is not planning a framework system. Microsoft, therefore, is more likely to include the necessary WBEM standards in its products, and leave the gathering and presentation to some of the framework systems that already exist. If Microsoft changes its point of view, it is likely to expand the SMS product toward a real management framework system.

Windows Management Instrumentation (WMI)

Windows Management Instrumentation (WMI) is part of the new driver architecture (Windows Driver Model) introduced in NT 5.0 and Windows 98. As the name indicates, WMI is the supporting instrumentation mechanism for hardware units on the Windows platform.

When the NetPC specification (covering PCs in which all the hardware components that are particularly exacting in administrative terms have been removed; see Chapter 1 for an in-depth definition) was announced, Microsoft also introduced WMI. However, WMI is not limited to NetPCs, but rather is an integral part of the NT 5.0 and Windows 98 operating systems.

In other words, WMI is the new standard for surveillance and control of the hardware units of each PC in the Windows environment. WMI is in full compliance with the requirements of systems administered via WBEM, and WMI enables administrators to create uniform and open access to management information from systems based on Windows 98 or NT 5.0.

> **Note:** WMI is an operating system interface that has access to properties and notifications from the units monitored. Likewise, WMI consolidates management particulars

from the underlying hardware components, their drivers, and their applications, and passes on this data in a coherent information base. This base meets the WBEM requirements and uses the DMTF CIM standard.

WMI (together with CIM-based information) enables you to carry out the following types of management tasks on Windows-based hardware and software via a WBEM-based management system:

- Monitoring and solution of errors and alerts in hardware and software

- Preventive maintenance

- Version and upgrade control

- Capacity planning and performance management

- Enhanced asset management and administration of security

- Operations management

- Automated management

Note that WMI is closely linked with the introduction of the new WDM drivers with regard to hardware. The WDM drivers likely will not replace all the current drivers for a long time. This is certainly true in Windows 98, where WDM is in a battle with the existing driver architecture on the most popular hardware units, and even finds itself in a poor starting position, because the WDM driver code will be operated more slowly than the corresponding code in the conventional Windows drivers.

Furthermore, the WDM driver classes in NT 5.0 and Windows 98 can be expected to cover only the following types of hardware units:

- Still life units (such as cameras, scanners, and video capture units), multimedia units (such as MPEG decoders, video capture units, sound bites, and DVDs), and broadcast architectures

- All types of data-input units—beginning with just the USB units covered by the Human Interface Devices (HID) specification (such as keyboards, mice, pointing units, and all kinds of games controls)

- The basic types of USB units (hubs, peripherals, and controllers)

- The basic types of IEEE 1394 units (controllers)

Still, no WDM driver classes are ready for traditional PC units: graphic cards and data-input units that are linked to a type of gateway other than the USB. So, the WDM driver classes are not compatible with existing mice, keyboards, and joysticks, unless they comply with the HID firmware specification.

New Facilities In NT 5.0

NT 5.0 has many functions and facilities that will delight administrators. Some of its most conspicuous assets are the following:

- Enhanced fault tolerance in most components (see also Chapter 6)

- A genuine directory service (see also Chapters 4 and 10)

From the perspective of server administrators, one of the truly great facilities is that upgrades and downgrades with the Domain Controller (DC) are now possible. Therefore, reinstating NT Server from the bottom is no longer necessary when carrying out more-radical changes of the domain, or changing the servers that will act as DCs. All that remains is to start the dcpromo.exe executable from the Win32 directory when the given server must change its status regarding the domain.

Task Scheduler, shown in Figure 7.11, is another great facility. Task Scheduler puts a more powerful and user-friendly interface on the facilities for arranging timetables for operating applications, relative to the previous Windows NT AT service and System Agent, which was part of the Windows Plus! package. The interface in NT Task Scheduler is identical to the interfaces in Windows 98 and Internet Explorer 4.0. The only real difference is that the NT version contains some enhanced security facilities.

The Scheduled Task Wizard (see Figure 7.11) makes embedding new applications in Scheduled Tasks very simple. The Wizard requests only that you choose the program from a list of registered applications (or by directly indicating the name of the executable file, batch file, command file, or script), stating when the program will be operated and in which security context it will be handled.

Moreover, as previously stated, Microsoft has promised to design a series of very simple user interfaces (dubbed TaskPads)—similar to the current Administrative Wizards in NT 4.0—for less-experienced administrators to use. The number of TaskPads Microsoft is currently designing, and whether they will be accessible from all NT Server versions when the products go into production, are not known.

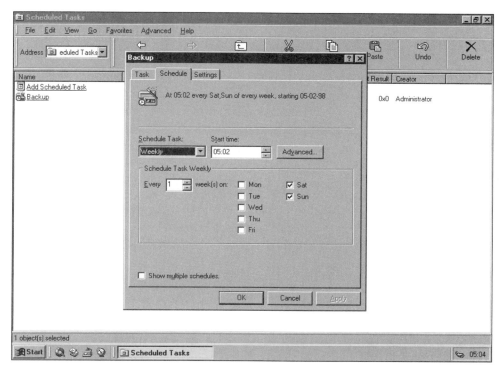

Figure 7.11
Task Scheduler is incredibly simple to use. Now there is no excuse for not arranging a timetable to operate the applications in the IT environment.

More To Come...

On several occasions (and even on its Web site), Microsoft has mentioned a product by the name of *Directory Service Administration*, which is the administrator software for the Active Directory. As such, it is supposed to give access to administer all objects in the Active Directory, including users, computers, printers, servers, organizational units, and so on.

The Directory Service Administration software allegedly will be available as both an MMC snap-in, and the Directory Service Web browser tool (sometimes dubbed DS Web) that gives the ability to administer Active Directory objects from any Web browser equipped with frames. Directory Service Administration also supports Kerberos authentication, which uses secret-key cryptography to keep passwords safe over networks.

Both of these programs currently are either being designed, altered, or dropped, as neither of them exists on NT Server 5.0 beta 1, nor are they mentioned anywhere in the beta documentation. The reason Directory Service Administration isn't mentioned in the beta documentation likely may be that the tool has changed its name to Directory Management, which seems to meet the specifications that Microsoft originally stipulated for Directory Service Administration. If this is the case, then the Web browser tool is the only thing that is missing, which may not be a problem, because Microsoft probably can use the corresponding tool from NT Server 3.51 and 4.0 (Web Administration for Windows NT Server). This tool can be installed on any server that is operating Windows NT 4.0 and the Internet Information Server.

Microsoft's Systems Management Server (SMS), a vital component in ZAW and a product in the Microsoft Back Office family, also remains to be added. SMS is a systems management application that gives access to automated distribution of software, inventory of software and hardware, and remote control of the computers in the IT environment. SMS is designed mainly to be a management tool for medium and large businesses, but it also is widely used in small enterprises because it integrates with many other management systems and can be integrated for third-party applications.

Because of the many software distribution facilities in NT 5.0, Microsoft SMS is not such a vital solution for pure NT 5.0 environments. Nevertheless, the coming SMS 2.90 (the current SMS version is 1.2) apparently has many new facilities for network management because of Microsoft's alliance agreement with HP, the purpose of which is to increase the integration between SMS and HP's OpenView to NT. SMS 2.90 should be ready before NT 5.0 is publicly available. So, many signs indicate that SMS will also offer several interesting possibilities for managing IT environments of the future.

Avoid The Hassle—Start Using MMC Now!

A closer look at the management applications for NT 5.0 shows that not many things are repeated from NT 4.0. Already, a majority of the management applications have been replaced with new ones that have a different appearance and functionality. Microsoft has repeatedly promised that the management applications, copied from NT 4.0 thus far, will be replaced with new MMC tools before NT 5.0 is available.

The change from NT 3.x or NT 4.0 to NT 5.0 is bound to be enormous for the server administrator. NT 5.0 has many new technologies to become familiar with (not least of which is Active Directory, which turns many of the fundamentals of a server domain upside down), as well as management applications that look different.

Therefore, rather than offering the joy of recognition after upgrading, NT 5.0 will offer the frustration of learning something new. Nevertheless, Microsoft states that the new management applications will make the daily routine of the server administrator vastly easier, after the initial confusion has subsided. I am sure that what Microsoft says is true—not so much because the new tools are easier to handle than the old ones (and quite frankly, they are, as they now have an entirely new user interface), but because all the Microsoft server applications will be furnished with MMC-based tools, and because the independent program developers will be forced to replace their current management applications with identical MMC-based tools (because MMC support is being made a prerequisite for obtaining a BackOffice logo).

On the other hand, Microsoft seemingly is doing everything it can to underestimate how tough changing to some completely new administrative tools actually is. Administrators are strongly urged to start accumulating expertise with MMC, which you can do by obtaining and experimenting with a beta version of NT 5.0.

Experimenting with MMC can also be done without NT 5.0. MMC v1.0 is available for download from the Microsoft Web site (**www.microsoft.com/management/ mmc/helpmenu_productnews.htm**). Version 1.1 is expected to be ready during the third quarter of 1998, whereas version 2.0 is planned for delivery in the fourth quarter of 1998.

The best way to learn, of course, is to work with the MMC-based tools on a daily basis. This already is possible, because both Microsoft SNA Server 4.0 and the applications in the Option Pack for Windows NT Server 4.0 use MMC-based tools. The Microsoft Option Pack consists of the following applications: Internet Information Server 4.0, Microsoft Transaction Server 2.0, Microsoft Message Queue Server 1.0, and Internet Connection Services for Microsoft RAS. The Option Pack has been available for download from the Microsoft Web site (**backoffice.microsoft.com/ downtrial/optionpack.asp**) since December 1997. So, no excuses exist for not getting familiarized with the MMC-based management applications.

Daily User Administration

On several occasions, Microsoft has stated that one of its most important goals for 1998 is to reduce operating costs in Windows environments. This statement has had an effect on the design of NT 5.0 and Windows 98.

The most noticeable consequence of Microsoft's attempt to reduce operating expenses is that NT Server 5.0 has a lot of new functions added that enable administrators to drastically reduce the costs of maintaining an environment consisting of NT Workstation 5.0 clients, compared with similar environments that are based on NT 4.0 (see Figure 8.1).

This sharp reduction in Total Cost of Ownership (TCO) in IT environments in which a combination of NT Workstation 5.0 and NT Server 5.0 are used is possible through a combination of the following:

- Better facilities for automating all components of programs (scheduling, Windows scripts, etc.)

- An increase in the overall administration capabilities of the environment (with MMC and other improvements)

- Easier data gathering for error detection, device failures, and so on

Moreover, Microsoft states that the combination of NT Server 5.0 and Windows 98 will mean a substantial reduction in TCO compared with relatively homogeneous Windows 98 environments (and with NT 4.0 and Windows 95 environments). But the TCO level will always be lowest in a purely NT 5.0 environment.

This chapter describes the NT 5.0 functions that Microsoft expects to lead to significant improvements of TCO in the Windows environment.

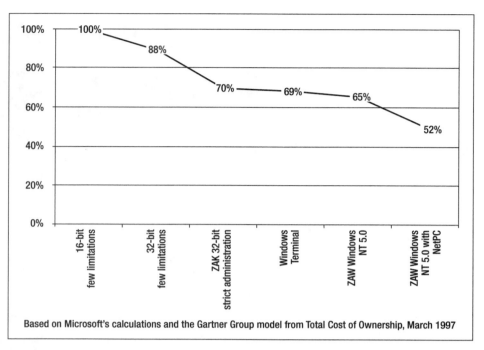

Figure 8.1
Microsoft's vision regarding TCO, from 16-bit operating systems to NT 5.0 NetPCs.

TCO And ZAW: Microsoft's Latest Mantras

Microsoft's initiatives to reduce operating costs, or TCO, is dubbed *Zero Administration for Windows*, abbreviated as ZAW. The Windows terminals and NetPCs, mentioned in Chapter 1, represent one side of the focus on reducing TCO as much as possible, and represent one of the cornerstones of the ZAW philosophy. This section will first explain ZAW and TCO, and then go on to discuss Microsoft's Zero Administration Kit (ZAK).

The Essence Of ZAW: IntelliMirror And Application Management

Microsoft believes that a purely Windows NT 5.0 environment (using NT Workstation 5.0 on the clients and NT Server 5.0 on the servers) will reduce TCO by up to 50 percent, compared with other Windows-based solutions. Microsoft hints that even more savings will occur in the long run.

This reduction in TCO is due to a series of drastic ZAW-oriented refinements of NT that have not been implemented in Windows 98. The primary objective of these initiatives is to eliminate an administrator ever needing to go to a desktop client to perform updates of the operating system or applications.

So far, the two biggest ZAW items in NT 5.0 apparently will be called *IntelliMirror* and *Application Management*. These two concepts (which Microsoft undoubtedly will advertise more about in the future) cover all facilities for mirroring the client's data on the server, and greatly enhance the installation of applications.

Yet, much uncertainty exists regarding whether Microsoft will put IntelliMirror and Application Management at the top of its agenda. Some confusion seems to exist within Microsoft regarding what constitutes the correct terminology for the ZAW-specific technologies. So, Microsoft may start using ZAW as a term that jointly covers all the new technologies in NT 5.0 that help reduce TCO. This book, therefore, refers to ZAW as the sum of all features and technologies that reduce TCO.

While some uncertainty remains in the choice of words, no doubt exists as to which functions Microsoft plans to include in NT 5.0. Regardless of whether the technology is IntelliMirror, Application Management, or something else, NT 5.0 gives the administrator the tools to guide the user through changes to applications and the environment, error detection, and so on, in a comparatively simple way—without having to leave the administrator's office chair.

Some rather new and very sophisticated capabilities for installing and uninstalling software (which is the primary source of many of today's administrative headaches)—combined with "intelligent mirroring" of the user's data, applications, system files, and the administrative setup of NT Server 5.0-based servers—constitute the core of NT 5.0's technology.

The new ZAW technologies in NT 5.0 present administrators with the following great advantages:

- *"No touch" administration of applications and operating systems*—As previously stated, NT Workstation 5.0 removes the need for an administrator to visit one or more PC clients for software-related tasks. The NT 5.0 installation service enables an administrator to send and update applications easily to every user or group of users. The applications are automatically entered or updated—either completely or partially, as needed—the next time the user logs on to the PC.

- *Exchangeable PCs*—Typically, when a client PC crashes and is replaced, the entire environment has to be rebuilt from scratch. With NT 5.0, handling such situations is fairly easy. Inserting an entire new copy of the work environment of the user (including data, applications, preferences, and administrative policies) is very simple and takes little time when the user environment is mirrored onto the server.

- *Policy-based administration*—Administrators can introduce various policies, such as individual desktops and operational access to applications for any user or group of users. To facilitate "roaming users" as much as possible, these policies follow users when they log on to any NT Workstation 5.0-based PC on the company network.

Additionally, the ZAW technologies give users these advantages:

- *Fully secured data*—If a client's PC is out of order or otherwise unavailable, the complete user environment can be reestablished quickly and easily (including data, applications, preferences, and administrative policies) simply by logging on to another, or a new, NT Workstation 5.0-based PC.

- *Support of "roaming users"*—Users can use their entire user environment, even if they roam to another NT Workstation 5.0-based PC on the network.

- *Offline directories*—Users have easier access to local or network-based resources when they are not connected to the company's network, such as on a portable computer while traveling. Personal data is synchronized automatically when the user logs on to the network again.

Microsoft emphasizes that an administrator may choose to limit the implementation of part of the ZAW functions just listed. They may pick and choose which features to implement, and for which users or groups.

How much of NT 5.0's ZAW technology will be assigned to Windows 98 is still unclear. Regardless, ZAW likely will take the form of an update to Windows 98, after NT Server 5.0 is released, according to Phil Holden, Products CEO of the Personal and Business Systems Group at Microsoft.

The Zero Administration Kit

For the traditional Windows operating systems—NT Workstation 4.0 and Windows 95—ZAW takes the form of the Zero Administration Kit (ZAK). ZAK enables the administrator to convert a traditional Windows PC to either of the following two scaled-down types of clients, with a considerably lower potential for errors and problems:

- *Taskstation Mode*—Designed for users who need to carry out only one or just a few similar tasks. Taskstation Mode enables an administrator to start an application (or perhaps a shell containing a group of applications) automatically when the user logs on to the network. Likewise, the administrator may make the desktop simpler than normal, so that, for instance, the user has access to only one application and is unable to see any shortcut icons, the Start menu, or the Taskbar.

- *Appstation Mode*—Intended for users who need to handle several applications, but who don't have the necessary skills to handle the full range in Windows. The principles are basically the same as in the Taskstation Mode, but the Appstation Mode is more flexible. The administrator decides how the desktop must look, whether any limitations are placed on the PC's hardware, and which applications are allowed to operate. Appstation differs from Taskstation in that Appstation is based on the user using the traditional Windows maneuvers, such as starting applications from the Start menu.

Both types of clients are based on the user's unique logon name for NT Server (provided the business uses NT Server as an operating system). Thus, ZAKs may be implemented for some business users, without other users ever noticing. This flexibility is great, as ZAW doesn't have to be an all-or-nothing implementation, and is adjustable to the comfort level of the NT administrator.

ZAK enables you to regulate and limit a user's access to the hardware and operating system resources of the PC (including access to install applications). The implementation of ZAK requires the administrator to be extremely knowledgeable. ZAK facilities presuppose an in-depth knowledge of the Registry, because ZAK is based on the Windows system policies and user profiles. Also worth noting is that the administration of user profiles apparently will remain unchanged.

The Zero Administration Kit is only the beginning of the ZAW initiative. ZAK currently requires in-depth technical knowledge from the administrator, but Microsoft's declared objective is to reduce these requirements considerably in Windows 98 and NT 5.0. Moreover, ZAK only helps to reduce the administrative overhead involved in using the fairly simple ZAW system. Thus, ZAK is not sufficient to fully meet Microsoft's ZAW vision: An administrator should never need to revert to a client PC in order to update software or diagnose errors—instead, the administrator should ideally be able do all of these tasks remotely.

Microsoft has done a lot to make its new operating systems more manageable in every sense, especially for "ordinary" Windows users. This effort to improve things by Microsoft is in addition to the current facilities for unattended setup (such as Install Wizards) and rudimentary tools for remote administration. For example, Windows 98 contains a host of new tools with which to gather status information and actual error detection (which might be of the active or the passive type), including the following:

- *Internet System Update*—Gets new drivers and file systems from the Internet.

- *System File Checker*—Verifies that the system files such as *.dll, *.vxd, and the like are not corrupted.

- *Microsoft System Information Utility*—Collects system hardware and software information for resolving configuration problems and troubleshooting.

- *Dr. Watson*—Intercepts Windows errors such as general protection faults, and provides detailed information on screen and in a log file.

- *ScanDisk*—Scans for lost clusters.

- *Automatic Skip Driver Agent.*

- *System Configuration Utility.*

Moreover, Windows 98 contains the Windows Update Manager, a Web-based driver-update tool that enables an administrator to identify outdated software applications and drivers and to download the right Service Packs, upgrades, and patches direct from Microsoft over the Internet. Update Manager is based on an ActiveX control and a database on the Microsoft Web site that jointly enable you to compare the hardware and software components of a PC against the information in the Microsoft database on drivers and error recoveries. Update Manager requires that the user actually agree to give Microsoft automatic access through the Internet to a large amount of data on the user's PC.

Finally, both Windows 98 and NT 5.0 are equipped with a scripting language (Windows Scripting Host) that can be operated from the user interface or a command. At last, administrators and more-advanced users can automate various actions. This is similar to the old MS-DOS scripts and batch files, but with Windows the scripts can be more powerful. For example, a script can be set up to automatically dial a network, download a file, email the file to a user, and then print it out on paper.

Additionally, Microsoft is still working on making its Windows user interface (shared by Windows 98 and NT 5.0) easier for ordinary users to work with and keep updated. This is the reason why NT 5.0 and Windows 98 introduce some changes that make their interfaces similar to Web browsers, and why they include a new service program.

Windows 98 is far from meeting the ZAW vision. But Microsoft's objective has never been to turn Windows 98 into the primary ZAW operating system platform—NT 5.0 has been selected to implement the ZAW vision.

> **Note:** Microsoft has the following to say regarding its ZAW vision: "Windows NT Workstation 5.0 will be the premier desktop operating system for businesses and organizations of all sizes. It will include the same key features as Windows 98, such as second-generation

Plug and Play and power management, as well as a 'Web integrated' graphical user interface. It will significantly extend the reliability, security, networking, and performance advantages that make today's version of Windows NT the most powerful enterprise desktop operating system. Most importantly, when combined with Windows NT 5.0, Windows NT Workstation 5.0 will be the only desktop operating system to support all of the manageability capabilities that help businesses reduce total cost of ownership (TCO) an expected 50 percent or more over other Windows-based environments."

Enhanced Application Management

Application Management, the installation and uninstallation of applications, is one of the two main prerequisites of ZAW. Installation and uninstallation of applications is handled via the Microsoft installation technology. The installation technology is a completely new transaction-based methodology with which to administer all the facilities generally associated with the life cycle of an application.

Ordinary users will notice the Microsoft installation technology because there are now two Add/Remove Programs icons, as shown in Figure 8.2. The first icon contains the two familiar tabs to install or uninstall programs, or to install extra operating

Figure 8.2
The NT 5.0 beta 1 Control Panel has two different Add/Remove Programs icons.

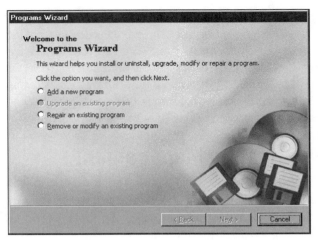

Figure 8.3
Clicking Add/Remove Programs—v2 in the Control Panel activates the Programs Wizard.

system components. The other icon (Add/Remove Programs—v2) starts a Wizard for installation, uninstallation/modification, upgrading, or repair of a program (see Figure 8.3). This is an extremely user-friendly guide, with facilities for installing, uninstalling (or modifying), upgrading, or repairing applications.

Microsoft's installation technology is a very sophisticated solution, and it provides a tangible step forward in handling applications on the operating system. It is geared toward administrators rather than users. Microsoft's installation technology contains the following functions:

- *Standardized package format and install service*—The installation technology is built into Windows, and it is responsible for handling installation, repair, uninstallation, and detection of components (defined as collections of files, entries in the Registry database, shortcuts, and so forth, all jointly administered).

- *Sturdiness*—Repairing applications, rolling back install transactions, and establishing redundant install points are all possible, to ensure that access to the full spectrum of facilities that administer the applications is always available.

- *Just-in-time (JIT) installations*—Microsoft's installation technology-management API enables you to tailor applications with which to install program components, when needed. This API contains all the necessary functions for detection and forced installation of the program components.

- *Administration based on policy*—Microsoft's installation technology is supported by the announcements of applications, which enables a PC client to appear as if a particular application has already been installed on the system, when it hasn't. If the user tries to start the application, it is automatically installed at that moment, and started. This means that interactive installations will take place only when a user is present (to set preferences, and the like), and that installations occur only on those clients that will be using that particular program (thus saving network traffic).

- *Lockdown support*—The installation technology is administered as a service on NT Server, which enables you to carry out application installations on the PC client, even if the user doesn't actually have the rights necessary to implement the installation of these applications.

- *Management and package API*—The installation technology contains a vast selection of functions that enable you to adapt applications to the needs of the organization. The API contains functions for reconfiguring, repairing, detecting, and forcing installation of applications and their components. Moreover, the API places a broad selection of functions at the software developers' disposal, so that they can manufacture packages and interconnect various components.

It is worth noting that Microsoft's installation technology facilitates the implementation of administrative requirements in network environments. This is done through facilities for optional installation (through "Just In Time" advertisements/publishing, discussed earlier in this chapter) and conditioned installation (through the allocation and assignment of various installation rights to groups and users) of all or part of the applications. Microsoft has also remembered to solve the small but irritating detail concerning rights of the NT Workstation: Installing applications, without having administrator rights to the particular PC client, is now possible, as the installation program is handled as a service on Windows NT Server. This permits automatic installations without the intervention of an administrator.

Built-in detection of components in NT 5.0 is the most important improvement regarding installation compared to NT 4.0. The lack of component detection is truly one of the worst problems regarding applications in NT 4.0—especially with DLLs that are used by several applications that, thus, can't be removed without risking the introduction of errors, and with dangling references in the system Registry. For example, uninstalling one application in Windows NT 4.0 (or Windows 95) can remove DLLs or other files that are required by other applications, thus making those applications fail. Built-in detection of components solves this problem in the best possible way: The operating system takes over responsibility for the installed components, thus enabling administrators to cope with any component dependence across several applications.

Microsoft promises that Service Packs for NT 5.0 will meet the requirements of the Microsoft installation technology, to make administering much easier than it is with

NT 4.0. Each Service Pack will be much smaller in size, because they can take advantage of all the components already installed on the system.

Although Microsoft's installation technology is sophisticated compared with what is available on the market, it actually is quite simple for applications manufacturers to work with. All that the manufacturers have to do is indicate the state of the application, all DLLs, all keys in the Registry database, and so on to the install service, and the installation technology will be able to distribute the application across a network. Since the manufacturers know the DLLs and Registry changes, they can easily supply this with their products so that it can be easily integrated into Microsoft's ZAW implementation.

The Downside

Although Microsoft's installation facilities are impressive when compared with available alternatives, it does have its shortcomings. A major shortcoming is that assigning applications at a more granular level isn't possible. For instance, you can install or announce an application only for a complete domain or an organizational unit, not to specific users or groups.

Moreover, you have to exercise great caution regarding the degree of freedom to install applications that you give users. With a bit of bad luck, the application might end up being installed on the server, which might come as an unpleasant surprise to the administrator if several users are involved. Microsoft is working on this. The solution is called *Server Intelligent Storage* (SIS), a server program that constantly safeguards against any waste of precious disk space that may occur when there are duplicate files on the server disk.

The worst limitation of Microsoft's installation facilities is a lack of version control. If a later version of an application is installed on the system, the earlier version is automatically overwritten, which doesn't support a situation in which one or more users need to use an older version of the application.

Last, but not least, you must note that using Microsoft's installation technology requires that the applications are built for the new installation API. This shouldn't be a problem in future NT applications, as support of Microsoft's installation technology will be introduced as a logo-bearing prerequisite. Soon, practically all third-party manufacturers will want to have the Windows logo on their products, and will thus make their applications compatible with the NT 5.0 installation technology.

Note: *The Microsoft installation technology doesn't solve the problems that already exist with the many different applications the company is currently using. So, a long* *transitory period will occur during which you won't be able to benefit fully from the new technology.*

Announcement Or Assignment Of Applications

As stated in the preceding section, NT 5.0 enables you to spread applications to clients across a network in two different ways:

- *Conditional installation* —You can assign applications to one or more users. When one of these users logs on to a PC, their desktop and Start menu are furnished with the icons assigned to their applications. The applications appear to be installed on the PC, even if they aren't. An assigned application isn't automatically installed until it is first activated, which occurs when the user selects the application. Thereafter, when the user activates the application, the installation is skipped and the application starts automatically.

- *Voluntary installation*—As opposed to assigned applications, published applications don't indicate in advance that they are installed on the PC. A published application is installed only if the user chooses it from Add/Remove Programs— v2 on the control panel, or if the user attempts to open a file that can't be handled by the local PC but can be read by the published application. The local PC finds the file types that can be handled by the various applications via the *Class Store*, the place on the network where all announced applications hide their attributes.

Spreading applications is monitored through policies similar to those of NT 4.0 and Windows 95, which is why Microsoft occasionally refers to the facilities as an integrated part of the "policy-based management." While Microsoft is expanding the number of policies, the System Policy Editor is itself being replaced by an MMC snap-in, called the *Group Policy Editor* (see Figure 8.4).

The Group Policy Editor enables you to establish user policies in a similar manner to the previous versions of Windows, but it also introduces a series of new policies. Thus, the Group Policy Editor is used to spread applications, introduce policies for computers and users, and administer scripts. The Group Policy Editor functions as a focal point for possible application-specific policies (implemented via ADM files, which is familiar from current versions of Windows).

The Group Policy Editor is integrated with the rest of the administrative environment and is based on the use of the hierarchical user structure of Active Directory. A policy must always be attached to a site, domain, or organizational unit, and automatically comprises all possible underlying levels of the directory tree, too. This integration makes implementing and administering policies easier than before, where the administrator might have had difficulties keeping track of things. It is worth

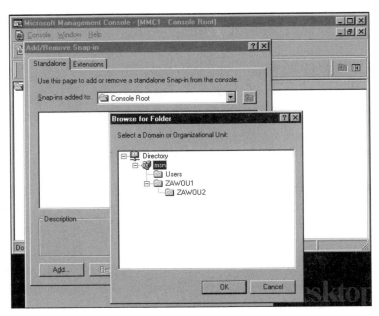

Figure 8.4
The Group Policy Editor is very simple to use. When the snap-in is added, you are asked which domain and organizational unit the policy is valid for.

noting that the inherited policies via the directory tree may easily become a source of enormous frustrations if all administrators are not fully informed of each others' actions. This puts bigger demands across the organization on planning and the consequences (or lack thereof) than what organizations currently are used to.

As with the current System Rules editor, the Group Policy Editor distinguishes sharply between computer and user-related settings (see Figure 8.5). Computer Settings covers all policies for users and computers that relate to the computer, and hence covers all users that log on to the computer, irrespective of their organizational affiliation in Active Directory. User Settings covers only the users that belong to the specified organizational unit.

Computer Settings in beta 1 comprises the following components:

- Client Application Settings
- Operating System Settings
    - Client Services
    - User Interface
    - Shared Desktop

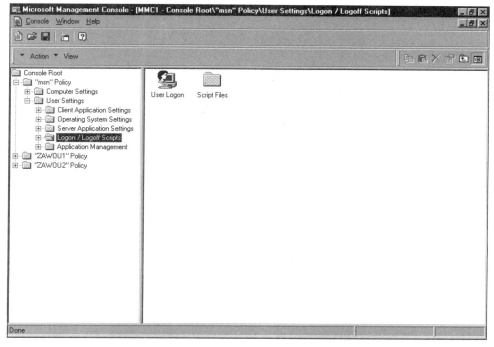

Figure 8.5
Policies have been added for the MSN domain and ZAWOU1 and ZAWOU2 organizational units.

- Files for Shared Desktop
- Shared Start Menu
  - Files for Shared Start Menu
  - Files for Shared Programs
  - Files for Shared Startup
  - Server Application Settings

User Settings also contains a vast number of options, as shown in Figure 8.6:

- Client Application Settings
- Operating System Settings
  - User Interface
    - Application Data
      - Files for Application Data

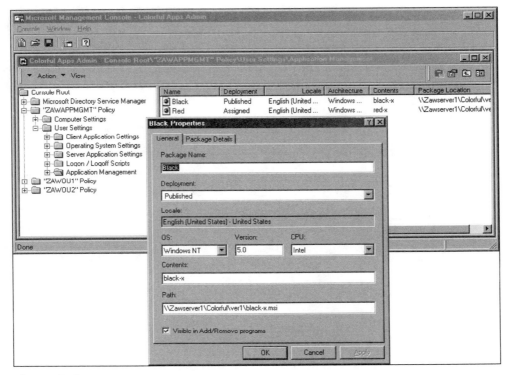

Figure 8.6
Incorporating new applications for a specific number of users is straightforward. It simply requires entering Application Management, pointing out the given Microsoft Install file, and perhaps changing a few of the settings.

- Desktop
  - Files for Desktop
- Favorites
  - Files for Favorites
- My Documents
  - Files for My Documents
- Network Neighborhood
  - Files for Network Neighborhood
- Printers
  - Files for Printers
- Recent

- Files for Recent
- Send To
  - Files for Send To
- Start Menu
  - Files for Start Menu
  - Files for Programs
  - Files for Startup
- Templates
  - Files for Templates
- Power Management
  - Monitor
  - System
- Server Application Settings
- Logon/Logoff Scripts
  - User Logon
  - Script Files
- Application Management

Discussing all of these functions would require too much information for the purposes of this chapter. Furthermore, Microsoft has announced that policies is one of the areas in which it plans to extend the range of functions significantly in NT 5.0 beta 2. For instance, the support of scripts in the Group Policy Editor in NT 5.0 beta 1 is limited to logon scripts. Thus, introducing user logoff and startup/shutdown of the PC isn't possible, which is one of the things Microsoft promises to include in the final version of NT 5.0. Currently, assigning applications via Computer Settings, which is an absolute prerequisite for obtaining suitable flexibility in spreading the applications, isn't possible.

In fact, the beta 1 version of Group Policy Editor leaves many unanswered questions regarding the functions that already are present, because they are addressed only peripherally. Also, some of these functions don't work as they should.

Finally, Microsoft has declared that the Group Policy Editor will be integrated with the Directory Service Manager snap-in. From the point of view of the administrator, it will function as an independently integrated part of Active Directory.

Mirroring The PC Onto The Server—IntelliMirror

In simple terms, IntelliMirror is a new cache system that has the entire network as its field of activity. It uses the local disk as a cache.

IntelliMirror functions like this: The built-in network redirector of NT 5.0 keeps a copy of the most frequently used network files on the hard disk of the local PC. When the user wants to use a specific network file, the redirector checks whether a copy of it already exists on the local system, and if so, whether the copy is absolutely identical to the network file. If they are identical, the local copy is used. This process saves time and bandwidth. If the files are not identical, the redirector retrieves the file from the network and updates the local copy.

This is precisely how the existing cache systems operate. The new addition is that if IntelliMirror discovers that the requested network resources are inaccessible, because the network is down or the PC has been taken off the network, the network redirector simply takes the requested file from the cache. This means that losing data because of operational failure on the network is no longer possible. Nor do you have to bother carrying the latest files home on your portable PC—you no longer have the hassle of updating the Briefcase.

Regarding portable PCs, IntelliMirror not only remembers the file name, but it also remembers the full UNC name, which means that the user always uses precisely the same file indicator, regardless of whether the PC is logged on to the network. This also means that IntelliMirror is always able to find its way back to the original file when the PC is logged on to the network again.

The IntelliMirror facilities are also the reason why, as of NT 5.0, Microsoft is trying to convince users that they should always save their data in the My Documents directory on the desktop. The My Documents directory is physically placed on the server, which means that it is always accessible to a user, regardless of which PC the user is logging in from. Immediately after the user logs on, the network redirector automatically copies to the client all their documents from the server directory.

IntelliMirror gives full support to users who move among different PCs or use PCs that are logged on to the network only part of the time—and IntelliMirror offers an improvement that actually is tangible to users.

One problem exists with IntelliMirror regarding NT 5.0 beta 1: Its facilities aren't implemented yet. So, predicting whether IntelliMirror will function as intended, or how far the cache system can be extended, currently is impossible.

Microsoft claims IntelliMirror makes changing PCs possible for a user, without the user noticing any difference in the access to network resources between the two PCs. So far, determining whether this requires a strong standardization of the computer and user settings through the Group Policy Editor, combined with the caching of files in My Directory, is impossible. Microsoft may have something new and smarter up its sleeve.

Windows Scripting Host

As with Windows 98, NT 5.0 has built-in support of *scripts* (the Windows name for *batch files*), something most experienced administrators have missed in the Windows environment. Until Windows 98 and NT 5.0 appeared, DOS batch files were the only method with which to carry out scripts in Windows.

NT 5.0 can handle scripts from the graphical user interface (through the wscript.exe program) and from the command line (via the cscript.exe program). So, you can start a particular script by double-clicking the script file in Explorer or by typing the name of the script on the command line.

Visual Basic Scripting Edition (VBScript) and JavaScript (JScript) render immediate support. However, Windows Scripting Host (whose starting/stopping options are shown in Figure 8.7) is designed in an open way, independent of language, so that expanding it to handle other scripting languages allegedly will be possible. On several occasions (including NT 5.0's Help facilities) Microsoft has hinted that scripting solutions would be designed by third-party suppliers for Perl, TCL, REXX, and Python.

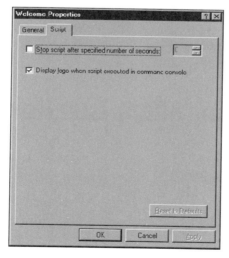

Figure 8.7
Currently, only two comparatively simple settings exist for the Windows Scripting Host. You have access to these settings by entering Properties on the shortcut menu for a script file or by starting the wscript.exe program.

Windows Scripting Host is designed as an executable component that calls the script interpreter (which so far can be either VBScript or JScript), which takes the form of an ActiveX control. Windows Scripting Host is supported by all the fundamental facilities in both scripting languages, including subroutines, functions, variables, strings, if...else clauses, and other flow-control statements.

Scripting Host also contains several new functions that can be called from scripts. These functions (implemented as methods of a special Shell object) enable scripts to create, read, write, and delete entries in the Registration database; create and change Windows shortcuts, directory network drives, and network printers; and even retrieve and change values stored in the DOS environment variables. Moreover, scripts that show dialog boxes with text and key buttons will be possible, as will be the capability to detect which key button was pressed. In other words, scripts can be made interactive.

Scripting Host scripts can also start other applications, scripts, and traditional batch files. Likewise, they can control applications supported by ActiveX scripting (such as Internet Explorer, Word, Excel, and PowerPoint).

The only shortcoming of Windows Scripting Host is that no built-in functions are provided to handle files. This means that the usability of scripts for purely administrative tasks is very limited, which is why Microsoft emphasizes so strongly that script facilities are a supplement to the facilities in Microsoft SMS.

On the other hand, Microsoft is truly trying to make system administration much easier through the script facilities. As previously stated, Microsoft wants to make adding scripts possible to practically any common event on all the clients covered by the NT 5.0 directory tree.

Improved User Administration

The hierarchical Active Directory service in NT Server 5.0 means that administering users, print queues, and so forth will be easier, because Active Directory enables you to have all network resources in one place and structure them logically.

However, an MMC superstructure seems to be missing that would allow users to simultaneously create, close, and correct several objects in the Active Directory from one management tool. While this small problem can be solved by designing some simple scripts in JScript or VBScript, operated through ADSI (which Microsoft has actually designed some demonstration copies of), Microsoft should provide NT 5.0 with some additional easily accessible facilities.

NT 5.0 offers a few more initiatives to reduce TCO. The first of these initiatives, designed to reduce costs for user support, is Active Directory Client User Interface. One of the most immediate results of this user interface is that it introduces a new directory in the Network Neighborhood, called Directory. (You can change the name to something more fitting.) This directory allows you to browse the whole directory tree, as shown in Figure 8.8.

But going down a directory tree to find resources is not very efficient. Certainly not if the tree contains more than 100 objects. This is why Microsoft has introduced a new Find category, accessible from the Start menu, to search *In the Directory* (see Figure 8.9). The In the Directory search enables you to find certain objects (users and groups, computers, printers, and so on) in part of or the whole directory tree. Figure 8.10 shows an example of a Find Printers—where print speed, color, paper size, double-side capability, and resolution can all be parameters of the search. The new Find options allow for searching based upon dates, file sizes, and text within files. You also may design some common findings and save them, so that all users can benefit from them.

These strong search capabilities are also used with the Add Printer Wizard and the Windows Address Book, which enables you to gather email addresses and other relevant address information in one spot. Windows Address Book enables you to structure the user data into groups and carry out findings on any LDAP-compatible

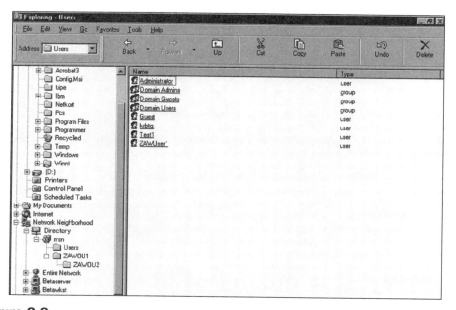

Figure 8.8
The Network Neighborhood in NT 5.0 has a new directory item added. This directory gives access to browse the entire directory tree.

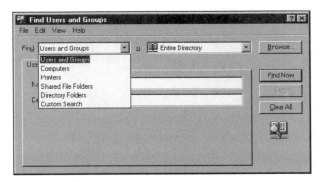

Figure 8.9
In the Directory, searches are easy and straightforward solutions for ordinary users.

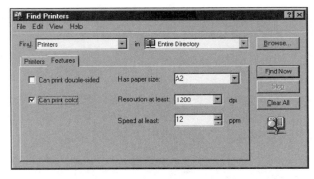

Figure 8.10
Some specialized parameters of the Find Printers command for printers.

directory service. For example, Outlook Express (which is LDAP-compatible) automatically looks for Find searches in the Address Book.

For businesses that operate in several countries, NT 5.0 is also truly multilingual. Microsoft can back up its claim that the API and the NT 5.0 program code are the same, irrespective of country. Built-in support is included in the standard version of NT 5.0 for the most common languages and type styles, as well as transparent support display and data input from various languages. Microsoft hopes that independent program manufacturers will seize this opportunity to create international versions of their software.

Honestly: It Is Much Better

As previously stated, the ZAW facilities in NT 5.0 are based on two cornerstones: facilities with which to install or update applications, and facilities to monitor the mirroring of settings onto every single PC (which will be possible largely via scripts).

Although Microsoft's overall philosophy regarding NT 5.0 is established, numerous unresolved issues remain in NT 5.0 beta 1 regarding the practical implementation of the technologies. Beta 1 contains only part of the facilities for installing and updating applications, and no IntelliMirroring whatsoever. Moreover, the possibilities of testing the facilities for administering applications are quite limited, because presently, no tools are offered with which to develop the Microsoft Install files (MSI files), which are a prerequisite for assigning and publishing applications.

Having studied the client-side items that Microsoft is planning, I fully appreciate why Microsoft speaks about NT 5.0 as the most important Windows operating system ever. Although foreseeing the full impact of Microsoft's facilities for automated installation of applications is impossible (especially the installation of new versions and corrections to the applications, as many shortcomings still exist in NT 5.0 beta 1), Microsoft certainly is going to succeed in substantially reducing TCO.

TCO is bound to improve for the following reasons:

- Introducing and administering policies for users and computers is much easier.

- Built-in facilities are provided for automated or semiautomated installation of applications, operating systems updates, and so forth.

- Design scripts are included to operate in Windows or from a command line.

- Mirroring the vital parts of clients' PC data (and possibly their settings) on the server is much easier.

You can add to this list the enhanced network operation of NT 5.0, greatly enhanced security facilities, and many other details discussed in depth in the following chapters.

The size of the total IT costs and operating clients will vary a great deal (as will how much the improvements will be reflected on the bottom line of the IT department, which, after all, is what is of the greatest interest). Remember that estimating optimum TCO results assumes that a business uses NT Server 5.0 and NT Workstation 5.0 on all PCs, which is bound to be a very powerful future selling point for both NT 5.0 versions. Conversely, this will be a source of irritation in many IT environments in which such a radical change is impossible to implement. Gauging the advantages that might be reaped by having a business change to NT 5.0 is not easy, because the efficiency of IT environments varies. I leave it to you to judge whether the decrease in TCO will be dramatic or just comfortable.

More Emphasis On Network Communication

Microsoft's introduction of Active Directory and its desire to establish NT as the ideal platform for distributed data processing have profoundly influenced the design of the network components of NT 5.0.

Probably the biggest upheaval is that Microsoft has retired WINS and is now focusing on Dynamic DNS (DDNS) for name resolution in TCP/IP environments. A second and almost equally big upheaval is that the present NT LAN Manager (NTLM) security methodology has been replaced with Kerberos. Finally, NT 5.0 is furnished with a functionality that supports the use of NT Server as an advanced network router.

NT 5.0 is certainly full of innovations, the common denominator of which is that Microsoft has started in earnest to concentrate on TCP/IP, which is in the process of being approved within the framework of the Internet Engineering Task Force (IETF), who are trying to implement changes to reduce protocol errors and unnecessary network traffic. Some elements of Microsoft's use of TCP/IP appear in Winsock 2, the Resource Reservation Protocol (RSVP), and tunneling. In addition, Microsoft has given the current NDIS architecture a series of expansions in functionality, including built-in support of Asynchronous Transfer Mode (including the vital LAN Emulation standard for using ATM on ordinary LANs) and many other intricacies of various familiar components.

The fairly simple conclusion to be drawn from these events is that Windows NT Server is seriously delving into the brave and ever-changing world of networking.

The Same Network Client?

The network client of NT Workstation 5.0, accessible through the network application in the Control Panel, offers the same basic functionality as the network client in

NT Workstation 4.0. Some things have been moved about among the five tabs in the network client program (Identification, Clients, Services, Protocols, and Bindings), which more-seasoned NT users may find frustrating, because many other things still look the same. Additionally, some changes have been made regarding the selection of facilities on the Protocols and Services screens. The available options from the Protocols screen are shown in Figure 9.1. The options available on the Services screen are Admission Control Service, ATM ARP/MARS Service, Dial-Up Server, File and Print Services, Roster, and SAP Agent.

The Services screen in NT 5.0 has fewer selections than in NT 4.0, which is due to the removal of many minor (but valuable) service programs—the contents in the tabs have been restructured and part of the service programs have been moved to the new Networking Options item in Windows NT Setup.

NT Workstation

The network client in NT Workstation 5.0 is basically the same as in 4.0. The only real difference is that NT 5.0 completely cuts its ties to the past by using TCP/IP as the standard setup. IPX/SPX is mentioned only with regard to its use as a connection to NetWare, and NetBEUI is mentioned only because you may need to use it to contact any Microsoft networks that use this protocol, and because its use is considered standard on minor networks with 1 to 200 clients.

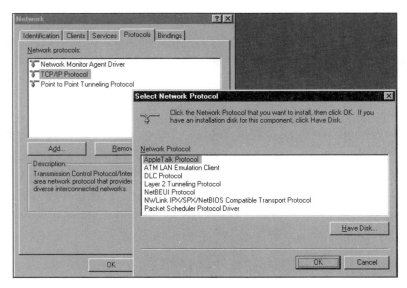

Figure 9.1
The new network protocols that are available in NT 5.0, accessed through the Network application in the Control Panel.

In conjunction with using TCP/IP as its standard protocol, Microsoft has done a lot to optimize the performance of the TCP/IP protocol stack. Furthermore, the new security facility for TCP/IP, IP Security, is introduced with a tunneling technology, Layer 2 Tunneling Protocol (L2TP), to establish the virtual Point-to-Point Tunneling Protocol (PPTP), which already is used in some of Cisco's network components.

NT Server

The changes in the TCP/IP protocol stack for NT Workstation 5.0 are nothing compared with the changes to NT Server 5.0. The vital TCP/IP infrastructure components for name resolution and security checks have been exchanged with some new technologies. (The old technologies are retained for backward-compatibility.)

Another exciting change is that all protocol stacks are being reprogrammed to be Plug and Play, which means that you can start and stop all protocol stacks in NT 5.0 without having to restart the computer. This is especially useful on servers and certainly is an added pleasantry on clients. You can add protocols such as TCP/IP or NetBEUI without having to reboot the server for them to take effect. This is just one of the many features that Microsoft has focused on to prevent unnecessary reboots, which require business applications to shut down. The more uptime systems can get in Windows NT 5.0, the more competitive it will be with other operating systems.

The ACPI power management facilities are intended to establish automatic wakeup of the system when a network packet arrives—regardless of whether the packet is from a LAN or an asynchronous line. This functionality enables clients to handle faxing and similar tasks in a more convincing, economical manner than is currently possible. This is especially true for laptop and palmtop computers, for which saving energy is important.

From WINS To DDNS

When you use TCP/IP as the primary network protocol in a Windows environment, you must have a unique IP address and a unique computer name. In addition, you must have access to *name resolution*, a mechanism that places computer names together with IP addresses, so that you can find an IP address from a computer name.

So far, Windows environments have used two very different naming conventions: NetBIOS and Domain Name System (DNS). Each of these two conventions use their own name-resolution mechanisms: Windows Internet Naming Service (WINS) and DNS, respectively.

The previous versions of NT Server required NetBIOS in order to have access to the services for sharing files and printers. If you wanted to use TCP/IP as a basic protocol in a Windows environment, NetBIOS had to be used over TCP/IP, and thus WINS had to be implemented, which was pretty frustrating because practically all other TCP/IP-based services (for example, the Internet) are based on DNS. But NT 5.0 marks the end of the NetBIOS era (which goes back to the LAN Manager product). NetBIOS and WINS are incorporated in NT 5.0 only to ensure backward-compatibility.

NT 5.0 will be using only one naming convention: DNS. Microsoft wants to offer dynamic allocation of names, so that a computer name can be registered when the client logs on, instead of manually creating all computer names in a database. To offer dynamic allocation, Microsoft introduces an entirely new version of DNS, called Dynamic DNS (DDNS).

To better serve countries that use more special characters than exist in the English alphabet, Microsoft introduces the *Unicode font* in DDNS. However, this decision has one serious drawback: The Unicode font has compatibility problems with standard DNS and DDNS implementations that are designed to use the English character set exclusively.

Like its predecessors, NT Server 5.0 contains the Dynamic Host Configuration Protocol (DHCP) Server program for dynamic allocation of IP addresses. The DHCP is an extremely efficient method for removing all challenges with TCP/IP setups, as users only have to state that they use DHCP, whereupon all TCP/IP setups are automatically read into their desktop computer. DHCP also enables you to alter TCP/IP setups on the network at a later time—which is becoming even more important in this rapidly changing world.

NT 5.0 DHCP Server contains the same functionality offered in NT Server 4.0 with Service Pack 2, which means that support now exists for superscopes. *Superscopes* enable you to group several scopes as a single administrative entity, thus enabling you to do the following:

- Use many different logical IP subnets on the same physical subnet

- Handle remote DHCP clients on the other side of BOOTP/DHCP relay agents, where the network on the other side of the relay agent also uses several logical IP subnets

You can read more about the transition from NetBIOS to pure TCP/IP—and thus about moving from WINS to DDNS—in Chapter 12.

Brave New Security

The shift from NetBIOS has also resulted in major changes in the authentication of network logons. Previously, security covering network logons was based on a variation of the NT LAN Manager authentication system (NTLM), which, as the name implies, has been present since the days of LAN Manager. NTLM is a bit inefficient—and quite hopeless at attaining a high level of security in distributed environments.

Consequently, the NTLM authentication system is being replaced in NT 5.0 with Kerberos, which is also a standard from the TCP/IP environment. Kerberos uses passwords for authentication, which makes establishing transitive trust relations—a vital part of NT 5.0's network infrastructure—fairly straightforward (see Chapters 13 and 14 for more information).

Lately, Microsoft's praise for Kerberos has been decreasing proportionally to Microsoft's increasing interest in public-key authentication. Yet Kerberos is the standard security system in NT 5.0, although you may be able to choose an X.509-compatible public-key authentication as an alternative. Kerberos is of special interest in connection with the NT 5.0 facilities for handling Smart Cards (which remove the main drawback with public-key systems: incredibly long passwords).

Chapter 11 takes a closer look at the many new security facilities in NT 5.0, including Kerberos and the public-key systems.

Admission Control Services

Admission Control Services (ACS) is one of the most significant innovations among NT 5.0's Services. ACS is Microsoft's first attempt to meet the need of current networks to reserve bandwidth for tasks that require more than just high reliability, such as transmitting multimedia that requires a constant bandwidth with few out-of-order packets and a low packet loss.

ACS enables applications that meet IETF's Quality of Service (QOS) standards to reserve a bandwidth or state a priority for their data transmissions. NT's built-in Winsock 2 interface establishes the conventions that applications need in order to negotiate the level of service required for parameters such as bandwidth and latency time. The facilities are accessible for programmers through Winsock's Generic Quality of Service (GQOS) APIs.

> **Note:** *Windows Sockets (Winsock) is an Application Programming Interface (API) that places itself between the protocol stack and the application, making both parts mutually independent, so that applications developers don't need to design for any specialties in the different implementations of the Windows TCP/IP protocol stack. Winsock is not a protocol, but rather an interface. Sockets originated in BSD Unix and was later adapted for Windows through Windows Sockets. A vast majority of the current TCP/IP applications for Windows, such as Telnet and FTP, use Winsock as a basis for their network communications. Winsock 2 was originally introduced in NT 4.0, but has become popular only recently.*

Likewise, ACS is a valuable tool for attaining more efficient use of the bandwidth that is accessible on a given subnet. ACS may be used to avoid more traffic being sent out than the subnet can handle. This may occur with applications that use a large bandwidth, such as multimedia that has live images and high-quality sound.

Importantly, ACS is the first phase in Microsoft's QOS strategy, which means that some facilities are still lacking and it isn't very user-friendly in its implementation. The ACS Properties card is shown in Figure 9.2. So far, ACS is limited to one subnet. ACS doesn't function in all routed environments, because this requires the router implementation of RSVP to have Subnet Bandwidth Manager (SBM) support, which is hardly the case for all routers.

ACS is operated by installing the Admission Control Services program on an NT 5.0-based system that is placed on the relevant subnet. On this ACS server, you state the parameter area for the various setups (including which TCP/IP subnet is the relevant one). You can define several ACS servers on the same subnet. All QOS reservation messages from clients and servers on the subnet are then sent to a specified primary ACS server, and any additional ACS servers function solely as backups for the active server.

Note: *The value of the Election Priority field determines which ACS server is the primary ACS server. The machine with the highest Election Priority is the winner.*

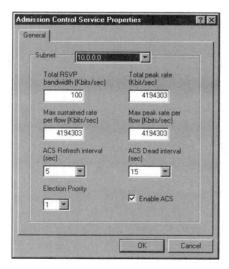

Figure 9.2
Setting up an ACS actually is quite simple, requiring "only" that you understand the special language it uses.

After the ACS server is fully installed, all the added NT 5.0 (and other) clients with an SBM-compliant network client can issue QOS requests to reserve bandwidth. The ACS server handles these reservations on a first come, first served basis. Thus, if no bandwidth remains, all subsequent reservation requests are turned down. Such a situation may occur if a few clients take up unreasonably large sections of the bandwidth.

The allocation of network bandwidth occurs by transmitting RSVP reservations from the ACS server. RSVP is a signaling protocol that enables a particular sender and receiver to establish between them the QOS route they want to use. The ACS server ensures that the RSVP message requesting the reservation of bandwidth is circulated to all routers and switches placed between the sender and the receiver, provided that the ACS server has approved the request.

RSVP has to be refreshed occasionally if the reserved bandwidth is to be maintained, because all reservations are kept in a "soft state" on the routers, meaning that they may change dynamically and are not hard-coded. This is important because topologies are likely to change often, and the soft-state design protects against transmission losses. Incidentally, RSVP is independent of protocol and is tailored for efficient handling of reservations for unicast (one-to-one communication) and multicast (one-to-many communication) traffic. So far, in an NT 5.0 environment, QOS can be used only with the TCP/IP protocol, because that is the only protocol ACS is capable of handling.

Extra Security On Network Packets

Another, equally exciting new facility, IP Security, is placed far away from the Network program. Microsoft has chosen to make IP Security accessible only through an MMC snap-in, based on the assumption that this facility must always be under the administrator's full control and close surveillance.

IP Security enables you to introduce strong encryption of network communications for the entire organization, or selected parts of it. Users won't notice this encryption on the packet level, nor will the encryption increase administrative costs significantly, because implementation is performed transparently by creating actual security policies for network communications. These security policies are stored in Active Directory and are made part of the policy regarding domains, which means that the security policy is allocated to all desktop computers that log on to the domain.

IP Security is based on Request for Comment (RFC) standards developed by the IETF IP Security taskforce (IPSEC). In the future, the NT 5.0 facilities for ensuring TCP/IP communication are likely to harmonize with other clients and servers. You will find a more in-depth discussion of IP Security in Chapter 11.

RRAS: Routing And Much Better RAS

Remote Access Service (RAS) has changed its name to Routing and Remote Access Service (RRAS) in NT Server 5.0. This name change shouldn't surprise NT observers, because RRAS already exists for NT 4.0 as an extra program component that can be downloaded from Microsoft's Web site. The functionality of routing in NT 5.0 beta 1 is identical to its functionality in NT 4.0. Whether this will apply to the final version of NT 5.0 is unclear.

 Keep in mind that RRAS occasionally operates under the name Windows NT Router (for example, when installing Services), which may be confusing.

RRAS offers high-caliber routing facilities: NT Router is supported by TCP/IP with Open Shortest Path First (OSPF)—to save bandwidth it sends only the transfer routing information that is new since the last transfer; Routing Information Protocol (RIP 1), which will be replaced with OSPF in the future protocols; and DHCP Relay Agent for IP. Figure 9.3 shows the protocol functionality. Routing of IPX/SPX with IPX RIP and IPX Service Advertising Protocol (SAP) is also possible. Additionally, access exists to some good packet-filtration facilities and an API, enabling third-party developers to add more functionality onto the product.

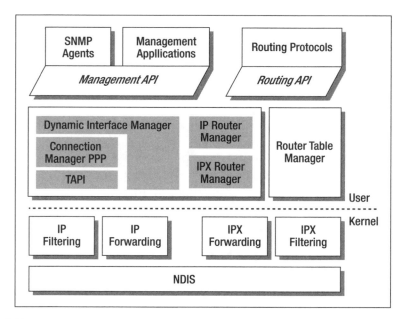

Figure 9.3
Windows NT Router contains both IPX and IP functionality.

Windows NT Router can operate on practically any network medium (from Ethernet and ATM, to Frame Relay, X.25, modems, and ISDN), with the possibility of demand-dial routing on WAN lines. The routing facilities are given support by Simple Network Management Protocol (SNMP) version 1-based management. The Router's user interface is shown in Figure 9.4.

Microsoft allegedly is working on incorporating Network Address Translation (NAT) and multicasting as fundamental parts of the operating system. However, no trace of such functionality exists in NT 5.0 beta 1.

The RAS facilities are revamped in NT Server 5.0. RAS is now supported by the Extensible Authentication Protocol (EAP), Bandwidth Allocation Protocol (BAP), and RRAS-prepared user profiles. EAP supports the introduction of new authentication methods in RAS, which is particularly interesting with regard to token-card security mechanisms. BAP provides the capability to dynamically add or eliminate extra links as required (which is relevant only when you use NT's multilinking facilities). The administrator must specify when and which multilink lines will be closed or added.

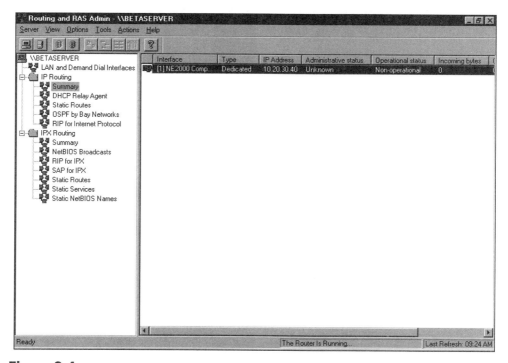

Figure 9.4
Windows NT Router is equipped with an easily accessible user interface, so configuring NT Server 5.0 to also act as a router is easy.

Finally, NT 5.0 offers a couple of features regarding tunneling, to establish virtual networks across unsafe networks (for example, the Internet). NT 5.0 is furnished with Layer 2 Tunneling Protocol (L2TP) and Point-to-Point Tunneling Protocol (PPTP). Likewise, NT Server 5.0 PPTP is furnished with facilities that enable you to define tunnels between servers (see Figure 9.5). Previously, it was only possible to use PPTP in client-to-client server setups.

> **Note:** A tunnel consists of a stream of network packets (with the information you want to exchange between two desktop computers), an encryption of these packets, and a transfer between two desktop computers of these encrypted packets as ordinary network packets. When these network packets reach the receiver, they are decrypted, and then processed in the normal way. Tunneling makes using the Internet secure when you need to transfer security-critical network communications.

More TAPI

NT 5.0 contains the new Telephony API (TAPI) version 3.0, shown in Figures 9.6 and 9.7. TAPI is Microsoft's interface for integrating different kinds of telephone-based solutions with Windows-based networks, so that one or more clients communicate with a server that functions as a gateway for the telephone network of the business. For

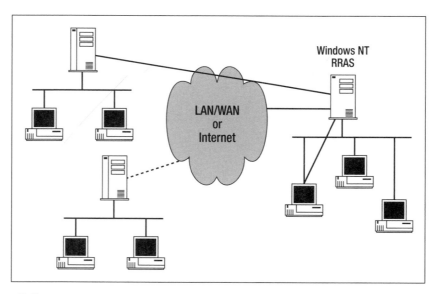

Figure 9.5
The Point-to-Point Tunneling Protocol (PPTP) in NT 5.0 has been expanded with server-to-server communication, so that secure tunnels now may be created for communication with local clients, between two servers, or to remote clients.

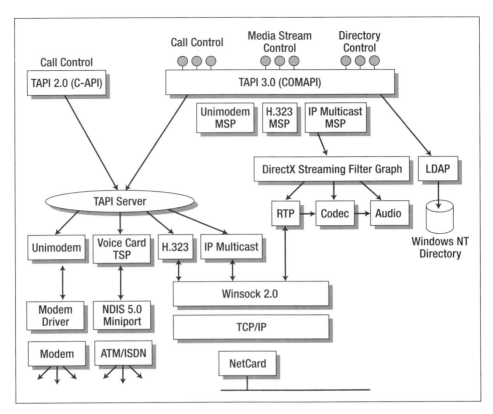

Figure 9.6
Microsoft's architectural diagram for TAPI 3.0. If you spend some time studying the diagram, you will discover that it isn't nearly as difficult as it might first appear.

instance, TAPI enables a business to integrate desktop computers with telephone functions, such as transfer of calls, voicemail, identification of calls, and telephone conferences.

Allegedly, NT 5.0 contains the technologies necessary to make a multimedia-equipped computer act precisely like a telephone unit. Support is provided from both Microsoft H.323 TAPI Service Provider and Microsoft IP Conferencing Service Provider, which means that any TAPI-prepared applications can use these two services. In addition, TAPI 3.0, like its predecessor, is furnished with a Unimodem driver with support for VoiceView modems (in other words, the capability to transfer voice and data simultaneously, and for the modem to answer voice calls).

H.323 is an International Telecommunications Union (ITU) standard for multimedia communication across networks. The standard version covers the control of calls, management, and the administration of bandwidth for point-to-point and multipoint conferences.

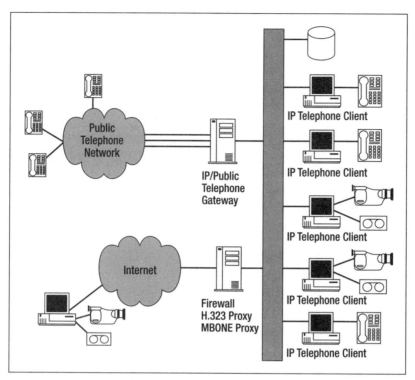

Figure 9.7
An example of how Microsoft expects to profit from TAPI within the business.

IP Conferencing is based on the capabilities of NT 5.0 using TCP/IP multicasting and the IETF Session Description Protocol (SDP) standard to announce IP multicast conferences on networks. The SDP descriptions are stored in Active Directory (more closely determined in the Internet Location Service Conference Server).

Microsoft's goal is to implement TAPI and IrDA (an infrared device) such that just one connection can handle living images, sound, and data. (IrDA uses infrared equipment to handle communication among several desktop computers, and on a level that is equal with other types of network communication.) In fact, Microsoft is approaching its goal with its introduction of Active Directory, which enables you to call a person through the network just as easily as by telephone.

Microsoft now needs a "killer application" to demonstrate the concrete value of their new design in order for it to gain general acceptance in the real world. NetMeeting has long been selected to fill this role. NetMeeting is used for teleconferencing over the Internet including audio/visual, chat session, and even an electronic whiteboard to share information. Yet, whether NetMeeting will fulfill Microsoft's hopes is far from certain, as there are many similar competing products out there.

Many New TCP/IP Details

As stated earlier, Microsoft has added various facilities to the Windows NT TCP/IP stack, which sounds promising, because although the previous TCP/IP protocol stack generally was very sensible, it wasn't complete in the minor details. This was perhaps due to Microsoft not yet understanding the logic underlying some of the finer parts of the TCP/IP protocol when it designed the original TCP/IP protocol stack for Windows NT. Hopefully, the new facilities Microsoft has added to its TCP/IP stack will round out the minor details so that it meets users' expectations.

Most importantly, DHCP support of the TCP/IP stack has been enhanced with regard to handling problems when allocating IP addresses from a DHCP server. If NT 5.0 is configured to fetch its IP address from a DHCP server, but can't make contact with any DHCP server, it will automatically invent an IP address—without bothering the user. This principle, called *autonet addressing*, is an enormous step forward, because the typical user doesn't understand DHCP errors. Previously, a DHCP error caused the desktop computer to be unable to connect to the network if the standard protocol on the network was TCP/IP.

Autonet addressing's self-allotted IP address lies in the private class A address compartment, version 10.x.x.x, which doesn't interfere with the Internet. Thus, communication is possible with any other desktop computers on the same subnet that also have a 10.x.x.x address. The TCP/IP stack chooses an IP address that isn't already occupied by another unit. This address is used until the TCP/IP stack detects a DHCP server, at which time it reserves a new TCP/IP address.

The autonet addressing principle not only behaves with more fault tolerance on the network, but it also behaves intelligently when it is quickly linked to two desktop computers. This makes the TCP/IP stack vastly easier to handle on small, peer-to-peer networks, because you no longer need to carry out any kind of configuration of the IP setup, unlike NetBEUI and IPX.

Allegedly, the DHCP support is also equipped with better handling and detection of conflicts in address allocation (the desktop computer doesn't crash; it just asks the DHCP server to allocate it to another IP address).

In addition, the new TCP/IP protocol stack is equipped with the following three new facilities that enhance the performance of the protocol:

- *Large window support*—Enhances TCP/IP performance when large amounts of data are en route (meaning they haven't yet been approved through acknowledgment packets) between two computers over a relatively long period of time. In communications based on TCP/IP, the *size of the window* (the maximum number of packets that can be sent in an uninterrupted sequence before an acknowledgment for the first packet in the sequence must be received) must, as a rule, be of a stable size. This is determined when the communication session is established between the two systems. Large window support enables the window size to be recalculated dynamically, so that the size can be increased during lengthy sessions in which large packets are transmitted. This facility means that several packets can be underway on the network simultaneously, thus enhancing the system's utilization of the effective bandwidth.

- *Selective acknowledgment*—This facility enables the network to overcome a congestion situation—or any kind of temporary disturbances—much more easily. Selective acknowledgment enables the receiver to receive a second time only those packets that cause problems on the sender's system. In earlier TCP/IP implementations, all the TCP packets sent after the erroneous TCP packet had to be retransmitted. Selective acknowledgment can restrict retransmission to the defective TCP packets only, thus increasing the effective bandwidth of the network.

- *Improved RTT estimation*—You can achieve enhanced performance by stipulating more precisely the Round Trip Time (RTT) interval, which is the time one packet takes to go from the sender to the receiver and back to the sender. TCP/IP performance depends on you knowing how long you have to wait for a packet, which is why more-precise RTT estimation brings about enhanced timeout values for the systems. This means you don't have to request to have a packet retransmitted too soon. The sophisticated RTT-estimation capability is particularly valuable on networks with high RTT.

Furthermore, the TCP/IP stack apparently is being furnished with support for Fast Retransmission and Fast Recovery of TCP attachments that experience loss of IP packets on the network. This mechanism enables the TCP sender to quickly detect a loss of a single packet, through special use of double acknowledgments of a dispatched TCP/IP packet. This mechanism is particularly useful when the network is congested. The principle of Fast Retransmission and Fast Recovery is simply that the sender retransmits just the latest TCP/IP packet that has not received an acknowledgment, thus avoiding having to enter TCP slowly—because one packet was lost. This generates better TCP/IP performance on the network, which is congested at certain intervals (for example, the Internet and most private WAN lines).

Finally, the TCP/IP stack offers support of multicast routing protocols such as Internet Group Management Protocol version 2 (IGMP), which currently has the status of a Draft suggestion, and Internet Control Message Protocol (ICMP) Router Discovery (RFC 1256), TCP large windows (RFC 1323), and Selective Acknowledgments (RFC 2018).

NDIS 5.0 And ATM Support

NT 5.0 offers a completely new version of the well known Network Device Interface Specification (NDIS) network architecture. The network-handling implementation is shown in Figure 9.8. NDIS makes up the interface between the protocol stack and the network card, ensuring that you can bind one or more protocol stacks to a variety of network cards and types of media.

NDIS 5.0 is just an extension of its predecessor. The main difference between NDIS 4.0 and NDIS 5.0 is that the new NDIS contains built-in support of ATM network cards. The interface to the network cards hasn't been changed, so existing NDIS 4.0 drivers to the network cards should continue to function well with NT 5.0. Backward-compatibility is reported to be just as good as in previous versions—Microsoft states that backward-compatibility should extend back as far as the NDIS 2.0 drivers (in other words, real-mode drivers) without any problems.

The biggest feature in NDIS 5.0 is its new and faster network technology, known as Asynchronous Transfer Mode (ATM). ATM works at a transmission speed of either 155 or 622Mbps, depending on the equipment. NDIS 5.0's inclusion of ATM should come as a welcome improvement to the many high-end users who have already started experimenting with ATM, and who have had recurrent problems with the network card producers' mutually incompatible drivers.

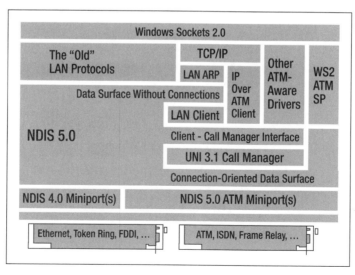

Figure 9.8
NT 5.0's implementation of network handling, including the new ATM support.

NDIS 5.0's ATM support is aimed at LAN Emulation (LANE) across ATM with User Network Interface-signaling (UNI-signaling). UNI-signaling is used to request connections on an ATM LAN. The present version of NT 5.0 uses LANE 1.0 and UNI 3.1. (Microsoft apparently doesn't intend to upgrade NDIS 5.0 to LANE 2.0 or UNI 4.0 prior to the production release of NT 5.0.) NDIS provides access to ATM through all the current LAN protocols and directly from Winsock 2. Likewise, Point-to-Point Protocol (PPP) dial-up across ATM may be performed, or TAPI applications may be developed that create and administer Virtual Circuits (VCs) on the ATM network.

Note that NT 5.0 gives the ability only to specify the ELAN name (ELAN is the Emulated LAN, used in ATM networks), which means that a LAN-Emulation Configuration Server (LECS) must be present in the ATM environment. This LECS must be configured with all ELANs accessible, as well as their associated parameters, type of media, ATM addresses for LAN Emulation Server (LES), Broadcast and Unknown Server (BUS), maximum packet size, and so on. All of this information is used by the LANE to route traffic on ATM circuits.

Services contains an ATM ARP/MARS Service (Address Resolution Protocol/Multicast Address Resolution Server), which gives you access to use TCP/IP directly across ATM—often referred to as *Classical IP and ARP over ATM*, or *MARS*, (compare RFCs 1577, 1755, and 2022). MARS is used for managing routing in clusters of ATM endpoints.

NT 5.0 enables you to use ATM in line with the more prevalent network topologies.

The following list includes some additional features hidden in NDIS 5.0:

- *NDIS power management*—This is necessary to implement Microsoft's OnNow ambition of establishing standardized handling of the increasing number of network cards that have automatic wake-up facilities.

- *Support of a single INF layout across Windows 98 and NT 5.0*—The new layout is based on Windows 95's INF files. Parts of the drivers to these two Windows platforms will continue to be different.

- *Mechanisms for transmitting some of the networklike OS tasks to the network card*—This might be the generation of TCP/IP checksum and Fast Packet Forwarding.

- *Broadcast Media extensions for handling high-velocity communication on one-way channels*—This is similar to the way in which television and radio signals are received.

- *Establishing attachment-oriented NDIS*—Previously, NDIS has been used only with attachless network technologies. However, handling attachment-oriented network technologies, such as ATM and ADSI, is now necessary.

- *Support of Quality of Service (QOS)*—Part of the Reservation Setup Protocol, QOS can guarantee that a throughput level is always reached. This is good for (among other things) customers that will be receiving network broadcasts, so that the image they receive isn't choppy.

- *Support of intermediate drivers*—Handling several layers of drivers may be necessary with broadcast services, the virtual network, arranging packets for QOS, and NDIS support of IEEE 1394 network units.

Additionally, NDIS 5.0 is prepared for Web-based management according to the Windows Management Instrumentation (WMI) standard, with its coupling with WBEM (Web-Based Enterprise Management). This will serve as a unifying method to share management information. Over 75 software and hardware vendors support WBEM.

Conclusion

Windows NT 5.0 demonstrates that Microsoft is concentrating its efforts exclusively on TCP/IP. NetBEUI is defunct, NetBIOS is included only to ensure backward-compatibility, and IPX/SPX is included to ensure smooth interaction with (and migration from) NetWare-based environments. So, the fact that NT 5.0 offers a whole range of exciting features on TCP/IP comes as no surprise. However, NT 5.0 doesn't yet contain any significant features in terms of software that processes the protocols—which are needed for NT to prove itself capable of handling distributed data processing in any type and size of IT environment. Perhaps additional features will be added in the production release of NT 5.0 for this arena, although details are not yet available.

But features aren't enough—stability and efficiency are necessary for NT 5.0 to be accepted as an efficient platform for building distributed IT environments. Whether the NT 5.0 TCP/IP protocol stack contains the requisite stability and efficiency can be answered only through time.

From Domains To Trees 10

I have said it before, and I will say it again: Active Directory is probably the biggest new feature in NT 5.0.

Active Directory is a completely new philosophy of how to view Windows NT-based solutions from the standpoint of clients, servers, and the network infrastructure. To implement Active Directory, you have to start from scratch in terms of design, implementation, and operating an NT-based IT environment. Active Directory turns the Windows NT networking world upside down. You have to start thinking in new ways when you change to Active Directory, because often you can't draw on past experience.

Understanding what systems of the future will look like—and Active Directory's important role as an NT solution in those systems—is the focus of this chapter.

This chapter begins by discussing the most important properties of *current* domain-based NT solutions, and then discusses NT solutions that are based on Active Directory. In this way, you should be able to cross the bridge between past and present, which is a prerequisite for making the transition from NT 4.0 to NT 5.0. This approach will be greatly advantageous in understanding the many new concepts and facilities of Active Directory.

After a detour in Chapters 11 and 12 to some of the other important subtleties included in NT 5.0, the discussion of Active Directory continues in Chapters 13, 14, and 15.

A Summary Of The NT 4.0 Solutions

As mentioned in Chapter 4, you shouldn't be deceived when Microsoft refers to its name service as Windows NT Server Directory Services, because it's still the same, familiar server-oriented service.

Windows NT 4.0 operates with a one-dimensional architecture in which all objects (users, print queues, servers, and so forth) are situated on the same level, which means users have to know the location of all the information and resources they need to use. Further, the network administrator has to create users on every server. The technology of *domains* enables administrators to avoid major administrative tasks by gathering all servers in the same domain, so that the user has to be created just once, in the domain.

The fundamental principles for security and administration in NT Server 4.0 are based on the same technology as in Microsoft LAN Manager. When LAN Manager was introduced in 1987, the structure was fully sufficient for administering small networks, but not for major solutions.

The establishment of desktop computers in large businesses has necessitated the introduction of server solutions that are based on PCs. These solutions are becoming more difficult to design, implement, and operate, because the technology of domains is getting older—but these difficulties can be avoided.

In domains, all resources are placed in a single, very flat area. All names in the domain must be unique, which can cause problems in large businesses that have many common employee names, such as Peter Smith and John Brown. Such name problems were solved on the Internet long ago through the use of a hierarchical name service that adds the particulars necessary to distinguish object names.

An NT 4.0 domain holds five fundamental administrative objects (shown in Figure 10.1): users, local groups, global groups, printers, and computers. New object types or object attributes can't be added to the domain database, which means master data from other server applications can't be integrated in the domain.

Thus, every application must establish its own domainlike functionality for administering users, security, and so forth. Microsoft Exchange is a good example of such an application. Even if Exchange is placed on an NT 4.0 Server, all Exchange users are defined and administered in two separate administrative databases—the domain's user database and Exchange's user database.

In an NT 4.0 domain, administrative rights to the domain's resources are granted on the basis of object type, and rights can't be granted on the basis of groups of objects or individual objects. Membership in one of the predefined NT domain groups dictates the user's administrative rights to certain types of objects in the domain.

The administration of an NT 4.0 domain is an all-or-nothing situation. The domain doesn't contain the flexibility necessary to allocate administrative rights to a partial number of objects. Therefore, you can't allocate the rights to administer a particular printer to a specific user. Instead, you have to add the user to the Print Operators group,

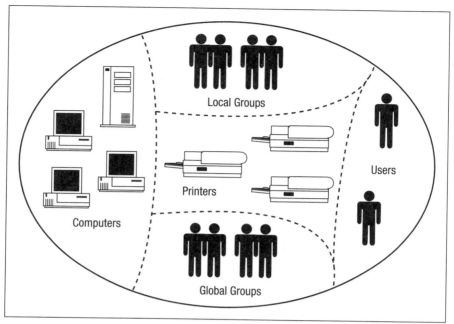

Figure 10.1
An NT 4.0 domain contains five fundamentally different types of objects. Administrative rights can be allocated only to every object type—new object types can't be "invented," nor can fields be added to existing object types.

which gives the user rights to administer all printers in the domain. The same principle applies for rights to administer users, and any other types of resources in the domain.

Trust Relations

NT 4.0 domains are independent, flat databases containing details about accounts. The original LAN Manager domain architecture didn't contain any capabilities to connect several independent domain databases. Thus, the resources in each domain had to be administered independently of one another.

Due to increasing limitations caused by the restrictions of the one-dimensional architecture of NT 4.0 (in its lack of a uniform administration for more domains), Microsoft introduced a superstructure that is based on the principle of domains, which expands the architecture so that it is two-dimensional. This attempt at repairing the fundamental problems of the principle of domains is known as *trust relations*.

A trust relation always covers two domains. Trust relations enable you to administer across several domains and allocate to users and groups in a domain the rights to resources—such as file servers and printers—that are part of the domain with which a trust relation has been created.

In short, with trust relations, users log in to their own domain only, but have access to resources in other domains that trust the user's domain (in other words, trust relations have been created). This saves the administrator from having to create the same user account in each of the domains for which the user needs to access resources. To enable users to exploit the defined trust relations, Microsoft introduced *global users* and *global groups*. Global users and global groups are the opposite of *local users* and *local groups*—the field of activity of the latter is limited to their own domain.

Two different types of trust relations exist:

- *One-way trust*—If a one-way trust relation is established that states domain B trusts domain A, then all global users and global groups in domain A are allocated rights to the resources in domain B. Because no corresponding one-way trust relation has been established from domain A to domain B, global users and global groups in domain B aren't allocated rights to resources in domain A.

- *Two-way trust*—If a two-way trust relation is established that states domain B trusts domain A, then all global users and global groups in domain A are allocated rights to resources in domain B, and vice versa.

These two types of trust relations are shown in Figure 10.2. One-way and two-way trust relations may also be combined, as shown in Figure 10.3. Here, a one-way trust has been established between the IT domain and the finance division and a two-way trust has been established between the IT domain and the human resources division. Thus, finance and human resources have full access to all the IT resources of the business, but IT only has access to the human resources division's information.

Trust relations are not *transitive*, which means that automatic delegations don't occur in the allocation of trusts. For instance, if domain B trusts domain A, and domain C trusts domain B, domain C doesn't necessarily trust domain A, even though both have established trusts with domain B. For domain A and domain C to trust one another, a specific trust relation has to be established between them.

The administrator must create trust relations manually to cover each relationship between the various domains. Thus, if a business has 9 domains that it wants to connect, so that users can be allocated resources across the domains, the administrator must create 72 two-way trust relations (9×8 trust relations). The formula with which to calculate the number of trust relations that are necessary to have all domains trust one another is fairly simple: If N is the number of domains, the administrator needs to establish $N(N-1)$ trust relations.

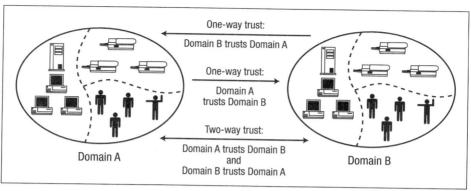

Figure 10.2
Trust relations can assume two forms: A one-way trust and a two-way trust.

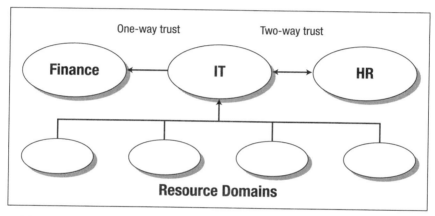

Figure 10.3
You can mix one-way and two-way trust relations, as needed.

As this formula clearly demonstrates, the number of trust relations grows exponentially as the number of domains increases. This can cause big installations to be lengthy and extremely boring tasks. For example, 100 domains requires establishing 9,900 trust relations, and 500 domains increases that figure to 249,500 trust relations, which is impossible to establish in real-world environments!

That anybody would establish a domain structure with more than 1,000 trust relations is unlikely (which would correspond to 32 domains), because the security implications would be enormous—administrative rights would have to be allocated to an unreasonable number of people, thus giving them widespread control of all the domains.

Synchronizing Domain Data

If you want to avoid single-point-of-failure locations when authenticating users under the domain login, you have to spread the domains' information efficiently to several servers. NT 4.0 Server meets this goal, because it is able to define several domain controllers for every domain. The following are the two types of domain controllers (shown in Figure 10.4):

- *Primary Domain Controller (PDC)* —The PDC can be used to authenticate users and alter the domain database. The PDC ensures that all changes to the domain database are replicated onto the BDCs of the domain. Each domain can have only one PDC.

- *Backup Domain Controller (BDC)* —The BDC can be used to authenticate users. It can't handle alterations of the domain database—such changes must be performed on the PDC. The BDC contains a full copy of the PDC database of the domain. A domain may have several BDCs.

The PDC is the heart of the domain—at any one time, the PDC holds a completely up-to-date version of the database of the domain, because all changes (creations, closures, and

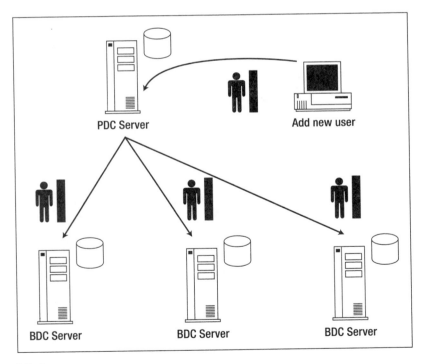

Figure 10.4
All changes to the domain database must be performed on the PDC, which then synchronizes those changes with any BDCs for the domain.

updates) in the domain must take place on the PDC. The PDC is responsible for ensuring that all information is uniform throughout the domain. The PDC does this at regular intervals by replicating all the changes on the domain's BDCs.

The division into a PDC and BDCs means that if the PDC crashes or is inaccessible, you can't alter the setups for the domain. Fortunately, users won't notice a brief problem with the PDC if one or more BDCs are present, because the BDC(s) can carry out a user login and authorize the use of resources in the domain (as well as any domains for which trust relations have been established).

If a PDC crashes for a longer period of time, however, everybody feels the effects, because the administrator can't work in the domain. In response to such situations, Microsoft built in facilities that enable a BDC to be promoted to the role of a PDC. Even so, you must use these facilities with great care, because reincorporating the previous configuration into the domain is still a challenging task in certain respects.

Microsoft defines four different domain models: the Single Domain (shown in Figure 10.5), the Single Master Domain (Figure 10.6), the Multiple Master Domain (Figure 10.7), and the Single Domain with Trust Relations. Table 10.1 shows Microsoft's calculation of each of these domain model's strengths and weaknesses (refer to the section "Domain Selection Matrix" in the *Networking Guide* from Windows NT Server 4.0 Resource Kit). Note that the number of user accounts (less than

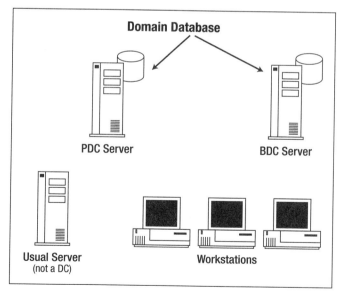

Figure 10.5
An example of a Single Domain solution.

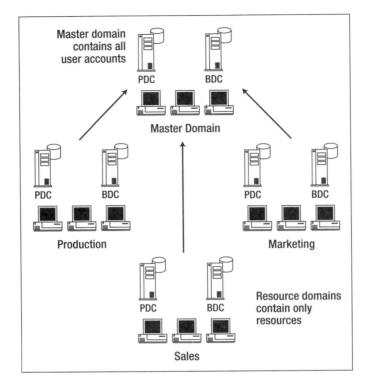

Figure 10.6
An example of a Single Master Domain solution.

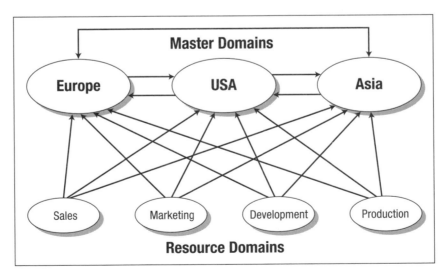

Figure 10.7
An example of a Multiple Master Domain solution.

Table 10.1 *Microsoft's four domain models and their properties.*

Property	Single Domain	Single Master Domain	Multiple Master Domain	Single Domain With Trust Relations
Less than 40,000 users	X	X	X	X
More than 40,000 users			X	
Administration of centralized user accounts	X	X		
Administration of centralized resources	X		X	X
Administration of decentralized user accounts			X	X
Administration of decentralized resources		X	X	
Centralized IT function	X	X		
Decentralized IT function				X

or more than 40,000) Microsoft provides serves only as a guide, because the precise size of the Security Account Manager (SAM) file depends on the number of user accounts, computer accounts, and group accounts.

The replication between the PDC and all BDCs in a specific domain takes place according to the *master-slave principle*, which means that the PDC (the master) replicates the same information out to every BDC (which, in this context, act as slaves). All updates of information in the domain databases of the BDCs must come directly from the PDC, although the network bandwidth might be used more efficiently if the updates came from another BDC. These problems are especially perceptible in computer environments in which the NT 4.0 domain also covers a WAN, particularly if some of the WAN locations have more than one BDC.

Master-slave replication generally isn't considered a very good solution, which is why most businesses have changed to the *multimaster principle* of replication (which NT 5.0 also uses), explained later in the chapter. The master-slave replication clearly limits the possibilities of scalability.

Restrictions

An NT 4.0 domain contains many tight restrictions. The following is a list of the most apparent restrictions:

- The number and content of the object types can't be extended, nor can you create actual integration (and hence administrative coherence) with user databases to other applications or services.

- Administrative rights can't be allocated to partial users and domains, which poses serious security risks, because users often receive more rights than they need.

- Trust relations don't solve any of the problems related to administering several domains. Despite their name, global groups must be serviced separately in each domain. Thus, administrators can't perform even the simplest of operations that span several domains, such as generating a member list for the global groups across domains, even if these domains are configured to act as one through defined trust relations.

- Print queues and other items depend on their physical placement, such that moving objects between two domains is not readily possible. They must be closed on one domain and created from scratch in the new domain, and new user and group rights must be allocated each time such a move is conducted. Nor can a disk volume be moved to another file server without changing the drive mappings on all the attached desktop computer clients.

- Microsoft's extension of the fundamental domain principle of NT 4.0 to a two-dimensional architecture doesn't solve the challenges of handling operations. Despite Microsoft's good intentions, the basic operations tasks are a nightmare in a big installation. In small installations, the nightmare isn't quite as bad, yet it is still a nightmare compared to the ideal situation.

- Replication among the domain controllers of the domain is inflexible, which might cause problems with scaling in large networks—or solutions in which the servers are separated by slow or expensive WAN lines.

- Each server can act as a domain controller only in a single domain. So, you easily can end up having many servers if you want to avoid single-point-of-failure points (which presupposes at least one BDC in every domain). In addition, you can't move the Domain Controller for a particular server between domains without going through the unpleasant process of reinstalling the operating system from scratch.

- The NT 4.0 domain structure is inflexible with regard to organizational changes. NT 4.0 Server doesn't contain the tools needed to divide and join the domain database, so altering the division of the domain is an immense task when it is first introduced. The same inflexibility applies to large upheavals within or between each section, if this requires users to move between two domains.

The Basic Philosophy Of Active Directory

I know that the many limitations of the NT domain that I just enumerated may sound like a funeral song, but this is deliberate. Although NT 4.0 has many positive aspects, you can't disregard the fact that the fundamental concept of the domain is full of problems, which makes operating the network environment more difficult than is strictly necessary.

Until NT 5.0 is released, you can't get around Windows NT 4.0 Server for strategic, tactical, economic, and technical reasons. Although NT 4.0 Server certainly isn't the optimal technical solution, it is better than its predecessor, LAN Manager.

Fortunately, NT 4.0's reign as the traditional, two-dimensional domain solution is nearly over. NT 5.0 contains a completely new three-dimensional solution known as Active Directory, which is a full directory service that completely eliminates the weaknesses of two-dimensional NT domains.

The fact that Active Directory is a full three-dimensional solution doesn't mean that domains disappear from NT 5.0. Microsoft includes domains in Active Directory to ensure backward-compatibility with the one- and two-dimensional domain-based solutions.

The four vital concepts of Active Directory are the following:

- *Domain*—The fundamental grouping of Active Directory. The domain contains numerous objects that can be structured hierarchically through Organizational Units (OUs). Moreover, an overall hierarchical structure can be established with the domains. At its foundation, the domain corresponds to the organizational idea of X.500, but the domain isn't defined in quite the same way, because you can't establish a hierarchy of organizations under the X.500 specification.

- *Organizational Unit (OU)*—Enables each domain to be split into a number of more manageable units. These administrative units are based on a hierarchical structure, making Active Directory a three-dimensional solution. The OUs of Active Directory correspond to the organizational idea of X.500, but the Active Directory OUs behave differently in a number of important respects.

- *Groups*—Collections of objects of the same type as used in the NT 4.0 domains. The idea of groups is contrary to the fundamental idea of directory services: Everything must be structured hierarchically, based on where the objects are placed in the directory tree. However, Microsoft chose to maintain groups as the fundamental basis for allocating rights to accessible resources.

- *Objects*—Objects can be a user or a resource, as in the NT 4.0 domains.

Moreover, Microsoft operates with a *site*, which is a collection of machines that are connected with fast and cheap communication equipment (this is typically a LAN). Sites are not an "ordinary" part of Active Directory (such as a namespace) as they are physical locations. But the term *site* is used frequently with regard to the design and description of Active Directory solutions, because the site is an integral part of establishing data replication environments.

Global Catalog

Active Directory introduces an entirely new philosophy, known as *Global Catalog*. Global Catalog contains all the objects from all the domains in a particular Active Directory domain tree, as well as a partial amount of the properties of each object. Inside, Global Catalog contains the same hierarchy as the domain tree.

Global Catalog can be used as a global address book (and, as such, it corresponds to Microsoft Exchange Global Address Book) for searches in the entire tree. If you can find all of the information that you are searching for in the Global Catalog, you won't need to define any LDAP references to other DCs. Note that a Global Catalog shows each user only those objects to which the user has access rights, which avoids any compromises that could occur in Active Directory's security level if all components in the domain tree were visible to everyone.

Having a Global Catalog in every site is advisable, because it provides a local place from which clients can perform all search operations. Active Directory automatically generates a Global Catalog.

Organizational Units

The OUs of Active Directory eliminate two of the tightest limitations in the current NT domain architecture, as shown in Figure 10.8. The OUs enable you to establish hierarchical naming, which supports descriptive names, such as J.SMITH. SALES.BAL.NETLOG rather than J.SMITH.

Hierarchical naming makes locating certain resources easier, because the names contain information about where the resources are placed. The capability to establish

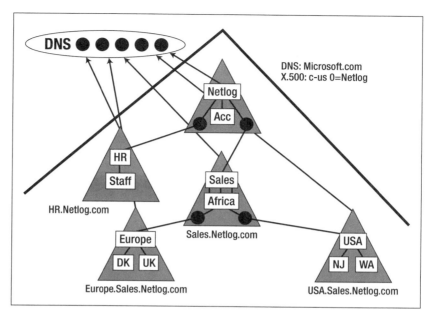

Figure 10.8
Domains enable you to establish a hierarchical domain tree on top of the hierarchical directory tree.

OUs results in improved administration, because administrative rights can be allocated based on a specific object type of the domain (previously, it was only possible to allocate to the entire domain).

In NT 5.0, administrative rights can be allocated to an entire domain, to a tree within the domain, or to a single OU. Thus, Active Directory enables you to allocate administrative rights based on a specific object or group of objects only if the object or group is placed within one or more OUs. Nor can administrative rights cover several domains, which is why Active Directory is administered as several independent domains, and not as a complete tree. This limitation makes handling Active Directory more cumbersome (and hence more expensive) than Novell NDS, for example.

Directory Schemas

Active Directory contains one other cornerstone of the X.500 model—the *directory schema*, which dictates how objects are kept in the directory. The directory schema enables new fields to be inserted in existing objects and new object types to be defined.

Active Directory uses a scaled-down version of the X.500 directory schema, consisting of object classes and attributes. The structure of Active Directory is fairly simple, containing very few rules regarding which objects are the most important and which attributes objects can contain. For instance, a user object can only contain properties associated with a user (email address, user profile, and so forth).

Rights And Heredity

Heredity in Active Directory is "by the book," meaning that all changes in the directory schema or changes to rights go into force automatically for the directory-tree level on which the change was introduced, as well as on all of its underlying levels.

Note that heredity in Active Directory is *static*, which means that the inherited changes must be included in all the objects that are covered through heredity. If many objects are covered, static heredity may generate, in extreme cases, some immense replications. This is why you should be very careful about having a domain move across a slow WAN line, and so forth. On the other hand, when working with users, static heredity causes Active Directory to be faster than a corresponding directory built on dynamic heredity.

Active Directory doesn't support using OUs as a basis for allocating resource rights, which is intentional by Microsoft, to ensure backward-compatibility with one-dimensional name services. As previously stated, Microsoft chose to maintain allocation of rights based on groups (and, if desired, a few users), even though this approach directly contradicts the fundamental concept of directory services, which states that everything must be related to the object's location in the directory tree. Consequently, administration of resources in Active Directory is more complicated than in competing directory services (such as Novell's NDS).

Microsoft probably intends to eliminate groups eventually, but completely eliminating them will require a comprehensive technical change in the core of NT (with regard to the security system). One positive note is that Microsoft's decision to maintain groups enables resource rights to be allocated across organizations, which may be practical for businesses that carry out numerous projects involving persons from many different working areas.

In my opinion, the optimum solution by Microsoft would have been to keep the concept of groups, but extend the allocation of rights to include OUs.

Please note that Active Directory can't distinguish between a local and a global group. However, support of local groups does exist (due to backward-compatibility). Yet, Microsoft recommends that you migrate to the Active Directory group objects, which is an extremely unpleasant task, because you have to repeat logon of users and rights to the resources involved.

Trust Relations With Active Directory

The concept of domains in Active Directory is very similar to that in NT 4.0. When you want to connect two Active Directory domains—such as when forming a domain tree—you do it through trust relations.

Active Directory removes the worst drawbacks of current trust relations. In Active Directory, trust relations in the domain tree are performed automatically, and the relations are *transitive*, which means that a trust exists between two domains if both have trust relations with a common intermediate domain. For example, if domain B trusts domain A, and domain C trusts domain B, then domain C also trusts domain A, even if no explicit trust has been established linking domains A and C.

By interconnecting domains in a hierarchical tree structure, corresponding to what is used for OUs, a fairly scalable and globally distributed architecture can be established. This architecture "accidentally" agrees extremely well with the fundamental principles of DNS, which was introduced as the new name service for the Active Directory environment, as shown in Figure 10.9.

The introduction of transitive trusts (shown in Figure 10.10) means that the number of trust relations necessary to create full trust throughout the domain tree is reduced from $N(N-1)$ to $N-1$, where N is the number of domains. As a result, creating large

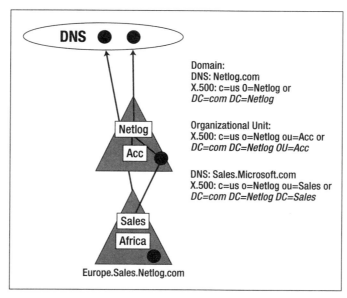

Figure 10.9

Naming in Active Directory is absolutely identical with the conventions for DNS names.

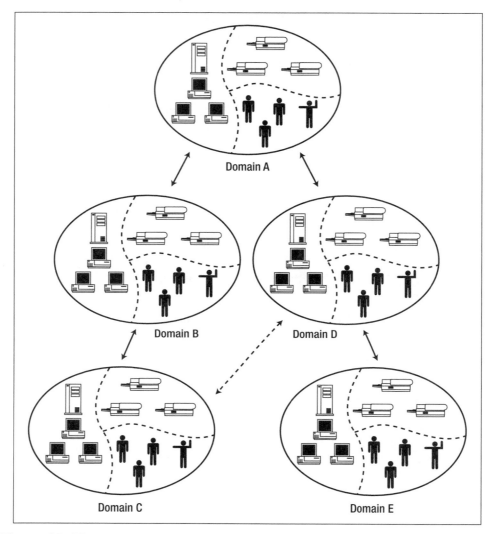

Figure 10.10
The use of transitive trust relations in Active Directory means that domain C actually trusts domains D and E—and thus is able to benefit from the resources in these domains.

domains is now feasible with NT 5.0. Taking the example from earlier in this chapter—500 domains would require 249,500 trust relations in NT 4.0 (impossible!), but now requires just 499 trusts with Active Directory. As if this isn't sufficient to create even very big domain trees, Active Directory also sets up a transitive trust relation for itself with the nearest parent domain in the domain tree (in other words, the domain that is situated immediately above the current domain) when the domain is entered into the tree.

Often, defining more than the minimal *N*-1 trust relations is wise, to obtain better performance when using resources that aren't placed immediately above or below the domain in the domain tree.

Partitioning And Replication

Novell NDS provides the capability to split the directory tree into one or more partitions, out of consideration for operating replication and limiting the extent of the replications. A partition contains a unique, partial amount of information in the directory tree, because no data may exist in more than one partition. On the other hand, you can establish an unlimited number of copies (or replicas) of each partition.

Active Directory doesn't enable you to split the directory tree into partitions. The whole tree is the smallest replication unit in Active Directory, which Novell has been quick to criticize. However, Novell's criticism doesn't seem fair, because Active Directory's capability to define domain trees from the standpoint of functionality is very comparable with NDS's partitioning facilities. Whereas NDS provides the capability to define only a single directory tree (which is based on a sophisticated tree structure consisting of organizational ideas and OUs), Active Directory enables you to define several directory trees, one for each domain.

The only real objection to working with two tree hierarchies (as in Active Directory, in which a domain hierarchy is established, and the domain also contains a directory hierarchy) rather than a single tree hierarchy (as in NDS, which has only one directory hierarchy) is that, as a rule, it requires the presence of more directory service servers.

If all single-point-of-failure locations in the directory service environment were eliminated, you would find, in most instances, that more servers with domain databases (in other words, domain controllers) would be required in solutions that are based on two tree hierarchies rather than one. To avoid single points of failure, you would need two copies of the domain database (in other words, two servers) for every single domain. Regarding partitions, you could get by with a copy for every single partition (one server per partition) and then connect all partitions at the same place (a server).

On the other hand, critics of tree hierarchies may express (with a certain degree of correctness) that this split is a more flexible and fault-tolerant solution than a tree hierarchy. The increased flexibility means that you aren't forced to use precisely the same directory schema on the various domains. And increased fault tolerance means that the domains function quite independently of one another, so that a critical problem in one domain won't affect the remaining domains (although some trust relations can break as a result).

With regard to fault tolerance, Active Directory contains a pleasant surprise compared with NT 4.0 domains: Active Directory eliminates the problem in NT 4.0 of the split into a PDC and BDCs, whereby the PDC may be a single point of failure and may be a source of performance problems for large WANs. In an Active Directory environment, only DCs are involved, which are completely equal to each other.

The change to using only DCs is a result of Active Directory's introduction of multimaster replication. *Multimaster replication* enables you to make changes to a domain on any NT 5.0 Server that contains a writeable copy of the domain database, and allows updates to the domain databases of the servers in the manner best suited for WAN lines.

As in earlier cases, the server can act as a DC only for a single domain, so you have to establish at least one DC server in every domain. In practical terms, at least two DC servers should be present in every domain, to ensure a reasonable degree of fault tolerance, should one of the DC servers become unavailable on the network.

On the other hand, you can easily promote a particular server to a DC or remove the DC component of the server. This provides greater flexibility in operating DCs than with the old NT domains.

While multimaster replication generally is considered the best replication solution in today's distributed environments, Microsoft has chosen to swim against the tide regarding the mechanism of *synchronization*, which determines which data should be replicated.

Most computers rely on time stamps as the basis for synchronization. The use of time stamps presupposes that all active units involved in the replication agree upon the exact date and time. Microsoft drops the time stamp in favor of a principle that allocates a counter to each object attribute, which is increased by one every time a change to the specific attribute occurs. Microsoft calls this counter mechanism *Update Sequence Number* (USN). If synchronization collisions occur between the USN figures (if the same attribute has been updated in two places between the latest replication), Active Directory then uses the time stamp as a "tie-breaker."

Dropping the use of time as the primary synchronization mechanism is quite a surprise, because Active Directory also uses Kerberos, which is based on all servers having a uniform perception of time. The idea isn't wrong: Replication certainly becomes more trustworthy by having two different synchronization mechanisms instead of one. However, complexity does increase. But this shouldn't be a deterrence, because administrators aren't likely to be involved in the day-to-day operations of replications, so they aren't likely to notice USNs or time stamps unless problems occur.

A Revolution—With Few Changes To The Basic Code Of NT

Although Active Directory constitutes a true revolution, regardless of your point of view, it causes remarkably few, and only minor, upheavals in the basic architecture of NT.

In NT 4.0, the domain database (whose architecture is shown in Figure 10.11) is kept in an encrypted flat file, known as the *Security Accounts Manager (SAM)*. Any interaction with the domain takes place through a special API, dubbed *NT Security (NTSEC)*.

The JET database also isn't new—it is already being used by Exchange 4.0, 5.0, and Access (in which the implementation allegedly differs somewhat from the Active Directory JET database). NT 5.0's use of the JET database instead of the Registration database to keep domain information was badly needed, because the Registration database (used to keep various operating system characteristics) is designed to store small-user and machine-specific amounts of information of a specifically defined size. Thus Registration databases lack various important functionalities of a database, such as indexing, advanced replication, and the capacity to be extended with new objects and attributes.

The shift to the JET database means that the scalability of the underlying domain information database is no longer a limiting factor. According to Microsoft, Active

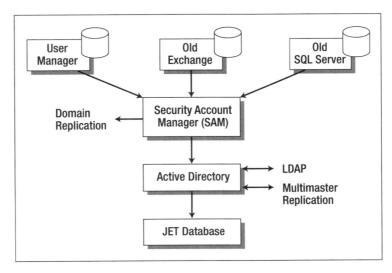

Figure 10.11
The NT domain architecture from a purely technical point of view.

Directory will be able to handle more than 1 million objects, whereas Microsoft gives an upper limit of 40,000 objects for an NT 4.0 domain.

Microsoft played it safe when developing Active Directory, adding no more new technologies in NT 5.0 than strictly necessary. The Directory Service layer (which contains the new multimaster replication service) and ADSI are the only true core operating system changes. The same is true for the security facilities, as NT 5.0 is based on precisely the same fundamental components as its predecessors: Security Descriptor (SD), Access Control List (ACL), Access Control Entry (ACE), and Security Identifier (SID). Consequently, Microsoft hasn't disturbed the all-important core security subsystem.

Microsoft introduces one other feature with Active Directory, called the *Globally Unique Identifier* (GUID). GUID, which is generated by the DC, is a very big, unique figure that is connected to each object in Active Directory. The unique GUID identifier (which can't be altered, once assigned) enables you to change the name of an object, or move it, without causing any kind of confusion in Active Directory.

The advantage of Microsoft's evident conservatism in its choice of technologies is that NT 5.0 should be absolutely reliable much sooner than if many new features had been added (especially compared to the time the transition to NT 3.5 took). Furthermore, you can continue using the familiar SAM-based solutions, if you want, until Active Directory is clearly ready to handle all the existing tasks.

And best of all, Microsoft's conservatism in its choice of technologies shows no evident disadvantages.

In Short

Directory Service is here to stay. It is a far better solution than what's available—both in theoretical and practical terms—for the challenges that network administrators encounter every day.

With Active Directory, Microsoft has produced a genuine directory service, which means that Windows NT Server 5.0 is a much more serious contender than its predecessor, NT Server 4.0, for handling very large and complex IT environments. (The difference between the directory services in the two versions is shown in Figure 10.12.) In this regard, note that Active Directory doesn't just improve the manageability of directory services, it provides a logical centralization—even if the system is physically decentralized. As such, Active Directory can act as the "glue" that binds together many distributed IT environments.

Active Directory also offers some very significant advantages to both the end user and the system developer. Some of Active Directory's most unique properties are a result of Microsoft combining the best features from DNS and X.500. Therefore, the DNS table isn't a separate database—it is placed directly in Active Directory, making Active Directory a very dynamic, safe, scalable, and easily expandable item.

Active Directory is easy to work with for software designers, because Microsoft has ensured that it is accessible on a high level of abstraction. Access to Active Directory is also possible through LDAP. This is particularly interesting for situations in which you want to communicate with other directory services, because LDAP is currently the only standard protocol that offers uniform access to many different directory services.

Finally, Microsoft designed Active Directory to be a strong and robust operational environment. Active Directory supports online backups, enabling you to return to a stable state, quickly and without the loss of data, should a crash occur. Furthermore, Active Directory enables you to replicate in a sensible manner, irrespective of the geography and bandwidth.

But don't be mistaken—Active Directory is a version 1.0 product, and thus involves a few risks and challenges, because it hasn't been implemented in a production environment. Yet Microsoft seems intent on devoting the attention necessary to Active Directory so that early bugs can be eliminated as much as possible. On several occasions, Microsoft has admitted that it is far from fulfilling its goal for Active Directory,

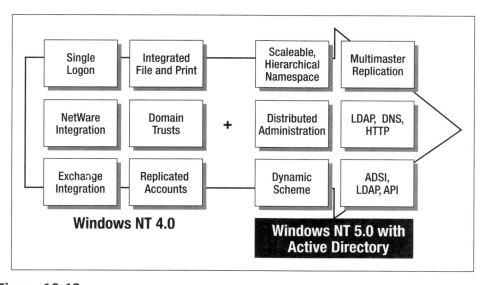

Figure 10.12
Microsoft's comparison of the Active Directory-based architecture of NT 5.0 to the "old" domain-based solution of NT 4.0.

which may be the best proof that Microsoft isn't underestimating the task before it. Only when Microsoft meets its target for Active Directory will it be ready to meet the world in earnest.

The discussion of Active Directory continues in Chapters 13, 14, and 15.

Security At Last

11

Security is a continuously discussed topic in the computer realm. Everybody understands the meaning of the word *security*—and everybody has an opinion about it, because security is fundamental for using computers in vital areas of business. Microsoft, too, has begun to talk a lot more about security, while also putting more emphasis on establishing itself in the high-end computer market.

NT 5.0 demonstrates that Microsoft is doing more than just talking. In NT 5.0, one of the leading security mechanisms previously used for authentication, NT LAN Manager (NTLM), has been replaced by a new system, Kerberos. Furthermore, a couple of new security options have been added—IP Security and an encrypted file system—and some expansions have been made to public key encryption, another vital security facility.

This chapter takes a closer look at NT 5.0's security capabilities. This chapter doesn't go into the possibilities of encrypting the NT File System (this is discussed in Chapter 16), and contains only a limited examination of the facilities for X.509-based public key encryption, because these facilities are already being used in NT 4.0 and have already been the subject of many discussions in connection with the Internet.

Kerberos: Straight From The Greek Underworld

If you delve into the mythological Greek underworld, Hades, you would be wise to show great respect for Kerberos. This three-headed dog guards Hades with six watchful eyes and many sharp teeth.

Luckily, the Kerberos of the real world is a somewhat more peaceful creature, whose task it is to guard the entrance to NT systems. Kerberos, which replaces NT LAN Manager authentication, is the new standard protocol for safe authentication of network users.

Kerberos' History

Originally, Kerberos (shown in Figure 11.1) was developed by scientists from MIT (Massachusetts Institute of Technology) in the 1980s as part of the Project Athena Network. Project Athena examined how to design, implement, and administer distributed environments. The first three Kerberos versions were used only for development and testing, which made Kerberos 4 the first version that gained popularity outside MIT. The original Kerberos program code has been accessible to the public on the Internet for many years.

Kerberos 4 has been implemented in many Unix and Internet-oriented systems, because Kerberos is one of the components in the Distributed Computing Environment (DCE) framework. As is often seen with new systems, Kerberos 4 turned out to have many restrictions. For example, Kerberos 4 was based on Data Encryption Standard (DES) encryption, the safety of which has been questioned over the years. Likewise, U.S. authorities have denied American software developers the right to export DES implementations, unless they apply for an export license for each buyer.

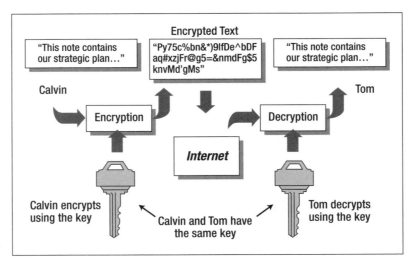

Figure 11.1
Kerberos is a shared-key encryption algorithm that is based on the use of the same password by the sender and recipient, which is why the password must not be known by other parties, if security is to be maintained.

Experience with Kerberos 4 led to the development of Kerberos 5, which, among other things, supports the use of *triple* DES encryption, as well as other encryption algorithms as needed. Kerberos 5 has been adopted as a standard by the Internet Engineering Task Force (IETF) in the form of RFC 1510. Even though many Kerberos 4-based products are still in use, the vast majority of current products (including NT 5.0) are based on Kerberos 5.

Kerberos is absolutely the most important security component in an NT 5.0-based network environment. Kerberos' authentication process is the very condition of a safe environment.

Instead of having three heads, the computer version of Kerberos offers a three-sided authentication process, with shared keys that enable network users to prove their identity, without compromising network security. Thus, Kerberos security is based on two fundamental concepts:

- *Shared keys*—The two parties involved share the same secret key, which proves that the users are indeed who they claim to be. The only prevailing "rival" for the method of shared keys is the public keys method. With public keys, one party holds two keys, one of which is publicly accessible (and is shared with those parties who should be given access to the system), and the other of which is private (and consequently is kept secret from anyone else, to maintain uncompromising security). The two keys combined can verify the identity of the user.

- *Three-sided authentication*—This authentication process involves three components:

  - The *client* (or the client application), which represents the user.

  - The *resource* that wants to make sure the client is legitimate. This resource is often a server.

  - A *central repository* with information about the clients. In most cases, the repository is a Key Distribution Center (KDC) service. The KDC database contains the identities and master keys (passwords) of all clients and servers that belong to the particular administrative domain. In Kerberos terminology, a domain is called a *realm*. To protect against unauthorized access to the data base, all master keys are encrypted with the server's private master keys, which in turn are protected by the administrator's local KDC password. You should understand that a physically secure KDC is an essential condition for an effective Kerberos security system. Sometimes, it's easier to physically steal the entire server to get the server's information than to electronically break into the KDC. This is why you should safeguard your KDC server to prevent physical theft.

Kerberos is built to use DES shared-key encryption for authentication of clients in unsecured networks (networks containing clients that are not physically secured). For this reason, all Kerberos communication that crosses the network is in encrypted form.

However, even though DES is a very effective encryption technique, its code has been broken several times. This is why Kerberos 5, as mentioned, offers the opportunity to implement other encryption algorithms (for instance, triple DES). But the DES encryption algorithm alone provides a level of security that is fully sufficient in most computer environments.

How Kerberos Works

The fundamental element in Kerberos is the *ticket*, which enables a user to set up a session with a specific server or service. Thus, a ticket is a certificate that is issued by the Kerberos service, certifying that the setup of a session between two parties is approved.

In addition, a very important kind of ticket exists, called a *ticket-granting ticket* (TGT), which removes the need for a client to be fully authenticated by the KDC each time a ticket is issued (in other words, each request for access to a network resource).

After a Kerberos server approves the client, the client receives a TGT. As mentioned, a TGT determines the authentication of the client every time the client requests a ticket for a network resource. In practice, when a request for access to network resources is received, the TGT is sent to the Kerberos server. If the TGT is valid, the server returns the requested ticket to the client, without asking any further questions.

TGT also eliminates the need to send passwords over the network, because the user is able to decrypt the ticket on the local client via the user's own password.

A Bit About Encryption

The word *encryption* originates from the Greek words *kryptos* (to hide) and *logos* (word), so encryption is far from a new phenomenon. Examples of encryption have been found that date back as long ago as the Egyptians' days of glory, 4,000 years ago, when some of the monument's inscriptions were encrypted. Two thousand years later, Julius Caesar used a simple form of encryption, too.

But not until the Second World War did encryption really become important to modern society. Since then, the value of encryption has grown concurrently with the progress of computers and communications media, because encryption is the most appropriate way to protect sensitive information against unauthorized persons.

The three central concepts in the field of encryption are:

- *Encryption*—Transformation of data, causing the meaning of the data to become unintelligible.

- *Decryption*—Backward transformation of the encrypted data to the original form.

- *Key*—A collection of signs, from which the encryption is made. Most often, the key must be used again to carry out a successful decryption.

In professional contexts, DES and RSA are the most commonly used encryption algorithms. DES and RSA (which stands for the inventors' initials, Rivest, Shamir, and Adleman) are acknowledged as the only algorithms, so far, that are of both practical use and sufficient complexity to make breaking their respective codes practically impossible. In other words, DES and RSA can be broken, but in most cases, the cost of breaking the code quite simply cannot compare favorably with the results. This is why, in practice, such algorithms are regarded as secure.

As opposed to the *practically* secure algorithms, *theoretically* secure encryption algorithms, unfortunately, have always proved too impractical for day-to-day use. The mathematician C.E. Shannon has proven that an encryption key, chosen completely by random and of the same length as the document to be encrypted, is theoretically secure—provided the key is used only once. In his demonstration, Shannon even used an encryption method that is as simple as any method can be—Vernam encryption—in which only the XOR (eXclusive-OR) operation is used for the physical encryption.

According to a former British agent, Peter Wright, and his book *Spycatcher*, the Russians availed themselves of such a theoretically secure encryption key during the Cold War. But the British broke the key, because the Russians had basically ignored the fact that the key, to be secure, could be used only once. The Russians had mistakenly used the same key in different parts of the world.

Tickets (and especially the TGT) must provide a high degree of security, which is why Kerberos always sets an upper limit to the number of times that a given ticket may validate accounts before the ticket expires.

Know Your DES

The Data Encryption Standard (DES) was established in 1977 by the American Bureau of Standards. DES is a 64-bit block encryption algorithm, which means that it encrypts 64 bits of the document at a time, based on a 64-bit encryption key. (In fact, the key only has 56 bits, because 8 of the bits are used to generate a checksum.)

According to the American standard, 16 *encryption transformations* (also called *rounds*) are carried out. Each encryption transformation consists of relatively simple transpositions and substitutions in groups of 4 bits. During each transformation, only 48 of the key's 64 bits are used, but the 48 bits are chosen randomly.

DES's working process means that each of the individual bits in a 64-bit block depends on the other bits, which also means that decrypting only part of the message isn't possible, even if part of the password is known.

Furthermore, DES is made so that the number of possible combinations of encryption keys is so large that finding the right encryption key is unlikely, unless a supercomputer is used for at least a year. So far, mathematicians have found no other method than this exhaustive search process—which in the worst case, requires going through all 72.058 trillion (2^{56}) possibilities.

But DES isn't always *DES*—several DES programs use less than the prescribed 16 transformations, which is an uneasy thought, because the security in DES depends on how many transformations the original document has undergone.

Already, in the early 1990s, Professor Adi Shamir demonstrated that breaking DES-encrypted documents that have undergone six and eight transformations is possible. On an ordinary PC, the encryption was broken in just three minutes and three seconds. (The only further condition was that the encrypted document was written in English.)

Fortunately, the standardized DES of 16 transformations is essentially different cryptographically from 8 transformations. But Shamir's attack on DES makes abundantly clear that the present encryption key length of 64 bits very soon should be increased to 128 bits, to further improve security in the world of ever-faster computers. Furthermore, Shamir's example shows that buyers of programs and hardware for DES encryption should make sure that their purchases follow at least the American standard.

How Kerberos Secures The Local Area Network

When a PC wants to access information on a server within the same domain, it must go through an authentication within the network. In practice, this authentication can be divided into a sequence of events between the client and the KDC.

Kerberos uses messages to give each Kerberos component the necessary information about what happens during the authentication process. As mentioned, many of these messages are encrypted and contain time stamps, to protect against anyone picking up the network packages with a traditional protocol-sniffing device and later sending them without the security system noticing anything unusual.

The following steps, shown in Figure 11.2, explain the typical sequence of events for authenticating a client against a particular server (or service):

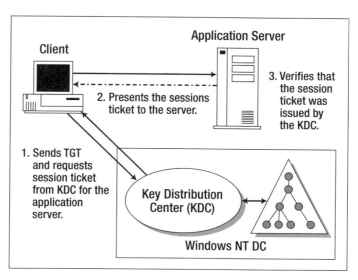

Figure 11.2
This is how the Kerberos authentication of the client against a given server takes place.

1. The client sends a plain-text message to the KDC, requesting a ticket to communicate with the KDC from that point on. The message from the client contains the user's name, the name of the KDC server or service, and a time stamp.

2. The KDC returns an encrypted message to the client. The message is encrypted with the client's password, and contains a time-stamped session key, to be used in relation with the KDC, and a general TGT, which the client can use to obtain future tickets for specific services within the realm of the KDC.

3. The client sends an encrypted message to the KDC in which it requests the right to communicate with a given server or service. The client encrypts this message with the session key that it received from the KDC. The message contains the name of the requested server or service, a time stamp, and the TGT. When the KDC receives the message, it can be certain that the request came from the client, because the message is decrypted by means of the client's session key. The KDC then produces a shared session key, which is used by both the client and the server. The KDC also produces a specific ticket for the server, which contains the session key, the name of the client, the address of the client's network interface card, the ticket's period of validity, and a time stamp.

4. The KDC sends a message to the client that contains the encrypted, shared session key and the encrypted ticket. The shared session key is encrypted with the client's session key, while the ticket is encrypted with the server's session key.

5. The client sends a message to the server to inform it that the client has the right to communicate with the server. (Whether the client can have its subsequent requests carried out is, of course, up to the server's security system.) The message contains the encrypted ticket that the client received from the KDC, and a time-stamp authenticator, which is encrypted with the shared session key. The server uses its own password to decrypt the ticket, which contains a copy of the shared session key and a few other vital pieces of information about the client. The server uses the shared session key to decrypt the time-stamp authenticator, to check when the client sent the message. If the client sent the message within the ticket's period of validity, and if everything else is in order, the server accepts the client's application.

6. After the server approves the client, the server sends an encrypted message, telling the client that it accepts the request to communicate. The message contains the time-stamp authenticator that the client sent to the server in Step 5. The time-stamp authenticator is still encrypted with the shared session key.

And now the communication between client and server can finally begin.

The first two of the preceding six events are superfluous when the client later wants to access another server or service, because the client can reuse the TGT until it expires.

How Kerberos Secures The Global Network

The authentication of clients across realms does not differ very much from the authentication within a realm. Each realm is equipped with its own KDC and ticket-issuing service. Instead of opening a separate account in each realm for the same user, Kerberos provides the capability for realms to approve each other's users, who can thus get access to servers and services within both realms (shown in Figure 11.3).

When authenticating across two realms, you merely carry out the following two steps prior to Step 3 in the client authentication, described in the preceding section. In other words, the following two events either replace the preceding Steps 1 and 2 (provided the client already has a TGT for the local realm) or are inserted between the preceding Steps 2 and 3:

1. The client sends an encrypted message to the KDC. This message contains a request for a session key, which makes communication with the KDC in the other realm possible.

2. The KDC sends the client an encrypted message, which contains a ticket to the KDC server in the other realm. Now, the client can contact the other KDC server directly and ask for a ticket to access the server or service it wants to use.

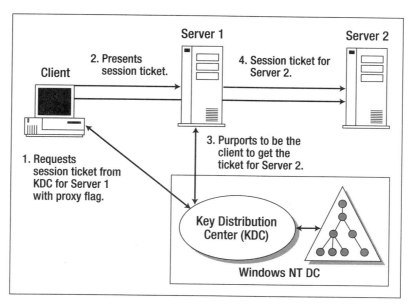

Figure 11.3
Kerberos authentication includes the capability to use resources from several different servers.

Naturally, the preceding two events apply only if the KDC in the client's own realm has a session key for the requested KDC—which requires that a manual registration between the two KDCs has taken place.

NT 5.0 includes the possibility for a client to access a realm that isn't immediately accessible from the local KDC. NT 5.0's Kerberos implementation can handle a hierarchy of realms, so that the client can contact a realm that has access to another realm, and so on. This trip through the hierarchy continues until the client locates the KDC it wants to use. The hierarchy of realms is based on the directory tree.

Nothing Is Perfect

In Greek mythology, the three-headed dog was cheated on some occasions, in spite of its deterrent nature. On one occasion, Hercules pulled the dog from the underworld to earth's surface, and on another occasion, Ulysses succeeded in bribing the dog with cake.

The computer version of Kerberos also is susceptible to trickery. Although Kerberos technology is an optimal solution to the security challenge of distributed environments, it isn't a completely watertight solution.

The biggest and most obvious risk is for Kerberos to fall for a password *dictionary attack* (an attack based on going through numerous commonly used passwords), made possible by a user choosing a far too simple and common password. Windows NT already contains some facilities to avoid such attacks, but those who have experience working with password-based computer security know that Windows NT's current facilities are inadequate to enforce a really effective security policy for passwords.

Another obvious weakness in Kerberos is that the KDC must be physically secured. Mistreatment of or inadequate security conditions around the Key Distribution Center causes a heavy reduction in security regarding client authentication.

Finally, the greatest risk of all is the human element. Experience shows that the vast majority of computer fraud cases actually are perpetrated by the company's own trusted staff members, against whom any security system is insufficient.

But, if nothing else, Kerberos definitely is the best current solution for a secure and easily administered security-authentication system for distributed environments. Kerberos is considerably better than NTLM authentication, the prevailing system prior to Kerberos. Kerberos gives clients proof that a server is what it claims to be, and introduces a time limit in the clients' access to servers across the network. Likewise, Kerberos routinely can be used to handle more domains, and is an acknowledged standard that can be used by many other control systems.

Public Key Systems

As mentioned earlier, public key encryption is the only widespread alternative to Kerberos' shared keys. Public key encryption is based on a division of the encryption key into two parts: a public key and a private key.

Superficially, Kerberos is the best method for securing confidence and integrity, whereas public key encryption is the most qualified encryption method for securing authentication and integrity. In other words, public key encryption is the most suitable system for determining whether a particular electronic document (for which it doesn't make sense to talk about masters and copies) comes from a particular person. In the pre-electronic world, the problem of integrity often was solved by entering information in such a way that adding or erasing information was difficult to accomplish without leaving traces. Authentication was defined by the signature (provided, of course, that it was a one-page document). In the age of electronic documents, ensuring that a particular document really came from a specific sender was not possible prior to the introduction of public key encryption, because a change doesn't leave palpable traces in an electronic document.

When securing authentication and integrity of data, the division of the encryption key works as follows:

1. A private key is issued that is known only by a certain sender. The private key can be used to encrypt information, in case the sender wants to assure the recipient system that the information it receives actually comes from the sender.

2. Simultaneously, a public key (a publicly accessible key) is issued. The public key can be used for encryption of messages that are received from the sender. This key enables the recipient to be certain immediately that the sender really is who he claims to be and that the sender is secure against others making changes in the document.

This working method is reversed (the sender encrypts the data with the recipient's public key, while the recipient decrypts data with his private key) if you want to use public key encryption to secure the confidentiality of data.

Currently, public key encryption is the standard method for digitizing signatures. A digital signature enables you to create an electronic copy of a master document that can't be changed without detection, and that demonstrably doesn't lose connection with its creator. This means that possible claims based on the contents of a document can be successfully defended or asserted in a court of law. These claims are verifiable because anyone in possession of the public key from the sender can read the document—and so indirectly make sure that the alleged writer actually created it. But the document cannot be re-encrypted without the writer's secret key.

RSA, described in the next section, is the preferred encryption algorithm in public key encryption.

A Bit About RSA

RSA is a public key encryption system that has the advantage of being able to publish a decryption key without compromising data security. RSA is almost obligatory for authenticating data, which is becoming more necessary as business deals and paying bills increasingly become electronic.

The RSA system is an *asymmetrical* encryption algorithm, which means that different keys are used for encryption and decryption (see Figure 11.4). The encryption key must be kept secret, while the other key can be made publicly accessible.

The public key consists of the pair (e,n) and the secret key of the pair (d,n). Here, n denotes the encryption key, which is the product of two suitably large prime numbers, p and q ($n=p \times q$). d and e must have the property that $(d \times e$-1) is divisible by

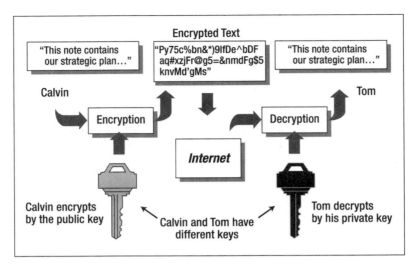

Figure 11.4

Public key encryption is based on the use of asymmetrical keys.

$(p\text{-}1)(q\text{-}1)$. The entire security in RSA depends on keeping p, q, and d secret. The e number may be known to the world, hence making this encryption scheme "public."

Mathematically, encrypting a document is easy and quick. Decrypting the document, however, is very hard without knowledge of the key. It could take several hundred years for someone to use computers to crack the encryption code. If M is a plain-text document, the encryption phase is defined by transforming the text M by using the encryption key n in conjunction with e (which is part of the public key). The conversion back to plain text is defined by taking the encrypted text, represented by C, and doing a mathematical transformation function using the encryption key n and d (which is part of the secret key).

The high degree of security of the RSA method is based primarily on the special properties of prime numbers when used in connection with computers. While finding large prime numbers with a computer is relatively easy, splitting up a large number into its prime number factors, p and q, is a task that requires intensive calculations.

RSA security can be further increased by choosing a *strong* prime number p, where $p\text{-}1$ has a large prime number factor r, and $p\text{+}1$ has a large prime number factor s. Furthermore, both $r\text{-}1$ and $s\text{-}1$ must each have a large prime number factor.

Unfortunately, such public encryption systems require much longer encryption keys than conventional encryption systems—and, consequently, they work considerably slower. Typically, each of the prime numbers p and q consist of 100 digits. Still, the most commonly used digit length in RSA (150 digits) is already being bypassed through the development of stronger computers. Newer RSA standards use a combination of 256-bit and 258-bit prime numbers for p and q.

Windows NT 4.0 already offers several services that are based on public key encryption, including Secure Channel Security (which implements the Secure Sockets Layer [SSL] protocol and Microsoft's Private Communications Technology [PCT] protocol), CryptoAPI, and Authenticode. NT 4.0 Service Pack 3 adds support for X.509 certificates and the Public Key Certificate Standard (PKCS).

> **Note:**   The contents of an X.509 certificate can vary. However, at a minimum, the certificate contains the user's public key and name (or alias); the certificate's date of issuance, date of expiration, and serial number; and the issuing Certificate Authority's name and digital signature. X.509 certificates are an International Telecommunication Union (ITU) standard that dates back to 1988.

The SSL algorithm has already become the de facto standard for connections between Internet browsers and Internet servers.

NT 5.0 increases the possibilities of implementing the Transport Layer Security (TLS) and Distributed Password Authentication (DPA) security protocols. TLS is the successor to SSL, which only means that SSL and some other IETF protocols have been combined, enabling them to offer a functionality rivaling the PCT protocol developed by Microsoft. DPA currently is being used for authentication of memberships at some of the largest Internet organizations—and Microsoft promises DPA will soon be implemented in its Commercial Internet System services.

Furthermore, NT 5.0 offers Certificate Server for issuing its own X.509 certificates. Certificate Server is part of IIS 4.0, and thus can already get access to NT Server 4.0 through the Option Pack. Microsoft also has promised that authenticating clients via SSL 3.0-based public key certificates will become possible.

Microsoft is targeting the SSL/TLS protocols at least as much as it is targeting Kerberos. Microsoft is following this course because it views the public key-based protocols as the only possibility for sufficient reliability and security when communicating across very unsecure media, such as the Internet—and Microsoft focuses a lot on its Internet products. In fact, Certificate Server is a good indication that Microsoft takes the prevalence of SSL/TLS seriously, because it developed Certificate Server for use in organizations that want to issue digital certificates directly to users, without being dependent on commercial Certificate Authority (CA) services.

How NT 5.0's Security System Works

As mentioned, Microsoft is making Kerberos the standard authentication mechanism for NT 5.0, which is why Kerberos is the center of attention when discussing NT 5.0's security model.

But how is Microsoft fitting Kerberos into NT 5.0?

Concerning the server, all domain controllers (DCs) are equipped with a KDC, and the Kerberos term *realm* corresponds to the NT *domain*. The KDC is integrated with NT 5.0's Active Directory service, which means that the KDC uses the Active Directory as a user-account database.

The familiar WinLogon service is used to log on to the NT domain (and consequently Kerberos) from NT Workstation-based clients. The WinLogon service is initiated when the user presses Ctrl+Alt+Delete simultaneously. These three keys typically are used to restart a PC, and so by pressing them during the logon process, NT prevents hackers from inserting a program that mirrors the logon screen but actually captures usernames and passwords. This means that the client goes through an authentication against the KDC, which ends in the allocation of a TGT after the client enters the correct username and password. The TGT is kept with other user logon information in the client's cache.

When the client wants to communicate with a service, the client looks for a valid ticket to the resource. If a ticket is not available, the client sends a TGT to the KDC and carries out the procedure described in the earlier section titled "How Kerberos Secures The Local Area Network."

The NT domain's security policy determines the time of expiration for the tickets. The standard is eight hours. If a ticket expires during an active session, the client automatically renews the ticket, without troubling the user.

Kerberos serves exclusively as an authentication protocol. It doesn't cover the access control component, which is still handled via the Security Identifiers (SID), Access Control List (ACL), and Security Descriptors (SD), as it is in NT 4.0.

Each Active Directory object has an SD, which contains the following information:

- The object's owner
- Which group or groups the owner belongs to
- The ACL for the object

Apart from an SD, all Kerberos 5-based clients can be authenticated against an NT-based KDC—or vice versa. In the current beta version of NT 5.0, Kerberos still has some compatibility problems with other platforms, but Microsoft promises that these problems will be eliminated in the final version of NT 5.0.

However, Microsoft definitely will be unsuccessful in eliminating one limitation, regarding the issuing of the basic information that identifies the client. The different implementations of Kerberos operate with different basic information, because the information typically is fetched from the underlying operating system. Microsoft's version of Kerberos, not surprisingly, uses SIDs, which are developed by Microsoft. This means that an administrator must set up local user accounts on an NT-based domain controller for each user from an outside system who needs access to the NT-based services.

However, remember that Kerberos can be replaced by SSI, if required, just as NT 5.0 still can understand and use the old NTLM service. Kerberos alternatives are shown in Figure 11.5.

Also note that Microsoft is cooperating with the IETF CAT (Common Authentication Technology) work group in order to finish an expansion of Kerberos RFC 1510, which supports the use of private-public key encryption methods. If Microsoft is successful in this project, a KDC will be able to determine the authentication of a

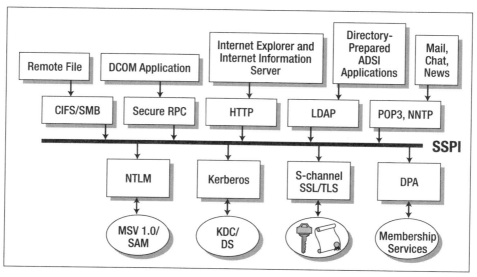

Figure 11.5
Microsoft plans for Kerberos to be the new authentication service, but several alternatives exist. These include the current widespread public-key-based SSL standard and Security Support Provider Interface (SSPI), a Win32 API that is used to isolate the applications' protocols from the security protocols.

request from a client via the client's public key—and subsequently return an answer in a secure way.

Microsoft's public key expansion for Kerberos, shown in Figure 11.6, is based on the user's X.509 certificate being created in advance in the User section of Active Directory. When the client requests a connection, the Kerberos service verifies the authentication of the message from the client by means of the public key, which is kept in the Active Directory. If everything is in order, the Kerberos service issues the requested ticket and encrypts it with the client's public key, which secures that only the correct recipient can access the ticket.

The public key expansion of Kerberos will enable an administrator to give a user outside the NT directory service access to NT resources. Therefore, Microsoft is certain to introduce support of public key-based authentication in the Kerberos implementation, no matter what happens concerning the standardization of security protocols.

Microsoft regards public key support as a necessary condition to, for example, log on to the system with a Smart Card—which Microsoft considers an important function that will be demanded by increasingly more companies in the future. The Smart Card

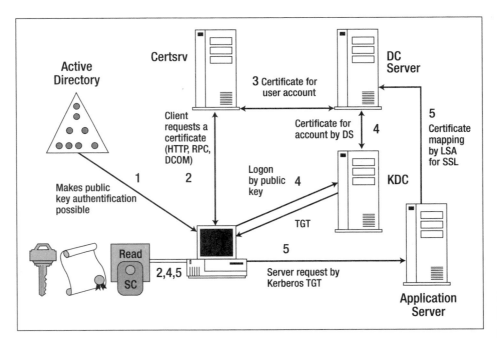

Figure 11.6
Microsoft intends to introduce public key authentication as a genuine alternative to Kerberos. However, this hasn't happened in NT 5.0 beta 1, so it's uncertain whether the implementation is going to look exactly like this.

function is so important to Microsoft that it has published a model of how to connect and use Smart-Card readers in connection with NT systems. The model is based on the Personal Computer/Smart Card (PC/SC) specification and NT 5.0's built-in SCard COM implementation (a collection of COM interface objects that can be used to build high-level interfaces or applications), which both utilize Smart Cards.

NT Security In Practice

Not only has Microsoft increased NT's security facilities tremendously, but it also has made these facilities considerably easier for the administrator to access. Almost all the security facilities have been joined in an MMC snap-in called *Security Configuration Editor*, which enables you to configure the security for the NT system and carry out periodic analyses of the system's security.

Security Configuration Editor, shown in Figure 11.7, enables you to configure and analyze the following items:

- *Security Policy*—Used to define access policies, including how and when users can log on to the system, the password policy, the general system object security, auditing installations, domain policies, and so on.

- *User Rights Assignment*—Used to control the group membership, privileges, users' rights, and so on.

- *Restricted Groups*—Used to configure membership to groups such as power users, printer operators, backup operators, and the administrator.

- *System Service*—Enables configuration of the security of the different services that are installed in the particular system.

- *Registry*—Used to make changes in the Registry's security values.

- *File System*—Used to set up the security for local file volumes and directory trees.

In practice, you work with Security Configuration Editor by defining Security Configuration Templates, which contain the installations for the security attributes for each of the areas mentioned in the preceding list. After doing this, these templates can be used to configure the security system and carry out security analyses on the basis of the template information.

The version of the Security Configuration Editor snap-in that exists in NT 5.0 beta 1 is, however, a very early version that lacks various functionalities. For instance, the Directory Security part is very limited in both its sphere of operation and user-friendliness. Microsoft promises, among other things, that user-friendliness in the final version of NT 5.0 will increase greatly via numerous predefined security templates.

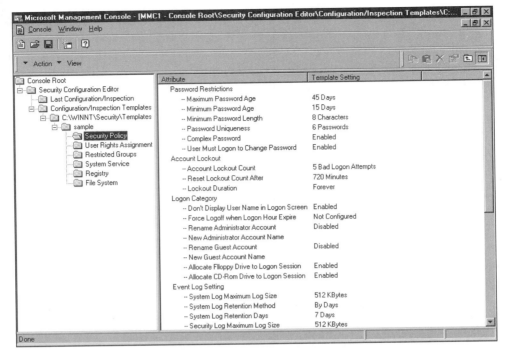

Figure 11.7
The very early version of Security Configuration Editor.

Security At The Lowest Level: IP Security

NT 5.0 contains a very fascinating new security technology called *Internet Protocol Security*—which is usually just called *IP Security*, or *IPSec* for short. As the name indicates, IP Security provides the capability to define security policies related to the network communication layer.

IP Security is completely independent of the other, more abstract security concepts that have been examined in this chapter and it completes NT's many other security concepts. IP Security can be used to increase the security in the entire NT environment, or part of it, to a higher degree than the other security concepts.

With IP Security, NT can be installed to automatically decrypt and encrypt IP network packages that go to and from the system—and thus protect the communications against network sniffing (a form of tapping a network communications line). IP Security can be installed to cover all or some of the machines on the IP network, as well as selected TCP/IP package types and TCP/IP ports.

IP Security can carry out encryption both with public keys, such as RSA, and with secret keys, such as DES. The standard version of IP Security offers the following encryption algorithms:

- *Diffie-Hellman (D-H)* —A public key algorithm in which the two parties agree on a shared key, without being encrypted during the key generation.

- *Hash Message Authentication Code (HMAC)* —A secret-key algorithm in which a secret key is combined with a hash function. The hash function can be either HMAC-MD5 (Message Digest function 5) or HMAC SHA (Secure Hash Algorithm), which produce 128-bit and 160-bit values, respectively, that are used as a signature for a particular data block.

- *Cipher Block Chaining (DES-CBC)* —A secret-key algorithm in which a random number is generated and used with the secret key in connection with the encryption of the data.

For the encryption itself, NT uses the following security protocols:

- *Internet Security Association and Key Management Protocol (ISAKMP)* —Before the IP packages can be transmitted among the computers, a *Security Association* must be established, which is a selection of parameters that define those services and mechanisms necessary to obtain the desired level of security.

- *Oakley* —The protocol that determines the key. The exchange of keys is based on the Diffie-Hellman algorithm.

- *Authentication Header (IP AH)* —Can be used for encryption of the IP packages. AH secures the integrity and authenticity of the packages. AH uses either HMAC-MD5 or HMAC-SHA encryption algorithms.

- *Encapsulating Security Protocol (IP ESP)* —Can also be used for encryption of the IP packages. ESP secures the integrity, authentication, and confidentiality of the packages. ESP uses the HMAC-MD5 and DES-CBC encryption algorithms.

The fact that IP Security is completely invisible to users and can be administered centrally means that, in practice, hardly any additional costs are incurred when implementing IP Security on the network.

Incidentally, IP Security is not limited to Windows NT machines on the network. IP Security is based on IETF RFC standards (RFC 1825, 1826, 1827, 1828, 1829, 1851, 1852, 2085, and 2104) and will probably establish itself among the other TCP/IP protocol stacks on the market. To protect against problems related to communications with systems that can't handle IP encryption, the present implementation of IP Security is set to work only when the recipient and the sender are NT 5.0-based systems.

IP Security In Practice

Implementing IP Security is surprisingly easy after you understand its basic principles. IP Security is administered from the IP Security Management MMC snap-in, as shown in Figure 11.8. IP Security's network implementation is based on three different types of policies:

- *Security policies* —Each composition of IP Security attributes is called a *security policy*. One security policy consists of negotiation policies and IP filters. The method to define IP filters is shown in Figure 11.9.

- *Negotiation policies* —Determining which security services are used in connection with encryption and decryption of the IP packages is called a negotiation policy. The choice is between IP AH, IP ESP, and a few possible alternate IP packages. The negotiation policies can be set up for more protocols, so that the

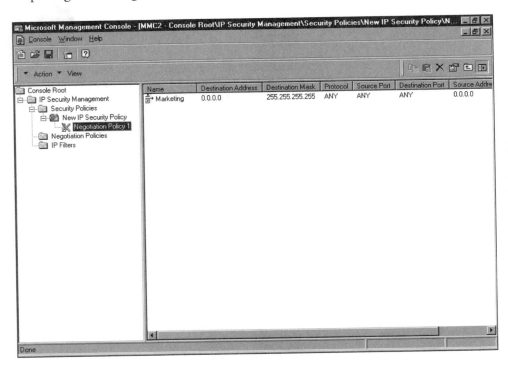

Figure 11.8
IP Security is administered from the IP Security Management MMC snap-in, which is easy to use once you have a general understanding of IP Security procedures.

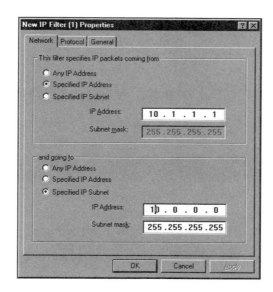

Figure 11.9
The IP filters are defined on the Network and Protocol tabs. The Network tab allows you to specify which IP addresses or IP subnets are covered by the filter (incoming as well as outgoing). On the Protocol tab, the filter's area of operation can be further narrowed to certain TCP/IP package types or TCP/IP ports (incoming as well as outgoing).

system automatically tries another protocol if the opposite party doesn't accept the first protocol.

• *IP filters*—These indicate a pattern against which each IP package is matched. If the IP filter matches, the negotiation policy defined by the security policy is used to send the given IP package.

As mentioned, all installations of IP Security are made centrally and apply for all NT 5.0-based systems that are connected to the particular Active Directory domain. This occurs because the installations are added to the domain's standard policies (which isn't the case with beta 1, where the user personally has to establish IP Security). You can also implement a particular security level on specific PCs by adding the IP Security installation to their domain policy in the Microsoft Directory Service Manager snap-in. So starting IP Security isn't at all difficult, because everything relative to clients happens automatically.

However, to implement IP Security, you must be a member of the administrative group and have rights in the directory tree to work with IP Security.

Genuine Security For Your Money

At a conference about information security and the spread of high-technology crime, William Moran, vice-president and senior product manager at the Chase Manhattan Corporation, complained as follows regarding the many new risks in connection with data security and integrity: "I liked it better back in those days when the data center was a fortress." Working with data security today isn't always nice, because client/server systems and intranets have made data far more distributed—to the delight of users and to the frustration of security professionals.

Many more sources of attack on security exist now than ever before—and there are a lot of unpredictable sources. Not surprisingly, this has allowed an increase in the number of attacks. In a survey by the Computer Security Institute and the computer magazine *Information Week*, an estimated total cost of $100 million was incurred in 1995 due to security breaches among the 563 participating U.S. companies. Almost half of these companies had experienced some sort of intrusion or unauthorized use of their systems within the past 12 months.

This survey is a good example of why the concept of security attracts a relatively large amount of attention from the computer market. Almost everybody involved in computer security agrees that the right security cocktail consists of two items: strong technologies and well-qualified computer professionals.

A large shortage exists of well-qualified computer professionals who possess a sufficient level of knowledge about, and interest in, the security area. However, computer suppliers have really begun to focus on strong security technologies for encryption and authentication.

Kerberos is presently the best authentication and encryption technology available that can be implemented across even very large companies. The same can be said about the IP Security technologies for network traffic and public key systems (which are based on X.509 certificates) in publicly accessible connections. The difference in security facilities between NT 5.0 and NT 4.0 is shown in Figure 11.10.

Many other large and small initiatives exist to increase security levels. For instance, the NT File System may be encrypted, and authentication of a program may be secured through the Authenticode technology. Incidentally, Microsoft promises that it will begin to use Authenticode for signatures of drivers, DLLs, and other vital

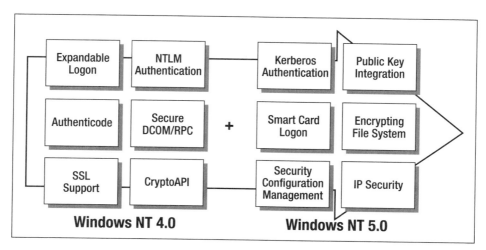

Figure 11.10
This is how Microsoft presents the security facilities of NT 5.0 compared to those of NT 4.0.

system components for Windows NT. Whether this will happen in the production version of NT 5.0, or any time soon, is uncertain.

In short, Windows NT 5.0 demonstrates on many levels that Microsoft is taking security as seriously as many of its customers.

From WINS To DDNS

12

Even though a network looks completely different today than it did 10 years ago, Microsoft's approach to the network has changed surprisingly little since it introduced its first network control system, LAN Manager.

Back in 1987, when Microsoft launched LAN Manager, NetBIOS and NetBEUI headed its networking agenda. And while NetBEUI has been met with increasing opposition during the 1990s, NetBIOS still holds its ground today.

But now Microsoft is ready to carry out a true revolution in its handling of networks, by eliminating NetBIOS in favor of completely focusing on all the prevailing standards and technologies of TCP/IP. With Windows NT 5.0, Microsoft aims at a "pure" TCP/IP implementation, which is based on the Dynamic Host Configuration Protocol (DHCP) and OSF DCE Domain Name System (DNS) standards—and thus eliminates Windows Internet Naming Service (WINS).

WINS and DNS are name services. *Name services* are used to connect names, which are more-easily accessible, to IP addresses, which are less accessible. WINS is the name service that is used for machines that use NetBIOS on top of TCP/IP, whereas DNS is the name service that is used for machines that use TCP/IP. DNS enables names rather than IP addresses to be used on the Internet.

DHCP is a standard for dynamic allocation of TCP/IP network addresses and various additional pieces of information that are used by the TCP/IP protocol stack. DHCP is an incredibly effective method of freeing users of all the challenges of TCP/IP installations, because the individual user only has to indicate that DHCP is being used, after which all the TCP/IP installations are entered automatically into the PC. Likewise, DHCP enables later changes to the TCP/IP installation to be a more practicable job, which is very important in this ever-changing world.

NT 5.0's implementations of DNS (which are really implementations of Dynamic DNS) and DHCP are the subjects of this chapter. For readers with a sufficient understanding of DHCP and DNS (and the predecessor, WINS), the examination in this chapter is deliberately made more "textbook-like" than most other chapters, so that you can benefit from the discussion, too.

NetBIOS Is Everywhere

You can't avoid NetBIOS in a Windows 95 or NT 4.0 environment. NetBIOS covers an interface and some name conventions that belong to the three upper layers of the Open Systems Interconnection (OSI) model (sometimes known as the OSI Reference Model). NetBIOS is the component that enables users to contact the services that are offered on the network, such as file sharing and printer sharing.

Note that NetBIOS doesn't arrange the actual connection to the network units. This happens in the lower layers of the OSI model. Traditionally, the lower layers in a NetBIOS communication have been handled by the NetBEUI protocol. Naturally, other protocols can be used—for instance, TCP/IP and IPX/SPX—as a foundation for a NetBIOS-based communication.

The similarity of the names NetBEUI and NetBIOS hasn't exactly made distinguishing them an easy task. Many people still have great difficulty distinguishing NetBIOS from NetBEUI, which is unfortunate, because they definitely shouldn't be mixed up. Just remember that NetBEUI is the network protocol and NetBIOS is the network-programming interface, which originally existed only for NetBEUI.

Microsoft started by using NetBIOS and NetBEUI as the standard protocols in its network solutions. NetBEUI was both the preferred network protocol in the Windows environment and the network protocol upon which Microsoft focused almost exclusively. As recently as 1993, Microsoft's Steve Ballmer was forecasting that a new version of NetBEUI (called JetBEUI) was going to make NetBEUI the most predominant future network protocol.

Today, no traces of JetBEUI exist, and Microsoft recently has been recommending that NetBEUI be totally replaced by TCP/IP. But until now, Microsoft's opinion was that NetBIOS should control access to network resources. Without NetBIOS, you can't do too much in a Windows NT 4.0 Server environment, which uses TCP/IP. Thus, without NetBIOS, using Net Use, Net View, Net Logon, and similar commands isn't possible, nor can you see any resources from other computers, such as with Network Neighborhood.

Somewhat surprisingly, Microsoft's continued use of NetBIOS on top of the TCP/IP protocol is supported by the Internet Engineering Task Force's (IETF) RFCs 1001 and 1002, which specify how NetBIOS is implemented on top of TCP/IP. RFCs 1001 and 1002 date back to 1987.

However, Microsoft's attachment to NetBIOS disappears with NT 5.0, in which NetBIOS is completely eliminated in favor of "pure" TCP/IP communication.

Registration And Resolution Of NetBIOS Names

NetBIOS names are used to identify the accessible resources on the network, in a user-friendly way. Asking for access to a server via a name rather than a network address (such as 149.555.12.12) is considerably easier for a user, because a numerical address doesn't remind a user of anything that will help him or her remember the address for future use.

Network resources are supposed to be registered dynamically when a computer or a service is started, or when a user logs on. However, you may create static registrations for certain NetBIOS names, if you want to do so. All NetBIOS names must be unique and may have a maximum length of 16 characters. However, Microsoft's network components enable you to specify only the first 15 characters of the NetBIOS name, because the last byte is reserved to identify the resource type.

When a user needs to access a NetBIOS resource, a name resolution must be carried out, which means that the system has to find the network address of the resource (for example, the IP address for TCP/IP-based networks) from its NetBIOS name. A network doesn't understand NetBIOS names, but instead works exclusively with network addresses.

In NT 3.0, domain name resolution was limited to LMHOSTS files (text files that map domain names to IP addresses) and ordinary broadcasts across the network. NT 3.5x and 4.0 added a special server service, WINS, to handle registration and resolution of NetBIOS names. NT 5.0 also contains a WINS server, as shown in Figure 12.1, but it is included mostly for backward-compatibility.

Windows NT 3.5x and 4.0 can use one or more of the following five methods to carry out a NetBIOS name resolution on a network that is using TCP/IP as the underlying protocol:

- *WINS*—A dynamic database that registers NetBIOS names and carries out searches.

- *Broadcast*—A signal sent out to the whole network, in which the particular NetBIOS resource is asked to identify itself.

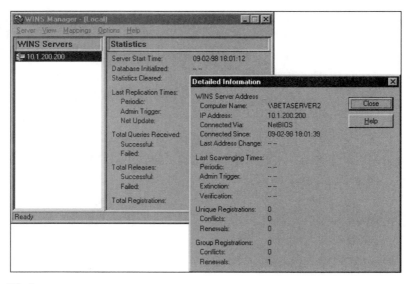

Figure 12.1
NT Server 5.0 also contains a WINS server, but it is included only to secure backward-compatibility, because Active Directory-based servers and clients use DNS for name resolution.

- *LMHOSTS file*—A file containing a number of entries that specify network addresses and the corresponding NetBIOS names for various resources. LMHOSTS files typically are used to give users access to NetBIOS services, even though no DNS or WINS servers exist on the network. LMHOSTS files can also be used, for example, to remove all the trivial broadcasts from the network or to embed names of machines that aren't registered in the WINS or DNS servers.

- *HOSTS file*—A file containing a number of entries that specify network addresses and the corresponding DNS names for various resources. HOSTS is the counterpart of LMHOST files with regard to "pure" TCP/IP machines. As with DNS, NetBIOS names can be registered in a HOSTS file.

- *DNS server*—A static database that can carry out searches on the basis of TCP/IP names (but also permits the indication of NetBIOS names).

The order in which the PC attempts to carry out the name resolution can vary, depending on the installation of the node type—the choice being either Broadcast node (B-node), Point-to-Point node (P-node), Mixed node (M-node), or Host node (H-node). The standard setup is H-node, whereby the attempt to carry out the name resolution is made in the order previously mentioned. NetBIOS is a very simple broadcast-based protocol, designed for use on small networks. As such, NetBIOS can't immediately cover more than one physical IP network (the area surrounded by routers). Each WINS server can immediately cover only one certain IP network. Thus, at least one WINS server must be placed on each physical IP network. In practice, however, WINS servers can take the form of a proxy server that only refers WINS name references to a WINS server on another IP network. Consequently, WINS has difficulty determining how to handle servers with more than one network interface board.

By building in facilities for replication among WINS servers, Microsoft has tried to ease the problems caused by NetBIOS's limitation to a singe IP network. The replication in WINS is based on a *multiple master model,* which means that each WINS server owns the entries registered on it and replicates these entries with its replication partners.

The replication of WINS servers is a two-way process, whereby each party has its own respective role—one server is a *push* partner relative to the other server, which is the *pull* partner.

You can establish a push rule between two WINS servers by indicating that the push partner must send a message (called a *trigger*) to the pull partner every time a certain number of changes have occurred in the push partner's WINS database. The replication itself is initiated by the pull partner. You can also set up a pull trigger by indicating that the pull partner must carry out a replication with the push partner at specified intervals.

Internet Or Unix Means DNS

On the "pure" TCP/IP networks (which are used, for instance, with Unix systems), another type of naming system is used, called *Domain Name System* (DNS).

DNS names basically work the same way as NetBIOS names. DNS is designed to produce more user-friendly identifiers for the resources on the network than those provided by IP addresses (which always are in the x1.x2.x3.x4 format, where x1 through x4 are integers defining the address, such as 10.1.4.1). You probably are already familiar with DNS names used on the Web, such as midi.com.

DNS is a well-known and widely accepted Internet standard for naming and registering resources, and it also can be used on private TCP/IP-based networks. DNS names are constructed in a slightly different way than NetBIOS names. DNS computer names consist of two parts: a computer name (called a *host name*) and a domain name. When these two parts are combined, they form a *fully qualified domain name* (FQDN). An example of a fully qualified domain name is ntbeta.microsoft.com, in which the computer name is ntbeta and the domain name is microsoft.com.

As mentioned, the Web (among other networks) is based on DNS names. This means, for example, that when the URL www.netlog.com is written in the Web browser, the browser treats the URL as a DNS name request. The request searches for a computer named www that is placed in the netlog.com domain. After finding the DNS server in which this computer is registered, the server sends an IP address back to the browser, which then can use it to contact Netlog's Web server.

Understanding DNS

Looking at DNS in a slightly more abstract way, it forms a distributed database system that provides a hierarchical naming system for identifying computers on the Internet.

DNS was designed to solve the problems that arose when the number of computers on the Internet grew drastically in the beginning of the 1980s. The fundamental specifications for DNS are defined in RFCs 1034 and 1035, which were accepted as IETF standards in 1987 and are still in force. But naturally, numerous updates of the DNS specification have occurred since then, which has resulted in some new RFCs. If you want to study DNS in depth, the minimum reading requirements are RFCs 1034, 1035, 1101, 1464, 1536, 1591, 1664, 1706, 1712, 1713, 1794, 1912, and 1995.

The conceptual name system on which DNS is based is a hierarchical and logical tree structure, called *domain name space*—which colloquially has become DNS. The top level in domain name space is administered by InterNIC (Internet Network Information Center; **http://ds.internic.net**). InterNIC is responsible for the delegation of administrative responsibility for parts of domain name space and registration of domain names. Domain names are administered through the use of a distributed database system, in which the name information is kept on name servers that are spread across the Internet. Every name server has database files (known as *zone files*) that contain the registered information for a chosen region within the domain tree hierarchy.

As mentioned, the names in the DNS database form a logical tree structure called the domain name space. Table 12.1 demonstrates how the top level (the top domain) in the Internet domain name space is implemented in the U.S. The global top domain is too large to display here, because it contains an abbreviation for each country outside the U.S. (such as .dk for Denmark and .de for Germany). The top domain currently is being expanded with numerous new areas because the Internet is gaining so much popularity that many existing popular names have already been taken.

Domain name space forms the entire tree structure—from the top level in the domain to the lowest level, where the computers are located. The tree structure must follow the conventions for representing DNS names: Each level in the domain (and the computer name) must be separated by a period.

In principle, every domain name can be considered a combination of one or more domain components. The following four domain components ordinarily are used:

Table 12.1   *The top U.S. domains in the Internet DNS hierarchy.*

Top Domain	Type Of Organization
.com	Commercial
.edu	Educational
.gov	U.S. Government
.int	International
.mil	U.S. Military
.net	Network
.org	Noncommercial

- *Top-level domain*—Always indicated farthest to the right in the DNS name. The top level typically consists of a name code of two or three letters that identify either a country or a type of organization, such as those in Table 12.1.

- *Second-level domain*—Consists of a unique name of varying length that has been formally registered by InterNIC for an individual or an organization connected to the Internet.

- *Subdomain name*—A registered domain can be divided further into a random number of underlying domains by adding sublevels called *subdomains*.

- *Host name*—Placed farthest to the left in the domain name, a host name identifies a specific computer on the network.

This hierarchical structure—and the capability to subdivide domains to match the needs of a specific job—is the leading concept for DNS domains. Microsoft's view of the DNS tree is shown in Figure 12.2. The hierarchical structure means that, in practice, the Internet will never run out of names, even if the growth doesn't stop until everybody on earth has registered their domain. The hierarchical structure also enables network administration to be divided in a manner that is logical and easy to understand—each organization on the Internet can be allocated authority for a large or small part of domain name space, meaning that the organization's administrator is responsible for the administration, subdivision, and naming in that part of domain name space.

Every time InterNIC accepts a new second-level domain, the particular organization is allocated authority to administer its own subtrees within that second-level domain, in the form of subdomain names, zones, and computer names.

A DNS name can consist of up to 255 characters. Each level in domain name space can consist of up to 63 characters and must be unique relative to the overlying level, to ensure that all DNS names in the world are unique—a necessary prerequisite for

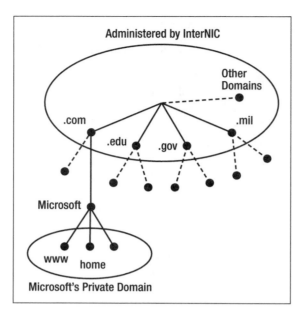

Figure 12.2
DNS is based on a hierarchical tree structure, which is shown here from Microsoft's point of view.

the execution of correct name resolutions. According to the RFC, for a domain name to be compatible across the Internet, it may consist only of the English alphabet, decimal numbers, and minus signs. No distinction is made between lowercase and uppercase letters in DNS names—it is *case-insensitive*.

A Bit About DNS Servers

The practical handling of domain name space happens through name servers, known as *DNS servers*. DNS is based on a client/server model, in which the DNS servers contain information about a part of the DNS database (the zone) and make this information accessible to clients (which are called *resolvers*). According to the DNS model, a client requests information about a DNS name from a DNS server, which can, if necessary, ask other DNS servers for the information if it doesn't have the information at its own disposal.

Besides handling requests, a DNS server has responsibility for one or more zones. A *zone* is the smallest administrative unit for a DNS server, and it can cover a large or small part of a domain name space. A zone can consist of a single domain or a domain with underlying domains (meaning second-level domains or subdomains).

A zone is rooted by a specific domain node, which is called the *root domain* of the zone. Each zone assumes the form of a file. A zone file consists of *resource records* (RRs), which are standardized divisions of the zone's configuration information. Among the RRs is the pool of DNS names and their corresponding IP addresses, which is where the name resolution has its starting point.

Importantly, a domain and a zone are different concepts, as shown in Figure 12.3. A *domain* refers to a single node and all the nodes placed under it in the domain tree. A *zone*, however, covers only those resource records that are delegated to a specific DNS server. A zone, as such, may coincide with a domain, but many zones may exist within a domain.

While the concept of a domain is what makes DNS a very simple and effective device, the zones are what make DNS effective to administer and use. By delegating zones to different DNS servers spread across the entire network, the speed of name resolution can be optimized, and administration tools can be placed exactly where events occur. Zone delegation sometimes also results in a more effective replication of the domain information.

If you want a specific DNS server to answer requests within a certain part of domain name space, it must be configured to have authority within that zone. This authority is configured with a special resource record called the *Start of Authority* (SOA), which

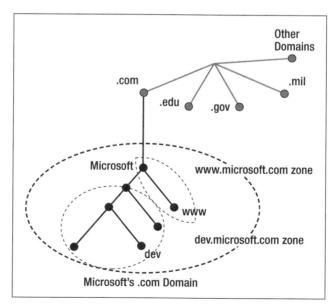

Figure 12.3
Knowing the difference between a zone and a domain is important.

typically is placed at the start of the zone file. An SOA record's presence in a server's zone file indicates that the server is the best source of information about the specific part of domain name space.

The following three different kinds of DNS servers are in operation:

- *A primary server*—This server contains the "original" copy of the data files for a particular zone, including resource records for all underlying domains and computer names. The server gets its zone data from its own local file. Changes for the zone are carried out on this server.

- *Secondary servers*—A secondary server receives data for its zone(s) from another DNS server. The process of receiving this replicated zone information (meaning the actual zone database file) is carried out through periodic *zone transfers* from the other DNS server.

- *Caching-only servers*—Unlike the primary and secondary servers, a caching-only server isn't associated with any specific DNS zone and doesn't contain any active database files. When first activated, a caching-only server doesn't have any knowledge of the DNS domain structure. But every time a caching-only server makes a request to a DNS server on behalf of a client, it registers the information in its name cache, which consequently grows over time to contain all the requests that have been carried out previously.

A primary server must be present for each zone. No secondary servers have to be present in the DNS environment, but including them is recommended, to secure the environment's operational stability. The method used to configure DNS environments are outlined in Figure 12.4.

In practice, at least one secondary server is recommended for each primary server that is established. But additional secondary DNS servers may be advantageous, depending on fault-tolerance requirements, the need for quick name references from distant locations, and loading.

Because the information in each zone is kept in separate files, the names *primary* and *secondary* are relative for each zone. A specific DNS server can function both as primary server for one or more zones and as secondary server for other zones.

Registration And Resolution Of DNS Names

A client making the request to the closest DNS server (also called *name server*), as mentioned, does the actual resolution of a DNS name to an IP address. Regarding the resolution of DNS names, remember that a DNS server can, in fact, also function as a client in relation to another DNS server. This actually isn't a rare occurrence.

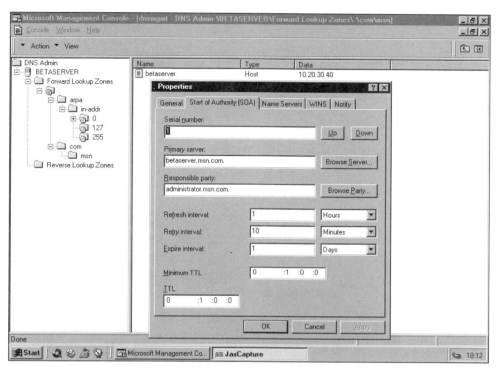

Figure 12.4
Microsoft's DNS server is an MMC snap-in in NT 5.0. Although the graphical interface enables you to make changes in the DNS files without a text editor, DNS does require a larger degree of knowledge than WINS.

If the DNS server doesn't have the information necessary to handle the request, it can use the following three types of name resolution to produce an answer:

- Recursion
- Iteration
- Caching

Recursion

A *recursive request* means that the client expects an answer to the question and will not be satisfied with a reference to another DNS server. So, through recursion, the DNS server takes over responsibility for the name resolution process and is under obligation to continue the recursive transfer of the request to other servers, until a positive or negative answer to the request has been established definitively.

A *positive answer* occurs when the DNS server finds the requested information. In this situation, the recursive server sends this information back to the client. A *negative answer* occurs when a server with authority indicates that the name or the requested data type doesn't exist. A *server with authority* is a DNS server that is configured to be either a primary or secondary zone server for the parent domain, where the requested DNS name should be placed in the domain tree.

Recursive name resolution puts all the work on the name server, which is specifically why the administrator must open that facility on many DNS servers. However, Microsoft's DNS server permits recursive name resolution as a starting point.

Iteration

In the strictest sense of the word, *iteration* can be called *nonrecursive name resolution*, because the requested DNS server answers the client request based on its best knowledge about the requested information. For example, the DNS's answer to the client may consist of references to those DNS servers that most likely have the answer, after which the client can make direct contact to those DNS servers as part of the completion of the name resolution process.

However, with iteration, the DNS server may also assist in carrying out the name resolution, besides simply returning the "best answer" to the client—but this isn't required.

For most iterative requests, the client is configured to contact other DNS servers in a domain name space, in case the local DNS server can't provide a complete answer to the request.

Caching

While the local DNS server processes requests, it will find a lot of information about domain name space. To increase the DNS performance and ease the pressure on other DNS servers, the local DNS server keeps this information in a local *cache*.

Caching can be particularly advantageous if the DNS server is on a network that is connected to the rest of the world with a slow line. *Caching-only servers* also are available, which are DNS servers whose only task is to carry out requests, embed the answers in the cache, and return the results. Such servers have no authority over any domains and contain only the information that they have intercepted while processing requests from local clients.

In each case of name resolution, the local DNS server checks its own zone information (the static DNS entries) and its cache (the dynamic entries stored in the cache) to find an answer. Even if no exact match exists for the requested address, you may be able to find some information about or a reference to a usable DNS server—and thus reduce the number of DNS servers attempting to find the answer to the request.

In a worst-case scenario for name resolution, the local DNS server starts from the top of the DNS tree with one of the root servers and works its way down through the tree until the requested data is found. However, this situation is abnormal, because the DNS server learns a lot over time while handling such requests—information that is placed in its cache.

But conversely, certain limits apply to what a cache can solve by itself. When the information is embedded in the cache, a Time-to-Live (TTL) value is also attached to ensure that the data is renewed within regular intervals—and that outdated information can't lie about in the cache forever.

However, on Microsoft's DNS servers, a few cache entries are loaded from the beginning and never become outdated or flushed out of the cache. These entries are references to DNS servers for the roots of the Internet (the .com domain, .org domain, and so forth), which should never change.

NetBIOS Vs. DNS

As a consequence of their different backgrounds, DNS and NetBIOS have different characteristics. DNS names are longer and the DNS structure is slightly more complex, because it is designed to cover the entire Internet. NetBIOS's intended use is only as a method of securing user-friendly names on small or medium-sized local networks.

The completely different designs of DNS and NetBIOS result in a world of difference between the practical handling of the two types of names.

DNS was designed from the start to produce high performance and stable operation on really large networks (as its very flexible zone structure demonstrates). Its hierarchical division of names also shows an intent to ensure both the best possible starting point for searches and globally unique DNS names, despite being checked only locally.

NetBIOS was originally built to cover only a single subnet (the area of the network surrounded by routers). Even though WINS repairs the worst problems with the administration of NetBIOS names on a TCP/IP network, it will never get it perfect, because NetBIOS was originally designed with small solutions in mind. Therefore, establishing and running a complex network requires an in-depth understanding of NetBIOS's name resolution and the function of WINS—and one of the following three compromises must be accepted from the start:

- Individual computers on each subnet can see only the units on their own subnet.

- A large amount of bandwidth (and a bit of structure) is required to keep all NetBIOS names updated across the network.

- Static installations must be carried out on each WINS server for all the resources with which communication must be possible (servers and the like) that lie outside the local subnet. This involves a relatively high risk of problems due to keying errors or changes in the structure that don't take into consideration all of the company's WINS servers.

Furthermore, WINS replication facilities are so weak that they don't contain any genuine security facilities (for example, to protect against false WINS servers). Likewise, experience with WINS has proven that it still isn't a completely stable solution. Although NT 4.0's WINS works considerably better than that of NT 3.51, an administrator still needs a lot of knowledge and experience to avoid the WINS database gradually being filled with outdated entries and such. Microsoft acknowledges that static entries shouldn't be set up in the WINS database, because problems will occur sooner or later with this setup.

DNS has only three disadvantages compared to NetBIOS:

- Due to the greater number of links and the use of separators (periods), DNS names can be a bit more difficult for ordinary users to understand. However, this problem is decreasing with the Internet's explosive prevalence and is close to being completely eliminated.

- DNS doesn't have the capacity to spread information from the primary to the secondary DNS server, in case of changes in the name table. Currently, DNS can only pull updatings of the information on the secondary servers within regular intervals.

- DNS only supports the use of static names, which means that DNS names on all resources (servers and the like) with which communication must be possible must be installed manually. This is practicable only for situations in which the number of changes is small and updatings occur only after large intervals.

DNS enables you to create solutions with greater fault tolerance than WINS, and DNS contains some far more advanced and flexible setup possibilities, enabling you to adapt the administration, operation, and security to your company's needs with much greater precision.

At most, Windows 95/98 and NT Workstation can be set up to look for two different WINS servers—a primary and a secondary WINS server. The two WINS servers are tried in turn, which means that the primary WINS server is always used first, and the Windows client tries the secondary WINS server only if the primary server doesn't respond.

DNS enables you to embed references to a random number of DNS servers in a prioritized order and, if necessary, indicate the order in which to search by domain suffix (in other words, indicate alternative domain names). Regarding the capability to indicate DNS servers, be aware that the Windows client also tries them one by one—the DNS server on top of the list is always used first, and the next DNS server is tried only if the top DNS server doesn't answer.

It's important to really understand the procedures for WINS and DNS, because the Windows client tries the next server in the row *only* if the first one doesn't respond. If the first server receives the request but can't find the name requested (and so sends a message back that the name is unknown), the Windows client will *not* repeat the same request to any of the other servers on the list.

DNS With NT 5.0: DDNS And More

Since IETF promoted DNS to the standard for name resolution on the TCP/IP protocol, many refinements of DNS have been suggested—and carried out. Some of the most important refinements are incremental zone transfers (RFC 1995), DNS NOTIFY (RFC 1996), improvements of the security facilities (RFC 2065), a new resource record type (RFC 2052), and Dynamic DNS (RFCs 2136 and 2137).

Incremental zone transfers means that you can obtain a more effective replication of zone files, because the data transfer can be limited to only the data that has been changed.

DNS NOTIFY is a push mechanism that enables the primary server to inform chosen secondary zone servers of changes to the zone file on the primary DNS server, which improves the data consistency across all zone servers.

Dynamic DNS specifies a method by which dynamic updatings (appending or deleting one or more entries in the DNS server's name table) of data are made on the primary DNS server, and are then spread in the normal way to the secondary DNS servers when they request an update. Incidentally, you may configure the primary server to accept updatings that are initiated by certain other servers. You may also set up various different conditions that must be met for a dynamic updating to be carried out. Apart from this, Dynamic DNS works in the same way as DNS.

DNS NOTIFY and Dynamic DNS remove the last two large disadvantages of DNS compared to NetBIOS: the limitation to static names and the lack of an on-demand replication mechanism. The removal of these disadvantages, combined with the numerous advantages of using DNS over NetBIOS, have resulted in Microsoft replacing WINS with DDNS in Windows NT 5.0.

Unfortunately, Dynamic DNS introduces a new disadvantage: The primary server for each zone becomes a single point of failure. The dynamic updatings can occur only against the primary DNS server for the given zone, which means that if the server is down, you can't make any updatings of the DNS database. Likewise, Dynamic DNS still needs to prove its worth with the many unpredictable situations that occur in real-world computer environments.

> **Note:** *This doesn't occur if you base the DNS infrastructure on the built-in DDNS server of NT Server 5.0 and use Active Directory's database as the data store. In this case, all the DDNS servers that also function as domain controllers can function as the primary DNS server.*

NT 5.0's DNS implementation contains support for a new resource record type, *service record*. The new service record can be used to specify those TCP/IP network services that are accessible within the specific zone. Thus, the service record enables clients to send a request seeking which servers offer a certain service within the local DNS zone. In NT 5.0, clients use the service record (among other things) to locate domain controllers that give access to Active Directory.

The structure of Active Directory assumes that each directory service domain has a corresponding DNS domain and that the DNS servers being used meet the previously mentioned RFCs. The DNS server in NT Server 5.0 meets these requirements.

The close connection between DNS and Active Directory means that you should plan the Active Directory structure before you install DNS on the network. Otherwise, you may have to carry out some unpleasant changes before implementing NT 5.0. Companies currently implementing DNS or NT Servers should study Chapters 13, 14, and 15 very thoroughly and make a plan for the transition to NT 5.0, to avoid unpleasant surprises later on.

DHCP: How To Remove The IP Headache Of The Internet

As mentioned earlier, the TCP/IP protocol is unavoidable. TCP/IP is a precondition for communicating on the Internet and it is the only real common denominator for all modern computer systems. So, if any de facto global network protocol exists, it is TCP/IP, which is why Microsoft focuses completely on TCP/IP in NT 5.0.

However, TCP/IP's overwhelming success doesn't mean that the protocol is completely free of problems. As most computer specialists probably know, configuring TCP/IP requires much greater qualifications than does configuring any of the two other popular LAN protocols, IPX/SPX and NetBEUI.

The installation of TCP/IP is a huge task for TCP/IP novices—which includes quite a few people, because TCP/IP was limited to Unix environments until just a few years ago. But few computer professionals can avoid TCP/IP any longer, due to the enormous popularity of the Internet.

TCP/IP has roughly the same source and characteristics as Unix—it is difficult to enter, but in return, incredibly useable and effective for its purpose.

TCP/IP requires a lot more administration than most other networking protocols, especially because of its need for consistent allocation of IP addresses, which can be an administrator's nightmare in the worst cases. For instance, if a company is connecting to the Internet and it doesn't already use a correct address space, it may need to do a complete reconfiguration of its IP addresses. The same is often true if a company wants a more thorough resegmentation of the network.

Unfortunately, the only way to escape inconsistent or wrong IP addresses of the past is through a lot of work performed by users. However, as previously mentioned, most users don't have sufficient knowledge to configure their own PCs for TCP/IP communication. But if it is done correctly from the beginning, all later changes can be made from the administrator's office chair. Acknowledging the increasing need for support, the world of TCP/IP has been expanded with a standard that enables you to change centrally almost all details in the TCP/IP setup for network-connected clients. This standard is called Dynamic Host Configuration Protocol (DHCP), a superstructure on the original standard Bootstrap Protocol (BOOTP). BOOTP originally was designed for the same purpose, but it has fallen far short of becoming the success once hoped for.

The really big advantage of DHCP over the older BOOTP is that DHCP supports dynamic allocation of IP addresses. This means that the system can automatically allocate IP addresses in the background for each computer as they are being connected to the network, instead of having an IP address reserved in advance by the administrators for each and every computer that might become connected to the network. With DHCP, you also can specify many more TCP/IP configuration parameters than with BOOTP.

DHCP solves the three biggest challenges on companies' budding TCP/IP networks: limited IP addresses, centralized configuration administration, and address conflicts. DHCP provides three different methods for allocating IP addresses:

- *Manually*—The administrator must enter MAC addresses (also known as Ethernet addresses) in advance and their corresponding IP addresses for all the legitimate PCs on the network. A MAC address uniquely identifies a computer with an Ethernet interface, but it does not indicate the computer's location like IP addresses do. MAC addresses consist of 12 hexadecimal digits such as 003ABE420F2A.

- *Automatically*—Removes the need to enter MAC addresses and IP addresses manually, because the DHCP server allocates addresses from a pool of IP addresses that it administers. Individual PCs are permanently allocated an IP address by the DHCP server.

- *Dynamically*—The DHCP server allocates IP addresses from an address pool under its administration, but the addresses are "on loan" only for a specified period of time (called the *lease period*). If the PC doesn't renew the loans before the end of the lease period, the IP address once again becomes part of the server's pool of accessible IP addresses.

A combination of the three allocation methods can be used on all network segments, but the last method (dynamically) is the most common setup for DHCP servers.

How DHCP Works

The working method for DHCP is fairly simple:

1. When a DHCP-prepared PC starts, it sends a DHCPDISCOVER broadcast message on the local network segment, which can also contain other information, such as a previously allocated IP address. If the client doesn't receive an answer (compare this to the next point), it keeps sending DHCPDISCOVER packages four times a minute for the next five minutes, or until it receives an offer. Incidentally, the DHCPDISCOVER message from the client is transmitted to the rest of the network, if the router is set up to do so (through the DHCP Relay Agent facility).

2. Each DHCP server that receives a DHCPDISCOVER message searches its tables for an allocation for this PC. If a server finds one, it answers with a DHCPOFFER message, which contains the IP address, the lease period, and other pieces of configuration information (for instance, the subnet mask and indication of routers). If no previous allocation exists, one or more DHCP servers answer with IP addresses belonging to the subnet on which the PC is placed, and that function as accessible IP addresses on the DHCP servers.

3. When the PC wants to accept an IP address, it returns a DHCPREQUEST message with an identification of the chosen DHCP server.

4. The server carries out an address registration and answers with a DHCPACK message, in which the IP address from the DHCPDISCOVER message is repeated and, concurrently, other pieces of possibly relevant information are sent (such as extra configuration parameters for the TCP/IP protocol). If the server doesn't accept the DHCPREQUEST message for some reason, it issues a DHCPNAK, after which the PC has to start again from the beginning.

Clients equipped with hard disks keep the allocated TCP/IP address with each subsequent start. The client will try to renew the lease of the address when half of the lease period is over. If the client can't get to the DHCP server with which it originally made the lease agreement, and 87.5 percent of the lease period has expired, the client tries to renew its lease of the IP address by sending a broadcast of the request on the network.

If the lease period expires without a resubscription, the client must immediately stop using the IP address and start a new negotiation of IP address via the previously described procedure.

DHCP Contains All Relevant Facilities

DHCP gives the network administrator an immediate opportunity to control all relevant parameters centrally, supervise the development on the network, and save a lot of boring manual administration work. However, DHCP does contain a couple of problems, as described next.

First, the DHCP specification is not completely rigid. For instance, the clients do not have to define all configuration parameters, even though the DHCP specification contains almost all of the many possible parameters in the TCP/IP protocol. Unfortunately, this condition means that a test of which parameters can be handled by the currently used client programs is required every time, to be absolutely safe against unpleasant surprises such as inconsistent or unknown parameters.

Second, DHCP is not integrated with DNS, which is felt more at the transition to NT 5.0 and which requires the presence of a DNS server. No exchange of information occurs between DHCP and DNS, despite the fact that, in principle, a situation may occur in which the DHCP server changes an IP address without the DNS server's knowledge (and thus without it updating its table). An exchange of information would ease the registration work, because DDNS needs roughly the same information that is already possessed by the DHCP.

But the largest problem definitely concerns the operation. The current DHCP specification doesn't enable you to establish any kind of warm backup servers relative to the DHCP service, because the DHCP standard doesn't contain a protocol for server-to-server communication. Thus, the only way to be absolutely safe is to divide the specific IP address space further into more separate parts (because the IP addresses on each DHCP server must be unique) and embed these address spaces in the different DHCP servers.

The only disadvantage to this procedure is that it is a poor utilization of the IP addresses and increases the overhead in connection with a DHCP registration. This also means that clients have to change IP addresses more often because the DHCP server that answers first may use another part of the IP address space than the previous DHCP server used. But this is a secondary consideration compared with the question of whether clients are always able to find a DHCP server to register against.

But help is on its way. The group working on DHCP is defining a server-to-server protocol that will enable the DHCP servers to appoint a server to be an "online reserve" for the primary DHCP server, which supposedly means that the same pool of IP addresses and common configuration installations are used for a particular subnet.

Finally, DHCP contains a gaping security hole. Currently, an unauthorized DHCP server may be established that can intercept client requests and return wrong configuration information. Incidentally, the problem of security is what has caused the updates to DHCP to drag on.

DDNS And DHCP Are The Future

As the TCP/IP protocol continues to spread and integrate with the Internet, the chances for any real alternatives diminish. In connection with TCP/IP, DHCP and DDNS can't be avoided if you want to obtain a flexible, stable, and administrable solution.

In the past few years, DHCP has really started to replace BOOTP. Every modern TCP/IP protocol stack is equipped with DHCP facilities, and a large number of commercial DHCP server products are available for almost any popular server platform. The same is true for DNS, which now is almost a precondition for getting a good connection to the Internet.

By comparison, DDNS currently is still taking its first tiny steps. But IETF's recognition of DDNS as an official Internet standard means that DDNS's position will only get stronger with time. Furthermore, Microsoft's (very wise) decision to implement DDNS in NT 5.0 definitely will help make the standard successful in the future.

Thus, Microsoft's choice of DDNS likely will prove so successful that it will stick to DDNS well into the next millennium. DDNS's success will be boosted if IETF takes action soon to close the last gaping holes in the TCP/IP administration tools: the lack of integration between IP addresses in the DHCP server and computer names in the DNS server, and the lack of opportunities to define backup servers with DDNS and DHCP.

Designing Your Network Environment With Active Directory

Having read Chapter 10, which discusses the many new ideas and terms related to NT 5.0's services component—Active Directory—you undoubtedly are wondering how to move on to the brave new world of Active Directory.

True, Microsoft needs to tie up a couple of loose ends in NT 5.0, such as details regarding Active Directory's implementation, and I don't think all of these loose ends will be resolved until well after the production version of NT Server 5.0 is released. But the basic properties and capabilities of NT Server 5.0 are clearly evident now. So, whether you are starting from scratch or have been given the task of migrating an existing domain-based NT installation onto Active Directory, this chapter should answer all of your initial questions on how to introduce this new environment. Likewise, whether you already know that your company will be changing to Active Directory or are just window-shopping, you are well advised to read this chapter very carefully, because numerous details need to be attended to in your network environment for Active Directory to be a success. If you start taking these details into account while designing your network, as outlined in this chapter, you and your company will avoid a lot of bother and frustration.

A prerequisite to reading this chapter is a firm understanding of NT domains and Active Directory—at least to the level of information provided in Chapters 4 and 10. If you come across a concept in this chapter that you find difficult to understand, leaf through Chapters 4 and 10 for clarity.

If you have difficulty understanding one or more of the NT domain concepts (which are explained more briefly than the corresponding Active Directory concepts, based on the assumption that most readers are already familiar with NT domains), please refer to the books supplied with NT Server 4.0 and the excellent Resource Kit for Windows NT Server. Also, bear in mind that handling the information in this chapter will be much easier if you already understand the concepts that are part and parcel of NT domains.

Migrating

Microsoft designed NT 5.0 to cater to organizations that already have a Windows NT Server-based environment that may want to migrate the entire organization, or part of it, to NT 5.0.

One of the great assets of migrating from an NT Server 4.0 environment to an NT 5.0 environment is the backward-compatibility of NT 5.0, as highlighted in Figure 13.1. NT 5.0 is entirely backward-compatible with the existing logon method, the security philosophy, and the replication schema, as the following explains:

- An NT Server 5.0-based Domain Controller (DC) can function as an NT 4.0-based Backup Domain Controller (BDC), which means that NT 5.0 can receive a copy of the user database from an NT 4.0 Primary Domain Controller (PDC), and thus handle logon authentication for all the existing clients. NT 5.0 can also act as a PDC.

- NT Server 5.0-based DCs can establish traditional trust relations with NT Server 4.0-based domains and handle pass-through authentication between domains, which means that you don't have to upgrade all existing NT domains (or any, for that matter) to Active Directory in the first attempt.

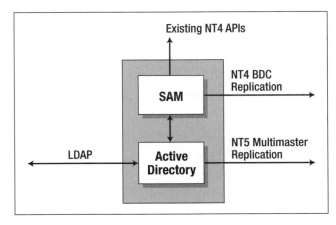

Figure 13.1
Windows NT Server 5.0 offers complete backward-compatibility for client authentication.

- Even if an NT Server 5.0-based DC acts as an NT Server 4.0-based BDC or PDC, it is able to handle login queries from Active Directory clients, too (in other words, Kerberos authentication).

In short, you can upgrade all servers from NT Server 4.0 to NT Server 5.0 without users sensing any changes. You can perform a gradual migration of the clients to Active Directory, one domain at a time.

The main point is that many migration options are available. Irrespective of your choice, a situation will never arise in the process of migration that requires massive migration to a later version of the operating system on servers and clients. Nor will you have to take down an entire domain when the DCs or the clients are being migrated. At most, each DC will be inaccessible during the time you are updating the operating system to version 5.0.

Be aware that after you establish Active Directory by upgrading an existing PDC to NT Server 5.0, the NT Server 5.0 DCs will continue to act as NT 4.0 PDCs and BDCs, until you intervene. To use only the latest NT Server 5.0-specific server functionality, you must specify that you want to change from a mixed domain to a native-mode Active Directory domain (see "The Recommended Migration Methodologies" in Chapter 14). Even if you switch to a native-mode Active Directory domain, you can still use NTLM authentication side by side with the new Kerberos authentication.

Because NT 5.0 contains full support of NTLM authentication, all current clients that don't use Kerberos are capable of using the server environment in the normal way. For example, they can be authenticated against, or use services from, NT Server 5.0-based servers.

The Transition To Active Directory

You should always remember the following details when planning a change to Active Directory:

- *A description of the site structure*—How the geographic corporate structure should be adapted to the logical network.

- *Stipulate the domains*—How to structure the logical network.

- *Stipulate the domain tree*—How to structure each area in the logical network.

- *Stipulate each domain's directory tree*—Define the Organizational Units' (OU) structure.

- *Clarify how network administrative rights should be structured and delegated.*

- *Stipulate the DNS structure*—How the DNS service should be designed.

Moreover, you need to consider carefully the number and division of servers, dimensioning the servers, dimensioning LAN and WAN, and so forth, which all relate to parameters that are specific to your company (in other words, the number of users, load profiles, uptime requirements, and current infrastructure-component recycling).

Also consider the existing corporate infrastructure when you are deciding whether to introduce Active Directory (and hence, by necessity, NT Server 5.0). You have to be very careful to implement an efficient and successful migration, whether it be from NT 4.0 domains to Active Directory, changing an existing DNS structure, or migrating from Novell NetWare 3.x or 4.x to NT Server 5.0. For more information on this topic, see Appendix A.

The Structure Of The Business

Before you embark on planning the setup of Active Directory, you must be quite clear about the physical structure of your organization's entire network (LAN and WAN), which is necessary to implement a solution that is optimized to your corporate infrastructure.

Clarifying the physical structure requires finding out how the various parts of the organization are connected, how much bandwidth these connections generate, how much of this bandwidth is already occupied for other purposes, and how much this bandwidth consumption varies in any given 24-hour period.

Often, dividing the network into LAN parts and WAN parts is sufficient, because a significantly higher bandwidth tends to be available on the LAN parts of the network. With this information, you can define the site construction of the business. However, knowing the bandwidth available on all slow WAN connections is also very desirable.

The term *site* was introduced by Microsoft to design and describe various Active Directory solutions. A site is defined as a bunch of machines that are connected with fast and cheap communication; in other words, much like a typical LAN area. Strictly speaking, in moderately sized networks that are based on Active Directory, *site* covers all attachments having a minimum accessible bandwidth of 128Kbps. Each site should have at least one DC. The difference between sites and domains is shown in Figure 13.2.

An *administrator* likely defines a site as one or more TCP/IP subnets.

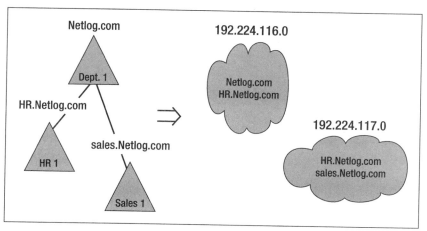

Figure 13.2
Remember that sites and domains are two mutually independent notions.

Sites won't be found in the central part of the directory (in other words, the namespace), because a site is a concept that describes the physical infrastructure. Sites are placed in a separate part of Active Directory, because they relate only to hardware components, such as computer objects and attachment objects (which are used to configure replication among various sites).

The network traffic within a site tends to be significantly higher than the traffic among various sites. The two main reasons are the following:

- *Client logon*—When a user logs on, the desktop tries to localize a DC on the same site as the desktop. When the logon process starts, the PC client receives its site membership from a DC, a statement of the site membership of the DC, and whether that DC is the closest in relation to the PC client. If that DC is not the closest one, the PC client may then choose to change to the closest DC. If the desktop is moved to another location, the first logon will be told that it no longer uses the closest DC, while at the same time receiving new site information.

- *Directory replication*—Many more opportunities arise to configure the replication itself and the replication routes among various sites than to configure within a site. This is based on the fact that replication among sites occurs more often than within a site. However, you can configure the time interval for replications within a site (the standard value is set to every 10 minutes) and the topology of replication (which is like a circle that you can traverse either way; in other words, a bidirectional circle).

Planning sites means to ensure that the bandwidth is sensibly used in places that have only limited (or expensive) bandwidth at their disposal. Several attachments can be defined between two sites. Then, after each replication is started, Active Directory chooses the attachment with the lowest price per unit of bandwidth (or, alternatively, the attachment with the highest bandwidth), so that the cheapest, or most effective, attachment is used (provided that it is available at the time).

However, planning is also a matter of determining which DCs you want the clients to use. As stated earlier, a client first tries to find a DC within the local site, and then chooses a random DC from another site to validate its logon. Be aware that, currently, if a client doesn't have contact with a DC from the local site, it can't state any site preferences for logon attempts. In fact, the client won't even bother to find the site that is closest to the physical network, but instead will choose one at random from the current list of DCs. The client will investigate at certain intervals whether a DC is available in the local site, and if one is, the client will use this DC for all successive DC queries.

Also realize that multihomed computers (units with more than one network card operating) always belong to a particular site, regardless of whether they use subnets that actually belong to several sites. To avoid undue confusion and frustration, place all the network cards on each multihomed computer in the same site.

Also note that the philosophy of *sites* already is used to reduce replication traffic across slow WAN lines in several other BackOffice applications. Unfortunately, the various BackOffice applications use different definitions of the term *site*. NT 5.0 introduces a new philosophy, wherein the site is not optimized to each application, but instead, the underlying TCP/IP network is used to decide which locations have good network connections. Microsoft has established that all BackOffice applications will gradually change to this definition of a site.

The Structure Of The Domain

The structure of the domain concerns the very opposite concept of site structure. A structure of a domain must be based on the organizational model of the business (in other words, the logical point of view of the business, which is the natural counterpart to the physical point of view). The site structure and the domain structure thus are two entirely separate concepts. A single domain may cover several geographical units, and a single site may contain users and resources that belong to several domains.

When establishing the structure of the domain, the primary design parameter should be the geography, or physical placement, provided that this design parameter is also used in the organizational model of the business. On the other hand, remember that the entire database of Active Directory must be replicated onto all DCs within the same domain. This requires a lot of bandwidth in large businesses, to handle all the replication.

If the business happens to be divided into organizational units that cover North America, Asia, and Europe, administered from three operational centers, establishing a structure with three domains would be most sensible. If the three units are administered from one place, one domain would work best, unless other important factors indicate otherwise. Note that the number of users should not determine the configuration, because (according to Microsoft) every Active Directory domain can hold up to 10 million objects and have a total size of up to 17 terabytes.

The following is a list of advantages of placing all objects in the same domain:

- All queries can be handled by any DC.

- No need exists to administer the relationship among several domains.

- The possibility to split up the domain into divisions, operational areas, departments, workgroups, and so forth, by means of OUs, remains an option.

On the other hand, having everything in the same domain is a bad idea, because the traffic of replication can be extremely cumbersome, as the entire directory database must be replicated to every DC. Moreover, you will have to use the same properties and common guidelines (for example, the security policy) everywhere in a domain. This can be a problem in a very decentralized corporate culture.

Somewhat helpful is the fact that Active Directory limits itself to replicating only the properties that have been changed. Likewise, you can plan how often replications must occur within a geographic site, and among sites. These facilities make creating separate domains for every single site unnecessary.

Depending on the size and dynamics of your organization, the task of replicating can turn into a very nasty experience, such that you are forced to divide Active Directory into several domains for everything to function harmoniously.

If you want more than one domain, you have to decide whether these domains should be placed in a domain tree or in separate domain trees. At first glance, the DNS name structure and the trust relations are the only differences between these two options, as both store the resources in the same Global Catalog. Users can have access to each others' resources (provided that this is allowed, and that trust relations are established among the separate domain trees). However, an Active Directory query for an attribute that isn't indexed in the Global Catalog will be executed only in the domain tree in which the user or the application carries out the search.

If you want a coherent DNS name structure or full searches irrespective of the Global Catalog's contents, you must choose a domain tree. Otherwise, establishing several domain trees may be an advantage.

When determining the structure of the domain, you must also consider the fact that domains contain OUs, a type of hierarchical branch beyond the domain trees. Every domain can be subdivided into a number of OUs that can contain users, groups, computers, printers, and other resources, as well as other OUs.

When you split the domain into a hierarchy, you no longer have to look at all the resources in a flat list. The OUs enable you to organize the objects into logical structures that fit into the way the business is organized. One possible goal for the OUs is to reduce the number of domains necessary by establishing an Active Directory solution that is identical with the corporate structure of the organization.

Consider the following subjects after you decide to split the network into domains and OUs:

- If the company operates with a very decentralized IT structure, such that different users and resources are administered by mutually independent computer staff, you should split the network into many different domains.

- If the network is split into two or more parts that are so slow that transferring replication traffic is impossible, these areas of the network should be split into a corresponding number of domains.

- OUs should be the primary tool with which to show details of the organizational structure of the business.

- OUs should be used to delegate administrative control over small groups of users, groups, and other resources.

- If the organizational structure tends to change fairly frequently, you should choose to use OUs. Any domains should be organized such that they don't need to be moved or divided too often. In other words, using the sites of the business as your basis to determine the number and location of the various domains often is most advantageous.

Thus, each domain must contain at least one DC. In general, you have to place at least one DC in every site that contains users or computers from the given domain, to ensure sensible performance for the users. This statement is based on Microsoft's own model of "99 percent queries and 1 percent updates" for Active Directory. By having a DC in every site, the users have a local server that can handle their queries immediately. On the other hand, you have to live with the traffic of replication, perhaps by configuring it to take place outside normal working hours.

Maximum performance normally occurs when a DC is present in every site that acts as a Global Catalog server. This enables the server to carry out queries for objects from all accessible Active Directory domains.

Migrating From The Old NT 4.0 Domains

Until NT 5.0, the versions of Windows NT Server have operated with the following four basic domain models:

- Single domain

- Single master domain

- Multiple master domain

- Single domain with trust relations (including Complete Trust)

In most instances, these four domain models are chosen to implement a network environment. However, a mixture of these options also can be implemented, because the domain models aren't built into the server software. The choice is all a matter of how the trust relations and domains are used.

Active Directory enables administrators to reduce the number of domains for all situations beyond the single domain model. As a rule, Active Directory provides two great advantages:

- Every domain is cheaper to administer, or fewer domains exist to administer. Handling a group of Active Directory domains is easier than handling the same number of domains in NT 4.0, because the transitive trust relations drastically reduce the number of trust relations. Of course, performing the day-to-day administrative tasks is cheaper with fewer domains.

- All users, groups, and resources can be put together into just one logical structure, which makes things more manageable for the administrator and the users. The ability to build a hierarchical structure with OUs also means that you can maintain, and perhaps refine, the splitting of the organization's objects to match its requirements.

Migrating From A Single Domain

When you migrate from a previous version of NT Server to NT Server 5.0, a single domain structure, as a rule, ends up being a single domain in Active Directory.

On the other hand, you can add functionality that was previously unavailable, through Active Directory's many features. In particular, the ability to set up a hierarchy of

OUs enables you to build a structure that is based on the corporate structure and delegate administrative rights on the basis of this structure.

Many businesses operate with several single domains, linked by trust relations. This solution is used mainly by the many decentralized businesses that lack a common IT organization. However, this solution is also used in many other organizations that don't intend to introduce an NT Server solution, because the multiple single domains solution has grown into something of a grassroots movement, often in the form of a Complete Trust. In other words, a full trust among the domains is established.

When migrating to Active Directory, you can maintain the current number of independent domains and link them via the NT 4.0-like one-way trust relations of Active Directory. After all, the transitive trust relations of Active Directory are much easier to handle than the trust relations of NT 4.0.

You are sure to achieve improved efficiency by changing the structure, either by bracketing together a series of domains (operating with a single domain and a relatively sophisticated directory tree), by gathering several domains in a domain tree (operating with several domains, all gathered in the same hierarchy), or by tying together the domains in a forest.

> **Note:** A forest consists of one or more different domain trees (and hence, different name structures). These domain trees use the same directory schema and Global Catalog and are mutually linked through transitive trust relations. By comparison, a domain tree is a hierarchy of domains with a connected name structure, which share the directory schema and Global Catalog, and are mutually linked through transitive trust relations.

You will need some very weighty arguments for maintaining a Complete Trust solution, which undoubtedly is the most complex domain solution in terms of bandwidth. However, as you may know, many other advantages exist to gathering the business into one common domain tree.

Migrating From A Single Master Domain

Migrating from a single master domain structure tends to start from the top of the structure. The master domain is migrated first, and then the resource domains are handled one by one.

If your business operates with a centralized IT unit, converting the single master domain structure into a single domain often is advantageous, because this rids you of all the administrative work involved in maintaining several domains. A business can maintain the organizational structure in the various domains via a hierarchy of OUs.

The hierarchy of OUs can be an identical copy of the old domain structure. In many instances, however, administrators take advantage of the opportunity to introduce an even greater level of detail, because Active Directory doesn't add any extra administrative costs for more domains and trust relations.

For an organization with a centralized IT structure, the advantages of migrating from a single master domain model to a single Active Directory domain are the following:

- Fewer domains to administer.

- Queries are handled faster and more efficiently, because all objects are collected in only one domain.

- Establishing a more detailed corporate network structure is possible, without causing any unpleasant administrative side effects.

- Delegating administrative rights that cater far better to the areas of each staff member is possible.

In more decentralized businesses, keeping a domain tree structure often will serve you the best. The same goes for businesses with a centralized IT structure in which each business entity is regarded as an independent unit that can be bought, sold, or moved at regular intervals.

The transition from the single master domain model to a domain tree results in the users and resources no longer appearing separate. All domains must contain the users and resources that actually appear within that domain.

Migrating From A Multiple Master Domain

The choice of using the multiple master domain model often is made either because the number of objects is too large for a single domain, because several geographic junctions exist (each with their own objects), or because the domain model agrees best with the corporate structure. Regardless of the reason for operating with the multiple master domain model, it is eliminated when Active Directory is introduced.

While Microsoft doesn't recommend that you place more than 10,000 objects on one domain at a time for NT 4.0, and actually has a theoretical limit of exactly 10,000 objects for the first version of NT Server (version 3.1), Active Directory should be able to handle up to 10 million objects. Having a large number of users no longer is a good reason for having a large number of domains.

Likewise, Active Directory enables you to split the network into different sites and establish a replication model among these sites. If the attachments among the largest sites are able to handle the load from occasional replications, you can consolidate the domains and reap all the administrative advantages mentioned earlier.

In fact, maintaining the existing domain structure is worthwhile only if the geographic structure agrees closely with the corporate structure. And even if the corporate structure agrees with the existing domain structure, you should consider the following possibilities when migrating to Active Directory:

- Unite all existing resource domains with the master domain that belongs to it, or move all the users to the domain to which they logically belong. This results in fewer domains and more administrative advantages.

- Preserve all existing domains and organize each of the existing master domains as the root in a domain tree. This is a good idea particularly if you want to give the administrators full autonomy over their master domains. Furthermore, the existing DNS name structure of the business is divided in the same manner as the existing master domain model. Depending on the requirements, you can compose domain trees in a forest or have them appear independent of each other. If you choose the forest, all users will have access to all resources, regardless of which domain tree they are placed in (because of the transitive trust relations). Defining NT 4.0-like one-way trust relations is possible only among dependent domain trees.

Migrating From Scratch To Active Directory

When you have the great privilege of starting from square one with the design of the Active Directory solution, you must concentrate on meeting the following five requirements:

- Build up a name structure that agrees with the corporate structure, so that the name structure makes sense and is readily accessible for users.

- Make handling later corporate changes easy, without expensive and complicated reorganizations of one or more domains.

- Design for possible future requirements caused by company mergers, corporate takeovers, or closer integration with various services (especially the Internet, which might have to be geared to the DNS name structure of the business).

- Provide efficient replication that is compatible with available network bandwidth.

- Ensure a certain degree of fault tolerance in all parts of Active Directory, so that users have the widest possible access to a local Active Directory server.

As a foundation for Active Directory, you should always rely on a design that operates with a single domain. From a purely administrative viewpoint, this is clearly the most appropriate method—if your company can limit itself to one domain and a fairly advanced hierarchy of OUs that can fully express the corporate structure.

A domain is the preferred solution because it usually is the cheapest solution in terms of administration. A domain is the cheapest solution administratively because all trust relations are set up automatically, and the domain constitutes the immediate security limit. Also, in most instances, the OUs are sufficiently powerful to represent the corporate structure.

The tradeoff is that the OUs don't appear in the DNS name structure. And if you have more sites, a solution consisting of only one domain is at a disadvantage, because you limit the possibilities of operating replication of the dynamic domain information between the DCs in two sites. In such instances, you should consider whether the corporate structure agrees better with being split into several domains that are all part of a domain tree.

On the other hand, I can't recommend that you gamble on forests of domain trees, several independent domains (or domain trees), or some of the other old domain models (single master domain, multiple master domain, or single domain with trust relations). You need some extremely good reasons to support choosing one of these solutions. And the only reasons that seem sufficiently weighty are either a very decentralized business (and IT organization) or an extremely dynamic corporate environment with constant selling and takeovers of autonomous entities.

Implementing a forest or a domain tree is a good idea with existing Active Directory solutions. The domain tree and the forest enable administrators to combine two existing domains—such as with a corporate takeover or merger—without having to go through an expensive and unpleasant transitory phase. Microsoft has already selected forests as the main auxiliary tool with which to handle mergers of businesses or perform an easy implementation of any NT 5.0-based solution at a grassroots level.

Furthermore, the introduction of old-fashioned, nontransitive one-way trust relations among standalone domains (single domain with trust relations) or domain trees can be a very useful facility. This solution may be used to link Active Directory domains among subsidiaries or close collaborators.

Determining The DNS Architecture

DNS provides the basic name services in the Active Directory environment, which means the DNS architecture must agree with the Active Directory hierarchy. This can be a challenge to businesses that have an existing DNS infrastructure, because Active Directory uses Dynamic DNS (DDNS).

How the actual DNS name structure appears depends on the architecture of Active Directory. But how the actual DNS architecture is set up depends a lot on any existing DNS environment.

When you design a new DNS architecture, begin by establishing a DDNS zone for each NT domain (for example, so that the domain sales.netlog.com lies within the DNS zone sales.netlog.com). At least one DNS server must be available in each NT domain. If you choose to create a DNS zone for every domain, that DNS zone ends up having all the gateways that must be used by the DCs of the domain—and thus, the DNS information that is frequently used should be present locally.

The DNS integration of Active Directory should be switched on, so that all DNS data will be stored (and thus replicated) throughout the Active Directory database. If the DNS zone is created in Active Directory, any DC may function as a primary server (with full read/write DNS authority). If, instead, you choose to use the DDNS server in a traditional manner, only one DNS primary server can exist, which must be accessible constantly for the clients to be able to register their DNS names. The DNS primary server becomes a single point of failure for the environment, which is an unfortunate situation, because the network then depends on the availability of just one server.

Having all DCs also appear as DNS servers isn't an absolute prerequisite. However, I recommend that at least one DNS server be available in every site that contains a DC—for bandwidth considerations. Often, placing clients in separate domains within the given DNS zone, based on which site they belong to, is advantageous (so that you may operate with the domains, such as germany.sales.netlog.com and sweden.netlog.com, for the clients). Because each domain still belongs to the same DNS zone, you still have a joint DNS database. These guidelines are the best solution for a DDNS architecture.

So, even though you don't have to turn upside down the existing DNS architecture, something must be done about the DNS servers. Above all, DDNS can support the DNS servers if all the client names don't have to be introduced manually in the zone file, which often involves outrageous administrative costs.

Microsoft recommends that you use the DNS server that comes with NT 5.0, so that you avoid any risk of incompatibilities or reduced functionality. DDNS is a fairly new standard, and Microsoft's DDNS implementation also supports the use of the Unicode font, which enables you to use special characters in the domain names (which isn't part of the DDNS standard).

Note that all the existing DNS zones don't necessarily have to be rearranged to DDNS zones in order to handle all the dynamic information for the NT domain. The name of the NT domain doesn't have to agree with the domain name of the DNS (for example, the NT domain sales.netlog.com could easily have the DNS name netlog.com). Thus, you can operate with DNS domain names—which are entirely different from the NT domain names—and have everything function via the DNS zone transfer.

The NT domain trees will always operate with a coherent namespace. This namespace can be placed in a joint DNS zone, or you can configure a DNS zone per domain. Several zones lower the replication traffic, so that most DNS queries can be answered on the local DNS server or on some of the DNS servers close by. A big DNS zone requires that DNS zone transfers be performed on a much bigger area, which means a larger volume of traffic. As a rule, you should operate with several zones in businesses that are very decentralized. In decidedly centralized businesses, the opposite is true. If a need exists for an incoherent namespace, you have to establish a forest rather than a domain tree.

Beware: Naming Is More Important Than You May Imagine

When talking about DNS name structures, you can't ignore the Internet. After all, DNS is the standard for name resolutions on the Internet. And experience demonstrates that if a business isn't already online to the Internet, it likely will be soon due to business pressure. This is true regardless of the current security demands of the business. As a rule, solving Internet security problems in a prudent manner is a headache for the IT department.

I can't emphasize enough my very strong recommendation that you consider the Internet when you are determining the DNS name structure of your Active Directory. Otherwise, the DNS name structure could quickly turn out to be a straightjacket. It can be reversed, but doing so is extremely unpleasant.

The following are the two fundamental ways to design the DNS name structure to accommodate the Internet:

- Two separate name structures—one for the internal network and one for the Internet

- One name structure for both the internal network and the Internet

The advantages and disadvantages of implementing two separate name structures are the following:

- A clear distinction exists between internal and external resources.

- The structure is easier to administer from an operational perspective, because the independent name structures can be administered separately, with no risk of overlap.

- The installation of clients is simpler. (Blocks for all internal names are put on the firewall.)

- The configuration of the proxy is simpler. (All names that end on the internal domain name will be defined as internal.)

- The logon name of the user is different from the email name, which the users are bound to find very puzzling.

- Both domain names must be reserved with the Internet authorities, to avoid name coincidences.

The advantages and disadvantages of implementing a common name structure are the following:

- The domain name can be the same on either side of the firewall. Therefore, registering a domain name is necessary only with the Internet authorities.

- The logon name of the user is the same as the email name.

- The configuration of the proxy is far more complex, because it must be told when a query needs to be sent out of the internal network.

- You must clarify how the clients on the internal network are to be guaranteed access to the Internet resources of the business. One of the better solutions is to create a mirror of the Internet resources on the internal network (which, however, requires that you always keep the resources up to date in two places).

- The structure is much more difficult to administer, because the administrators must know the difference between internal and external resources, to avoid unpleasant mistakes.

- The DNS domain looks different to users, depending on whether they look at it from the internal network or through the Internet. For reasons of security, some intranet resources are bound to be made inaccessible for Internet users.

Prepare For The Future Today!

Although your company may not be ready to change to Windows NT Server 5.0, taking a closer look at some of the fundamental components for the Active Directory-based environments of the future is still very worthwhile. If you prepare for the capabilities (and qualifications) of Active Directory now, you will be in a far better position when migration is launched. And, believe me, Microsoft will do everything in its power to make sure migration occurs as soon as possible on all NT installations.

Regarding the fundamental components, you are well advised to take special note of DNS: Active Directory and the DNS namespace are two sides of the same coin. So, if a namespace hasn't already been set up for your company, you should seriously consider how Active Directory should appear (and perhaps have the DNS name reserved with the Internet authorities). If your company doesn't already have a ready-made DNS solution at its disposal, I advise you to start looking around to see whether changes are necessary. And, if so, implement them at a convenient time.

You should also consider what effect Active Directory is likely to have on the future network load. For example, you should think about any slow WAN lines, which are bound to be loaded down with replication activity, and so forth. Active Directory may prove to pull in the opposite direction of the existing network architecture, because Active Directory aims at linking and integrating the entire business far more than current domain-based solutions (such as NT 4.0, or the widespread Novell bindery-based solutions of yesterday).

Moreover, you should consider the current clients: While you are migrating to Active Directory, upgrading the client operating systems may be worthwhile. So, you should take a closer look at your company's current philosophy of distributing changes and carrying out upgrades of the actual operating system.

Finally, you should focus a bit on the political challenges within your company—how divisions, departments, and so forth should be placed relative to each other within Active Directory. Clarifying who is to be placed at the top of the tree, and other such matters, may turn out to be quite a challenge.

But don't despair. My experience from implementing the Novell hierarchical directory service (NDS) is that most things become evident after you determine the corporate structure. All things considered, the starting point is more favorable with Active Directory than with NDS, because of its great flexibility and many capabilities, especially its very simple—and quite flat—NT domain structure.

If you are about to set up a Windows NT Server 4.0-based solution, you will be helped significantly if you take all the preceding information into consideration. When establishing new NT solutions, you especially should consider how difficult the transition is going to be from your type of domain to Active Directory. In most instances, you can't do much, because the NT 4.0 domains are not very flexible. Consequently, only one solution will agree with all (or most) of your particular situation's demands. But, even so, I advise you to give it some thought, because referring the resources and users to their own separate domains (which is the case in single master domain and multiple master domain philosophies) doesn't make sense when you know that this split is troublesome in an Active Directory environment.

The Reality Of Active Directory 14

The last chapter focused on the design of Active Directory solutions, primarily the planning involved before migrating from domain-based solutions. This chapter discusses the details of that migration by covering the following:

- How the various Active Directory mechanisms function in practice

- How migration to Active Directory should be carried out

- How users in the operating environment are likely to experience Active Directory

The description of how Active Directory works is very theoretical at this point, because the production version hasn't been released for companies to start using. Experience with Active Directory currently is limited to two test installations, because companies aren't going to implement the first beta of a server operating system on a production computer installation.

The Active Directory Domain Model

The domain trees of Active Directory may be viewed either logically or physically. The physical view focuses on the division of the namespace for the domain tree (the physical architecture of the directory). The logical view focuses on the trust relations between the domains, or trees (the logical architecture of the directory).

In Active Directory, a domain serves as a partition in the namespace. All domain controllers (DCs) in the same domain hold the entire directory for the domain, and their databases are identical. Replication of objects always takes place at the domain level. DCs never replicate domain objects for DCs in other domains. This turns a domain into both a name context and a partition in the namespace.

A domain tree of Active Directory consists of a hierarchy of domains, each with trust relations up to the parent domain and down to all the child domains. This is another way to say that trust relations exist with the domains above and below a specific domain in the hierarchy. Each domain may contain a hierarchy of OUs, which are organized in the same manner as the domain tree.

So, two structuring mechanisms are available in Active Directory: the domain hierarchy and the OU hierarchy. This hierarchical two-tiered structure provides a lot of flexibility in the design and administration of the domain trees. This flexibility is a result of Microsoft's intent to enable every business to create an IT infrastructure that matches its organizational structure.

In Windows NT 5.0, a domain is a partition of a namespace, marking out the boundaries for the joint security policy. The security policy of the domain defines how powerful passwords must be, the length of time before a password is reused, the lifetime for Kerberos tickets, and so on. When creating a security principal in a domain, the principal is allocated a *Security Identifier* (SID). Part of the SID contains an identifier for the domain in which the SID was issued, which helps make easier the task of finding which domain contains the particular user or group and whether that person or group can be allocated access to a particular resource.

Thus, a domain is a physical security boundary, and full administrative control can be assigned only to individual domains.

The Logical And Physical Structure Of A Domain

The logical structure of a domain doesn't have to match the structure of the network, nor that of the business. The concept of a logical and physical structure of a business is shown in Figure 14.1.

Active Directory registers the physical topology of the network via the *site* concept (see Chapter 13 for more information on this topic), which provides an area in which all units are tied together with high-speed attachments. The philosophy of the site is that the physical organization of the network must be designed such that all clients having access to Active Directory receive the maximum benefit from the physical layout.

NT 5.0-based clients and servers use sites to ensure that an inquiry is handled by units within the same physical area, if possible. For instance, when a client attempts to log on, Active Directory uses the TCP/IP address of the client and any accessible site information to reach a DC placed on the local site, if possible.

Moreover, the site topology is used to optimize replication among the DCs, described as follows:

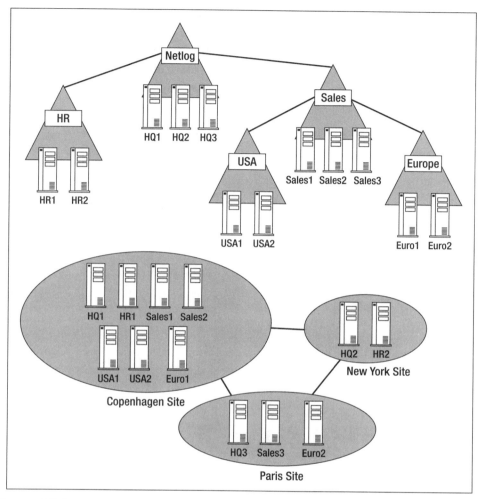

Figure 14.1
Domains and their sites don't have to be identical, because they concern two different matters—the logical and physical structure of the business, respectively.

- *Replication among various sites*—While installing a DC into a site that doesn't already have a DC from the domain, replication attachments to a DC in another site must be created automatically. This ensures that the DC is connected to the other DCs for the domain. If necessary, you can reconfigure the replication attachments and adjust the setups. In the beta 1 release of NT 5.0, this automatic creation of replication attachments isn't completely developed, although the necessary attachments can be established manually, through the Microsoft Site Replication Manager MMC snap-in.

- *Replication within the same site*—While installing a DC into a site that already has at least one DC that covers the given domain, a ring topology for replication among the DCs is automatically created. The topology defines how directory updates should flow among DCs. The ring structure ensures that at least two replication routes exist between each pair of servers, so that replication functions satisfactorily even when a DC crashes.

Because of the requirements of replication, two networks that are connected with a fairly slow attachment should be defined as two different sites.

In order for a replication environment to be flexible, it must allow you to move servers among different sites, change the setup of the replication attachments between the servers, define subnets for each site, and adjust the setup of replications (for example, when and how often replication should occur). Windows NT 5.0 provides for all of these capabilities.

Adjustment of the replication setups for replication among various sites has several parameters—compared to replication within the same site. Within the same site you can use simple SMTP connections or Exchange processing rather than the Remote Procedure Call (RPC) normally used for replication.

So far, the capabilities of the replication tool interface (Microsoft Site Replication Manager, shown in Figure 14.2) can only be speculated upon, because none of the functionalities previously listed are quite ready for NT 5.0 beta 1.

Replication Of Active Directory

Active Directory is based on multimaster replication, which is why all DCs are equal. The distinction between the Primary Domain Controller (PDC) and the Backup Domain Controllers (BDCs) has been removed in the replication implementation of Active Directory. This equality means that all objects can be created and modified on any DC in the domain and then be replicated out onto the remaining DCs.

However, a few (very rare) operations remain in which the DCs are unequal, specifically those operations in which changes are introduced that have an impact on the entire domain tree (for example, when adding or deleting a domain and altering a domain schema). Such operations require a *lockout mechanism*, to be absolutely certain that the alteration has been spread to all DCs in the domain, before attempting to introduce a new, comprehensive change globally.

The lockout mechanism in Active Directory consists of one of the DCs being appointed *Floating Single Master* (FSM). The FSM role may be moved among various

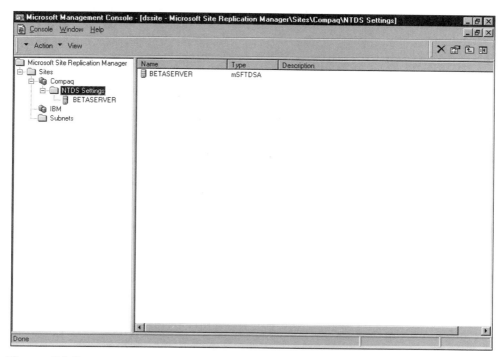

Figure 14.2
The MMC snap-in (Microsoft Site Replication Manager) that handles replication.

DCs, but only one FSM can exist at any given time. If a DC having the FSM role crashes, another DC will be promoted to take over the FSM role.

The replication mechanism in Active Directory isn't based on time but rather on a far simpler mechanism, known as *Update Sequence Number* (USN). A USN is a 64-bit number that is maintained by each Active Directory server. Every time a change is introduced in the Active Directory database on a particular server, its USN is incremented. The change and the increase of the USN is performed as an atomic operation (in other words, both parts are either implemented or fail together).

The directory database of every DC contains a table with entries to the server's own USN and the latest USNs from all its replication partners (which are all servers within the given site, and any other replication partners to which the administrator has defined attachments).

At the beginning of a replication cycle, each of the replication partners sends its own USN number. This number is used to filter out the changes already introduced on the two servers. A USN table, prior to its replication, is shown in Figure 14.3.

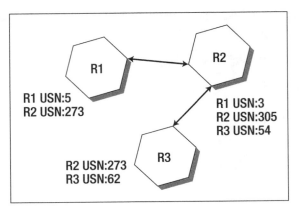

Figure 14.3
A USN table prior to replication.

The replication cycle on each of the servers means the following:

- If the USN number received from the counterpart is equal to the corresponding entry in the USN table of the server, the server does not ask to receive information about any changes from the counterpart.

- If the USN number received from the counterpart is higher than the corresponding USN table entry of the server, the server asks to receive all the changes that have occurred between the given USN number in the USN table and the USN number stated by the counterpart. This means that if server A has a USN entry of 58 for server B, and server B has issued a message that its USN number is 60, then server A asks to receive the changes that correspond with the USNs 59 and 60. When the server introduces the changes in the database of the directory, it increases its own USN number with the number of changes performed. At the same time, the USN number of the counterpart is entered into the corresponding entry in the USN table.

The USN methodology makes restarting the server after a crash very simple, because both the local USN and the USNs of the replication partners are performed as atomic operations on updates and replications. This means that loss of data on the local directory, in principle, can't occur, and that the server is immediately brought in synchronization with that of the replication partners, by repeating the normal pattern of replication. The USN table after replication is shown in Figure 14.4.

Active Directory's replication system allows loops in the replication topology in the form of several routes among the servers, which serves to enhance performance and the accessibility of the entire system. This is why Active Directory's replication sys-

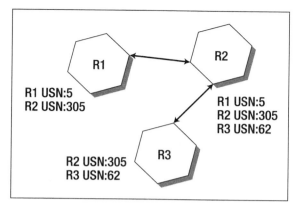

Figure 14.4
The USN table after replication.

tem is called a *propagation dampening mechanism*, which prevents changes from propagating endlessly among the servers—with a subsequent loss of bandwidth and diminished overall network performance.

The philosophy of the propagation dampening mechanism is that an up-to-date vector is maintained on every server. The up-to-date vector contains a list of USN pairs stating the highest USN for an originating write, received from a specific server. An *originating write* comprises an update performed on the specific server, and doesn't occur from replication. The up-to-date vector contains all servers on the particular site, along with any other replication partners to which the administrator has defined attachments.

The propagation dampening mechanism causes each replication to be slightly more advanced than was first described in this book. Immediately prior to the transfer of replicating data (in other words, when the server has ascertained that one or more new changes are present on its replication partner since the latest replication), the up-to-date vector is transferred to the replication partner, which uses it to filter out superfluous data, because the given attribute has already been updated. Although all changes of the attribute are superfluous, the USN numbers of the replication partner continue to be updated in the server's USN table.

In a multimaster replication system, such as Active Directory, the same attribute can be updated on two or more different replicas between each replication. When an attribute is changed a second time, with the changes from the first attempt being distributed to all replicas, a collision of replications is caused. Such collisions are detected through the use of the version numbers, which are valid for every single attribute that is contrary to the server-specific USNs.

The version number for an attribute is recorded every time a change of the attribute occurs. Replications don't cause the version number to be recorded, because this number is entered into the replication of the attribute.

When a replication collision occurs, the two DCs involved decide which of the attributes should be kept in the database of the directory, in the following manner:

- *First, on the basis of the version number*—Active Directory always chooses the attribute with the highest version number, assuming that the attribute with the lowest version number is obsolete. This might not always prove to be the right solution, but it does provide a definite decision (if the version numbers aren't the same).

- *Second, on the basis of the time schema*—If the version numbers of the altered properties are the same, and the values of the attributes are different, the DC uses the time stamp to choose which property should be kept in the database. The time stamp is always inserted with every property and version number. The property with the latest time stamp is chosen. For this solution to function satisfactorily, all timers on all applicable DCs have to be synchronized. Even if they are synchronized, the time stamp isn't necessarily always the right solution. Nevertheless, using the time schema is a good method with which to resolve replication disagreements.

- *Third, on the basis of the buffer size*—In the extremely unlikely instance that the version number and the time stamps are identical, the DC performs a binary memory-copying operation and compares the buffer sizes. The larger buffer size is the winner. If two buffers generate the same result, then the attributes are completely identical, and thus discarding either one of them is fine.

Note that all decisions for replication collisions are logged, and the administrator may choose one of the attributes that was originally rejected.

Naming

Active Directory offers support of several different well-known types of names, including the following:

- *RFC822 names*—These consist of the type *name@domainname* (for example, **akaplan@interaccess.com**) and are familiar to most users of Internet email addresses. Active Directory provides an RFC822 name for all objects, which can be used for email addresses and login accounts.

- *HTTP URL names*—Active Directory has built-in support for Web browser access via the HTTP protocol and Microsoft's Internet Information Server (IIS). For example, *http://domainname/path/page* specifies a route to a Web page, and should be familiar to users of Web browsers. Access can be gained to the contents of Active Directory via HTTP URLs. The *domainname* indicates the server that operates Active Directory, and the *path/page* is the path through Active Directory to the desired object. For example, the following is an HTTP URL that specifies an Active Directory page: **http://www.netlog.dk/User.ASP?path=Salesdivision/ OU=Presales/OU=Projects/CN=MortenStrunge**.

- *LDAP URLs and X.500 names*—Active Directory has built-in support for LDAP inquiries from LDAP clients. LDAP names are less intuitive than the well-known Internet names, because LDAP names use the X.500 naming convention called *attributed naming*. An LDAP URL contains a statement of the server that operates Active Directory and the attributed name of the object. For example, the following is an LDAP URL that specifies an Active Directory page: **LDAP:// Server1.netlog.dk/CN=MortenStrunge,OU=Projects,OU=Presales,OU= Salesdivision,O=netlog,C=DK**.

- *UNC names*—Active Directory also has Universal Naming Convention (UNC) support, which currently is very popular on Windows-based networks. UNC names can refer to volumes, printers, and files. In Active Directory, a UNC name consists of the domain's DNS name, the path of the requested object, and the object itself (such as **\\Server1.netlog.dk\Sales\Project\Netlog\internet\Excelfiles\ budget98.xls**).

In practice, most users come in contact with RFC822 and UNC names, whereas HTTP URL names are limited to users who use Active Directory through Web browsers. As a rule, LDAP names are hidden behind an application—which is just as well, because these names are extremely difficult for ordinary users to relate to.

Apart from these name formats, Active Directory also introduces two of its own defined formats:

- *Active Directory Canonical Names*—Correspond to the route from the root of the tree to the object (such as **/DK/Netlog/Salesdivision/Presales/Projects/ MortenStrunge**).

- *Active Directory Service Path Names*—Reverse LDAP URL names (such as **LDAP:// Server1.netlog.dk/C=DK/O=netlog/OU=Salesdivision/OU=Projects/ CN=MortenStrunge**).

From NT Domains To Active Directory

Microsoft states that in NT 5.0 beta 1, migration from an existing NT domain to Active Directory always begins with the PDC of the NT 4.0 network, as shown in

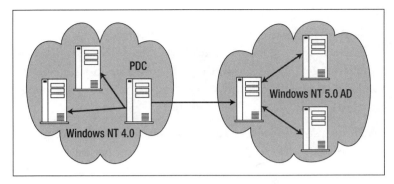

Figure 14.5
The only method to migrate from domains to Active Directory (in NT 5.0 beta 1) is the PDC method, which very likely will end up being the most popular migration methodology.

Figure 14.5. After upgrading to NT 5.0, the PDC can present itself as an NT 5.0 DC for other NT 5.0-based servers, and as an NT 4.0 PDC for all the existing NT servers. In other words, existing servers and clients can't tell the difference between the new NT 5.0-based PDC and the old NT 4.0-based PDC; the NT 5.0 is 100 percent backward-compatible.

For NT 5.0, Microsoft undoubtedly will recommend the PDC-based methodology the most. However, Microsoft indicates that the production version of NT 5.0 will have the capability to migrate out of an existing NT domain in a less drastic fashion— by upgrading one or more BDCs, as shown in Figure 14.6. The advantage of this

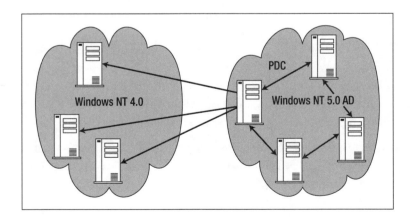

Figure 14.6
The BDC method might be a fitting name for the other method used to migrate from domains to Active Directory. The BDC method contains a series of restrictions that makes the PDC method more preferable.

method is that the NT domain is maintained, and no fundamental changes are made in the functionality of the computer environment. On the other hand, the administrator doesn't gain any new functionality by migrating to Active Directory in this fashion. In fact, the only noticeable change is that NT 5.0 tools can be used for queries.

The BDC method isn't discussed any further in this chapter, because, until the PDC is migrated onto NT 5.0, no changes to Active Directory occur. The way in which Microsoft will implement this migration methodology is still unclear.

When the PDC is migrated onto NT 5.0, two different ways to continue are available, in principle. The first method is to upgrade all other servers to the NT Server 5.0 operating system immediately after the PDC has been changed. The second method is to install Active Directory on the PDC and not change the current appearance of all other NT servers in the foreseeable future.

Both procedures are passable methods. Nevertheless, the best strategy is probably something in between these two extremes. If more than one NT 5.0 DC exists, the fault tolerance concerning Active Directory information is enhanced (if a DC fails, another DC still has a full copy of the Active Directory database). If an old BDC is maintained, you are assured of a fallback if problems still crop up with the interaction between NT 5.0 and the servers that use older versions.

When planning a migration, you should consider whether you can obtain a noticeable advantage by introducing a changed division for the domain in Active Directory, compared to the current domain solution. Because of the many restrictions regarding domain-based solutions, they tend to reach a compromise among several opposing requests, and thus aren't the best possible solution for Active Directory, which is a different (and more flexible) entity.

Before upgrading, you must facilitate the transition from WINS to DNS. WINS enables Windows-based clients that use NetBIOS to localize resources on the TCP/IP network. WINS support is included in NT (for both clients and servers), but it isn't a requirement in a purely NT 5.0 environment. Often, using WINS during a transitory period may be necessary on old NetBIOS-based Windows clients and servers. Over time, using WINS should be reduced proportionally to the migration of clients and servers to the DNS environment, until eventually all WINS servers can be discontinued.

Next is the question of how and when to tackle clients. To benefit the most from Active Directory, and avoid using Active Directory and NT Server 5.0 as an updated version of NT 4.0 Server, the client operating systems for Windows NT Workstation 5.0 must be upgraded or an Active Directory network client must be added onto any Windows 95- or Windows 98-based PC.

The Recommended Migration Methodologies

Microsoft recommends that you begin migrating a PDC for the following reasons:

- The domain is immediately incorporated into the domain tree of Active Directory, although it is still used as an NT 4.0 domain.

- The administrator can begin to use the new administrative tools and create Active Directory objects and OU hierarchies. When migrated, the structure and the objects are regarded according to their purpose on all units of Active Directory, while older units can't see the OUs, and thus regard all objects as belonging to an ordinary, flat structure.

After an upgrade has taken place, all objects are kept in Active Directory. Thus, other Active Directory-prepared servers and clients can log on to the server, and all old servers and clients can see the difference on the NT Server 5.0-based DC and the old PDC, because NT 5.0 also contains NT LAN Manager (NTLM) functionality. Figure 14.7 shows the appearance of the NT domain before migrating to NT 5.0. Figure 14.8 shows the appearance after an upgrade of the PDC to NT 5.0. Figure 14.9 shows the appearance after an upgrade of the BDC to NT 5.0. Figure 14.10 shows the appearance after changing from a mixed mode domain to a native mode Active Directory domain.

The administrator will experience the following two improvements of functionality by changing to a native mode Active Directory domain:

- Groups can be placed within groups. In the old domain-based model (and in a mixed mode domain), only global groups can be inserted into local groups. In

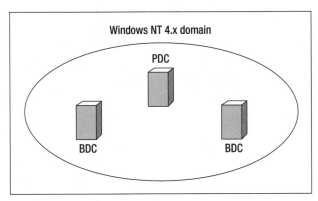

Figure 14.7
The original appearance of the NT domain that is going to be migrated.

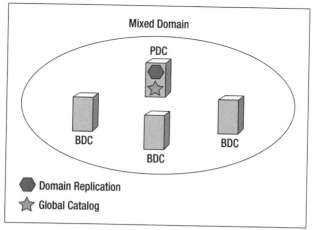

Figure 14.8
The NT domain after upgrading the PDC to NT 5.0.

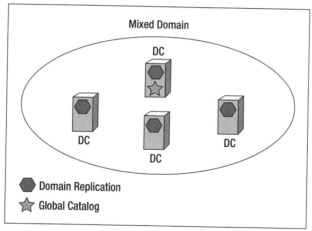

Figure 14.9
The NT domain after upgrading the BDCs to NT 5.0.

Active Directory, only global groups are accessible in the entire domain tree. On the other hand, Active Directory enables you to insert groups, but not until you change from a mixed mode domain to a native mode Active Directory domain.

- The old domain-based clients can take advantage of the transitive trust relations and are given access to resources all over the domain tree, in line with Active Directory-prepared clients. Incidentally, this enhanced access to other parts of the domain tree is the only change that old clients notice when moving from a mixed mode domain to a native mode Active Directory domain.

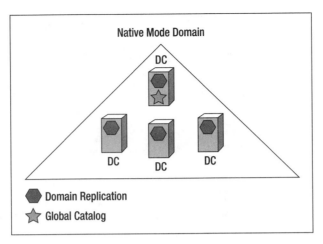

Figure 14.10
The NT domain after changing from a mixed mode domain to a native mode Active Directory domain.

The change from a mixed mode domain to a native mode Active Directory doesn't take place automatically, as shown in Figure 14.11. To change from mixed mode to native mode domain, start the Microsoft Directory Service Manager MMC snap-in, choose Properties for the specific domain, and then click on the Mode tab. If the Mode tab doesn't appear, the domain is ready to act as a native mode Active Directory domain.

With migration, all information from the existing NT domain is transferred to the new NT 5.0-based PDC during installation. For instance, the existing users, computers, and built-in local groups are placed in the following common name objects: Users, Computers, and Built-in. The built-in global groups and user-defined groups, moreover, are placed in the common name object Users.

However, the one exception to this rule is that the security policies (for example, the requirements for passwords and setup of revision/auditing) are not moved along to the NT 5.0 server. If a new Active Directory domain tree is created while setting up the server, the standard values for the security policies are used, and if the server is incorporated into an existing domain tree, it inherits the security policies of the parent domain.

Two Alternative PDC-Oriented Migration Methodologies

As previously stated, Microsoft recommends the method of migration with PDC upgrading. Yet Microsoft mentions two slightly different, more mainstream models

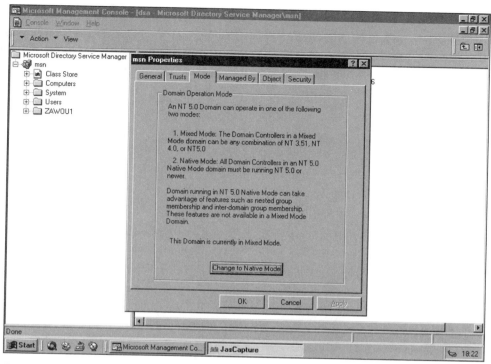

Figure 14.11
The administrator has to initiate the change with the Directory Service Manager.

for migration. These models are particularly usable for environments in which the stability of NT 5.0 may be insufficient for use as a PDC. Remember that the PDC constitutes a potential single point of failure in the old domains, thus leading to its instability.

The philosophy of the first alternative migration model is that—as in the migration Microsoft recommends—the old PDC is replaced with an NT 5.0-based server and, if desired, migration of the remaining servers is commenced. Thus, one of the existing (or perhaps a completely new) BDCs simply has been set aside immediately prior to starting the migration. This means that you have a complete copy of the domain database from the point in time when the BDC was removed from the network, and that you can promptly reestablish the entire NT domain up to that point by removing the PDC and turning the safe BDC into the new PDC.

If any problems occur while migration is carried out, you simply remove all NT 5.0 servers from the production environment and introduce the safe BDC as the new PDC. The only drawback with this method is that all changes are lost that are being implemented while the safe BDC is away from the network. To minimize this loss, you may temporarily attach the BDC at frequent, short intervals during the migration process, to update its copy of the domain's database. This generates a corresponding increased risk of the BDC's domain database suffering from the same problem, which is why you should reestablish it. Large IT environments are recommended to operate with two safe BDCs, whereby one BDC is not touched while the other is being updated at intervals.

The second alternative migration model consists of removing the PDCs that are going to be migrated from the production environment, before migration begins. Then, in peace and quiet, you can perform migration of the PDCs and establish a domain tree of Active Directory, without causing any consequences to the operating environment.

After the PDCs are migrated, you can try to add clients and more servers onto the domain tree. If the migration continues to function according to plan, the PDCs will be ready to be moved back to the production environment.

The main advantage of using this second migration model is that the production environment is completely unaffected until after the new PDCs are thoroughly tested and seem reasonably stable. Moreover, even very large domain trees can be shaped without disturbing the production environment. One downside to this model is that you need a sufficient number of extra servers at your disposal for the model to work. Probably the biggest drawback is that changes in the domain's databases can't be made until the new PDCs are ready for use.

Adding Resource And User Domains

As mentioned in Chapter 13, if you use the single master domain or multiple master domain model, slightly changing its structure while migrating to Active Directory often is worthwhile. At the very least, this change means that you place users and resources in the domain where they belong. In the extreme cases, you eliminate second-layer domains (in other words, the resource domains).

If you merely want to transfer users to the correct domains, you can't avoid the task of finding out which users need to be moved to other domains. This task can be extremely unpleasant if, for some reason, you don't want the master domain and the resource domains to belong to the same domain tree, because you can't readily move users between two domains that don't belong to the same domain tree. Figure 14.12 shows a typical multiple master domain of NT 4.0, and Figure 14.13 shows the new structure after migrating to Active Directory.

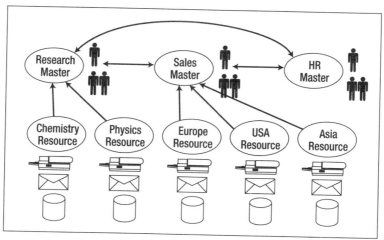

Figure 14.12

A good example of a typical multiple master domain found in NT 4.0 installations.

If you want to eliminate second-layer domains, you will expend blood, sweat, and tears performing the following required tasks:

1. Migrate the PDC in the master domain to NT Server 5.0.

2. If you are replacing second-layer domains with OUs in the master domain, you have to create the OUs. Then the users and groups can be moved from their current container objects into the correct OUs.

3. Migrate the PDCs of the resource domains to NT Server 5.0. These servers aren't immediately incorporated into the master domains, because the security setups must first be moved from the resource domains to the master domain. Unfortunately, this transfer doesn't take place automatically, because of the local grouping of the resource domains.

4. All resource domain servers (and hence their computer accounts and local groups, if any) that don't act like PDCs or BDCs should migrate into the correct OUs. The old resource domains and their corresponding PDC/BDCs must not be closed, because these components are responsible for handling the SIDs that each of them has issued.

5. All local groups from each resource domain—which must also be in the new Active Directory domain—must be transferred into the master domain. The groups that have been moved act like other groups in the master domain.

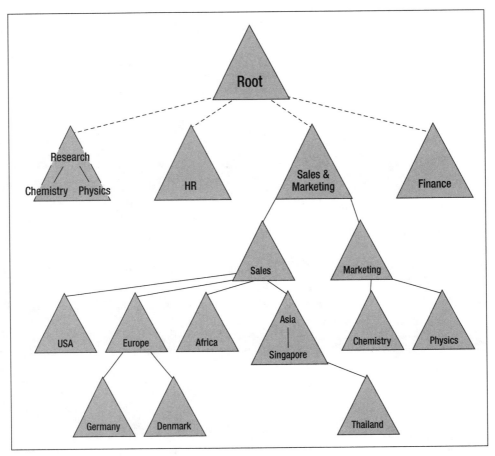

Figure 14.13
What the domain might look like after being migrated to Active Directory. The new structure is far more detailed, more intuitive, and considerably easier to administer.

6. Finally, all clients are moved from the resource domains to the master domain. For Windows 95/98 clients, this is done by changing the name of the computer's workgroup. Windows NT Workstation clients first must be removed from the old domain and then added to the master domain. A new computer account is then created in the master domain. At the same time, the network software should also be upgraded to the Active Directory-prepared clients (in other words, NT Workstation 5.0 or the separate client for Windows 95 and Windows 98).

7. You may now eliminate the resource domains, which you can do either by removing all PDCs and BDCs in the resource domain or by migrating every single server onto the master domain.

If you haven't created any local groups in the resource domains—which must be migrated to the master domain—then you can simplify matters by following the preceding procedure, taking into account that NT Server 5.0 can't automatically migrate this information. If any local groups in the resource domains aren't going to be reused, you can skip Step 3. Then, Step 5 simply involves migrating the resource domains' PDCs directly into the correct OU.

Choose The DNS Namespace With Care

When determining the namespace of Active Directory, you must be very aware of the following considerations:

- Which replication traffic the namespace indirectly entails (in other words, the domain structure of Active Directory, and the restrictions on the server's DNS structure).

- Which organizational changes—with a consequent change in the namespace—cause a change of Active Directory's domains. This is an expensive and very unpleasant task.

- The capability of the namespace to be developed in line with the organization.

- Establishing naming conventions, and the possible restrictions that they may cause.

If only one domain or one domain tree exists, then the DNS namespace, by definition, has a joint root domain and possibly a series of underlying domains. Only when you operate with many domain trees can you have many different root domains.

In the most common instance (a domain or a domain tree), Active Directory is grouped under a joint domain name, which should always be registered with an Internet authority, to prevent unpleasant identical names. Having identical names may exclude users from accessing any Internet resources that happen to use the same name. Users should be familiar with the name of the root domain, because, as a rule, it is part of their logon name and email address.

The first layer of underlying DNS domains is established to minimize replication of Active Directory (by limiting the number of replication attachments) and should represent the "geopolitical" limits of the network. The names of these domains should be established as widely as possible, so that they don't have to be changed at the first organizational change within the business. Often, allocating domain names on the basis of geography is advantageous, rather than on the basis of the names in the organizational diagram. Depending on the name of the root domain, you can choose to use the existing ISO 3166 two-letter country codes, which are also used on the Internet. These codes are the standard abbreviations, such as UK for the United Kingdom, IL for Israel, DE for Germany, and so forth. In big, global organizations, however, domains often have to be divided further, into continents. These continent abbreviations should be at least three letters, to avoid them being identical to the ISO 3166 codes. These domain names should be added together with any other relevant structuring mechanisms (such as trade partners, subsidiaries) at this level.

In large organizations, the other domain layer will also help minimize replication of Active Directory. Again, using geographic domain names might be a good idea, because this is the best way of safeguarding against problems with organizational changes within the business. If the other domain layer represents countries, using the ISO 3166 two-letter country codes is best.

This division of domains is continued for just as long as domains or OUs remain in Active Directory.

Changing names on OUs is far more manageable than changing names of Active Directory domains, so you only have to define some loose standards for OUs instead of giving each unit a name. In an organization with several decentralized computer functions, this also has the positive side effect that the local information department managers feel that they also have a certain say in their own situation.

If you use only one Active Directory domain, naming is pretty straightforward when deciding on the name standard for the first domain. Please note that this is true only if you are sure that you will never have to establish new domains. Otherwise, you should seriously consider introducing a DNS namespace that has space available to establish a domain tree. For example, the name of the root domain would correspond to the name of the domain tree, and the first domain layer would indicate the name of the domain.

Moreover, right from the beginning, you must decide whether you intend to use a namespace that takes the organizational structure or the organizational geography as its basis. Pros and cons are inherent in both structures.

Just a well-intentioned (and hard-earned) bit of advice on naming: Never underestimate the political turmoil that the choice of the name standard for every domain layer will create. Practically everybody in an organization will have his or her opinion regarding the setup. So, it can be a highly charged subject that may lead to a political battle. An IT division is well advised to avoid getting embroiled in it. My best advice to you is to take the safest route: Choose a name standard that is based on geographical facts—it is easy to administer and hard for others to argue against.

The user's point of view often is the weightiest argument against implementing a domain standard based on geography. So, you should always consider in advance whether a domain standard based on the organizational structure is a sound alternative to naming based on geography. The organizational structure has much more logic in it, which makes it easier for the users to remember. Likewise, you should consider how often users will be required to use the full domain names.

In addition, some naming conventions must be established. When migrating work sites to NT 5.0, you may be very tempted to use the same names as used previously. The only problem with this is that the old names meet the NetBIOS name standard, which isn't identical to the DNS name standard. In DNS names, no distinction is made between lowercase and uppercase letters, and you are limited to using the English alphabet, the numbers 0 through 9, and the hyphen character (-).

However, in defiance of the DNS standard, Microsoft has chosen to allow use of the far more expansive Unicode character set (which also includes all special letters from the European character set) in its DDNS server. If you choose to benefit from the Unicode character set, realize that it actually makes parts of the DNS solution incompatible with the Internet.

A Bit About Clients

If you want to benefit the most from Active Directory, you need to use Active Directory-prepared clients, especially if you want to carry out queries against Active Directory to find particular objects on the network.

In NT 5.0 beta 1, the following Active Directory clients exist:

- The built-in client in NT 5.0

- An add-on client for Windows 95 or Windows 98-based clients

The add-on client contains Kerberos Logon & Security Support Provider, an altered NTLM-authentication, LDAP 2.0, and ADSI 2.0. Additionally, you must install the DFS client, which provides the ability to use any fault-tolerant file systems and to allow caching of the client.

Currently, the add-on client is pasted onto the NT client. Yet Microsoft acknowledges that the present client contains only part of the facilities that are planned for the production release. For instance, a user interface will be introduced for Active Directory searches in the final client.

For Active Directory searches, you can develop a series of predefined searches that will benefit users. Administrators must realize that a world of difference exists between working with a domain tree versus working with a forest of domain trees. If you work with domain trees, searches always interfere with the domain tree, because the DC automatically refers to all its underlying domains (starting from the root).

When you are dealing with a forest of domain trees, the search stops after the domain tree is searched, because no references to the other domain trees in the forest are returned. This lack of references is due to the fundamental difference between forests and trees: Forests are operated with a disconnected namespace in which the names of the parent and child domains aren't directly related to each other; trees do not have this limitation.

The Fundamental Prerequisites For A Good Operating Environment

If you want an operating environment to run smoothly, you need to remember the following important items about an Active Directory environment.

Above all, you should always administer the rights to the various users through groups. Never administer user objects directly. To avoid confusion and problems, I recommend that you define a large number of groups in Active Directory from the outset (before the first user is created) and draw up guidelines for using these groups. Remember that you can create a hierarchy of group objects when a change is made from a mixed mode domain to a native mode domain. With a hierarchy of group domains, you may, for instance, have a group that defines the joint rights for the sales division and that defines various subgroups (such as secretaries, sales assistants, sales people, sales managers, heads of sales) that automatically inherit the joint rights. You then simply need to allocate the group object that corresponds with the job title on the user's business card.

Administrators must understand Active Directory's distributed-security philosophy, which will enable them to implement Active Directory correctly—and save a lot of work. If they don't understand this philosophy, the business is at risk of important information being destroyed or stolen. The distributed security philosophy operates as follows:

- Always assign rights as high up as possible in the OU tree, which achieves the maximum effect with the minimum effort. The access rights that are allocated need to be suitable to the underlying objects.

- Use inheritance to spread access rights into the OU tree. Inheritance is the whole secret behind directory services. All objects under a particular object immediately inherit that object's assigned rights, which makes inheritance an immensely powerful and extremely efficient tool.

Active Directory enables you to delegate rights extremely efficiently and flexibly, which is a valuable tool with which to limit administering security to cover only a well-defined part of the entire business, and to place the rights and duties closer to end users, which reduces the TCO. Naturally, you allocate rights to administer a small number of users or groups only to the relevant staff member, who isn't given the ability to administer accounts in other divisions of the organization.

Delegating the responsibility for creating new users or groups is defined on the OU level or in the container that creates user accounts. Group administrators of an OU won't necessarily be able to create and administer accounts for another OU within the domain, but domain-encompassing setups and access rights defined on a higher level in the directory tree may cover the whole tree through inheritance of access rights.

The following three ways exist to define the delegation of administrative responsibility:

- Delegation of rights to change properties of a particular container; for example, LocalDomainPolicies in the domain object.

- Delegation of rights to create and delete child objects of a specified type below an OU, such as users, groups, or printers.

- Delegation of rights to update certain properties on the child objects of a specific type below an OU. For instance, the right to Set Password on User objects.

The Directory Service Administration user interface facilitates viewing the delegation information for a specific container. Adding new rights can also be accomplished simply and easily by choosing to whom you want to delegate the rights, and then choosing what rights they need.

Not everything in Active Directory is necessarily easy, however, such as the following:

- Foremost, you can't administer users based on where they are placed in the hierarchy of Active Directory. This still must be done through groups (but Microsoft has introduced a hierarchy, through the ability to embed groups within groups).

- Administrative rights can't cover multiple domains through trust relations, and the like. Therefore, Active Directory's environment is administered as a series of independent domains—not as a fully continuous directory tree—with regard to administrative rights. The same is true for resources, because Microsoft states that resource ACLs can't be spread over multiple domains.

The Operating Environment

The administration of objects in Active Directory (for example, users, groups, volumes, print queues, and the domains themselves) is handled through the Microsoft Directory Management MMC snap-in. As you might expect, everything can be managed from this snap-in. But, so far, moving users among different domains isn't possible. Microsoft promises to have this in order prior to the production release of NT Server 5.0.

Moreover, administering security in Active Directory is just as easy as you might expect, as is implementing backups of the Active Directory database. With the backup tools that come with Active Directory, starting the backup is just a matter of checking the Backup Directory Services box.

The new DC philosophy of NT 5.0 enables you to promote servers to the status of DC, without reinstalling the operating system. In fact, promoting a server that is already a member of the domain to be a DC is amazingly straightforward. You simply run the Domain Controller Promotion wizard program (dcpromo.exe) and answer some simple questions. The only requirements are that the server already be attached to the domain, and that the particular domain already operate as a native mode Active Directory domain.

As you have seen, two kinds of trust relations (administered by the Microsoft Domain Tree Management MMC snap-in, shown in Figure 14.14) support Active Directory:

- Explicit one-way trust relations to the NT 4.0 domains

- Two-way transitive trust relations between domains that are part of Active Directory's domain tree

The transitive trust between domains in NT Server 5.0 makes the administration of trust relations between the domains much more simple than in NT Server 4.0. Domains that are members of the domain tree define a two-way trust relation to the parent domain in the tree. All domains implicitly trust the other domains in the tree. If certain domains don't need to operate with two-way trust relations, you can define one-way trust relations.

Note that inheritance in Active Directory is static, which means that any inherited changes must be added to all the objects covered by inheritance. In the extreme, this may mean that some large replications must be performed to implement the inherited changes. Thus, you must be very careful not to have a large (or very dynamic) domain run across a slow WAN line, or some similar setup. The fact that tools don't exist yet for scheduling and refining multimaster replication makes matters worse, but Microsoft promises that such tools will be in the production version of Windows NT Server 5.0.

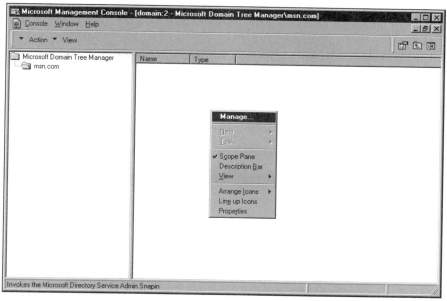

Figure 14.14
The administration of trust relations for each domain (and the security policies for the domain and the adjoining computers) in the domain tree is performed through the Microsoft Domain Tree Management MMC snap-in.

Moreover, Microsoft hardly mentions handling synchronization of time between servers and clients. Synchronization isn't absolutely required when the environment is in operation, but it is recommended nonetheless, because time is one of the parameters to solving replication collisions. This is troubling, because the current time-synchronization facilities of NT 4.0 (the NET TIME command) leave much to be desired.

Global Catalog

Active Directory contains Global Catalog, a special service and database for handling searches in the directory. Global Catalog enables users to find an object, regardless of which domain it is placed in, by searching for certain specific properties.

Global Catalog is designed to handle queries on objects everywhere in the domain tree, quickly and with the minimum use of bandwidth. Because Global Catalog contains information on objects from all domains in the domain tree, a query on an object from another domain is carried out promptly and without bothering very many DCs.

Global Catalog is kept on some specific servers that act as DCs within the environment. The administrator indicates whether a given DC should also contain Global Catalog by checking a box in the Site/Replication Manager tool, which is shown in Figure 14.15.

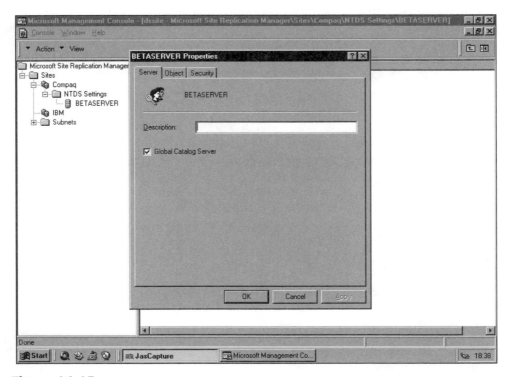

Figure 14.15
Choosing whether a specific DC should also act as a server for Global Catalog is quite straightforward.

Realize that Global Catalog doesn't contain a full replica of all objects in the entire directory—it contains an entry for all objects, but it doesn't contain all the attributes of the objects. You have to limit yourself to the most likely search properties, such as the name of the user, when doing a search in Global Catalog. The administrator can add extra properties to Global Catalog, if necessary.

You also need to be aware of Global Catalog's restrictions, because Global Catalog is the reference that is used for all searches. A query will be performed less efficiently if one or more of the attributes indicated aren't present in Global Catalog: You may have to go through the entire domain tree, negating the very reason that Microsoft incorporated Global Catalog. In addition, you may also come across a significant restriction when searching in forests. While the domain trees are searched completely, a search for a forest will be complete only if the attributes outlined actually exist in Global Catalog. If they don't exist, the search with all the attributes will be performed only in the domain tree from which the users or the application carry out their search.

Some Practical Closing Remarks

I'm sure that Active Directory (like its competitors for directory services) will start off having the greatest impact in large businesses and organizations that have global interests and a complex IT infrastructure.

But this doesn't necessarily mean that Active Directory isn't of interest to small and medium-sized businesses. Although the positive impact will be less significant for these businesses, the impact is bound to be bigger for these businesses in the future. Above all, Active Directory signifies a general enhancement of network security, including much needed strengthening of the replication facilities and more manageable administration. Administration is more manageable due partly to the capability to group user accounts according to geographic criteria, partly to the capability to delegate rights of administration on a more limited scope, and partly because of MMC.

Active Directory contains yet another very promising innovation: The capability to define new attributes and objects, which can be used for anything that you can imagine.

Additionally, Active Directory has a very strong potential of being integrated with other IT components and strong capabilities for distributing software within a network environment. To fully reap the benefits of these two facilities, the rest of the networked environment has to adopt the NT 5.0 operating system, which currently seems likely (see also Chapter 15), but will take some time.

Note that Active Directory isn't advantageous only for network administrators. Whereas most directory services tend to focus only on administration, Active Directory focuses just as much on helping users, who will notice the efficient search facilities and gradually also sense Active Directory through its powerful integration with other IT components in the business.

ADSI: The Vision Of The Future

The philosophy of directory services is quite interesting to administrators because it provides the capabilities to expand the schema, create and define new types of objects with new properties, and allocate attributes to existing objects.

For instance, you can store a vast number of properties (name, telephone number, login name, and password) through the attributes for user objects. But you can also expand the user object schema by adding new properties, such as salary, current projects, date of employment, and perhaps a scanned image. These capabilities are available in directory services because it is based on *orientation principles*—everything is hierarchically structured (like a tree that is turned upside down, with the root at the top and all the branches underneath). The hierarchical structure means that by combining an object's name and location in the hierarchy, it will always be identified in the directory tree.

Very few computer professionals truly understand directory services, and even fewer have any experience using it, which is part of the reason it hasn't caught on yet. But the primary reason directory services hasn't gained popularity is that no well-defined and broadly supported standard exists by which to communicate with directory services. So, independent software manufacturers are left high and dry regarding the technological direction of directory services.

Although most applications producers have adopted the X.500 definition for the fundamental components of directory services, opinion seems divided regarding the practical implementation of directory services. Microsoft Active Directory is not an exception to this rule. But Microsoft has developed its *Active Directory Services Interface* (ADSI), with the objective of making interface design for other solutions easy.

Microsoft's focus on integrating Active Directory with other implementations of directory services and various kinds of software solutions is the topic of this chapter.

Also included is a discussion of the more precise nature of ADSI and how you can implement ADSI to create small macros and similar types of batch routines to automatically handle the administrative tasks of Active Directory.

Defining Active Directory

Before discussing ADSI and all of its components, Active Directory must be defined, because you have to understand Active Directory to be able to use ADSI.

I have waited until this chapter to give you the definition of Active Directory because it is very abstract and difficult to understand. The earlier chapters should have given you a fundamental appreciation of directory services, so that you can fully understand this chapter.

The X.500 data model has very much inspired Microsoft to develop the Active Directory data model. Active Directory can hold objects that represent various elements, which are described by means of their attributes (properties).

The object universe in Active Directory is defined by the *directory schema*, which is a collection of rules that sets the structure and coherence in the various levels of the directory. Active Directory will likely become popular, because it combines information from many directory services (Lotus Notes, NetWare bindery, Novell NDS, NTS DS, X.500, and so forth) to appear as one consolidated directory service. This solves one of the major problems facing network administrators and users of heterogeneous directory service environments. In such environments, each directory has its own application interface, making administration a potential nightmare. Also, users need logons for each directory service, which makes working in such an environment difficult. Hopefully, ADSI will fix this problem for the majority of heterogeneous network environments, so that directory services will become more popular with users, developers, and administrators.

The directory schema consists of two types of objects: object classes and attributes (properties). Each object in the directory is an instance of one or more of the object classes defined in the directory schema. For example, the directory schema may contain an object class for users, which means that each user account on the network is represented by an object in this object class.

> **Note:** *Classes are collections of attributes that identify the information an object may contain. Classes are just ideas. Attributes contain the real information that is stored in the directory.*

The directory schema is the formal definition of all the objects and attributes that can be created in the directory. Defining the object classes that are to be stored in the directory and the attributes that can be part of the object classes creates the directory schema. The directory schema thus defines which attributes are mandatory for an instance of an object class, which attributes are optional, and which object classes can be a parent to the particular object class.

The directory schema consists of the following three tables:

- Object classes

- Attributes

- Syntax objects (the type of information, such as integral number, character string, or whether the attribute can have more than one value)

Thus, when defining a user, the Active Directory schema contains a class called *user objects*, which contains attributes that can be created for the user, such as first name, last name, and password. Please note that the directory schema is implemented as a multitude of object class instances that are stored in Active Directory's database, which means the directory schema can be updated dynamically with new attributes and object classes.

You may remember that the schema is expanded with new object classes and attributes, and that it may add attributes to the existing object classes. The snap-in that is used to create attributes is shown in Figure 15.1. Third-party manufacturers may use this tool to incorporate their own data structures into the directory, and use Active Directory to store the master data of their applications. This often saves a lot of manual work (and the unnecessary duplicate registrations that make keeping data consistent more difficult), because the directory already holds the information that may be necessary for the application. Moreover, Active Directory's flexible security model enables you to define some very fine-meshed security setups, which may also rest on the organizational structure already defined in Active Directory.

The directory schema supports inheritance, enabling administrators to set up new object classes so that they automatically inherit all object information from an existing object class, by making the new class into a subclass of the existing object class. If the existing object class later is changed, all its subclasses automatically inherit the changes.

Microsoft also states that removing attributes and object classes from the directory schema should be possible, but this capability hasn't been implemented in NT 5.0 beta 1.

Active Directory In Practice

Windows NT 5.0 contains a standard directory schema that defines a vast number of object classes, such as users, groups, computers, domains, OUs, and security policies.

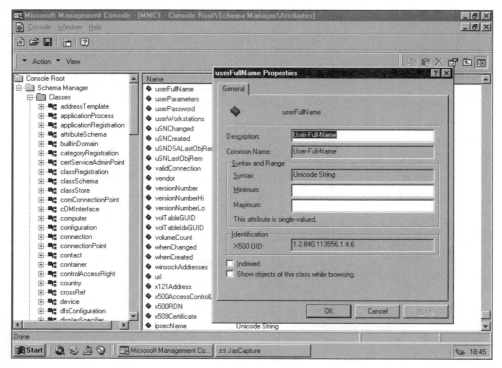

Figure 15.1
You can perform a dynamic update of the directory schema: The objects can be created either through the Directory Service Schema MMC snap-in or with a third-party program.

Thus, the directory schema designates that Active Directory may consist of one or more domains and that each of these domains generally may be split into container objects and leaf objects. *Container objects* are known as organizational units (OUs) in Active Directory terminology, which include, by default, the following objects: computer, country, domain, locality, namespaces, organization, and organizational unit. Container objects behave as an overall concept, with certain characteristic features (attributes), and various *leaf objects*, including the following: alias, file service, file share, group, print device, print job, print queue, resource, service, session, and user. These leaf objects automatically inherit the characteristics of the container object.

In addition to the directory schema and the information contained in the container and leaf objects of the domain, Active Directory's domain database contains *metadata*, which indicates where all Global Catalog servers are placed. Metadata is similar to the list of all the company's domains and domain trees under Active Directory.

External security suppliers, such as Kerberos and Secure Sockets Layer 3.0 (SSL), provide authenticity and security to enable safe communications with Active Directory. These external suppliers use the Security Support Provider Interface (SSPI), which is designed to enable the use of other similar suppliers of security equipment, when available. Figure 15.2 shows how SSPI fits into the entire communications model.

As previously stated (Chapter 14), Active Directory gets support from many different object-name standards, enabling users to use the notation with which they are most familiar when they refer to a directory object.

Microsoft's entire Active Directory design strategy is based on the fact that businesses already use other directory services (such as Lotus Notes, Exchange, or NDS) on their applications and operating systems levels. This is a strategic decision by Microsoft for the following two reasons:

- Novell, Active Directory's closest competitor, is placed in a less favorable light. Although Novell can offer the more-thoroughly tested and refined NDS directory service and a gateway with access to the directory through Lightweight Directory Access Protocol (LDAP), Novell hasn't done anything yet to address the logical questions that crop up regarding the practical application of the LDAP gateway. (For example, the email applications of Netscape Communicator or Microsoft Internet Explorer may be used to search for telephone numbers and email addresses in the NDS database. However, not much more functionality is available without customizing your functionality through programming. And so

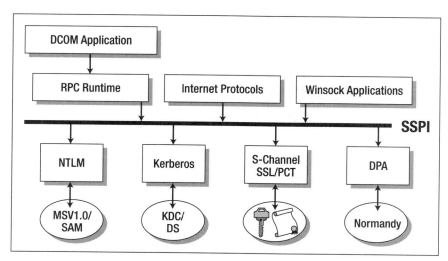

Figure 15.2
NT 5.0 introduces the SSPI API with which to handle authentication and other security.

far, Novell doesn't offer much assistance, such as code directories or documentation, to develop applications for NDS with respect to LDAP.) By contrast, Microsoft is spending a lot of energy both to develop the necessary tools for designing applications that use Active Directory's services and to adapt the existing code to take advantage of ADSI.

- If Microsoft's ADSI strategy is a success, applications manufacturers will be able to benefit from gateways for any purpose imaginable—and thus move Microsoft a step further toward creating a simple, universal directory service. This means that Active Directory's technology will be positioned at the core in the exchange of data among existing and future directory services. This strategy is particularly smart, because no Active Directory code will be available until NT 5.0 is available in stores. And Microsoft benefits much more if companies wait for Active Directory to be released with NT 5.0 instead of choosing some other directory service product already available in stores.

If Active Directory lives up to its promises, it will certainly be a more obvious choice than its closest competitor, Novell NDS, to serve the role of a metadirectory for many different products. This fact (combined with the ADSI facilities) could greatly help Microsoft win customers who have already chosen another brand of directory service.

Novell realizes that Microsoft's directory service has a much better position regarding programming capabilities. In response, Novell has created the Java Naming and Directory Interface (JNDI), which is a 100 percent pure Java API for NDS, based on the CORBA object standard. Novell continues to show little interest in gathering data from other directory services in the NDS database. It claims that it will gather such data after the LDAP standard is more mature, which might prove to be too late.

Introducing ADSI

As the preceding section mentions, Microsoft has designed a sophisticated interface specification for Active Directory, known as Active Directory Services Interface (ADSI).

Contrary to what is normal for directory service interfaces, ADSI is built as a generic directory service interface, without any dependence on a particular directory service or computer language. Naturally, ADSI works very well with Active Directory, because of the flexibility of both products with object definitions. To define, view, and extend ADSI objects, the Schema Management tool is used, which enables administrators to modify class container objects, property objects, schema container objects, and syntax objects. ADSI's design is based on Microsoft's Component Object Model (COM).

ADSI thus constitutes a very simple, yet very powerful, object-oriented interface for Active Directory. ADSI enables programmers and administrators to design directory-prepared applications in a fairly straightforward manner by using high-level tools, such as C++, Visual Basic, and Java. Moreover, ADSI is fully scriptable, so that you can operate it with VBScript, JavaScript, or Perl. Many administrators are bound to prefer these scripts over actual computer languages.

ADSI supports third-party schema extensions, so that software developers can make their own object properties for their particular applications. ADSI also provides two additional methods for extending objects: directory extensions and provider schema extensions. Directory extensions are created to manipulate directory objects. Provider schema extensions enable you to use a provider's extensible schema for extending ADSI objects.

Thus, ADSI isn't limited to Active Directory—it is an open environment, in which you can add support for other types of directories, regardless of whether they are based on LDAP, NDS, the Active Directory protocol, or something else. Because ADSI's design is based on an abstract model of the fundamental components in any directory service—presented in the form of a single directory service interface—you can query, summarize, and administer the resources in a directory service, regardless of which network environment is associated with a particular resource.

The uniform interface of ADSI makes performing administrative tasks—such as the creation and deletion of users or the administration of printers—easier in environments that have many different directory services. If all queries go through ADSI, you don't have to worry about the trivial differences among the various directory services. Thus, you can utilize the same program code immediately on all the directory services for which an ADSI provider is developed. This uniformity is shown in Figure 15.3. The current version of ADSI comes with services for NT domains, NDS, Novell bindery, and LDAP.

Although ADSI is developed primarily to handle genuine directory services, such as NDS and Active Directory, ADSI also functions with network environments that don't offer directory services, such as the NetWare bindery (the older versions of NetWare) and NT 4.0 domains. Microsoft has constructed an ADSI provider for these environments.

Although Microsoft intends ADSI to be the primary interface for Active Directory, it isn't the only route to Active Directory. Active Directory also has support from the LDAP C API (RFC 1823), which is a low-level interface for C programmers that is more difficult to tackle than ADSI. This interface enables you to implement client access to an LDAP server. Furthermore, access to Active Directory via the Messaging API (MAPI) protocol is possible, which means that old MAPI applications still function as intended within an Active Directory environment.

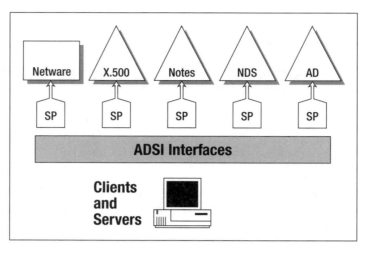

Figure 15.3
ADSI provides a uniform interface for programmers and administrators, and you can add support for various directory services through service providers (not to be confused with ISPs—Internet Service Providers).

LDAP Provides Maximum Openness

The main reasons for using a directory service are to establish a joint storage place (also known as a *repository*) for the information that is used to authenticate and set up the various components and to keep track of and administer the privileges of users and applications to access this information.

A repository with access to services, servers, database systems, and other applications must have a communications attachment between users (or server applications) and the specific directory service for the repository to make any sense. And for the implementation of this communications attachment to be practical, it must be well defined and compliant with an accepted standard.

The market apparently has chosen the Lightweight Directory Access Protocol (LDAP), which originally was designed for researchers at the University of Michigan as a simplified method for clients to utilize X.500-based servers. LDAP soon attracted so much attention that a standardization group was established under the auspices of the Internet Engineering Task Force (IETF), which included representatives (in force) from Microsoft.

The latest version of LDAP is version 2 (described in the RFC 1777 and RFC 1778 guidelines). LDAP 2 describes how a client and a server can exchange X.500-based messages across a TCP/IP-based network. The authentication must be through either regular unencrypted text passwords or a Kerberos-based authentication service.

On the downside, LDAP doesn't yet handle server-to-server communication between several different directories. But hopefully the next version of LDAP will eliminate this restriction. LDAP 3 is expected to include specifications for a replication protocol and for communications between directories with various directory schemas. Also, LDAP 3 will include the capability for directories to alter each others' directory schemas via LDAP messages. Moreover, authentication is expected to be extended with support of the current Secure Sockets Layer (SSL) standard and the Simple Authentication and Security Layer (SASL), which hasn't been developed yet.

Although LDAP 3 is currently being designed, three of the biggest suppliers of network software (Microsoft, Netscape, and Novell) have announced that their products will have built-in support for LDAP 3 as soon as the standard exists. So, LDAP currently seems likely to establish itself as the standard for communications attachments among different directories.

Not surprisingly, Active Directory uses LDAP for client access and to communicate with other server applications. Active Directory also supports part of the Directory Access Protocol (DAP), the Directory System Protocol (DSP), and Directory Information Shadowing Protocol (DISP). Microsoft states that the server-specific part of its LDAP implementation is geared to handle directory synchronization and interoperability with other applications (and other operating systems or directory services). Because the standardization for replication hasn't been completed yet, Active Directory doesn't contain a proprietary replication protocol.

Microsoft promises that when a standard for replicating within the LDAP framework exists, it will be incorporated into NT 5.0. Microsoft hopes that LDAP 3 will be ready well before the production release of NT 5.0, and Microsoft is working closely with the IETF to make sure that it is ready.

ADSI: Exciting And Straightforward—If You Know Active Directory

ADSI not only establishes a uniform interface for programmers and administrators, it also enables you to provide access to various application services and actual directory services. These interfaces enable you to design applications and automate administrative routines that function across many different commercial and customized network solutions.

Windows NT, NetWare, and other network operating systems have their own APIs for access to and administration of network resources. ADSI simply adds a uniform layer on top of these APIs, so that you no longer have to use different Software Development Kits (SDKs) or learn different APIs to be able to design solutions for mixed network environments. ADSI enables you to abstract objects and interfaces from the underlying directory service. In addition to the abstraction layer, ADSI introduces some uniform COM objects and interfaces.

Although the preceding information may make using ADSI seem complicated, it actually isn't too difficult to use. You may already be familiar with the COM technology because it is also used for ActiveX components and in conjunction with the DCOM object model (see Chapters 5 and 17 for more on this topic), and if so you will pick up ADSI easily.

But how does ADSI work? Both the ADSI software and the services can operate on the local PC. You don't absolutely have to install any ADSI components onto the servers in the IT environment. When a program call comes from ADSI, it always happens after the program's own API of the server; after all, the server can't see ADSI. The standard platform for ADSI currently is Windows NT, although the ADSI application can also operate on Windows 95/98.

As its basis, ADSI contains the standard container and leaf objects shown in Table 15.1. (Recall that object types can be divided into container objects and leaf objects.) Container objects may contain leaf objects *and* other container objects, whereas leaf objects can't contain any other objects. New object types can be added by expanding the schema, just as it is done for Active Directory.

Table 15.1   *ADSI's standard container and leaf objects.*

Standard Container Objects	Standard Leaf Objects
Namespaces	User
Country	Group
Locality	Alias
Organization	Service
Organizational Unit	Print Queue
Domain	Print Drive
Computer	Print Job
	File Service
	File Share
	Session
	Resource

ADSI comes with the following four services:

- ADSNW.DLL for handling NetWare bindery

- ADSNDS.DLL for NDS

- ADSNT.DLL for NT 4.0 domains

- ADSLDP.DLL for NT Server 5.0 and LDAP servers

ADSI may be used for most popular server and network operating systems. ADSI corresponds most closely to Active Directory in its terminology, design, structure, and names.

As a foundation, you can use Visual Basic 4.0 (32 bit), Visual Basic 5.0/6.0, Visual C++ 4.2, and Visual J++ with Java Virtual Machine (JVM) to develop ADSI applications. But realistically, you can use any other development environment that can be bound, and utilize the interfaces for COM objects. Thus, you can use NT's built-in Windows Scripting Host (WSH) tool to design VBScript batch commands or scripts. WSH provides a robust and flexible scripting language environment to 32-bit Windows platforms, blowing past the old MS-DOS command language.

WSH is started with either the WSCRIPT.EXE command (in Windows host mode) or with the CSCRIPT.EXE command (in the command shell-based host mode). WSH currently works with both Visual Basic scripts and Java scripts, and Microsoft states that it will be adding interfaces for Perl, Python, REXX, and TCL.

Microsoft has developed several small ADSI-based VBScripts for WSH that show how to automate your standard operations. The scripts are available for free downloading at **www.microsoft.com/management/wsh.htm**. They are all excellent examples for learning both VBScript and JScript. The following is a list of the available scripts and a description of what they do. (*.vbs* represents a VBScript, *.xls* represents an Excel spreadsheet, and *.js* represents a Java script.):

- *addusers.vbs*—Adds users (contained in the addusers.xls Excel spreadsheet) to Windows NT through ADSI.

- *chart.js and chart.vbs*—Both show the contents of an Excel spreadsheet.

- *delusers.vbs*—Deletes users from Windows NT who are listed in the delusers.xls Excel spreadsheet.

- *excel.vbs and excel.js*—Display Windows Scripting Host properties by creating an Excel spreadsheet.

- *network.js and network.vbs*—Using the WSH Network object, these scripts display network properties, such as usernames, total connects, and total disconnects.

- *registry.js and registry.vbs*—Add or delete entries in the system registry.

- *shortcut.js and shortcut.vbs*—Create a desktop shortcut to the Notepad application.

- *showvar.vbs*—Displays all environment variables.

If you study the program codes of these scripts more closely, you will notice that designing these types of scripts isn't absolutely straightforward. For example, the code for delusers.vbs, which is used to add and remove a number of users listed within an Excel spreadsheet, is shown in Listing 15.1.

Listing 15.1

The delusers.vbs script demonstrates the power of the Windows Scripting Host language.

```
' Windows Script Host Sample Script
'
' -------------------------------
'                 Copyright (C) 1996 Microsoft Corporation
'
' You have a royalty-free right to use, modify, reproduce and
' distribute the Sample Application Files (and/or any modified
' version) in any way you find useful, provided that you agree that
' Microsoft has no warranty, obligations or liability for any Sample
' Application Files.
' -------------------------------
'
'This script deletes users from the Windows NT DS
'via ADSI. The script reads an EXCEL spreadsheet (DelUsers.xls) that
'contains a page of users to delete.
'
'The sample uses the directory root LDAP://DC=ArcadiaBay,DC=Com,O=Internet
'Change the directory path in the Excel spreadsheet to match your DS
'before running this sample.
'
'To add users, run ADDUSERS.VBS with
'%windir%\"Your Samples Directory here"\AddUsers.XLS.
'To Delete users, run DELUSERS.VBS with
'%windir%\"Your Samples Directory here"\DelUsers.XLS.

    Dim oXL
    Dim u
    Dim c
    Dim root
    Dim ou
    Dim TextXL
    Dim CRLF
    dim oArgs
```

```
'Get the command line args
set oArgs=wscript.arguments

CRLF = Chr(13) & Chr(10)

'If no command line arguments provided, prompt for file containing
'users to add/delete
If oArgs.Count = 0 Then
    TextXL = InputBox("This scripts reads an Excel spreadsheet and " & _
        "deletes users from the Windows NT DS via ADSI." & CRLF & CRLF & _
        "Before starting, change the DS root in the EXCEL spreadsheet " & _
        " to match your DS."& CRLF & CRLF & _
        "Type in the path of a file containing users to add or delete" & _
        "Sample Add User file: ADDUSERS.XLS" & CRLF & _
        "Sample Delete User file: DELUSERS.XLS" & CRLF)
'Else file containing users is the first argument
Else
    TextXL = oArgs.item(0)
End If

If TextXL = "" Then
    WScript.Echo "No input file provided. Stopping script now."
    WScript.Quit(1)
End If

'We will use ou to control loop, so set initial value to null
ou = ""

'Start EXCEL and display it to the user
Set oXL = WScript.CreateObject("EXCEL.application")
oXL.Visible = True

'Open the workbook passed in the command line
oXL.workbooks.open TextXL


'Now do deletes
'
'Activate the Delete page
oXL.sheets("Delete").Activate

'Set the cell cursor to the DS root
oXL.ActiveSheet.range("A2").Activate 'This cell has the DS root in it

'Show it to the user
'WScript.Echo oXL.activecell.Value
```

```
    root = oXL.activecell.Value
    oXL.activecell.offset(1, 0).Activate

    'Until we run out of rows...
    Do While oXL.activecell.Value <> ""

        'If the requested OU is different
        If oXL.activecell.Value <> ou Then
            ou = oXL.activecell.Value

            'Compose the new ou path...
            s = "LDAP://" + OU + "," + root

            'Show it to the user
            WScript.Echo s

            'Get the new container
            Set c = GetObject(s)
        End If

        'Compose the user name
        uname = "CN=" + oXL.activecell.offset(0, 1).Value + " " + _
          oXL.activecell.offset(0, 2).Value
            ' wscript.echo uname
            'Delete the user
        Call c.Delete("user", uname)
        oXL.activecell.offset(1, 0).Activate ' next row
    Loop

    'Done.  close excel spreadsheet
    oXL.application.quit
```

The preceding script uses an Excel spreadsheet, called delusers.xls, that you can create or modify to drive the program to loop through and delete users. Table 15.2 shows a sample spreadsheet.

As you can see, the flexibility and power of these scripts are in an entirely different

Table 15.2   *The delusers.xls spreadsheet with sample entries.*

DS Root	First Name	Last Name	Email	SAM Account	Phone
OU=TestOU1	Todd	Kaplan	**Tkaplan@interaccess.com**	ToddKaplan	1-800-555-5243
OU=TestOU1	Ari	Kaplan	**Akaplan@interaccess.com**	AriKaplan	1-800-555-5244
OU=TestOU1	Rachel	Greene	**Rgreene@interaccess.com**	Rachel-Greene	1-800-555-5245
OU=TestOU1	John	Hurley	**Jhurley@erols.com**	JohnHurley	1-800-555-1212

class than the old DOS batch scripts. However, some additional user-friendly design tools are needed that can intermediate between the ADSI and WSH. Currently, regular text editors, such as Notepad, are used to create these scripts. Undoubtedly, some of the many NT-design entrepreneurs out there are working full-steam to meet this upcoming demand.

Good Ideas That Require A More Mature Product

The market prospects for Active Directory and ADSI seem extremely bright. Many independent program designers are experimenting on integrating Active Directory into the next versions of their NT-based server applications.

Almost every company in the computer business has backed ADSI, except for some of Microsoft's biggest competitors in the market for directory services. Some of the businesses that support ADSI are Cabletron Systems, Inc., Cheyenne, Compaq, Computer Associates, CompuWare, Control Data Systems, Digital Equipment Corporation, Novell, Siemens Nixdorf, Symantec, and Worldtalk. Furthermore, Novell has made the extremely exciting announcement that it has ADSI services for NDS. ADSI likely will be better supported by NDS than Microsoft's current (and somewhat limited) service. Because ADSI has been available for some time, the worst errors and problems of functionality are bound to be removed and solved once NT 5.0 is ready.

Don't be deceived by Active Directory's present status—Microsoft most likely won't achieve its goal to establish before late 1998 a directory that can provide reliable handling of all network applications and services. I simply can't believe that a new product such as Active Directory (or the Netscape LDAP-based Directory Server 3.0, for that matter) will suddenly prove to be the panacea for all that a business requires of its directory service. All the kinks could take a while to straighten out, most likely not until sometime in the latter half of 1999.

Meanwhile, LDAP and ADSI (which, after all, is more thoroughly tested than Active Directory) should be able to meet the most frustrating drawbacks of handling several different directories. LDAP version 3 needs to be ready soon, because it is required for the integration of the various directories.

Likewise, LDAP enables users of the Internet and intranets to have access to basic information in one directory via standard Web browsers or email clients. Currently, you can use the Internet/intranets to change information in the directory, without third-party products. This can be managed because numerous complete LDAP products are already available on the market that enable network administrators to handle directory data from distant locations, with sufficient security through authenticated access.

After reading this chapter, hopefully you can understand why ADSI and Active Directory will help not only Microsoft, but developers, third-party companies, and all businesses that incorporate this technology.

NTFS Version 5

16

The first version of Windows NT supported three different file systems: File Allocation Table (FAT), High Performance File System (HPFS), and NT File System (NTFS).

FAT should be familiar to everyone from the DOS and Windows environments, because FAT is the default disk format for those environments. HPFS probably is lesser known, because it is the product that resulted from the joint effort of IBM and Microsoft in developing OS/2. NTFS, as its name indicates, is designed especially for the Windows NT environment.

Microsoft's ideal is for all Windows NT systems to be based on NTFS. FAT and HPFS file formats are primarily intended as migration routes from other operating systems, and for backward-compatibility until that migration occurs. Microsoft states that HPFS has already become obsolete, which is why it isn't included in Windows NT 5.0.

Thus, Microsoft limits itself to NTFS for developing new, sophisticated facilities that require something extra of the file system that the FAT or HPFS formats can't handle. NTFS is the right choice if your goal is to attain maximum integration with the rest of the operating system. For instance, only NTFS offers granular operation of security (such as detailed operation of rights and revision of changes linked to the files), very large disk support, and support of the Unicode font.

This chapter describes the new facilities in NTFS 5, which is part of Windows NT 5.0.

The Biggest Features: Disk Quotas And Dynamic Disk Storage

The latest version of NTFS has many new items; the two major new features are built-in support for disk quotas and the capacity for dynamic disk storage.

Disk Quotas

Ever since Microsoft introduced the $QUOTA metadata file into the NT 3.5 operating system, the speculation has been that NTFS would soon be equipped with support for disk quotas. *Disk quotas* enable administrators to designate an upper limit for how much disk space each user is allocated. So far, plenty of third-party tools have been developed with added functionality for NT disk quotas.

The developers of these third-party tools should be very concerned about their entire market basis, because NTFS 5 introduces support for allocating disk quotas to each user for specific disk volumes. The disk-quota specifications are stored in the $QUOTA file in the new $Extend metadata directory on its associated disk volume.

Before utilizing disk quotas and all their related features, the file system has to be updated from NTFS 4 to NTFS 5. Microsoft hasn't indicated yet whether the future production release of NT 5.0 will still require manually upgrading from NTFS 4 to NTFS 5, but Microsoft will make an error in judgment if it doesn't make this upgrade process automatic. The older versions of Windows NT have difficulty reading NTFS 5, so problems might arise when working with moveable disks or using dual-boot partitions with pre-NT 5.0 versions. But many similar compatibility issues have occurred in the past for which Microsoft didn't want to make automatic changes an option for new features.

Regardless of whether the upgrade from NTFS 4 to NTFS 5 in NT 5.0's production release is manual or automatic, the process should be quite straightforward. If you do have to perform the update manually, you simply have to start the command toolbar convert.exe, shown in Figure 16.1, with the command **Convert** *<drivename>* **fs:NTFS /v**, where **/fs:NTFS** means upgrade to the NTFS file system format automatically, and **/v** means *verbose mode* (to give feedback during the upgrade process). The upgrade to NTFS 5 is performed when you reboot the system. You can check the type of volume (FAT, FAT32, or NTFS) by running chkntfs.exe on the command line. Specify **chkntfs.exe** *<drivename>* to determine a volume's format.

Figure 16.1
*The **Convert** command is used to upgrade a volume to NTFS 5.0.*

Disk quotas are easy to assign and manipulate. The administrator decides whether to use the disk quotas only as a *soft-surveillance* tool (no limits are set for users; the system warns you only if a certain consumption of space is exceeded) or as an operating tool to prevent users from using more than a specified number of megabytes on the disk. Part of the quota functionality is a new tab that appears in the Properties window, shown in Figure 16.2, for the Disk Management MMC window (which is described in more detail later in this chapter). Here, you can start and stop quota supervision for each disk volume. Also, you may define both the limit of disk space and the warning threshold (the point at which a warning message is sent to the user for exceeding a limit that is approaching their quota). Note that you may actually deny users from exceeding the quota, or just issue warning messages by checking/unchecking the box labeled Deny Disk Space To Users Exceeding Quota Limit.

> **Note:** The disk consumption of every user is calculated on the basis of file ownership. However, after a user joins the Administrators group of the local computer, any files that the user creates belong to the Administrators group—disk quotas cease to function for users who join the Administrators group.

When a user exceeds the warning value of the disk quota, an event is written into the Event log so that the administrator is notified, but a user isn't given a warning message until he or she attempts to exceed their disk quota. The warning takes the form of the familiar, unfriendly Insufficient Disk Space message.

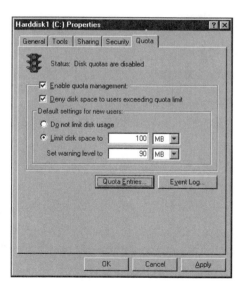

Figure 16.2
After you upgrade to NTFS 5, a new Quota tab appears on the disk drive's shortcut menu. Admittedly, the tab is also available when using NTFS 4, but it is useless unless the drive is upgraded to NTFS 5.

The Quota tab enables you to specify a standard quota for all new users. However, you can also adjust the quota for each system user by using the Quota Entries tool, shown in Figure 16.3, which is activated when the Quota Entries button is clicked on the Quota tab. Note that the Quota tab defines quotas for disk volumes, whereas the Quota Entries tool is for defining quotas for user accounts or user groups.

Unfortunately, NT 5.0's disk-quota facilities suffer from a serious administrative drawback: You can't allocate disk quotas to individual disk drives—only to volumes. Thus, you have to create a disk quota for every logical volume, which can be extremely confusing because you can't set up equally narrow limitations on every drive (provided that this refers to global disk consumption).

Moreover, the administrator isn't given the capability to individualize whether specific users can be refused access to exceed their disk quota, which is somewhat inflexible. This property, without exception, applies to all disk quotas on a particular drive. This means that an administrator must choose either to have every user potentially get a warning message or to have every user potentially be refused file creation after exceeding their quota; no mixture of the two options is available for each disk volume. Nevertheless, Microsoft promises that certain extensions to the disk-quota facilities will occur prior to the production release of NT 5.0: It plans to introduce facilities for global remote administration of disk quotas.

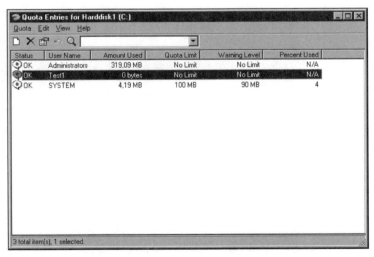

Figure 16.3
The Quota Entries tool enables you to adjust the quota installations for individual users and to determine quickly how much disk space each user's files occupy.

Dynamic Disk Storage

Dynamic disk storage is another innovation offered in NT 5. As its name implies, *dynamic disk storage* enables you to assign or remove disk space from the various volumes (and thus the logical drives), or to add new disks without having to reboot the operating system. Neither MS-DOS nor other versions of Windows (apart from NT 5.0) can handle disks that use dynamic disk storage. Therefore, you are faced with an all-or-nothing decision: Either have dynamic disk storage and incompatibility with non-NT 5.0 operating systems or simply don't use dynamic disk storage.

Using current disk-storage methods is still an option in NT 5.0—Microsoft refers to it as *basic storage*. Microsoft promises that upgrading a basic disk to dynamic disk storage will be feasible in a later beta version. Currently, you can only create a new volume defined as dynamic disk storage, and not update an existing volume.

Dynamic disk storage differs much from the current method of storage, which is why new terms and definitions are being introduced. The most important term regarding dynamic disk storage is *volume*, a storage unit consisting of space on one or more physical disks. A volume can be formatted or assigned a logical drive name, such as C:. Five different types of volumes exist:

- *Simple volume*—Consists of space on a single disk. A simple volume may consist of a single area on the physical disk or several areas that are "clipped" together. A simple volume can be extended to cover several physical disks, which turns it into a spanned volume (described next).

- *Spanned volume*—Consists of space on several physical disks. You can concatenate the disk space on up to 32 disks in a spanned volume.

- *Mirrored volume*—A fault-tolerant volume in which the data is copied onto two or more physical disks. If a disk has an error or becomes unavailable, you can still access the data through the other disk(s). Mirroring is also referred to as *RAID-1*.

- *Striped volume*—Data is spread evenly over two or more disks (a data unit is written rotationally onto every disk). *Stripe size* defines how large each chunk of disk space should be, such as 8K. Striping is also referred to as *RAID-0*.

- *RAID-5 volume*—A fault-tolerant volume in which the data is striped across three or more disks with a parity value, which enables an administrator to reconstruct the data if a crash occurs. If a physical disk does have an error, data that was placed on the disk can be recovered, based on the data that remains and the parity values.

Microsoft also promises to introduce two other volume types when NT 5.0 beta 2 is released: the *system volume*, containing the hardware-specific files necessary to input

NT, and the *boot volume*, containing all the NT systems files placed in the \WinNT and \WinNT\System32 directories. These two volume types enable administrators to separate the fundamental NT components from the other files on the disk level. Until this happens, though, bootable disk areas can be established only via basic storage.

Moreover, the Disk Management MMC snap-in, shown in Figure 16.4, provides the capability to administer the disk systems on all Windows NT 4.0 and NT 5.0 computers, with administrator rights to reach throughout the network.

To create a partition, you use the Create Partition Wizard, whose first screen is shown in Figure 16.5. With the Create Partition Wizard, you can specify whether to create a primary partition (using free space), an extended partition, or a new logical drive.

After you determine the type of partition you want to use, you need to specify the partition size. The Wizard ensures that you keep the size between the maximum and minimum values, based on the free space of the drive and system overhead, respectively (see Figure 16.6).

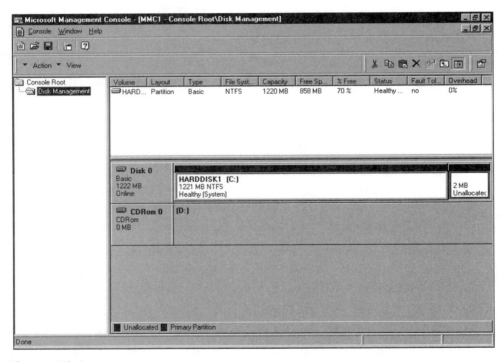

Figure 16.4
NT 5 also introduces an MMC snap-in (Disk Management).

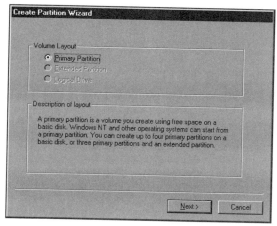

Figure 16.5
The first screen of the Create Partition Wizard, which is part of the Disk Management MMC snap-in.

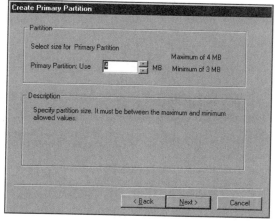

Figure 16.6
The second screen of the Create Partition Wizard, used to determine the partition size.

After you determine the partition type and size, the third and final screen of the Create Partition Wizard appears. In this window, you do the following:

- Assign a drive letter (C:, D:, and so forth) to the partition.

- Format the volume.

- Apply a label to the volume.

- Determine whether the file system will be NTFS, FAT, or FAT32.

- Specify the allocation unit size.

- Decide whether to compress the file system.

Encrypting On The File System Level

From a security perspective, the greatest innovation of NTFS 5.0 is its built-in support for encryption, so that any sensitive data on the disk can be protected effectively against unauthorized users. NTFS provides sufficient security when Windows NT is in operation. Problems occur when unauthorized users can physically access the machine, outside of Windows NT, by booting another operating system (for example, DOS) and using programs, such as NTFSDOS, that ignore the installation rights of NTFS.

Encrypting File System

NTFS 5's encryption is completely transparent and can be used on all NTFS 5-formatted drives. The encryption doesn't occur in NTFS itself, but rather through an accessory component called *Encrypting File System* (EFS), which is executed automatically when a user tries to execute an encryption-related operation. This ensures that EFS doesn't take up memory on systems that don't use the encryption facilities.

EFS is based on public-key encryption. As its basis, EFS uses the Data Encryption Standard (DES) encryption algorithm and a 56-bit encryption key. This key may be reduced to 40 bits when shipped or used outside of the United States, to conform to strict U.S. encryption-export regulations. EFS is designed to utilize other encryption algorithms, too.

EFS ensures that accidentally encrypting the files from which the system boots (thus making the entire system unusable) is impossible. EFS refuses to encrypt files that are either located in the root of the drive or have the systems attribute activated. As a rule, activating the systems attribute to prevent encryption does work, but by no means is it a watertight guarantee against making a costly error. Therefore, my advice is as follows: Never encrypt anything placed on the system directories of NT!

EFS is invoked from the shortcut menu for files and directories, as shown in Figure 16.7. Files and directories may be encrypted from either of the following two points within the user interface:

- Through Windows NT Explorer, thus providing access to the basic encryption and decryption facilities. The shortcut menu for the selected objects contains an Encrypt menu option if the objects have not been encrypted, and a Decrypt menu option if they have already been encrypted. Encrypting a directory doesn't encrypt the existing files and subdirectories; it encrypts only future files and subdirectories.

- Through the **Cipher** (shown in Figure 16.8) and **Copy** commands from a DOS window, command line, or Windows script, which provide access to the full encryption and decryption facilities. For instance, **Cipher** has the capability to encrypt directories so that all files subsequently added are encrypted and all underlying subdirectories are immediately encrypted. Two new options—export and import encrypted files—have been added to the **Copy** command. These new commands are vital prerequisites for maintaining security while copying files, because the file objects are automatically decrypted during ordinary copying.

Encrypting and decrypting takes place quite rapidly in NTFS 5.0. When you have an encrypted file open and are working on it, you don't notice that it is an encrypted file. However, unauthorized users will have no doubt regarding whether a file is encrypted when they attempt to open one.

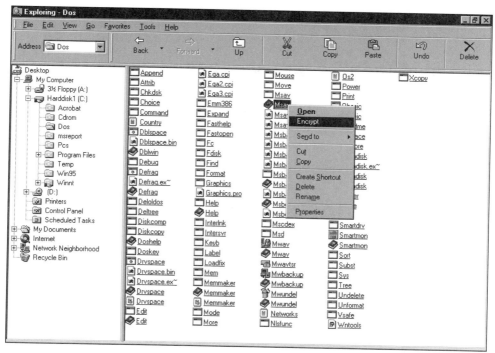

Figure 16.7
EFS hides itself on the shortcut menu for files and directories as an option to Encrypt or Decrypt.

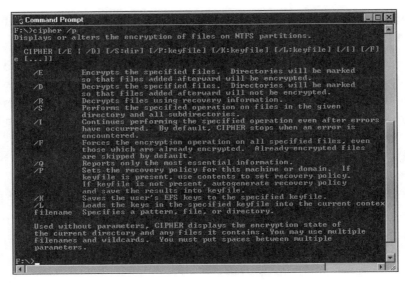

Figure 16.8
The format of the **Cipher** *command, with its keywords, which is used to display or encrypt files that reside on NTFS volumes.*

Encrypted Data Recovery Policy

Before you begin to encrypt a file or a directory, you must realize that encrypted data files can't be recovered easily. If a reading error occurs in an encrypted file, it may be lost, regardless of whether a backup file exists. To overcome this data-loss situation, Microsoft has introduced the *Encrypted Data Recovery Policy* (EDRP). An EDRP file contains the personal key against which all encrypted files on the relevant computer are encrypted.

The EDRP file represents an enormous security risk, because it contains all the encryption keys, but it also provides sufficient fatal-error recovery to make the effort of keeping it protected worthwhile. In other words, benefits outweigh its risks in some cases.

Microsoft accounts for the security risk by making sure that EDRP can be linked to a domain-encompassing security policy, so that every user has access to use the EFS only if the administrator gives them permission. Thus, unauthorized users won't have a chance to view the EDRP file, as long as the organization has a domain-encompassing security policy. Under such a security policy, the EDRP file covers the entire domain and is accessible only to the administrator, thus removing all elements of danger from the sphere of the user.

Currently, maintaining an EDRP file is possible only through the **Cipher /P** command, but Microsoft promises to have an MMC snap-in that can maintain EDRP files by the time the production version of NT 5.0 is released. Also note that a new EDRP file is automatically generated every time the **Cipher /P** command is activated. So, you should use the command only once and then save the file generated in a safe place (and on a disk media that isn't prone to data loss).

Other NTFS Improvements

Windows NT 5.0 provides a multitude of new improvements for granting permissions in NTFS (as well as FAT and FAT32).

Permissions

The Permission Entry screen from the Disk Management MMC, shown in Figure 16.9, enables the administrator to grant or revoke various security options. Permissions may be applied to any group of users in the form of the following seven object groupings:

- This folder only
- This folder, subfolders, and files
- This folder and subfolders
- This folder and files
- Subfolders and files only
- Subfolders only
- Files only

You can set many of the permissions, including delete, execute file, traverse folder, and many more. Hundreds of combinations of objects and permissions are possible, each of which may be granted to, or revoked from, any group of user accounts.

Junction Points

Junction points are another exciting new feature within NTFS 5.0. Similar to DFS junction points, NTFS junction points are designed to gather various different volumes onto one logical drive.

Junction points can be used to transfer access of data automatically from a local volume to a distant volume, or to join together several volumes within the same logical drive name. NTFS junction points are transparent for the applications, unless the application specifically requests to have the particulars of the junction points.

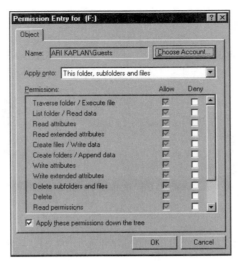

Figure 16.9
The Permission Entry screen defines security for disk volumes and files.

This can improve the distributed environment for many applications. For example, a large database can have drive space distributed across many servers, and the database software acts as if it is all on local disks. The **cdsli** command or an MMC snap-in can be used to view junction points.

Sparse Files And Reparse Points

NTFS 5 contains support of sparse files and reparse points. *Sparse files* are files in which the actual data contained in the file doesn't match its listed size (shown with the **DIR** command, for instance). Sparse files can save space, because NTFS can allocate disk clusters only to the parts of a sparse file that contain valid data (the parts of the file that don't contain valid data are assumed to contain all binary 0s). *Reparse points* are symbolic links that can point at files or directories on the same or other disks.

Distributed Link Tracking

Microsoft has jazzed up the distributed link tracking service, which finds shortcuts (pointers to files) and OLE chains (pointers to Object Linking and Embedding objects) to NTFS files that haven't been moved or renamed. The new distributed link tracking service can also recover lost file chains in the following instances (or combinations of these instances):

- The file has been moved between two NTFS 5 volumes that are placed on computers belonging to the same domain.

- An NTFS 5 volume has been physically removed from an NT 5.0-based computer to another NT 5.0-based computer belonging to the same domain.

- An NT 5.0-based computer with an NTFS 5 volume has changed its name, while still belonging to the same domain.

- The share on which the NTFS 5 file is placed has changed its name.

This list for lost file chains also applies to lost OLE chains.

Auditing

One more nice feature of NTFS is its impressive auditing capabilities. Similar to selecting the permissions for a file or directory, you can select events that trigger Windows NT 5.0 to record information to an audit trail. You select the permission (such as deleting a file) for a particular group. Then, you can select whether the auditing is for a success or a failure, such as whether a file is successfully deleted or an attempt to delete it failed. The administration of auditing is handled via the Auditing tab of the Access Control Settings window within the Disk Management MMC. Figure 16.10 shows the setup for when Power Users fail to delete files and Everyone (a default group for every user account) successfully takes ownership of the folder and files within the folder.

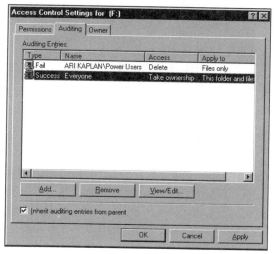

Figure 16.10
The Access Control Settings for an NTFS volume: the Auditing tab.

Timeout Counter

Finally, Microsoft promises to add a timeout counter, a minor but very pleasant detail that may be of great importance on computers with many disks. NTFS 5 will support placing this timeout counter into the **Autochk** tool (which is the version of **chkdsk** that operates when the system starts), similar to the OS Loader facilities, so that there is better disk performance. (This option isn't available in NT 5.0 beta 1.)

Focus On Backup Facilities

NT 5.0 offers an entirely new infrastructure for making backups that, contrary to its tape drive-centered predecessor, is media-centered. This means that users no longer have to choose a certain tape drive (and frequently also a certain tape) to perform a backup operation, but instead just have to state which media the backup should be transferred to. The system then decides which tape drive should be used to perform the backup operation. This new backup infrastructure is known as *Windows NT Media Services*, shown in Figure 16.11. Windows NT Media Services is still in its

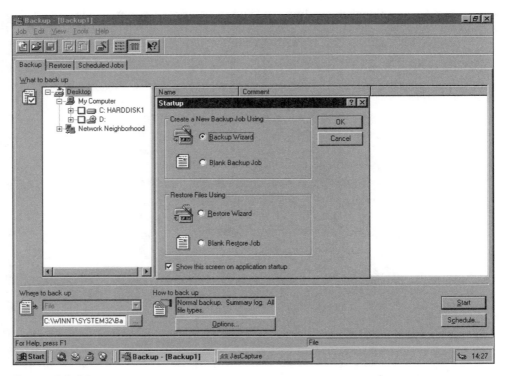

Figure 16.11
Windows NT's own Backup program has had a thorough facelift. It also is enhanced with some new functions—a backup of Active Directory is now possible.

early stages—for example, it supports only 8 mm, 4 mm, and Digital Linear Tape (DLT) tape drive media. (DLT is used for fast tape rates up to 2.5Mbps.) Whether the tape-centered work method will be removed, partially or entirely, from the final version of Windows NT Media Services is still unclear.

Many administrators have been waiting for a media-centered work method. Media Services enables administrators to implement multidimensional backup systems, which are systems on several backup levels. These systems have the capability to copy older files onto ever-slower (and hence cheaper) backup media, because the older files are, the less need there is for fast access in many environments. Microsoft promises that the final version of Media Services will be supported by two-level *Hierarchical Storage Management* (HSM), a data storage system that manages data on media such as tape drives and optical disks, which are less expensive than hard drives. Microsoft expects that third-party companies will add support for three or four levels of HSM shortly after the production release of NT 5.0.

Media Services supports shared access through a combined API (which is necessary for working with tape robots). This means that applications no longer need to be written for the specific backup units. You can have access to all the linked-up backup units by communicating with a homogeneous API user interface. This API acts as an abstraction layer and should make the management of backup schemes much easier, especially in environments with multiple backup products.

The facilities in Media Services are handled through the Media Services Management MMC snap-in, which, alas, is very unreliable software in beta 1. In most instances, I was incapable of gaining access to the tool without receiving a nasty message telling me of an applications error causing the entire MMC console to crash. But that's what beta versions are for; I am looking forward to seeing the new features (and bug fixes) in beta 2.

Enhanced Disk Tools

NT 5.0 contains an enhanced version of the backup system in the beta release. As it did with the previous version, Seagate Software will develop the newest release, which is a scaled-down implementation of its much-praised Backup Exec application. The new NT Backup program contains a series of new capabilities to design and install the backup jobs. Tape spanning, which is used to back up large files, such as a 2GB file onto two 1GB tape drives, is not supported in beta 1.

Disaster-recovery support has also been incorporated into NT 5.0, which means that—assuming the backup system can be connected to the computer—the backup system can recover the underlying operating system. Thus, you can then start the computer in the normal manner and recover the remaining data. Disaster recovery also enables you to recover an entire computer onto a new computer, which is necessary when a computer is completely broken and can't be restarted.

Beta 1 of NT 5.0 contains an early version of the Defragmentation tool, which will be part of NT 5.0. The NT 5.0 Defragmentation tool is a scaled-down version of the Diskeeper defragmentation tool by Executive Software, which allegedly is the only network defragmenter available on the market. One of the most significant differences between NT 5.0's built-in Defragmentation tool and Diskeeper is that Diskeeper's defragmentation operates automatically across several computers, whereas NT 5.0's Defragmentation tool does not. The tool functions on the local FAT, FAT32, or NTFS formatted file systems.

NTFS Keeps Its Promises

NT 5.0 includes some other enhancements regarding file handling. Microsoft's enhanced support of the FAT file format to also cover FAT32, which is used by Windows 95 OSR 2 and Windows 98, is very important. These FAT and FAT32 files are likely to reside on PC platforms that are being upgraded to NT 5.0. The same support applies to the Universal Disk Format (UDF) file system, which is designed to handle data from DVD and CD media, thus supplementing the CD-ROM File System (CDFS), used on CD-ROM players.

Finally, you can implement Fibre Channel, thereby increasing the accessible bandwidth to 250 percent of the Ultrawide SCSI (from 40 to 106Mbps, which might even be as high as 212Mbps, if the duplex possibilities of Fibre Channel are included). Fibre Channel provides a vast increase in the number of units that can be connected (from about 10 serial/parallel connections to 127 units via the USB), and entirely removes the tight limitations on direct connection distance (jumping from 75 feet to 5 miles).

Fibre Channel solves the headaches caused by deciding where to place servers, disk towers, and backup systems, which are issues that server administrators address every day. The disks can remain in safe storage in the central data center (where professionals skilled in tending to disks and making backups regularly are located), despite the fact that it acts as a distributed resource.

Nevertheless, the advantage of changing to Fibre Channel isn't too great as far as performance. Quite a lot of disks and disk controllers are necessary to reach a transmission speed of 40Mbps or even 20Mbps (which are the theoretical maximum speeds for Ultrawide SCSI and Ultra SCSI, respectively).

As you learned in this chapter, a series of new, exciting facilities have been added to NTFS version 5, as well as a much-needed backup boost. These functions by themselves are sufficient reasons to consider upgrading the company's servers from NT 4.0 (or earlier versions) to NT 5.0.

More On DFS And DCOM

NT 5.0 contains two new technologies that are bound to be an important ingredient in many of the server installations of the future: Distributed File System (DFS) and Distributed COM (DCOM).

So far, these two technologies have not attracted much attention on the market or with current users of Windows NT Server. They mostly have been limited to use by true NT connoisseurs, because Microsoft hasn't advertised them much—yet. Microsoft may be hesitant to advertise DFS and DCOM simply because these technologies aren't easy to describe in simple terms, which might make preparing a marketing campaign quite difficult.

Another reason Microsoft may be withholding a publicity launch of DFS and DCOM is to avoid revealing in advance too much about the NT 5.0 DFS and DCOM improvements. Microsoft wants to be cautious that it doesn't promise something it can't deliver. Current DFS and DCOM versions are already available for Windows NT 4.0—DFS has been available to download from Microsoft's Web site since December 1996, and DCOM is built into Windows NT 4.0.

NT 5.0 does introduce many new features regarding DFS and DCOM, but these innovations are more difficult to "popularize" than the technologies themselves.

DFS = Fault Tolerance And Greater Clarity

The leading principle of the DFS technology is actually quite simple: Group together several logical disk partitions or volumes from many different servers to act as one unbroken logical drive. DFS is able to do for servers and shares what file systems do for hard disks—it provides uniform access to a basically identical collection of storage areas (in other words, disk sectors).

DFS breaks with the time-honored principle in PC environments that a disk partition should always appear as a logical drive, to be readily accessible to users. This change is most welcome, because problems already exist in the more complex environments, due to all the drive mappings that a user may require within the 22 options available on a conventional PC (A through Z, in which A, B, C, and D are normally reserved for floppy drives and local hard drives).

The improvement to the environment that DFS provides is shown in Figures 17.1, 17.2, and 17.3. Figure 17.1 shows how a company's data can be spread out over many unrelated shares in a networked environment, leading to confusion and disorder when looking for files or collecting data. Figure 17.2 shows the same shares in a logical DFS configuration, which is a much better organized structure. The physical implementation of Figure 17.2 is shown in Figure 17.3, which demonstrates how several servers, each containing one or more shares, can contribute to a DFS environment. Note that the servers can run on different operating systems—not just Windows NT—although DFS is accessible from Windows NT Workstation 4.0/5.0, Windows NT Server 4.0/5.0, and Windows 95/98. Each DFS structure has its own root located on one server, and from each root, multiple branches may be located on multiple servers.

DFS can solve another, even larger problem than the limited number of drive letters. DFS contains the potential to ensure more flexible, fault-tolerant, and scaleable operating situations than is possible with other current technology. The following are the limitations of non-DFS technology:

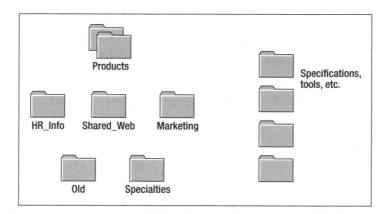

Figure 17.1
The data in everyday use is commonly spread out across many different shares. This figure may have an abundance of shares, but exaggeration tends to enhance the understanding of DFS.

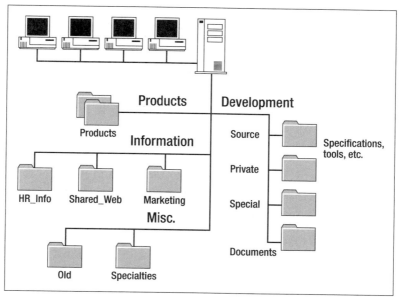

Figure 17.2
Collecting all the unrelated shares and disk partitions from Figure 17.1 into just one share may be easier and it reduces the confusion in searching for a file.

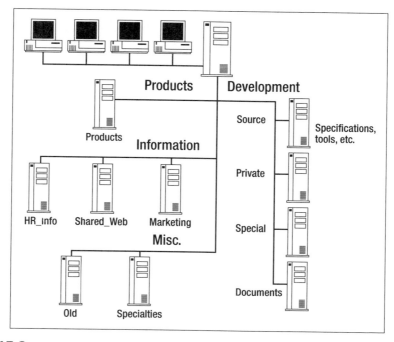

Figure 17.3
It is important to understand that the shares and partitions can be spread across several servers, and some of these servers may not use NT.

- *Limited flexibility and scalability*—Creating shares that cover more disk capacity than a particular disk controller can handle is almost impossible (because a partition tends not to stretch over several disk controllers).

- *The lack of fault tolerance*—RAID solutions or not, each logical drive is a potential single point of failure in itself. Currently, if a crash occurs, you can't duplicate the drive onto another server's disk system to reroute the clients onto this drive automatically.

- *Lack of scalability in terms of performance*—Each share is linked to a certain disk partition administered by a particular computer. This means that you can't scale performance of the solution if the number of readings and writings are increased beyond what the disk system or file server are able to handle.

- *Lack of user-friendliness*—The user's comprehension generally correlates to the number of shares. At most, a user tends to be able to distinguish among just a few drive letters, which is why large enterprises with many file servers run a risk of their users being overwhelmed by the many places where relevant data is stored.

As you can see, several good reasons exist to look more closely at the DFS technology.

How DFS Functions

With DFS, shares from many different servers can be located within the same file structure (or the same logical drive, published as a single share). DFS provides the following significant advantages compared with other current file systems:

- One hierarchical file system can be constructed, the contents of which are spread out on all the company's servers. The mere fact that the number of drive letters is reduced is a great relief to users.

- The fact that the file system is spread over several servers increases its flexibility and scalability, because you can always increase disk space and performance by adding new shares and file servers.

- Greater fault tolerance (and scalability with regard to performance) can be attained for directories with read-only files, because DFS enables you to replicate a specific area in the file structure into many different shares. When a user requests a file from this area within the file structure, the request is passed on to one of the attached shares. This creates a higher degree of fault tolerance, because all the servers involved are unlikely to crash at the same time. Also, you can increase performance by adding more servers.

DFS also enables you to incorporate within the file structure—on equal terms with the other shares—shares that don't operate on NT-based servers. The only prerequisite is to include an NT redirector to the particular file system. All you need is just one Windows NT server to be present to establish a DFS solution.

Note that DFS is not a new file format—it is merely the software that enables you to collect many different shares in a single file system (and hence a single share). Although DFS might seem like an innovation to most people, several other well-established file systems within the world of Unix have the same functionality as DFS, including:

- *Andrew File System (AFS)*—Designed by researchers from Carnegie Mellon University.

- *Network File System (NFS)*—Designed by Sun Microsystems, NFS enables computers to act as servers for local files and as clients of remote files across a network.

- *Open Software Foundation (OSF)*—An attempt to develop an open solution for multiple environments.

- *Distributed Computing Environment (DCE)*—Robust in security and fault tolerance for large networks.

- *Symbolic links*—A popular facility in the Unix file system.

The DFS Architecture

The DFS architecture is easy to understand: The central component in DFS is the DFS *root*, which is the local share that constitutes the basis of the DFS file structure and that receives and processes all client searches in the directory structure. Any NT 4.0 or NT 5.0 share can be transformed into a DFS root.

The DFS root stores the information regarding the various shares—including mappings of logical names to physical resources—in the *Partition Knowledge Table* (PKT). The PKT is cached locally onto the clients, to achieve a higher lookup speed (and to lower the load of the DFS root). All page objects directly below the DFS root—all the disk partitions acting as subdivisions to the root—can either be in the form of a common share (from the same computer or other computers) or a DFS root. The remaining DFS roots have to be placed on another server, because only one DFS root can be defined on each server.

The attachment to each share is known as a *junction point*, which can also be thought of as a logical connection between two separate network points. Figure 17.4 shows the overall DFS architecture, including how junction points function to bridge two servers, and the root-branch structure for each server.

A page object that is a DFS root is known as an *inter-DFS chain*. Note that all page objects are DFS roots, because they act somewhat differently than ordinary shares.

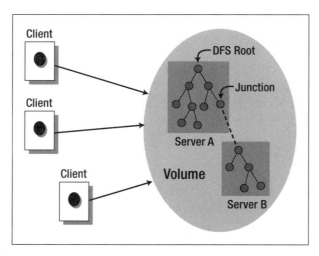

Figure 17.4
An overall picture of a DFS implementation.

When a user uses an inter-DFS chain, the client sees the DFS root of the page object as the valid DFS root. This underlying DFS root takes over responsibility for all directory lookups from the client from this point within the file structure.

Two important terms that deal with DFS junction points are *alternate volumes* and *downlevel volumes*. Alternate volumes provide the capability to duplicate a certain junction point and enable several shares to be added onto the same junction point. This is useful if you want to leverage the duplicate volumes, mounting both shares at a single point, which improves the availability of data if one volume becomes unavailable. Alternate volumes cause a lot of problems, unless the added-on shares are completely identical (making it impossible to write to these shares), because DFS chooses randomly among the shares listed. The alternate volumes are not automatically kept in synchronization, so you have to manually make sure that they are synchronized (through replication or other means). At most, 32 alternate shares can be identified for each junction point.

All shares that don't come from a server that is operating with NT Server 4.0 or NT Server 5.0 are regarded as *downlevel volumes*. A downlevel volume can enter into the DFS file structure, but can't act as DFS roots or junction points for other shares. For example, Windows Workstation 4.0, Windows 95, and Windows for Workgroups are considered to be downlevel volumes.

A DFS file structure looks exactly like any other NTFS-based or FAT-based file structure. Thus, you can establish a site indication in the DFS structure via a *Universal Naming Convention* (UNC) name. UNC is a format that is used to identify resources uniquely, such as files and printers on a LAN. The UNC format is *Servername**Dfs-root**path**file*.

With this information in mind (and the fairly straightforward DFS administrator tool), establishing DFS file structures, similar to what is shown in Figure 17.5, is quite simple. Figure 17.5 shows a straightforward DFS structure, including all UNC names, alternate and downlevel volumes, roots, and junction points. The next section briefly explains the process of creating and maintaining DFS volumes.

Creating DFS Solutions

There are several ways to configure DFS. The most rudimentary method is to use the dfscmd.exe command within a command prompt window. All options, which include the capability to map, unmap, add, remove, and view shares, are shown in Figure 17.6.

The dfscmd.exe command is flexible, but it is far from being user-friendly. Microsoft has a few applications that make administering DFS much easier through a GUI interface. The DFS administrative tool, shown in Figure 17.7, is used to create and

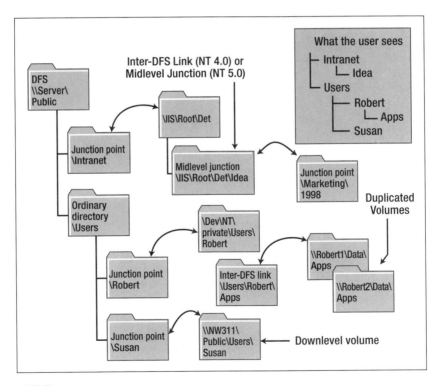

Figure 17.5
After you create a diagram of the file structure you want, similar to this one, establishing the file structure is just a matter of practice.

Figure 17.6
The dfscmd.exe command, run from a command prompt window, enables you to create, manipulate, and view shares.

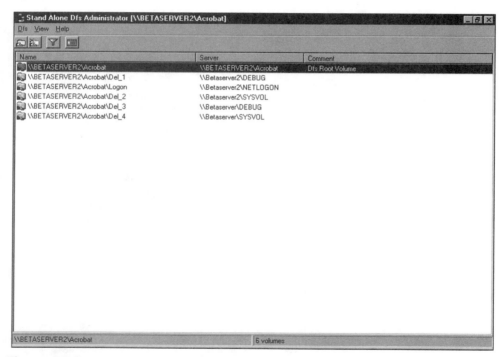

Figure 17.7
NT 5.0 beta 1 contains a slightly modified version of the "old" DFS administrative tool. Microsoft promises that beta 2 will have an MMC snap-in for the DFS.

manipulate DFS structures. NT 5.0 beta 2 promises to have an MMC snap-in for the administration of DFS.

Your first step in creating a DFS structure is to create a DFS root. Click the Network icon in the Control Panel. Select the Services tab and then select Host A DFS On Share and select the share name. You can also use the DFS administrative tool to perform this function. The DFS administrative tool can be called either by typing "dfsadmin" from the "Run" command line or by clicking Start|Programs|Windows NT Administrative Tools|Dfs Administrator. Use one of the following options in the DFS administrative tool to create a share, as shown in Figure 17.8:

- Create A New Fault Tolerant Dfs In This Domain

- Join An Existing Fault Tolerant Dfs In This Domain

- Create A Stand Alone Dfs On This Machine

If you select the third option, you need to select a share to host a DFS. You can browse the directory tree to select a folder, as shown in Figure 17.9. After you select the folder (the "shared_folder" is selected in Figure 17.9), click Create Share.

After selecting a share to create, you are prompted to enter several options for the share, as shown in Figure 17.10, including the following:

- *Share Name*—The name of the volume on which to allow sharing.

- *Comment*—A description of the volume.

- *User Limit*—Either set to Maximum Allowed or Allow ? Users to select the number of users that may simultaneously use files that are on the share.

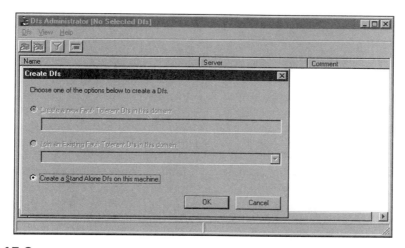

Figure 17.8
By using the DFS administrative tool, you can create a DFS root or a shared volume.

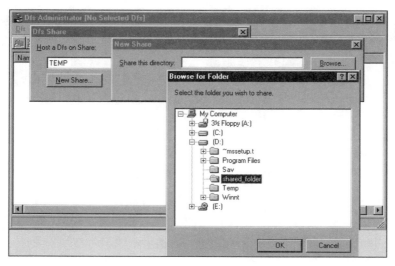

Figure 17.9
The DFS administrative tool can create a standalone DFS share on the machine.

Figure 17.10
The options that may be set during the creation of a DFS share, either by using the DFS administrative tool or by choosing the Sharing option in Windows NT Explorer.

- *Permissions*—A separate pop-up screen that is used to either allow or deny full control, change, and read to any groups that exist in the domain.

Using Windows NT Explorer is another way to bring up the screen to modify options. By right-clicking a folder, a list pops up that contains Rename, Delete, and so forth. One of the options is Sharing. When you select this option, the screen shown in Figure 17.10 appears for the volume, from which you can enable or disable sharing, along with the other options.

One addition that Microsoft made to the operating system is a caution message that appears when you attempt to delete a shared volume. The warning is that other users may be using the files in the folder.

Many other tasks may be performed with the DFS administrative tool, including the following:

- *Add a new volume to the DFS*—Select the volume under which you want to add the new volume, click Add To DFS, and then enter the path and volume name for the options labeled When A User References This Path and/or the Send The User To This Network Path.

- *Remove a volume from the DFS*—Select the volume to remove and click Remove From DFS.

- *Create an alternate volume path*—Select the volume to which you want to add an alternate path, and then click Add and enter the path of the shared directory to add under the Send The User To This Network Path.

- *Delete an alternate volume path*—Select the volume that has the path that you want to remove, look in the Send The User To This Network Path category, select the network path that you want to remove, click Remove, and then click OK.

- *Save the DFS tree*—Select Save As, enter the file name, and then select Save. This is useful for recovering a DFS tree if you lose data or some type of server crash occurs.

- *Restore a DFS tree*—Select Load, and then browse for the DFS file (that was created previously by using the Save As option). Click OK.

DFS must be separately installed on Windows 95/98. The necessary DFS functionality is built into Windows NT 4.0/5.0.

Two Obvious DFS Solutions

DFS can be useful in many situations, but DFS really stands out in two frequently encountered situations.

The first situation is when you run out of disks in the file server cabinet or on the disk controller. If you are unable to introduce a new server with a new share, you can only do the following:

- Acquire a new server with a higher disk capacity. This means an unpleasant migration of all setups and data from the existing server.

- Exchange the disks in the file server with something bigger. This also involves an unpleasant migration of all setups and data from the existing server.

- Establish an external disk tower. This works only if the disk controller is able to handle even more disks.

DFS provides a much more pleasant option: Leave the existing file server in peace and add a new server that takes over handling part of the existing file system. This solution is extremely easy to implement, and the user obtains enhanced performance. Furthermore, this solution is attractive financially if you consider the cost of migration (and the risk of economic loss if something goes wrong during the migration).

A second situation in which DFS proves to be highly useful is in a very decentralized business in which every department or subsidiary has its own file servers and doesn't want to change this setup. Yet, if even more users need to have access to files across the departments, the only solution is to define a multitude of drive mappings to the various shares. Furthermore, a drive-mapping standard for the entire company probably needs to be introduced. This may cause a major upheaval in most departments, and the users may find coping with such an upheaval extremely difficult.

DFS, however, enables you to collect all shares into one file structure, in which every subdirectory is assigned a descriptive name (such as marketing, sales, production, and so forth) that corresponds to one of the decentralized servers. The one file structure might even be relative to the original shares in every department, so that users have to experience only one of their old, familiar shares suddenly giving access to the remaining shares within the company.

Current Problems And Future Improvements

DFS does have its problems and limitations, the worst of which are the following:

- The DFS root is a poor environment for fault tolerance, due to its single point of failure.

- Currently, you can't introduce duplication of shares that are also written to, unless you are prepared to gamble (which I don't recommend, regardless of how good your replication solution is). This translates to low scalability and low fault tolerance for writeable directories.

- Currently, DFS-prepared clients exist only for Windows 95, Windows 98, NT 4.0, and NT 5.0.

- DFS does not protect against recursive junction instances, in which server 1 has a junction to server 2, and server 2 has a junction back to server 1.

- DFS has difficulty cooperating with Microsoft Cluster Server. Ironically, DFS ceases to function when the system operation is passed from the primary server to the backup server.

Beyond these limitations, one other detail is important with regard to the Windows 95 client. The current DFS client for Windows 95 and Windows 98 can't handle types of servers other than Microsoft's, and it suffers from a fundamental limitation in the length of path names (the file name combined with the path name must be less than 250 characters).

NT 5.0 beta 1 solves some of these problems, as follows:

- You can choose between creating fault-tolerant DFS in the given Active Directory domain and a standalone DFS (the type of DFS available in NT 4.0). Fault-tolerant DFS means that the DFS root can be placed on all the DCs in the given domain of Active Directory. This removes DFS's worst constraint thus far: the single point of failure for the DFS root.

- An alternative to the inter-DFS chains is being introduced. This new type of junction for shares that also act as a local DFS root is known as the *midlevel junction*. In a midlevel junction, the original DFS root always handles all the directory lookups, irrespective of whether the user moves down in a page object that is a DFS root.

Microsoft plans for the production version of Windows NT 5.0 to have the following facilities:

- NT 5.0-based clients will be able to make an intelligent choice among several duplicated servers, based on the site-date of Active Directory. If two servers are placed in different sites, the client will automatically prefer the server that is placed in the same site as the client.

- DFS will use the replication facilities of NT 5.0 to spread around all file changes among duplicated servers. Microsoft believes that this will enable duplication of servers that write to the directories involved.

- NT 5.0 contains a new Dfs Administrator tool that takes the form of an MMC snap-in.

- DFS will function, as was Microsoft's objective, with Cluster Server.

- More DFS roots may be defined on the same server.

DCOM Technology

Distributed COM (DCOM), previously known as Network OLE or Distributed OLE, is Microsoft's extension of the COM portfolio to cover networks, too. In short, DCOM is a standardized method with which to communicate among object-oriented programs.

For example, DCOM opens the possibility of using object-oriented components placed on PCs other than the local one. You can distribute both your data and your processing power among several servers, in locations that make business sense. As such, DCOM is a basic prerequisite for the functionality in the ActiveX environment and enables all existing "well-behaved" OLE applications to readily function across networks, both over LANs and over the Internet.

DCOM is part of NT 4.0/5.0, and the corresponding Windows 95/98 component can be downloaded from Microsoft's Web site. DCOM implementations are also available for the following systems:

- Apple Macintosh
- Java
- Sun Solaris (Sparc) 2.5
- Linux 2.0
- HP/UX
- DEC Alpha Unix
- Digital OpenVMS
- IBM OS/400
- Siemens Nixdorf SINIX
- SCO UnixWare
- IBM AIX from Software AG

DCOM also supports many protocols, including TCP/IP, IPX, SPX, and HTTP, and works with many languages, including C/C++, COBOL, FORTRAN, Java, Perl, REXX, and Visual Basic.

A very important part of DCOM is its mechanisms that enable you to include attachments to components and to create new instances of the components. These mechanisms are commonly called the *activation mechanisms*. As a basis, you must state where a particular DCOM component is placed on the network. This can be done either by editing the Registration database or with the DCOM Configuration Tool, which is invoked by running dcomcnfg.exe at the command line or within a command prompt window.

When the DCOM Configuration Tool is invoked, three tabs appear: Applications, Default Properties, and Default Security. The default tab, Applications, provides a list of applications that may be used with DCOM, as well as the opportunity to

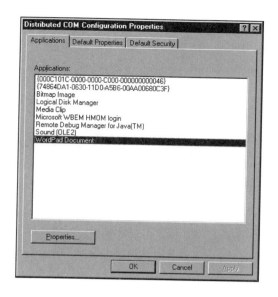

Figure 17.11

The DCOM Configuration Tool provides a complete view of which DCOM components are present on a client. You can view a specific DCOM component more closely by pointing to it and selecting Properties.

modify their properties, as shown in Figure 17.11. By opting to modify the properties, an object's Properties screen appears.

The following six tabs appear on the Properties screen:

- *General*—Shows the general properties of the DCOM application, including the application name, the application type (local server, and so forth), and whether the path is local or remote

- *Location*—Helps DCOM locate the correct computer for an application. Figure 17.12 shows the Location tab, on which you can select to run the application either where the data is located, on the local computer, or on a remote computer. If you select more than one option, DCOM uses the first option in which it finds the application.

- *Security*—Defines the three options for application security: access (who can access the application), launch (who can launch the application), and configuration (who can change the security configuration for the application). You can also control the Registry Value Permissions for the launch option, which is shown in Figure 17.13. You can either allow or deny different groups to launch the application.

- *Identity*—Defines under which user account the application is run. It may be either the interactive user, the launching user, a system account, or a specific user.

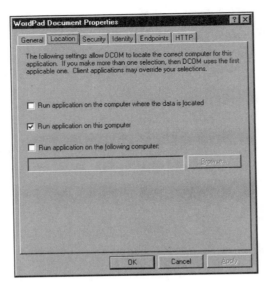

Figure 17.12
When you choose a DCOM component, six tabs appear, providing you with a series of installation options.

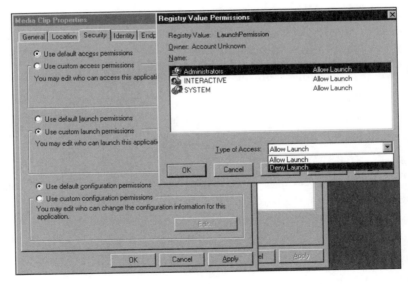

Figure 17.13
You change the Registry Value Permissions for DCOM security in this screen of the DCOM Configuration Tool.

If you choose a specific user, you may select the user and, optionally, add a password that must be entered before launching the application.

- *Endpoints*—Select the various DCOM protocols and endpoints. According to the screen's text, this is "The set of protocols and endpoints available for use by clients of this DCOM Server. The system defaults entry indicates that the default set of DCOM protocols and endpoints for the machine will be used." When you add an endpoint, you can assign it as either static or dynamic (through an Internet range of endpoints or an intranet range of endpoints), along with the protocol sequence, shown in Figure 17.14. The following is a full list of supported protocols:

  - Connection-oriented NetBIOS over TCP

  - Connection-oriented NetBIOS over IPX

  - Connection-oriented NetBEUI

  - Connection-oriented TCP/IP

  - Connection-oriented named pipes

  - Connection-oriented SPX

  - Connection-oriented DECNet transport

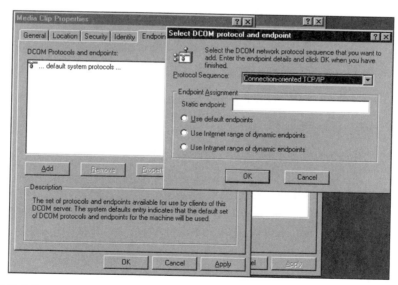

Figure 17.14
The endpoint screen for the DCOM Configuration Tool.

- Connection-oriented VINES SPP transport

- AppleTalk DSP

- Datagram UDP/IP

- Datagram IPX

- DCOM over HTTP

- *HTTP*—Allows or denies HTTP usage with DCOM. This is to access and/or launch the application.

The preceding information describes the six tabs of the DCOM Configuration Tool's Properties screen. As previously stated, the two other tabs of the DCOM Configuration Tool are Default Properties and Default Security. The Default Properties screen provides the opportunity to change both the default authentication level, which specifies the packet-level security, and the default impersonation level, which specifies whether applications are allowed to perform tasks as the client, and whether applications can determine the identity of the calling client. The authentication levels are None, Call, Connect, Default, Packet, Packet Integrity, and Packet Privacy. The impersonation levels are Anonymous, Delegate, Identify, and Impersonate.

The Default Security screen of the DCOM Configuration Tool is used to define the default access, launch, and configuration permissions of the particular DCOM application. The configuration permissions determine who may modify the OLE class configuration information. Figure 17.15 shows the various configuration permissions, which includes 10 special access types. The access capabilities are Read, Full Control, and Special Access.

Microsoft is working on removing the necessity for anyone other than truly advanced administrators to use the sophisticated and extremely complex DCOM Configuration Tool—or a corresponding MMC snap-in, which Microsoft promises will be ready for the production version of NT 5.0.

All data pertaining to activation mechanisms is thus transferred to Active Directory and is treated similarly to the user's master information. The DCOM code directories are then supposed to retrieve activation information automatically from Active Directory, so that any change of a DCOM component is automatically spread across all Active Directory-based clients.

But, so far, NT 5.0 doesn't seem much beyond the familiar Windows NT 4.0 DCOM function. This is substantiated by the fact that Microsoft has hardly mentioned DCOM in relation to NT 5.0 beta 1, which isn't a particularly good sign that the final version of DCOM will be implemented into NT 5.0.

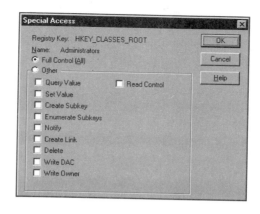

Figure 17.15
The Default Security screen of the DCOM Configuration Tool controls who may access and launch the DCOM application, and contains 10 special access types that may be set.

DCOM Vs. CORBA

The distributed object software industry has two major contenders vying to become the industry standard: DCOM from Microsoft and Distributed System Object Model (DSOM) from IBM. The DCOM object model is basically ActiveX, while DSOM's is the Common Object Request Broker Architecture (CORBA). DCOM and DSOM have similar functionality—they both are used to create objects, and they both enable objects to be manipulated in a binary-standard manner, thus supporting language independence. Microsoft uses DCOM/COM for the controls (such as ActiveX) in all Windows operating systems, and IBM uses DSOM/SOM for their OS/2 controls.

This section describes some differences between the two implementations. These are fairly new technologies, and many changes will occur in the next year. Because of this lack of finality, many businesses have not settled upon one or the other for their strategic plans. Many businesses have created ad hoc combinations of technology, because they are unsure where the distributed object market is headed.

Perhaps the most obvious difference between DCOM and DSOM lies in their respective support for protocol transports. As previously listed, DCOM supports a variety of protocols, whereas CORBA supports only TCP.

Security is also a big difference between DCOM and CORBA. DCOM supports (in Windows NT 5.0) Kerberos Version 5 security, DCE, NTLM (which is used by Windows NT 4.0 and earlier), IPSEC, and SSL/Public Key encryption. By comparison, CORBA only supports SSL/Public Key encryption. As Chapter 11 discusses, Kerberos is an important security consideration, which appears to give DCOM at least one strategic advantage over CORBA, especially with the security concerns posed by the Internet. Companies are looking closely at what security configurations each environment can handle.

Language support is another area where DCOM has the advantage over CORBA. Both support C/C++ and Java. CORBA supports ADA, but DCOM doesn't. However, DCOM supports COBOL, FORTRAN, JavaScript (and other scripting languages), Perl, REXX, and Visual Basic. CORBA doesn't support any of these languages. Considering the sheer number of programmers (Visual Basic alone has several million), DCOM seemingly has a significant advantage over CORBA. Recalling the IBM versus Apple competition, IBM succeeded largely due to the number of applications developed for its systems, not necessarily for technological reasons. DCOM appears to have both advantages.

Additionally, DCOM supports Windows NT services, such as message queuing, asynchronous communications, and transaction processing (including two-phase commits, which are necessary to ensure that transactions updating data on several servers either all commit or all roll back, so that the data is always in a consistent state). DCOM also has great scalability, fault tolerance, and various types of advanced load balancing.

DFS And DCOM: This Is Only The Beginning

The fact that few people know about DFS is a shame, especially because so many situations occur in which DFS can solve some of the problems for which administrators currently have no other solutions. Yet, I am absolutely convinced that a change is going to occur. Undoubtedly, DFS contains some pretty unique and practical facilities. After administrators and program manufacturers recognize DFS's attributes, it should become widely popular. Likewise, Microsoft hasn't aggressively marketed DFS.

I encourage you to start experimenting with DFS, or at least to be aware of its potential. DFS is sufficiently sturdy to implement in an actual business environment. So, why not get cracking?

DCOM won't appear soon. Although DCOM is ready for use, it is so far from being complete that using it in a business environment is too much of an administrative burden for IT personnel; thus, it likely won't become widely popular in its current form. How Microsoft tackles this issue effectively prior to releasing NT 5.0 should be interesting.

The Many Old And New Services 18

Windows NT Server 5.0 offers some new add-on services: Microsoft Transaction Server and Microsoft Message Queue Server are included in NT Server 5.0. These add-ons make the NT platform more qualified to handle distributed environments.

Furthermore, NT Server 5.0 contains the latest version of Internet Information Server 4.0 (IIS), which also contains Index Server and Certificate Server. Microsoft has released an Option Pack for NT 4.0 that contains all of these add-on services (plus a few extra details). The release notes for the Option Pack are available from Microsoft's Web site at **www.microsoft.com/windows/downloads/contents/products/nt4optpk/ntsvroptpkrelnotes.asp**. In addition to the Option Pack is the Microsoft BackOffice Suite, shown in Figure 18.1.

This chapter describes the add-on services and provides a complete review of the Windows NT 5.0 command prompt and batch file commands.

Transactions With NT: Microsoft Transaction Server

The vast majority of traditional client/server systems are based on relational database systems and, thus, are data-oriented, because client software is based on Structured Query Language (SQL) queries, which use a Windows environment, often through the ODBC interface. SQL is operated by a Relational Database Management System (RDBMS), such as Oracle, Sybase, Informix, or Microsoft SQL Server. The data-oriented procedure is extremely efficient and is based on the powerful and well-known technology of the RDBMS. The database maintains the data and allows multiple users to view and manipulate the data, while keeping everything in a consistent mode. Databases also provide an extra degree of fault tolerance, in case hardware is corrupt or fails.

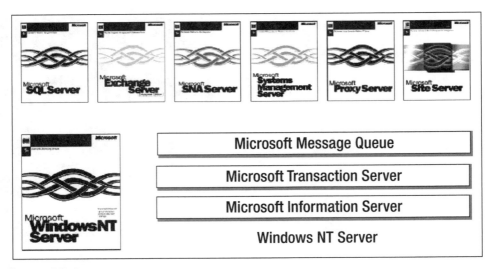

Figure 18.1
Microsoft's view of the division between NT Server 5.0 and BackOffice.

RDBMS applications may have limitations when handling large systems in which the use of queries consumes much of the total system and network resources and creates long logjams on the database system and network. Likewise, procuring the necessary information on how to use the data is fairly complicated, and permissions of who may view or manipulate data must also be maintained. This is a very complicated matter, because maximum access and performance of a system requires that you have sound, detailed business and technological knowledge of all parts of the system's dynamics.

The data-oriented approach also has a risk of security problems, because security in an RDBMS is based on access to data, and not always access to functions or business procedures (depending on the database vendor).

The alternative to sending SQL queries directly against an RDBMS is to insert a Transaction Processing (TP) monitor between the RDBMS and client. The TP monitor originally was designed to meet some rather tight Online Transaction Processing (OLTP) requirements and to provide an infrastructure for developing, implementing, and administering applications.

Microsoft Transaction Server is Microsoft's transaction processing tool. It is scalable, robust, and performs well with Internet and intranet applications. By running on the Internet, communication costs can be dramatically reduced. There is an MMC snap-in provided in Windows NT 5.0 to manage the Transaction Server, as shown in Figure 18.2.

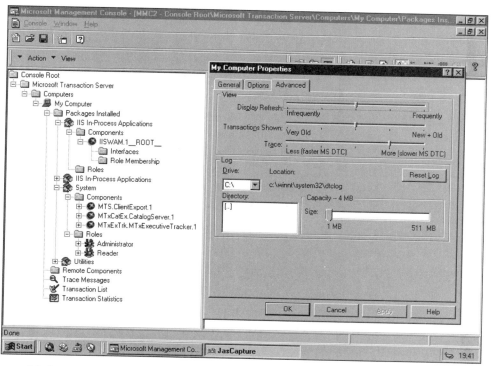

Figure 18.2

Microsoft Transaction Server also has a powerful snap-in.

The TP monitors match the main requirements that arise when constructing large client/server systems, notably the two-phase commit. This special procedure provides the capability to link several operations in such a way that each operation is performed only if all the operations are successful. If just one operation misses, all the other operations are rolled back.

A TP monitor also acts as a type of middleware that shields the database system from the client. Within a TP monitor in the environment, the RDBMS is completely invisible to the client. So, data can be moved around various RDBMSs, without users being involved. Thus, the inclusion of a TP monitor means that you don't depend on one particular database system for your business processing. However, this introduces an equally great dependence on the TP monitor.

A TP monitor contains a series of transaction objects that can be called by the client. The manner in which the TP monitor operates is thus applications-oriented. This procedure reduces logjams, because the transmission mainly consists of calling transaction objects—not the actual data—between the client and TP software.

Usually, most of the data exchange occurs between the TP monitor and the RDBMS, which tends to have a larger bandwidth at its disposal than do clients, because the RDBMS is centrally situated, perhaps even on the same server. Likewise, the TP monitor facilitates handling SQL code updates, because a transaction object acts as a "black box," from the client's perspective.

Security is enhanced by the TP monitor, because the basic control unit is now a transaction, not merely a table in a database. Users can be assigned access rights on the basis of business procedures (functions) that are considerably more similar to real-world problems. A user can have access to one transaction and be refused access to another, even though both transactions update the same data (these transactions may update the same data in different methods).

The TP monitors have a strong market position due to their long background in OLTP environments and their ability to collect information that is relevant for optimizing performance. Any good TP monitor also collects particulars on user patterns, such as answering times and resource consumption.

The preceding considerations partially underlie Microsoft's incorporation of Transaction Server in NT 5.0. Microsoft concludes that the TP monitor procedure is vital to attaining the desired sturdiness and independence of data in a distributed IT environment.

The other fundamental difference between Transaction Server and an ordinary TP monitor is that Microsoft's TP monitor doesn't have SQL operations as its main focus. Transaction Server is designed mainly to handle DCOM/COM-based program components.

Microsoft Transaction Server 2.0 introduces transaction layers for DCOM/COM-based applications, enabling manufacturers to produce transactions based on ActiveX components and the Active Server Pages (ASP) code. Besides having tools for collecting ActiveX components in transaction units, Transaction Server also handles the necessary creation and deletion of components.

Like other TP monitors, users don't immediately notice Transaction Server, but should notice it indirectly through increased sturdiness and performance. Manufacturers and administrators really feel the difference of Transaction Server, because they are provided with some badly needed facilities with which to interconnect and administer components. Not noticing Transaction Server is easy, because it is integrated almost seamlessly with IIS 4.0.

Message Queues With NT 5.0: Microsoft Message Queue Server

Most TP systems are very good at administering fairly static data, because this data tends to need no support in instances when it is movable from one server location to another. This includes, for example, status information that must be exchanged between one or more systems.

These TP systems sometimes have problems with the client/server concept because a client/server implementation implies a need to transmit data between applications across various operating systems and communication protocols; complete security of maintaining data integration while it is being moved; and that data is delivered correctly. Also, the problem needs to be solved of applications having to await a response from the receiver system before being able to continue operating. Conversely, if one of the many systems in the IT environment crashes, a guarantee against data loss is needed. The risk of crashing increases as a business buys more systems.

Thus, an unsatisfied need exists to extend the client/server systems beyond the point that can be reached with remote procedure calls (RPCs) to databases. This need is met through a fairly new type of middleware system known as a message queue server.

Message queue servers are geared to handle movable data. A message queue server shields applications from the complexity of the network, enables standard message methods for online and batch messages, and sets no limits to the application structure. A message queue server enables an application to continue its task undisturbed, without speculating about whether the message is received. A message contains a type of data (or a request or response for data) that both the sender and receiver understand.

Microsoft's Message Queue Server consists of two independent components:

- Several queues in which messages are stored until they are sent

- Queue Manager, which handles the following: its own queues and queues belonging to applications; link-ups to other queue managers; a front-end API; and tools that give the administrator the ability to communicate with Queue Manager

Message Queue Server constitutes a "shoot and forget" mechanism, meaning that an application must only identify which queue it wants to send the message to, leaving the rest to Message Queue Server. As long as the application doesn't require an immediate confirmation of the message's receipt, the application continues treating data, assuming that the message will eventually reach its destination. This procedure is the default setting, but you can specify that an acknowledgment message should be returned that reports whether the message was received. This is useful in many situations, such as when a network is down or laptops are disconnected from the network. When the network connection is reestablished, Queue Manager ensures that all messages are properly delivered.

A good message queue server has many different queue mechanisms, ranging from standard mechanisms, to mechanisms that handle fairly uncertain data and on-the-spot delivery. Microsoft Message Queue Server meets this standard. Microsoft promises that Message Queue Server will be part of NT 5.0, regarding it as a component that is as indispensable as a TP monitor for distributed IT environments. MSMQ 1.0 is included in Windows NT 4.0. However, not a single trace of Message Queue Server is found in NT Server 5.0 beta 1. You'll have to wait to see what the production version offers.

Web With NT: The Internet Information Server

The remaining three add-on services, Internet Information Server 4.0 (IIS), Index Server 2.0, and Certificate Server 1.0, are all designed to be used for Web applications and Web servers.

Internet Information Server 4.0

IIS 4.0 is an update to Microsoft's popular Internet Server. IIS 4.0 can be used as a Web server, News server, and FTP server, and is an efficient upgrade of IIS 3.0. However, IIS 4.0 doesn't currently support Gopher, which is included in IIS 3.0. This doesn't matter much, though, because Gopher's usefulness has diminished with the advent of the Hypertext Markup Language (HTML).

Only the most significant features of IIS 4.0 are mentioned in this chapter, assuming that you are already familiar with the basics of IIS. An exciting new feature of IIS 4.0 is that you now can create transaction-based Active Server Pages scripts, which means that scripts can be handled as atomic transactions (where they do not depend on the success or failure of other transactions) that are administered as usual by Transaction Server. Furthermore, administrators undoubtedly will appreciate the new and quite advanced MMC-based tools that come with IIS 4.0.

Many manufacturers and administrators are also certain to appreciate the fact that most of IIS 4.0 is implemented as a DCOM/COM object. Scripts for IIS 4.0 can be written with Windows Scripting Host or any other computer language that is capable of handling DCOM/COM objects. Microsoft Script Debugger is another useful addition.

Besides IIS 4.0, the Internet server component of NT 5.0 is equipped with Microsoft Certificate Server 1.0 and Microsoft Index Server 2.0.

Certificate Server 1.0

Certificate Server enables a server to establish and use its own unique digital certificates. Optionally, Certificate Server can issue and administer certificates, carry out authentication of users, and have users log on to their existing NT user accounts.

Index Server 2.0

Index Server, shown in Figure 18.3, indexes the contents of a Web site and then lets users search the index that it generates. Index Server is capable of indexing all text

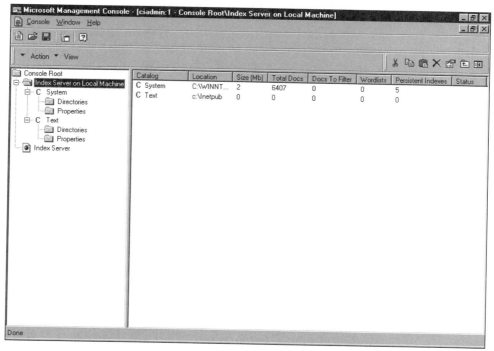

Figure 18.3
Index Server is surprisingly easy to operate. It may also be used to index the contents of a normal server, which may then be made accessible through IIS.

and all properties of documents stored on the server. Clients can make inquiries via a Web browser by filling in the spaces on a simple form. By having all text indexed, the results of a client's search is returned extremely quickly.

Index Server is controlled through the Index Server Manager MMC snap-in. You can view and modify indexing properties of the files and directories that are indexed. Dozens of options are available, such as filtering files to index, adjusting Registry settings, and configuring catalogs.

The Windows NT Command Prompt

Ever since MS-DOS first came out, an ever-increasing number of commands have been created that can be issued in various versions of the command prompt and batch files. These commands enable you to control the Windows NT environment more finely, and in some cases, more precisely than is possible through the various add-on services, system utilities, and MMC snap-ins. Batch scripts can be used to automate a business function, repeat frequently used commands, create user-friendly menus, perform tasks when a user logs in (login scripts), or perform any chain of commands. Program flow can be controlled with conditional logic (such as with **FOR** and **IF** commands).

This section describes all the available commands that are used with the Windows NT command prompt. These command all can be used with batch or script files. Each command is presented in alphabetical order, followed by a brief explanation of its functionality. To see a full list of all options (which could constitute a 400-page book in itself!) see the Windows NT 5.0 online help screens.

Some commands don't do anything in Windows NT and the MS-DOS subsystem, but are kept nonetheless for purposes of backward-compatibility with files from MS-DOS. These nonfunctional commands, which are not described in the following list, are **break, buffers, driveparm, fastopen, lastdrive, nlsfunc, share,** and **verify.**

The following is a list of the commands for Windows NT 5.0:

- **append**—Enables you to specify additional directories whose contents then appear as if they are appended to the current directory. This is done with the **append** environment variable (similar to **PATH**). The **append** command typically shouldn't be used for data files that are modified.

- **arp**—With TCP/IP protocols, looks in the address resolution protocol table (ARP), which uses the IP-to-Ethernet (or token-ring physical address) translation tables. It can display the IP, ARP entries, and physical addresses. **arp** can also add or delete ARP entries.

- **assoc**—Specifies the file extension to associate with the file type.

- **at**—Enables you to schedule (start and stop) tasks to run on either local or remote computers. You can specify both a time to run the task and whether the task should be repeated at specified times/days. You can specify a log file to review the results of the scheduled run. Typical files to run are programs (.EXE, .COM extensions), batch programs (.BAT or .CMD extensions), or Windows NT commands.

- **backup**—Used to back up one or more files from one disk (floppy or hard) to another disk. You can specify to back up subdirectories, enabling multiple files to be copied easier. The **backup** command gives five different exit codes for programming control, which is especially helpful for scheduling backups.

- *Batch commands*—The following commands are used for program control in batch programs (such as BAT files): **call, echo, endlocal, for, goto, if, pause, rem, setlocal,** and **shift**. They are explained in more detail throughout this section.

- **cacls**—Used to display and modify a file's Access Control List (ACL). You can grant or revoke users' read, write, and full-control access to files.

- **call**—Used to call one batch program (that has .BAT or .CMD as the extension) from within another. You can pass parameters to the other batch file with the **call** command. Advanced programmers can have a batch file recursively call itself (hopefully providing an exit clause).

- **chcp**—Displays or changes the number of the active console code page that the Windows NT console uses. This is used for language considerations. For example, Multilingual support uses the number 852 and Russian uses 869.

- **chdir (cd)**—Changes the current drive and directory.

- **chkdsk**—Locks a specified drive and checks it for errors (such as bad sectors). It can also check files for fragmentation and provide status reports.

- **cls**—Clears the screen.

- **cmd**—Opens a new Windows NT command interpreter and executes new commands within it. After **cmd** is finished, control is returned to the original window.

- **codepage**—Infrequently used, because it is retained only for backward-compatibility with old MS OS/2 version 1.3 (and earlier) releases. It changes the code pages (character sets) for the computer, and must be placed in the OS/2 C:\CONFIG.SYS file. Like **chcp**, Multilingual support uses the number 852, Russian uses 869, and so on.

- **color**—Sets the default console foreground and background colors, using a hexadecimal code. You should not set the foreground and background to the same color.

- **comp**—A powerful command (similar to the Unix **diff** command) that compares the contents of multiple files and shows their differences in either hexadecimal, decimal, or character format. Also, either the line within the file or the byte offset from the start of the file can be displayed, along with the information. You can also choose whether you want the comparison to be case-sensitive.

- **compact**—Compresses or decompresses files and directories on NTFS partitions. It can be specified for subdirectories as well. Also used to display existing compression settings.

- *Conditional processing symbols*—Enable you to issue commands based on the results of another command, issue multiple commands from the same prompt, and to act based on the results of a command. The double ampersand symbol (&&) runs the command after && only if the command preceding && succeeds. The double pipe (||) does the opposite: it runs the command after || only if the command preceding || fails. Other conditional processing symbols include the single ampersand (&), semicolon, comma, and caret (^). The single ampersand is used to separate multiple commands that are on one command line. The semicolon and comma are used to separate multiple parameters. The caret signifies to take the character following the caret literally (**you^&me** is interpreted as you&me), to avoid the character from being processed as a conditional processing symbol.

- **convert**—Converts a FAT volume to NTFS format. You can't convert the current drive. You can select a *verbose* mode to get feedback on the progress of the conversion.

- **copy**—Popular command used to copy files to another location or to combine multiple files into one file. Includes options to convert from long names to short names (8dot3 format).

- **country**—Changes the supported language information for the MS-DOS subsystem, including time zones, date formats, currency formats, and so on, which are used in the **backup, date, restore**, and **time** commands. The **country** command should be added to the CONFIG.SYS if you want the changes to be permanent.

- **date**—Enables you to view or change the system date.

- **debug**—Brings up a special Debug utility, which is used to debug and test MS-DOS executable files. Several dozen parameters may be used to perform debugging and testing.

- **device**—Loads device drivers into memory for the MS-DOS subsystem.

- **devicehigh**—Loads the specified device drivers into the computer's upper memory area, to free up more of the computer's conventional memory.

- **devinfo**—Used with OS/2 to set a particular device to use code pages. It specifies the type of device (keyboard, monitor, printer, and so forth), the model of the device, and the file name that contains the code page information. The command needs to be put into the OS/2 C:\CONFIG.SYS file.

- **dir**—Shows a listing of files within a directory (and optionally subdirectories). You can specify which information to display (extension, date the file was last created/modified, and size). You can opt to show hidden files and designate a sort order for the display.

- **diskcomp**—Used to compare the contents of two disks. Can be used only with floppy disks (not hard disks or network drives). **diskcomp** is simplistic insofar as it doesn't actually display the differences, but it does report whether any differences exist.

- **diskcopy**—Used to copy the contents of one floppy disk to another floppy disk. Can be used only with floppy disks (not hard disks or network drives). The destination need not be formatted; if not formatted, **diskcopy** formats the floppy disk first.

- **diskperf**—Used to start and stop various disk performance counters, which are programs that measure the performance of drives (both regular and striped drives). The information is used to determine how to spread data among various drives, and whether new hardware is needed to improve disk performance.

- **dos**—Used in the CONFIG.SYS file, specifies whether the MS-DOS subsystem should link to the upper memory area or the high memory area (HMA).

- **doskey**—Starts the Doskey utility, a simple line editor that is used to repeat previously typed Windows NT commands, edit command lines, and create macros. The macros are great for repeating often-used commands.

- **dosonly**—Forbids any non-DOS-based applications from executing within the command prompt.

- **echo**—Displays a message or specifies whether commands should be echoed back to the screen. **echo** is important for displaying feedback during interactive sessions.

- **echoconfig**—Displays messages during the processing of the MS-DOS subsystem CONFIG.NT and AUTOEXEC.NT each time the MS-DOS subsystem is started. Must be in the CONFIG.NT file to be used. If not in the CONFIG.NT file, the processing messages are not displayed.

- **edit**—Starts the MS-DOS Editor utility, which is a simple text-based editor that is used to create and modify ASCII text files.

- **edlin**—Starts the Edlin utility, which is a basic line-oriented text editor that is used to create and modify ASCII files. Personally, I prefer **edit** to **edlin**, because **edlin** requires you to memorize many shortcut commands.

- **endlocal**—Used in conjunction with the **setlocal** command. **setlocal** starts the localization of batch-file environment changes, and **endlocal** ends it. After **endlocal** is encountered, environment variables are restored to their state prior to **setlocal**.

- **exe2bin**—Used to convert executable files (with the .EXE extension) to binary format, which is useful to developers.

- **exit**—Exits the command interpreter.

- **expand**—Decompresses compressed files and directories.

- **fc**—Compares files and displays the differences between them. Similar in functionality to the **comp** command. You can choose whether you want the comparison to be case-sensitive.

- **fcbs**—Specifies how many File Control Blocks (FCB) may be opened simultaneously by the MS-DOS subsystem. An FCB basically stores file information; thus, the value defined by **fcbs** determines how many files may be open simultaneously.

- **files**—Similar to **fcbs**, limits the number of files that can be accessed simultaneously from the MS-DOS subsystem. The maximum value allowed is 255.

- *Filter commands*—A variety of filter commands exist, which are used to filter and sort output generated from a command. As in Unix, you redirect output from one command into the filter command by using the less-than sign (<). Windows NT 5.0 has three filter commands: **more** (displays output one screen at a time), **find** (displays only specific output and acts as a case-sensitive filter), and **sort** (alphabetizes the output based on the ASCII character set).

- **find**—Powerful command that searches files for a text string and displays all lines that include that text string. Don't confuse this with the Unix **find** command, which looks for specific file names and extensions. You may specify whether the search is case-sensitive.

- **findstr**—Even more powerful and flexible than **find**, **findstr** is used for advanced text searches for strings in files. For example, you can specify that the string being searched for is at the beginning or end of a line, or that no lines contain text, other than the string being searched for.

- **finger**—Used to view personal information about a user account on either the local server or a remote server. For example, **finger akaplan@interaccess.com** shows information about this book's author. Exactly what information is displayed depends on what the user or administrator has established on the server.

- **for**—A batch command that repeats a command for each file/text string within a set of files/text strings.

- **forcedos**—Runs a program in the MS-DOS subsystem mode, with the capability of parameters being passed. This is useful for old programs, such as games that run only within MS-DOS.

- **format**—Formats floppy disks in FAT format and hard drives in either FAT or NTFS format. You can specify the format size of the disk or drive.

- **ftp**—An interactive file-transfer utility that uses TCP/IP to copy files to and from remote computers (which can be running Unix, Windows NT, or many other operating systems). The remote server must be running an FTP server service. With the advent of the Internet, hundreds of thousands of free and shareware programs are available with the **ftp** utility.

- **ftype**—Shows or modifies how file extensions relate to file types. For example, you can associate DOC files with Microsoft Word, so that Word is automatically launched when opening DOC files.

- **goto**—Batch command that skips to a specified label contained within a batch script (or Windows script). This is useful in the logical flow of a program.

- **graftabl**—Like the **chcp** command, **graftabl** displays or changes the number of the active console code page that the Windows NT console uses. This is used for language considerations. For example, Multilingual support uses the number 852, and Russian uses 869. The difference is that the **graftabl** command is used in graphics mode, not window mode.

- **graphics**—Prints the displayed content of the screen. You need to specify the printer type, or Windows NT will look for the GRAPHICS.PRO file.

- **help**—Provides online information on the specified command, or on all commands. Please use the **help** facility for more information on all commands described in this section.

- **hostname**—Shows the name (or IP address) of the current computer that identifies that computer over a network.

- **if**—Batch command that controls the logical flow of a batch script. If the specified condition of the **if** clause is true, then the command that follows the **if** condition is executed.

- **install**—Installs (loads) a memory-resident program into memory, along with any parameters that are to be passed to the program.

- **ipconfig**—Shows TCP/IP network configuration values, such as the IP address, subnet mask, and default gateway values. With DHCP on Windows NT 5.0, **ipconfig** is important because it enables you to see your IP address, which is dynamically generated.

- **ipxroute**—Shows both SAP tables for file servers and IPX router statistics.

- **keyb**—Sets the keyboard layout for non-English language configurations. **keyb** should be placed in the CONFIG.NT file.

- **label**—Displays or changes the volume label and volume serial number of a disk.

- **libpath**—Used with OS/2 subsystem to define which directory or directories contain dynamic link libraries (DLLs). **libpath** is similar to **path**, but is used only to search for DLLs. It needs to be in the CONFIG.SYS file.

- **loadfix**—Ensures that a program is loaded above the first 64K of conventional memory, and runs the program. In the command **loadfix [drive:][path] filename**, **[drive:][path]** specifies the drive and directory of the program, and **filename** specifies the name of the program.

- **loadhigh (lh)**—Loads the specified program into the upper memory area, to free up conventional memory. **loadhigh (lh)** is like the **devicehigh** command, but is used for programs rather than device drivers.

- **lpq**—Shows the print queue status for LPD servers, including what print jobs are in progress and waiting to be printed.

- **lpr**—Prints a file on the specified LPD server.

- **mem**—Shows the free and used memory of the computer, as well as all programs in memory, along with their sizes.

- **mkdir (md)**—Creates a directory in the specified drive and path.

- **mode**—Does many different things, all relating to the configuration of system devices and ports. **mode** is used to configure printers, baud rates and other information regarding serial communications ports, the display type of the command prompt window, and the key repeat rate of the keyboard.

- **nbtstat**—Shows statistics for TCP/IP connections using NBT (NetBIOS over TCP/IP).

- **netstat**—Shows statistics for TCP/IP network connections. For example, **netstat** shows the IP addresses of people logging on, along with network traffic information.

- **net**—Dozens of options are available for the **net** command, which views or modifies various Windows NT networking options. Pass either a **/y** or **/n** to specify yes or no; otherwise, you are prompted. Table 18.1 shows all the options for **net**, along with a brief description of what each option does.

Table 18.1 *The options for the **net** command.*

Command Option	Description
net accounts	Updates user account logon requirements (passwords, logon time constraints, and so forth)
net computer	Adds and deletes computers in a domain database
net config	Shows network settings for a specified service
net config server	Shows settings for a specified server service
net config workstation	Shows settings for a specified workstation service
net continue	Starts up services (FTP, TCP/IP, and so forth) that were in suspend mode
net file	Shows all open shared files and file locks on the specified server
net group	Shows (and changes) global groups on Windows NT Server domains
net help	Shows help topics for network commands
net helpmsg	Shows help documentation relating to a particular Windows NT error message number
net localgroup	Shows (and changes) local groups on the server
net name	Shows, adds, and deletes aliases that are used by the Messenger service
net pause	Suspends services (FTP, TCP/IP, and so forth) that are running
net print	Shows (and changes) print jobs
net send	Broadcasts messages over the network (assuming that the Messenger service is running)
net session	Shows and disconnects sessions on a local computer
net share	Shows (and changes) shared resources
net start	Starts up a service, such as FTP publishing service, Remote Access Connection Manager, SNMP, and UPS

(continued)

Table 18.1 *The options for the **net** command (continued).*

Command Option	Description
net start alerter	Starts the Alerter service, which broadcasts alert messages across the network
net start client service for netware	Starts the Client Service for NetWare service
net start clipbook server	Starts the ClipBook Server service
net start computer browser	Starts the Computer Browser service
net start dhcp client	Starts the DHCP Client service
net start directory replicator	Starts the Directory Replicator service
net start eventlog	Starts the event logging service
net start file server for macintosh	Starts the File Server for Macintosh service
net start ftp publishing service	Starts the FTP Publishing Service
net start gateway service for netware	Starts the Gateway Service for NetWare service
net start lpdsvc	Starts the LPDSVC service
net start messenger	Starts the Messenger service.
net start microsoft dhcp server	Starts the Microsoft DHCP Server service
net start net logon	Starts the Net Logon service
net start network dde	Starts the Network DDE service
net start network dde dsdm	Starts the Network DDE server service
net start network monitor agent	Starts the Network Monitor Agent service
net start ntlm security support provider	Starts the NTLM Security Support Provider service
net start print server for macintosh	Starts the Print Server for Macintosh service
net start remoteboot	Starts the Remoteboot service
net start remote access connection manager	Starts the Remote Access Connection Manager service
net start remote access isnsap service	Starts the Remote Access ISNSAP Service
net start remote access server	Starts the Remote Access Server service
net start remote procedure call locator	Starts the RPC Locator service
net start remote procedure call service	Starts the Remote Procedure Call (RPC) Service
net start schedule	Starts the Schedule service
net start server	Starts the Server service
net start simple tcp/ip services	Starts the Simple TCP/IP Services

(continued)

Table 18.1 *The options for the **net** command (continued).*

Command Option	Description
net start snmp	Starts the SNMP service
net start spooler	Starts the Spooler service
net start tcp/ip netbios helper	Starts the NetBIOS over TCP/IP service
net start ups	Starts the Uninterruptible Power Supply (UPS) service
net start windows internet name service	Starts Windows Internet Name Service
net start workstation	Starts the Workstation service
net statistics	Shows the server/workstation statistics log—this includes response times, errors, password violations, and so on
net stop	Stops a Windows NT network service (FTP publishing service, TCP/IP, and so on)
net time	Shows (or changes) the system clock; it can be synchronized with other computers in the network
net use	Shows computer connection information, or connects/disconnects a computer with a shared resource
net user	Shows (or changes) user accounts, including setting and expiring passwords, home directory, and profile information
net view	Shows computers, domains, and resources being shared by the specified computer

- **nslookup**—Shows Domain Name System (DNS) name server information in either an interactive or noninteractive mode. **nslookup** can also find computers on a network, finger users, and other similar network searches.

- **ntbooks**—A GUI-based help book on Windows NT information. It is very helpful as a supplement to this book for finding specific information about Windows NT and its add-on options.

- **ntcmdprompt**—Starts the Windows NT command interpreter from the command prompt or from within an MS-DOS application.

- **path**—Sets the **PATH** environment variable, which directs Windows NT to search in several directories for a file. **PATH** is critical to locate files; otherwise, you would have to specify where executable files are located or change to their directory.

- **pause**—Temporarily suspends a batch script; when the user presses a key, the batch script continues.

- **pax**—Brings up the Portable Archive Interchange (PAX) utility, which is used to copy files and directories. CPIO and TAR interchange specifications, which are common backup formats in the Unix world, are available.

- **pentnt**—For the Pentium chip only, **pentnt** checks for floating-point division errors, which were more common when the Pentium first hit the market.

- **ping**—Tests the TCP/IP network connection to a remote computer by sending test network packets and timing how long a response, if any, takes.

- **popd**—Used in conjunction with the **pushd** command. **popd** changes the directory to what is stored by the **pushd** command. This is useful for keeping track of which directory a batch file started in.

- **portuas**—Loads all LAN Manager 2.x user accounts (from the NET.ACC file) into the specified Windows NT user accounts database; used mainly during a conversion from LAN Manager OS/2 to Windows NT.

- **print**—Sends the contents of a file to a device such as a printer.

- **prompt**—Customizes the appearance of the Windows NT command prompt. You can put in any text, in addition to directory information, time, and so on, to make the command prompt environment better for users.

- **protshell**—Windows NT and the OS/2 subsystem don't use this command. It is accepted only for backward-compatibility with files from MS OS/2 version 1.3 or earlier.

- **pushd**—Used in conjunction with the **popd** command. **popd** changes the directory to what is stored by the **pushd** command. This is useful for keeping track of which directory a batch file started in.

- **qbasic**—Starts the Qbasic utility, which is a Basic computer-language interpreter. Basic is a flexible language that is much more powerful than batch programs.

- **rcp**—Works only from Unix to a Windows NT computer, and is used to copy files over the network. It is different from **ftp** in that no user or password is needed. Only the IP address of all NT computers that are allowed access must reside in the .rhosts file on the Unix machine.

- **recover**—Attempts to recover data from a disk with bad sectors. It can't recover data in bad sectors, so you probably have to reenter data or text, if possible.

- **rem**—Lets you put remarks (which are just text messages) in files.

- **rename (ren)**—Changes the name and/or extension of a file.

- **replace**—Copies all files from one directory to another, replacing any files that already exist.

- **restore**—Restores files and directories that were backed up by using the **backup** command. It works for floppy or hard drives.

- **rexec**—Runs commands on remote computers. It is different from **rsh**, in that the user is prompted for a password.

- **rmdir** (**rd**)—Deletes a directory and all files and subdirectories within it.

- **route**—Adds, deletes, modifies, or prints network routing tables.

- **rsh**—Uses the RSH service to execute commands on remote servers. **rsh** is powerful, because you can distribute programs or update many client machines from a centralized location.

- **set**—Shows (or changes) Windows NT environment variables, such as **PATH** and **PROMPT**.

- **setlocal**—Used in conjunction with the **endlocal** command to keep track of environment variables. **setlocal** starts the localization of batch file environment changes, and **endlocal** ends it. After **endlocal** is encountered, environment variables are restored to their state prior to **setlocal**.

- **setver**—Alters a file and associates an MS-DOS version number (such as 3.3, 4.01, 5.0, and so forth) with it. This helps Windows NT work with version compatibility issues.

- **shell**—Changes the command interpreter for the MS-DOS subsystem. You can specify your own command interpreter and pass parameters to it. However, unless you have some very specific needs that aren't covered by the default Microsoft shell, you don't need to use this command.

- **shift**—When parameters are passed to a batch file, they are recognized as %0 for the first parameter, %1 for the second, %2 for the third, and so on. **shift** rotates the positions of these parameter representations. The value of %0 is removed, %1 is copied to %0, %2 is copied to %1, and so on.

- **sort**—Takes in information, sorts it, and redirects the results to the screen, a file, or another device.

- **stacks**—Manipulates data stacks that are used with hardware interrupts. **stacks** can run in a second window (maximized or minimized), giving that window a processing priority. **stacks** shouldn't be issued by general Windows users, because it requires knowledge of both hardware and software, and can impede your environment if improperly issued.

- **subst**—Assigns a letter to a particular path, to create a virtual drive. Be careful of which directory you use this for, because it can't be used with some commands, such as **restore**, **diskcopy**, and **chkdsk**.

- **switches**—Changes an enhanced keyboard layout to work as if it were a conventional keyboard, for compatibility with some programs. **switches** should be placed in the CONFIG.NT file.

- **tftp**—A scaled-down version of **ftp**, which transfers files to and from a remote computer. The difference is that the remote computer must be running the TFTP service, instead of the FTP service. Also, **tftp** isn't interactive and has fewer options (just the basic **get** and **put** commands for a file).

- **time**—Shows (or changes) the time from the system clock.

- **title**—Changes the title of the command prompt window, which is shown in the border at the top part of the window.

- **tracert**—Shows the route that is taken to connect from the local computer to a specified remote target computer. It does this by sending Internet Control Message Protocol (ICMP) packets over the network and using the feedback to determine what route it took.

- **tree**—Shows the directory structure of a path, similar to the tree that is shown in the Windows Explorer utility. It can be displayed in either a text or graphics format.

- **type**—Shows the contents of a text file. If you expect more than one page to appear, use **type** in conjunction with the **more** filter command, so that you can see the file one page at a time.

- **ver**—Displays the Windows NT version number.

- **vol**—Shows the disk volume label and serial number for formatted floppy disks.

- **winnt, winnt32**—Installs Windows NT 5.0. After starting, various GUI screens appear, to guide you through the installation process.

- **xcopy**—Copies files, directories, and subdirectories from one place to another. **xcopy** is more powerful than the **copy** command, because **xcopy** keeps directory structures intact. You can selectively copy files that meet criteria, such as the last date the file changed. **xcopy** works with FAT or NTFS formats, and may copy files and directories from one type to another.

As you can see, the Microsoft Windows Command Prompt allows for powerful and flexible programs and routines to be written. These programs, which may be run manually or scheduled with a multitude of applications, can make your Windows NT environment much more robust.

Can Little News Be Good News?

Microsoft Message Queue Server, discussed earlier, is the only new innovation to add-on applications that is planned for NT 5.0, but the current beta version doesn't include a trace of Message Queue Server.

Whether the inclusion of Message Queue Server in NT 5.0 is good news or bad news depends on your point of view. I think NT 5.0's inclusion of a transaction monitor and message queue server is good news, because both are vital middleware products for distributed IT environments. Also, by incorporating these items into NT 5.0, the program manufacturers have some standards against which to write their applications within these two areas. Knowing that the NT 5.0 add-on services will first undergo thorough testing on NT 4.0 systems via Option Pack is also good news. The transaction monitor and message queue server must be very sturdy for businesses that use a distributed environment.

Yet, Microsoft's inability to "invent" more new add-on services is discouraging, particularly because Microsoft's Hydra solution was originally intended to be an add-on service. However, Microsoft recently announced that Hydra will be an independent product in the Microsoft BackOffice family. But Microsoft still has time to invent some new add-on services for NT 5.0 before (or even after) it goes into production.

BackOffice And Other Server Applications

Microsoft is aware that the success of Windows NT 5.0 isn't automatically guaranteed, even if Microsoft provides a strong product with many new functions. Microsoft's current commercial success in the server market is due largely to a far wider variety of server applications being produced for NT than are being produced for its closest competitors. Microsoft realizes that NT 5.0 runs a greater risk of becoming a flop—or at least of not being the overwhelming commercial success that Microsoft hopes for—if the server applications are unable to utilize the new facilities of NT 5.0.

Microsoft initially distributed NT 5.0 only to members of the Microsoft Developer's Network (MSDN). Microsoft's release of NT 5.0 at the Professional Developer's Conference in September 1997 certainly wasn't a coincidence because it gave application developers time to learn the NT 5.0 changes and apply its new features to their products.

Ever since beta 1 of NT 5.0 was released, Microsoft has worked hard to get a consistent message across to all third-party manufacturers: You must start integrating the technologies (especially Active Directory and the MMC snap-ins) of Windows NT 5.0 now if you want to keep up with the market.

Microsoft has announced that the BackOffice applications will be equipped with support for Active Directory and MMC snap-ins soon after the release of NT 5.0. Support for these two technologies seems to be a likely requirement for a company to use the coveted BackOffice logo for its products. Snap-ins for SQL Server 7.0, Microsoft Exchange Platinum, SAM 2.0, and other products reportedly are going to be available.

What Is BackOffice?

Microsoft BackOffice refers to a suite of business products that are bundled and sold as an additional option for Windows NT. BackOffice 4.0 has been available for quite a while with Windows NT 4.0. BackOffice 5.0 will likely be released in tandem with the production version of Windows NT 5.0. The following are the most significant Microsoft products included in BackOffice, which are all described in this section:

- *Exchange Server*—Provides messaging services

- *Internet Information Server*—Used to operate a Web page on the Internet or on a company's intranet

- *Systems Network Architecture (SNA) Server*—Enables NT to connect with SNA systems

- *SQL Server*—Relational database that is used to enter, store, and analyze data

- *Systems Management Server*—Automates software distribution and management of remote computers

- *Proxy Server*—Serves as a firewall between a corporation's internal data and the Internet, protecting the company from potential hackers, and improves performance with network caching

- *FrontPage98*—Used to create and maintain Web pages through versatile creation wizards

- *Site Server*—Used to host Web pages on an NT Server

> **Note:** BackOffice shouldn't be confused with Windows NT Option Pack, which includes the Certificate Server, Message Queue Server, Index Server, Internet Information Server, and Transaction Server. These products are described in Chapter 18.

All BackOffice products are Internet-ready and can take advantage of the NT Option Pack. All are designed with Microsoft's Total Cost of Ownership (TCO) in mind, with easier management through browser-based administration, MMC snap-ins, and reporting tools. The most important BackOffice applications are described next.

Exchange Server

This groupware product is based on routing email in a business. Exchange Server provides the typical emailing capabilities, such as a central management console, group mailing lists, calendar scheduling, and bulletin boards. It also provides good security, encrypted messages, and various security levels.

Other features of Exchange Server enable it to act as a router, so that email messages (and other messages) are passed through an NT Server that is running Exchange Server and then on to their destination. Replication is another great feature, whereby data is redundantly distributed to multiple servers, so that a business can keep running if one of the servers crashes, needs servicing, or otherwise becomes unavailable. Replication also improves network traffic.

Internet Information Server

Internet Information Server (IIS) is one of the most popular Web server products on the market. It is used to maintain a Web page on the Internet or on a company's intranet. Its great commercial success stems primarily from the fact that it is powerful enough to handle huge Web pages and runs on the relatively inexpensive NT Server (compared to Unix and other operating systems).

Not only does IIS provide support for Web pages, it also provides other Internet/intranet services, such as the following:

- An FTP feature that enables files to be transferred across the network in either binary or ASCII format.

- A Gopher feature that supports the outdated Gopher protocol, which uses a basic menu system that is similar to the old Bulletin Board Services (BBSes). The widespread use of HTTP on the World Wide Web has made Gopher obsolete.

- A Usenet feature that supports newsgroups, which are organized into various subjects (from surfing to Howard Stern fans to people interested in NT 5.0), enabling people to post messages, reply to other messages, and so on. The newsgroups on the Internet are becoming so popular that some Web pages act as interfaces to the newsgroups. For example, **www.dejanews.com** is an excellent starting point, if you are interested.

Internet Information Server is also popular because it is easy to use—administrators manage their Web site through a graphical management center. Also, IIS makes it easy to review statistics, such as how many users are viewing each Web file.

SNA Server

The Systems Network Architecture (SNA) Server enables NT to connect with SNA systems, most notably IBM's AS/400 system and various mainframe systems. SNA originally was an IBM network-protocol set, created in the mid-1970s. SNA now includes Advanced Peer-to-Peer Networking (APPN), which connects mainframes to minicomputers, workstations, and desktop computers.

SNA Server 4.0 not only enables companies to keep their current mainframe configuration (if they have one) and connect it to their NT servers, it also connects mainframes to TCP/IP, NetBEUI, and other network environments. For example, the SNA Server supports connectivity to IBM's DB2 database server, IMS data, and

CICS (Customer Information Control System), IBM's transaction monitor. SNA Server 4.0 allows businesses to keep their legacy data and setup while extending to a Microsoft NT environment.

Some other features of SNA Server 4.0 include COM Transaction Integrator (COMTI), which integrates Microsoft Transaction Server (MTS) with CICS/IMS by automatically converting COBOL programs into MTS objects and methods, and PU Pass-thru Service (a PU is a physical unit), which enables an NT Server to act like an IBM 3174 cluster controller. NT 5.0 will provide Management Console snap-ins for the SNA Server.

SQL Server

SQL Server is an industrial-strength relational database that is used to enter, store, and analyze data. SQL Server, and databases in general, can be used to maintain company data and perform some or all of its business operations. Databases may be used as order-entry systems, to store human resources and manufacturing information, for product tracking or sales analysis—basically a company's information infrastructure. Higher-end databases, including SQL Server, can be used as a data warehouse, with which sales and marketing managers can forecast and analyze information via user-friendly Online Analytical Processing (OLAP) tools.

SQL Server ensures that multiple users can view and manipulate data, without interfering with each other, and that all users have consistent data views. For example, if one user updates a record, other users don't see the changes until the user commits the update transaction to the SQL Server. Also, a sophisticated locking mechanism ensures that data is consistent. For example, if two people in different states simultaneously try to book a flight from Chicago to Tel Aviv, the database ensures that they don't get booked in the same seat, by locking the seat record first for one of the two people.

High-end databases such as SQL Server are popular for mission-critical applications, because data can be recovered up to the very millisecond that a disk or server crashes. *Transaction logs*, which keep track of all transactions and their time of execution, make this possible. Also, backups of data may occur while the database is running, allowing applications to run 24 hours a day, 7 days a week. Imagine an air-traffic-control system or a nuclear power plant having to shut down its systems for backups!

SQL Server is *scalable*—the size of the disk usage, memory usage, and number of processes can be changed dynamically. Data may be stored on several servers, but appear to be in one location when a user accesses the database. For performance improvements, various types of indexes may be created to make data querying faster, and statistics may be gathered so that the SQL Server engine can make informed decisions regarding which indexes are helpful for various SQL queries.

Note: *Hundreds of topics may be discussed for SQL Server, and databases in general. If you want to learn more, many books are available.*

SQL Server is Microsoft's integrated database solution. It is in competition with other high-end databases from such companies as Oracle (the largest database company in the world and the second-largest software company, behind Microsoft), Sybase, and Informix.

Systems Management Server

Microsoft Systems Management Server (MSMS) automates software distribution and management of remote computers, among other features. Basically, MSMS provides administrators a central location from which to manage their environment.

The remote features of MSMS enable administrators to troubleshoot problems on remote computers without leaving their desks. An administrator can take control of the remote computer, enabling the administrator to demonstrate visually the problem being discussed on the phone. This is a great improvement from a simple phone call, for anyone who has used a help desk. The capability to review files, the registration database, and other such information remotely is a great advantage.

MSMS also includes an inventory management center that shows which software programs (and versions) are distributed, and where they are distributed. The inventory management center makes keeping track of licensing issues much easier, and helps the administrator determine which clients need to have their software upgraded.

The distribution of software to remote clients likely will be replaced in NT 5.0 with the IntelliMirror architecture, described in previous chapters.

Future Compatibility Between BackOffice And Active Directory

Microsoft's declared goal is to integrate its entire BackOffice family of server applications with Active Directory, and it gives three good reasons why it wants to meet this goal:

- So that all objects can be viewed in a uniform manner
- So that the whole company can have a single, central administrative location
- To reduce the TCO for each application

Microsoft's Plans

The benefits of using Active Directory in BackOffice are shown in Figure 19.1. So far, Microsoft hasn't declared a plan of how and when changes are going to occur to the NT 5.0 standards for the various BackOffice applications. Undoubtedly, Microsoft intends this process to move quickly, because the previously listed advantages of such an integration are a real improvement for users (and likely a boost to Microsoft's sales). Currently, Microsoft is busy convincing third-party manufacturers that they should include the same standards in their own products.

Integration of Active Directory and BackOffice applications isn't simply a matter of each application saving its property data in the Active Directory database. Integration also involves, significantly, establishing greater uniformity in the architecture of the applications and, indirectly, tidying up the current confusion regarding the central terminology of the BackOffice applications. The new administrative tools for the server applications will be based on the MMC snap-ins.

The word *site* is a good example of the inconsistent terminology used across the BackOffice applications. The definition of a *site* in SMS is very different from the definition used in NT Server 5.0 (or Exchange Server). The SMS definition of site isn't tied to bandwidth (although bandwidth may be a restricting factor regarding the overall architecture), but instead is used in relation to creating a container for managing objects.

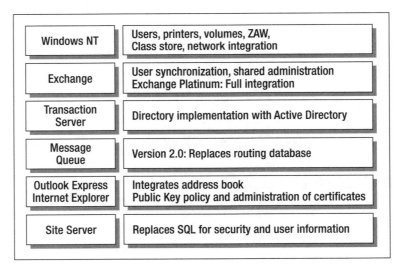

Figure 19.1
Microsoft's vision of the benefits gained by integrating Active Directory and the BackOffice family.

Microsoft reckons that it can integrate the next version of Exchange Server (currently code-named *Platinum*, but likely to be called version 6.0) with Active Directory. Microsoft promises to make Exchange Platinum ready for delivery within 90 days after the release of NT 5.0, thus becoming the first BackOffice application offering full integration with Active Directory.

Even though Windows NT 5.0—and thus Active Directory—may still be far from being a commercial reality, Microsoft has actually published a white paper stating how it imagines integrating the next version of Microsoft Exchange with Active Directory. Microsoft's thoughts are worth studying more closely, because what it is planning for Microsoft Exchange is bound to coincide with what happens to the other server applications in the BackOffice family in the coming years.

The Perfect Example: Microsoft Exchange Platinum

The current Exchange version (version 5.0) contains a few Active Directory-like functions: Support by Active Directory Services Interface (ADSI) and full implementation of the LDAP 3.0 draft specification, with read/write functionality for clients and the possibility of directory synchronization with other LDAP servers. Exchange Server has been equipped with multimaster replication.

Exchange currently lacks full integration with Active Directory. Microsoft states that full integration with Active Directory will offer Exchange the following advantages:

- Improved replication, through less consumption of bandwidth (because Active Directory replicates only the altered properties) and more sophisticated replication topology.

- Enhanced security, through a greater degree of details (Active Directory supports assigning rights on both the object and attribute levels) and faster security checks (because every object knows in advance whether a particular user has the rights necessary to perform a specific operation).

- Extension of the directory schema via programming to ADSI. Microsoft plans to replace the current Exchange Directory API with ADSI, even if Platinum is backward-compatible with the Exchange Directory API.

- Moving users among different sites is much easier, because sending all email to the new location is simply a matter of altering an attribute for mail routing.

All the information that is currently stored in Microsoft Exchange will be moved to Active Directory when an upgrade to the Platinum version occurs. This data consists of the following two areas, which are treated very differently:

- *Exchange receivers*—This information will be stored in the domain container of Active Directory. The Exchange mail tray will be implemented via a mailbox attribute that provides the email address and specifies on which Exchange server the email must be placed. Thus, any Active Directory object (for example, servers) can be linked to a mail tray, which is an innovation. Distribution lists will consist of a new object class that is linked to a mail tray, and will correspond to the current distribution lists.

- *Configuration information*—All the information that currently is placed on the directory of Exchange and the Registration database will be moved to Active Directory. This is done through a new container, called *Configuration*, which contains all configuration information. This container is replicated to all Active Directory servers within the organization and can also be switched elsewhere.

Exchange Platinum will operate with the same site definition as Active Directory, and so the site definition for Exchange in the underlying domain structure is removed. Therefore, Exchange sites no longer exist, only Active Directory sites. This means that when an Exchange Platinum server is installed, it automatically will be placed (based on its IP address) in the site where it is physically located. Likewise, the Exchange mail-routing mechanism will benefit from the site information, thus generating an optimum message topology.

All administrative tools in Exchange Platinum will be based on MMC snap-ins. The administration of Exchange receivers is carried out via an Exchange-specific extension to the Microsoft Directory Service Manager MMC, which already is the primary administrative tool for all objects within the domain. The configuration information will take the form of one or more MMC snap-ins.

Microsoft has already explained how it will ensure a flexible upgrade route from the current Exchange version to Exchange Platinum. You will be able to log on to Exchange Platinum from Exchange 5.5 clients (or even Exchange 4.0 and 5.0 clients) that are equipped with a new Platinum-prepared Service Pack, because the client can be rerouted automatically to the nearest Active Directory server.

Microsoft promises that you won't lose any data while upgrading from a previous Exchange version to Platinum. Moreover, Microsoft states that you can perform very easy implementations of Platinum while maintaining one or more existing Exchange Servers, without any significant negative impact on the operating environment. The only requirement for maintaining older Exchange Servers is to install a new Platinum-prepared replication agent on the existing Exchange Servers. The replication agent ensures the following:

- The upgraded Exchange servers will appear in the old Exchange site *and* the new Active Directory site.

- The changes in the directory will be transferred between the two directories (the old Exchange directory and Active Directory) via the replication agent.

- The Exchange Platinum servers can handle both Exchange MAPI clients and Internet clients.

- All users (all users still placed in the old Exchange directory) can be administered from the same spot via Exchange Platinum.

Opening A New Market Area

Parallel with Microsoft's efforts to have third-party manufacturers include built-in support for the new NT 5.0 facilities in the next versions of their products, Microsoft is expanding the market for applications. The new drive includes branch solutions (frequently called *vertical solutions*) and business applications (also known as *horizontal solutions*). Having conquered the market for standard solutions, Microsoft has picked vertical and horizontal business solutions as its next high-growth area, which is necessary considering Microsoft Office's immense market share for office suites (which includes Microsoft Word, Excel, Access, and PowerPoint). Microsoft's combination of Microsoft Exchange and Outlook also has a sharply rising market share in email solutions.

Rather than venturing into the attractive business-solutions market on its own, Microsoft has entered into strategic partnership agreements with applications manufacturers that are already prominently positioned in these areas. As part of these partnership agreements, outlined in Table 19.1, the program manufacturers commit themselves to integrating their products with the Windows DNA architecture (see Chapter 5), and thus the Windows and BackOffice platforms.

Primarily, these initiatives serve to open an incredibly large market area for Microsoft's basic platforms, such as operating systems and BackOffice server applications. Secondly, support of the NT 5.0 key technologies in all of these business solutions will be introduced. After this integration is available on several of the most frequently used business solutions, Active Directory undoubtedly will be much closer to winning the struggle to become the most prominent directory service on the market.

To ensure efficient administration and high visibility of the Windows-based business solutions, as well as efficient handling of Microsoft's standardization initiatives within the various solutions, Microsoft has established an entirely new unit called the

Table 19.1 *Microsoft's strategic partnerships with applications manufacturers.*

Solutions Area	Alliance Partners
Financial systems	CODA, Sage, OBIC Business Consulting, Exact, Platinum Software, Ramco, Great Plains Software, Solomon Software, State of the Art, Systems Union, and User Friend
Human resources management	Aurum, Clarify, Royalblue CIS, Scopus, Siebel, Success Technologies, and Vantive
Handling of documents	Documentum, Eastman Software, FileNet, Mosaic, and PC Docs
Electronic trading	Trintech and Sterling Commerce
ERP-systems (Enterprise Resource Planning)	Baan, Fourth Shift, J.D. Edwards, Marcam, Peoplesoft, and SAP AG
Financial benefits	Infosel, Prologic, and Sungard Capital Markets
Health	IDX Corporation, IMNET, Picis, and Shared Medical Systems
Production	Intellution, Intergraph, Siemens Automation, Wonderware, and Verifone
Trade	ICL Retail Systems, MICROS Systems Inc., and Ouroumoff Informatique

Application Developers Customer Unit (ADCU). At its inception, ADCU had more than 550 employees (200 in the U.S., approximately 250 in Europe, and approximately 100 in Asia), a very globally oriented organization.

To get an impression of Microsoft's venture into the business-solutions area, browse **www.microsoft.com/industry/welcome.htm**.

Others Plan To Integrate With Active Directory

The general structure of Active Directory can be used for purposes other than server applications. An obvious alternative is to integrate Active Directory with the active network components present in the IT environment. This can be used to enhance security, because only authorized users with access to the physical network are allowed to introduce detailed access policies for users or to divide the business into several virtual LANs that cover only certain users (regardless of physical location on the network). Some of the benefits of integrating with Active Directory are shown in Figure 19.2.

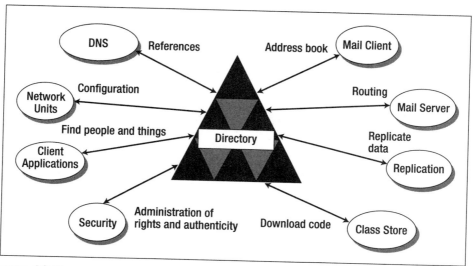

Figure 19.2
Active Directory offers seemingly unlimited possible uses, such as integration with network components.

During a presentation at the Microsoft Professional Developer's Conference in San Diego in September 1997, Microsoft and Cisco gave a practical example of how policies can be used. The routers of the example business were programmed to guarantee QOS (Quality of Service) for certain end users via Active Directory, instead of having to alter the setup in every single router.

Cisco, the world's biggest supplier of network components, is already ensuring that its network components are very closely integrated with Active Directory. Cisco has obtained a license for Active Directory and has announced that it will be ready to deliver its Active Directory software not later than 90 days after the release of Windows NT 5.0.

Cisco's software is a complete porting of Active Directory to Unix. This porting's first use will be to incorporate Active Directory support into its Internetwork Operating System (IOS), on which the majority of Cisco's network products are based. The porting can also be used to include Active Directory in all other types of Unix-based solutions (including Unix operating systems), which Cisco has said little about thus far. However, Cisco certainly has the rights to market and sell the Unix version of Active Directory to all interested parties.

Another 23 network applications manufacturers have announced that they support the efforts of Microsoft and Cisco to expand Active Directory's directory schema to cover modeling, configuration, and administration of network services involving active network components. The list of network producers includes 3Com, Ascend, Cabletron, Compaq, Digital, Fore, Hewlett-Packard, and Intel.

These 23 network producers have a compelling reason to join: They want to avoid the appearance that Cisco is the sole manufacturer focusing on Active Directory and, hence, Microsoft solutions. These companies haven't committed to anything, so far, so support for Microsoft and Cisco's efforts isn't costing them anything.

A Good Chance Of Being A Success

If Microsoft can maintain (and extend) the number of partnerships regarding vertical and horizontal business solutions, and if Windows NT 5.0 turns out to be a sturdy system, how can anyone compete with Active Directory? Novell, Banyan, and others haven't refined their directory services sufficiently in recent years to avoid having the majority of applications manufacturers plan to include support for Active Directory in their products.

Since 1995, Microsoft has been running the "Designed for BackOffice Logo" program, which requires vendors to meet several requirements before their products can use the BackOffice logo as a selling point. Figure 19.3 shows the overall requirements to receive a BackOffice logo. Microsoft's logo program has been immensely successful for all parties involved, because Microsoft is assured of receiving standard functionality from Independent Software Vendors (ISVs) and Original Equipment Manufacturers (OEMs), and the ISVs and OEMs get to use the logo as one of their sales features. Over 600 applications have BackOffice logos for Windows NT 4.0, and the number is sure to increase after NT 5.0 goes into production.

At the Tech-Ed '98 conference in June 1998, Microsoft introduced the new changes to its BackOffice logo program, which provide guidance for the eventual release of NT 5.0, including BackOffice 5.0. The new requirements, which will be changing throughout the year, can be viewed at **www.microsoft.com/backoffice/designed**. The requirements aren't expected to be stable until November 1998.

Some of the most conspicuous third-party developers on the market (SAP, Baan, and Peoplesoft) have already announced that they have selected Windows DNA, and hence the Windows and BackOffice platform standards, which indirectly leads to supporting Active Directory. Moreover, HP has announced a cooperative project with Microsoft to create solutions that make working over the Internet safe. Consequently, HP will incorporate support of Active Directory in a series of its products. No such products have been named yet.

Also note that designing sound, robust, distributed applications (the very essence of DNA—Windows Distributed interNet Applications) is possible without a directory service such as Active Directory. Don't forget that Microsoft has some tangible

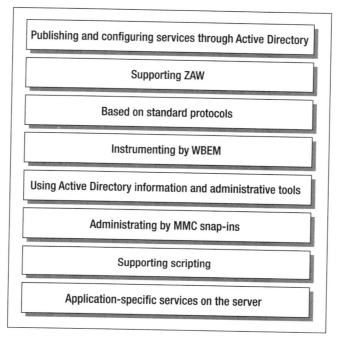

Figure 19.3
The overall requirements for the BackOffice logo with Windows NT Server 5.0. The independent program manufacturers have their work cut out for them.

advantages if Active Directory and MMC become widely popular. Third-party manufacturers can't ignore this fact when they weigh the advantages and disadvantages of integrating their applications with Active Directory.

Revolution At A Price

20

Windows NT 5.0 is the biggest update of NT so far. NT 5.0 finally removes the last traces of the LAN Manager heritage from NT. Bill Gates, the founder of Microsoft, is quite right when he states: "It's fair to say Microsoft has bet its future on Windows NT Version 5."

Windows NT 5.0 marks the beginning of the end of the competing Windows 95/98 platform (which originates in the world of DOS). Microsoft's declared goal is for Windows 98 to be the last version of the "old" Windows. The future belongs to Windows NT. In fact, Gates declared in June 1997, that Microsoft planned to invest over $1 billion in Windows NT before it is released.

With its increased focus on Windows NT, Microsoft is also trying to tighten its proprietary legal hold on the letters "NT." In late 1997, Microsoft's lawyers started contacting businesses that use "NT" either in their Internet address or as part of their company or product names, notifying them that they should refrain from using the letters "NT" to market their products. Microsoft likely is focusing on using the letters "NT" more often in its marketing, to expand its trademark from "Windows NT" to include the most frequently used abbreviation, "NT."

The Market Says "Wait And See"

Microsoft would like to have most large businesses lined up to buy Windows NT 5.0 when it's released, so that Microsoft can safely introduce the NT operating system on its clients and servers shortly after NT is released.

But the market isn't that simple. Whereas Windows NT Server 4.0 gained a solid position in the server market in 1996, NT Workstation 4.0 hasn't quite caught on. Less than two years have passed since Windows NT was launched, and fewer NT Workstation 4.0 licenses have been sold than Windows 95 licenses in the same time period.

According to most independent computer-market observers, the majority of businesses are biding their time with regard to making a decision on NT 5.0. In fact, an article titled "Betting On The New NT," appearing in the October 13, 1997 issue of *Information Week*, reported the results of a survey that shows, out of 100 IT managers responding, only 30 percent planned to evaluate an NT 5.0 beta installation. In the same survey (which allowed multiple answers to be selected), 70 percent of the managers said they didn't plan to evaluate an NT 5.0 beta installation, and 18 percent reported that they were uncertain. For the question of whether these IT managers planned to carry out a major introduction of NT 5.0 during the first year of its release, 25 percent answered affirmatively, 54 percent said "No," and 21 percent were uncertain.

The current version of Windows NT is doing excellently, with an increasing market share and numerous applications manufacturers supporting the platform, but the whole world isn't geared toward NT in the manner Microsoft would like to see. Despite the success of NT, Microsoft clearly hasn't taken over the market for server operating systems, nor is it likely to do so in the foreseeable future.

Considerably more users globally are using NetWare—approximately 55 million—than are using NT, because Novell has dominated the market for network operating systems until fairly recently. Even though Novell's market share has dropped from 75 percent to approximately 60 percent, it hasn't been knocked out—Novell expects to sell over $1 billion of its NetWare and intraNetWare products in 1998.

Furthermore, the lucrative Unix market is a strong contender for large applications solutions. Although NT has advantages regarding standardization, choice, underlying hardware platform, and software solutions, Unix still has a strong position regarding scalability, sturdiness, and fault tolerance, and the vast amount of accessible Unix expertise tends to be a decisive factor regarding the choice of large solutions for servers.

Moreover, many businesses still find choosing Windows NT too risky for large, business-encompassing applications servers. Experience demonstrates that Unix is the best bet for truly scalable database solutions, big servers for the Internet, Online Transaction Processing System (OLTP) solutions, and large client/server solutions throughout a company. Unix has developed and gained experience over two decades, and it is available from all the major computer vendors. One of the largest Internet server applications around, Apache, is a freeware program that runs on Unix.

Moreover, some variants of Unix can be scaled effectively to 32 or more processors. And, most importantly, more than 10,000 applications are available to choose from for Unix. By comparison, Windows NT offers only a few thousand applications, more limited scalability, and less than Unix's 20 years of business experience. However, the range of applications and expertise that comes with NT is increasing greatly. NT 5.0 is also introducing a series of bundled functions that previously had to be bought separately, and at great cost. The world of Unix has its attention focused on Windows NT Server as its most dangerous threat.

Microsoft is targeting the market that mainly uses Unix-based solutions, regarding them as potential Windows NT customers. Thus, not coincidentally, in 1997, several prominent Unix vendors (notably Silicon Graphics, IBM, Hewlett-Packard, Digital, and Intergraph) started selling solutions based on NT Workstation as an alternative to their own Unix-based solutions. The decision by these companies is based primarily on the fact that they are trying to maintain their own market shares in the low-end workstation market, which currently is being strongly attacked.

Microsoft Stakes A Lot On NT Server Selling To Large Businesses

As previously stated, Windows NT 5.0 is the central component in the emerging series of products for large businesses. NT Server 5.0 ensures that all Microsoft products will be better positioned in large and complex IT environments that have a great demand for overall coordination, scalability, manageability, and sturdiness.

Whereas NT Server 4.0 is so straightforward that independent departments and workgroups can readily establish their own servers without any support or oversight by the central IT department, NT 5.0, and particularly Active Directory, require a far greater level of standardization across the entire business for them to be used for mission-critical business applications. Thus, independent departments can't establish differing server setups.

The overall scalability of the IT environment has been enhanced considerably with Active Directory. Likewise, the scalability of each individual system has been enhanced through a series of new hardware and software initiatives (see, Chapters 3 and 6). By introducing the MMC snap-ins, also designed for third-party applications, Microsoft has boosted manageability enormously.

Yet one doubt remains: sturdiness. NT 5.0 certainly contains a series of new initiatives, such as Active Directory, DFS, Cluster Server, and the addition of a job object in the NT nucleus, aimed at providing sturdiness and enabling administrators to designate how many resources a particular process uses. These initiatives should enhance the sturdiness of the environment. But sturdiness isn't simply a matter of new technology—other crucial factors are experience, elimination of program errors, advanced operational tools, and good programs that work. These factors can't be evaluated until the NT system is used in real-world operating environments.

Microsoft's focus on large computer environments means that NT has become more complex, which makes greater demands on the administrator responsible for configuring it into smaller solutions. Windows NT Server 5.0 may not be any more advantageous than its predecessor in fairly simple networks, because if a business buys NT Server 5.0, it also needs to introduce both a fairly complex DNS service (instead of the simpler WINS) and Active Directory.

In installations with less than 25 users, Microsoft's Small Business Server is likely to be of great importance, because SBS attempts to make installing a server and handling the day-to-day administrative tasks easier. NT Server 5.0 very likely will appear in a Small Business Server version in the future.

NT Workstation 5.0 Isn't Ready For Real Business Solutions

When NT 5.0 beta 1 was released, Microsoft warned that its program code was designed for program manufacturers, and quite rightly so. Although the beta version contains practically all the facilities and technologies promised by Microsoft, NT 5.0 is far from being sufficiently tested in true business environments.

A series of major and minor details still need to be tuned: Microsoft needs to solve the issue of server migration facilities from NetWare to NT (see Appendix A), and the Active Directory leaves a lot to be desired. Many details regarding replication are unfinished, and I suspect that Active Directory can't yet tackle a bigger and more complex setup. This is only a guess on my part, because I haven't had an opportunity to establish a large Active Directory environment with a real user load; without such testing, Active Directory's reliability and efficiency can't be realistically measured. I don't have much negative to say against Active Directory, because all the tests I have performed on it so far have been positive.

However, NT 5.0 lacks some of the facilities that ordinary users consider absolutely vital. For example, upgrading directly from NT 3.51 or Windows 95 OSR 2 isn't possible in the beta version of NT 5.0—only from Windows 98 or NT 4.0.

The worst shortcoming is that NT 5.0 has considerable problems handling some very popular office applications, such as Lotus Freelance Graphics 96, McAfee antivirus programs, and even Microsoft's Access 95, PowerPoint 95, and Project 95. The Office 98 suite does work well, however.

NT 5.0's stability still needs much work regarding the migration from Windows NT 4.0 or Windows 95. Problems arise when installing Windows NT 5.0 on top of systems that already have one or more of the following applications installed:

- Borland Delphi
- ClarisWorks 4.0
- CorelDRAW! 6
- Corel WordPerfect Suite 7.0
- Lotus SmartSuite 96
- Macromedia Freehand 7.0
- Micrografx ABC Graphics Suite
- Microsoft Encarta 97
- Microsoft FrontPage 97
- Microsoft Internet Explorer 3.0
- Microsoft Money 97
- Microsoft Office 97
- Microsoft Visual Studio 97
- Netscape Navigator 3.0
- Netscape Navigator Gold

Most PC clients include at least one of these programs and thus confront this problem. Microsoft readily admits that it is working on solving these problems, while at the same time emphasizing that the current version of NT 5.0 is designed primarily for software manufacturers and hardware producers. Consequently, backward-compatibility with office applications hasn't been at the top of its list of priorities.

Microsoft can't solve on its own the problems regarding migration of applications. A migration from Windows 95 or Windows 98 often requires a *migration Dynamic Link Library* (DLL), which is a specially designed component that ensures both that a particular application doesn't vanish when upgrading to NT 5.0 and that it is still recognized by the system after the upgrade.

The migration routine in Windows NT 5.0 is designed to identify the applications installed and to call the corresponding migration DLLs during the different phases of the setup process. For instance, migration DLLs can be used to transfer applications files and keys from the Registration database, replace some of the components that exist with later components, and perform any other tasks that are necessary for an application to operate just as well on Windows NT 5.0 as on Windows 95/98.

Microsoft clearly states that the applications manufacturers are responsible for designing the migration DLLs for their own applications. Microsoft expects that most of these manufacturers will have migration DLLs ready for their own products (or have later versions that don't require migration DLLs, because they support NT 5.0) well before the release of Windows NT 5.0.

Unfortunately, Microsoft has renounced in advance any kind of distribution of migration DLLs in conjunction with NT 5.0, which requires that you refer to the third-party producer's Web site. This may be aggravating to large businesses that use many different applications.

Can The Problems Be Solved?

Microsoft anticipates that all the issues outlined in this chapter (plus several other details) will be solved prior to the release of beta 2. Many of my colleagues in the trade don't agree with me when I say that Microsoft will have NT 5.0 ready for launch in the first quarter of 1999. I have no doubt that Microsoft will do all it can to make this happen.

Things may still go wrong. NT 5.0 will be the biggest version of NT, as well as the most important version in terms of marketing. Microsoft originally intended NT 3.1 to be 3.1 million code lines, yet it ended up containing 6 million code lines. NT 4.0 has 16.5 million code lines, and NT 5.0 beta 1 has 27 million code lines (see Figure 20.1).

In simple terms, NT 5.0 contains 27 million potential points of error. The fact that something so complex can function so well is amazing. The question that remains is how well it will function in a large, dynamic environment.

The incredible array of hardware and software components certainly doesn't simplify NT 5.0. Microsoft's hardware laboratory is investigating potential compatibility problems by testing NT 5.0 against systems from more than 300 different manufacturers. This includes 405 graphics cards, more than 1,400 printers, 374 network cards, and over 2,600 modems that were tested while preparing NT 5.0 beta 1 for its release. New hardware components are allegedly being tested every day.

This testing has already had an impact on NT 5.0, because NT 5.0 offers many more built-in drivers and a more intelligent installation routine than its predecessor.

The demands on the underlying hardware are just as high for NT 5.0 as they are for NT 4.0. In other words: Don't implement Windows NT 5.0 on a PC with less than 32MB RAM, 800MB disk space (the operating system alone takes up approximately

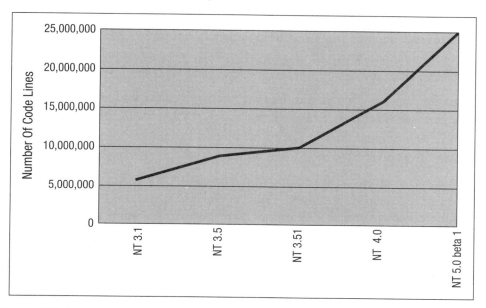

Figure 20.1
*The growth in the number of code lines from NT 4.0 to NT 5.0 is enormous.
Microsoft has to work very hard at maintaining a low level of errors.*

200MB of disk space), and a fast Pentium processor (at least 133 MHz). Having a bigger processor is also a good idea if the computer needs to handle more than basic office applications.

Microsoft's Gain Has Been Impressive

Although Windows NT currently is far from being the foremost product on the market for workstations and servers, it is having an impact on the computer industry.

The overwhelming success of Windows NT has forced Microsoft's competitors to change their strategies and expectations over the past 12 months. IBM has created a new hardware division that is devoted entirely to selling NT-based systems. Likewise, IBM's company for systems integration, Global Services, is focused on the NT market, realizing its enormous potential. The IBM software division is also focusing many of its efforts on porting its applications to NT. IBM's reversal from offering only their own proprietary systems has been so effective that IBM currently is the biggest vendor, by far, of NT applications, which exceeds 100.

Computer Associates, the software conglomerate, has joined forces with Vanstar Corporation, one of the true heavyweights in the market for integration services, for the supply of management solutions for NT environments. And Microsoft has entered into an alliance agreement with the auditing firm KPMG Peat Marwick, with a goal of establishing a group of consultants that focus entirely on Windows NT and NT-related solutions.

The market heavyweights have shifted their energies to the area of NT. The market survey institute Dataquest estimates that the direct and indirect turnover of Windows NT will amount to $12 billion in the year 2000, and the development and integration fees for Windows NT will produce an additional $8 billion.

Whether Microsoft succeeds in keeping its promise to deliver NT 5.0 by early 1999 should be very exciting to follow. Windows NT 5.0 is Microsoft's biggest special-brand project thus far, and if the first version of NT 5.0 is error-free and delivered within the time limits stipulated, it will be a great achievement.

If Microsoft comes up short, it won't be the first time that it doesn't keep to its schedule, certainly with regard to its operating systems. Windows 95 appeared very late in 1995, and the same trend carried through to Windows 98 (which launched on June 25, 1998), originally dubbed Windows 97.

So why should NT 5.0 be dead on arrival? After all, it has many more features than Windows 98, for example. But if Microsoft manages to have NT 5.0 ready as a reliable product by early 1999, it truly will have pulled off a successful revolution.

Migration From NDS To Active Directory

Microsoft's closest competitors in the market for network operating systems and server operating systems (Banyan, Novell, and IBM) are currently offering directory service solutions. These solutions have been on the market sufficiently long to be thoroughly tested in real-world business environments and have any bugs and problems fixed. Active Directory currently is a great new feature only with regard to NT. It has one serious drawback in comparison to its competitors: Because Active Directory is new, it is an untested product, with all the potential errors and problems that poses.

In technological and marketing terms, NT Server's biggest directory service competitors are Novell's NetWare products. The older NetWare 2.x- and 3.x-based systems (based on a flat user database known as a *bindery*) cover the largest section of the networking market. The latest version of NetWare (4.x) offers a directory service called Novell Directory Service (NDS), a competitor to Active Directory. If Active Directory isn't successful for some reason, NDS gains a great advantage, because NDS can also be used on Windows NT Server.

This is why in recent years Microsoft has vehemently dismissed all technical attacks from Novell. Microsoft has taken the trouble to design and create a migration route to Active Directory from NDS and the older bindery-based NetWare systems, so that businesses no longer will depend on Novell in their Microsoft environment.

Migration from NDS to Active Directory takes place through a special MMC snap-in known as the *Directory Service Migration Tool*, which is briefly outlined in this appendix.

A Strong Tool In A User-Friendly Wrapping

Undoubtedly, the Directory Service Migration Tool, shown in Figure A.1, is extremely important to Microsoft. Consequently, Microsoft has joined forces with the Cheyenne Directory Management Group (previously known as Preferred Systems), which has a reputation of having the best NDS experts outside of Novell.

The Cheyenne Directory Management Group is responsible for the NDS products *DS Standard* and *AuditWare*. AuditWare is a Windows-based tool that is designed to carry out NDS reporting and security analysis. DS Standard is a Windows-based, offline NDS management tool that enables changes to be introduced in a back-end database, rather than in the live NDS database. DS Standard complements the built-in NDS tools and is quite clearly the best third-party administrative tool for NDS. All complex NDS installations have DS Standard in their toolboxes, which is the reason why NDS is the most frequently sold item of its kind worldwide.

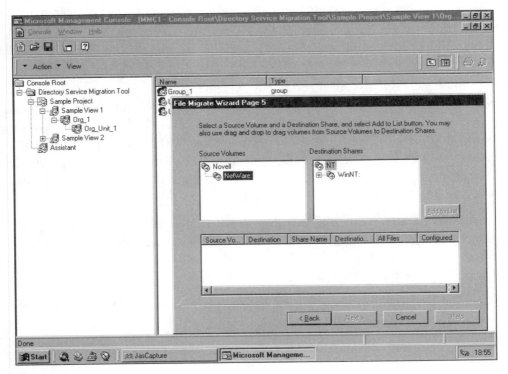

Figure A.1
The Directory Service Migration Tools MMC snap-in.

NDS is second to none. The new Directory Service Migration Tool is able to carry out a nondestructive migration of NDS (in other words, the existing NetWare environments can proceed even if all of their data has been transferred to Active Directory) as well as a bindery. The Directory Service Migration Tool also enables an administrator to alter the existing data on an offline copy prior to migration to Active Directory. The capability to transfer data between NDS/bindery and Active Directory in a nondestructive manner is a great asset in more-complex situations, because the result is a much smoother transitory period when users are located in two places.

The only prerequisite for starting migration to Active Directory is to have the Gateway (and Client) Services for NetWare (GSNW) and Directory Service Migration Tool installed on the server. The GSNW (which also installs the Microsoft IPX-compatible protocol stack) provides the necessary communications channel between Windows NT and the NetWare resources.

Migrating To Active Directory

If you want to perform a migration of users, groups, and the structure of the directory, follow these steps:

1. Establish a new view in the Directory Service Migration Tools MMC snap-in (see Figure A.2) by choosing View From NetWare on the shortcut menu for "Sample Project". This starts a wizard that enables you to choose the NetWare resources that you want to migrate.

2. Modify your offline database. After the NDS or bindery resources are placed in an offline database, you can add, delete, or alter the properties of each object. The toolbox that enables you to do this contains some fairly sophisticated search-and-replace functions, which means that you don't have to carry out more manual alterations than strictly necessary. However, one object property is usually handled manually: The user's password, which is the only object property included in the migration.

3. Configure the offline database in Active Directory (see Figure A.3). After the offline database has the structure and content that you want, you can write the data into Active Directory. This requires that you state which parts of the offline data should be migrated and where this data should be placed within the Active Directory hierarchy.

4. Verify that the new Active Directory data has the format that you want. You now can start using the data that was transferred to Active Directory with your usual MMC snap-in tools. The final version of the NT 5.0 Directory Migration Tool will enable you to use the offline database to migrate the files.

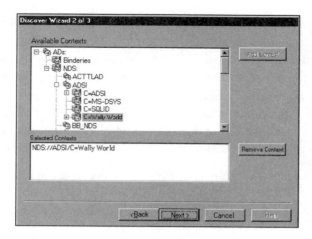

Figure A.2
Migrating NDS or bindery data to Active Directory is straightforward. This shot is taken from the Microsoft prerelease version of the Directory Service Migration Tool's user manual, due to the unavailability of an NDS server.

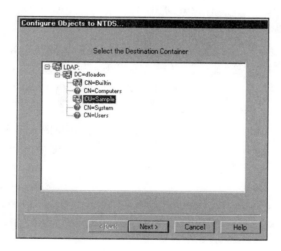

Figure A.3
The third step is to decide where the offline database should be placed in Active Directory. This screen, too, is taken from the Microsoft prerelease version of the Directory Service Migration Tool's user manual.

The Battle Of The Migration Tools

With Active Directory, Microsoft has created a genuine directory service, which means that Windows NT Server 5.0 will be an extremely strong competitor for very large and complex IT environments.

The Directory Service Migration Tool potentially can make the migration from Novell NDS (or bindery) to Active Directory easy and efficient. This should cause some exciting developments between these two directory services in the coming years. The Directory Service Migration Tool could well prove to be the Trojan Horse that makes moving from NDS to Active Directory so simple that administrators will consider such a change.

However, Active Directory has a long way to go before it's a serious competitor to NDS's efficient migration tool. A business that already has a well-functioning infrastructure that is based on NDS probably won't be inclined to consider changing to Active Directory until it has proven its worth in practice.

Microsoft's alliance with the Cheyenne Directory Management Group has led to some very positive developments for Microsoft, including Cheyenne's recent announcement that it is developing a DS Standard for Windows NT Server 5.0. Among other things, the DS Standard for NT will contain enhanced auxiliary tools to implement migration from the NT domain to Active Directory, several smart tools to enhance the handling of daily administration, and advanced facilities for backup and recovery of Active Directory's database.

Index

413

D

N

O